Women
in the
Church

Andreas J. Köstenberger is assistant professor of New Testament at Trinity Evangelical Divinity School. *Thomas R. Schreiner* is professor of New Testament at Bethel Theological Seminary. *H. Scott Baldwin*, a missionary with the Evangelical Free Church, teaches at Singapore Bible College. Köstenberger and Baldwin earned Ph.D. degrees from Trinity Evangelical Divinity School, Schreiner from Fuller Theological Seminary.

Women in the Church

A Fresh Analysis of 1 Timothy 2:9–15

Edited by Andreas J. Köstenberger,
Thomas R. Schreiner,
and H. Scott Baldwin

Baker Books

A Division of Baker Book House Co
Grand Rapids, Michigan 49516

Published by Baker Books,
a division of Baker Book House Company
P.O. Box 6287, Grand Rapids, Michigan 49516-6287

Printed in the United States of America

Library of Congress Cataloging-in-Publication Data

Women in the church : a fresh analysis of I Timothy 2:9–15 / edited by Andreas J.
    Köstenberger, Thomas R. Schreiner, and H. Scott Baldwin.
      p.   cm.
    Includes bibliographical references.
    ISBN 0-8010-2020-4 (paper)
    1. Women in Christianity—Biblical teaching. 2. Bible. N.T. Timothy, 1st, II, 9–15
  —Criticism, interpretation, etc. I. Köstenberger, Andreas J., 1957– . II. Schreiner,
  Thomas R. III. Baldwin, H. Scott.
    BS2745.6.W65W65   1995
    227′.8306—dc20   95-39701

Contents

Contributors

H. Scott Baldwin, Ph.D., Lecturer in New Testament at Singapore Bible College.

S. M. Baugh, Ph.D., Associate Professor of New Testament, Westminster Theological Seminary in California.

Harold O. J. Brown, Ph.D., Professor of Biblical and Systematic Theology, Trinity Evangelical Divinity School.

Daniel Doriani, Ph.D., Associate Professor of New Testament and Dean of the Faculty, Covenant Theological Seminary.

T. David Gordon, Ph.D., Associate Professor of New Testament, Gordon-Conwell Theological Seminary.

Andreas J. Köstenberger, Ph.D., Assistant Professor of New Testament, Trinity Evangelical Divinity School.

Thomas R. Schreiner, Ph.D., Professor of New Testament, Bethel Theological Seminary.

Robert W. Yarbrough, Ph.D., Associate Professor of New Testament, Covenant Theological Seminary.

Introduction

The battles over gender issues in the church in recent years are signs of a world that has strayed from God. Whatever God's design was for a humanity made up of men and women, it was not one of division and strife, but one of beauty and harmony. Since God exists, and since he made human beings male and female, these distinct genders must have been created for a purpose, and we should expect to be able to understand this purpose. It is obvious, however, that at the present time confusion largely prevails.

How can we recover God's vision for manhood and womanhood? For evangelical Christians, the answer lies in searching the Scriptures. But who among us is truly open to the biblical message? Who can claim to be free of the trappings of culture and tradition? Too often debates have been characterized by one of two extremes: easy answers to very complex questions or a confusing array of alternatives. Are we really doomed to a single choice between a dogmatism that is intransigent to genuine dialogue and a pluralism that has yielded the very possibility of settling difficult issues such as the roles of men and women in the church? Or should we, for the sake of evangelical unity, declare this matter to be potentially divisive and thus off-limits for truly broad-minded Christians, in order not to jeopardize the movement's vigorous growth and expansion, as one influential recent spokesman has advocated?

The contributors to this volume believe that while it is essential to do justice to the complexity of the issue, we need not throw away our confidence so quickly. We believe that as we do our best to interpret the Scriptures, both individually and corporately, the Spirit of God desires to guide us in our search for authentic gender identities. We are convinced that as we do so, we will be rewarded with a greater sense of understanding and security in God's design for men and women. We will find a deeper appreciation and experience of what it means to be a woman or a man created by God in his image, and a unity of purpose among those who share God's vision.

Issues as complex as these can hardly be resolved, or even be adequately dealt with, in one book. Our ambition is more modest. In an age when even interpreters committed to the authority of the Scriptures apparently cannot agree on the most elementary issues of interpretation, we propose to begin once more with a passage that (at least here most commentators agree) is one of the main dividing lines between various interpreters.

Two convictions have guided the group of scholars collaborating in this book. First, wherever possible, new evidence must be summoned to resolve the interpretation of a complex passage. As a result, the contributors have made every effort to engage significant new material in studying difficult words and grammar as well as in exploring the historical-cultural background of 1 Timothy 2:12. Second, we should use all the interpretive tools available to us in proper balance. Since this new evidence still needs to be properly interpreted, ultimately the decisive factor is a proper hermeneutical method. For this reason chapters in this book are devoted to the different areas of interpretation of 1 Timothy 2:12. All the contributors are convinced that 1 Timothy 2:9–15 prohibits women from teaching or exercising authority over men in the church. Despite this consensus on the basic meaning and application of the text, there remain some differences of opinion among the contributors regarding both the interpretation and application of the text. The discerning reader may be able to detect where we differ on some of the details.

We have attempted to construct the book so that the chapters appear in a logical sequence, beginning from the historical-cultural background informing 1 Timothy and concluding with some of the hermeneutical and cultural issues for today's church. In chapter 1 Steven Baugh investigates the religious background of Ephesus, examining carefully whether the assertion that the Ephesian church was threatened by feminism can withstand scrutiny. In order to interpret New Testament letters properly, the genre of the particular letter under consideration must be ascertained. Otherwise, our interpretation of the particular data in the letters may be askew. David Gordon sets the landscape for us in his chapter (2) on the genre of 1 Timothy. In some texts the meaning of a particular word is especially crucial in determining the interpretation of the text as a whole. The debate on 1 Timothy 2:12 has focused on the meaning of the word αὐθεντεῖν. Since this word is used only once in the New Testament, any new data or methodological clarity should be of significant help in interpreting the term. Henry Scott Baldwin, using the resources available through computer technology, has completed what is now the most thorough and up-to-date examination of the term. He presents his results in chapter 3. Not only has the meaning of specific words been the subject of controversy, but the relationship and significance of the two infinitives διδάσκειν and αὐθεντεῖν have been subject to dispute as well. More specifically, how should we understand the relationship of these two infinitives to one another in a construction in which they are joined by the Greek word οὐδέ? Andreas Köstenberger, in chapter 4, breaks new ground in analyzing the structure of 1 Timothy 2:12. Köstenberger, in an extensive study of both biblical and extrabiblical literature, collects and analyzes the texts that are parallel to 1 Timothy 2:12 in their structure. He explains the relevance of these parallels for the structure and meaning of 1 Timothy 2:12.

The first four chapters of this work function as a necessary prolegomenon before the interpretation of 1 Timothy 2:12 is presented. A full interpretation of this verse in context is needed, so that the reader perceives how the passage should be understood as a whole. Thomas Schreiner, in chapter 5, presents an interpretation of 1 Timothy 2:9–15 in which he takes into account the research presented in chapters 1–4. He also seeks to dialogue extensively with contemporary scholarship on the meaning of this text, since the text should not be interpreted in a vacuum.

Our work is not done, of course, when an interpretation of a text has been presented. The hermeneutical significance of the text for today's world must also be gleaned. This is particularly significant since some will inevitably object that this book only deals with one passage of Scripture. No book can accomplish everything, of course, but Robert Yarbrough in the sixth chapter investigates some of the most pertinent hermeneutical and cultural issues that pertain to the interpretation of 1 Timothy 2:12. In particular, he deals with the three larger issues relating to the interpretation of 1 Timothy 2, that is, our culture's liberalized views of women, the putative meaning of Galatians 3:28, and the alleged tie between women's subordination and slavery. In the seventh chapter, Harold O. J. Brown places the discussion into a larger cultural, social, and philosophical framework. Indeed, it is not merely accurate exegesis and proper hermeneutics that determine our passage's validity for the present day. Brown's essay, building on the contribution by Robert Yarbrough, makes clear some of the factors that have powerfully prevented larger acceptance of the "historic" interpretation of 1 Timothy 2:12. The book concludes with an epilogue by the editors and an appendix by Daniel Doriani on the interpretation of 1 Timothy 2:12 in the history of the church.

We are convinced that one's view of male and female gender identities and roles in the church really matters, and we pray that God will guide his church in the apprehension and application of his good gift of manhood and womanhood. May God renew us according to the image in which he made us in the beginning. This is needed for our own deeper fulfillment. This we seek for the sake of a world estranged from

God, which needs to see redeemed and renewed women and men in Christ—that they may believe that God was in Christ reconciling the world to himself.

Andreas J. Köstenberger,
Thomas R. Schreiner,
and H. Scott Baldwin

1

A Foreign World:
Ephesus in the First Century

S. M. Baugh

In some ways, the culture of ancient Ephesus was surprisingly like our own. The Ephesians, like all Greeks, had a passionate devotion to the gymnasium that resembles the current interest in fitness centers (cf. 1 Tim. 4:8). Athletes, musicians, and actors sometimes acquired astronomical fame and fortune, just as they do today.[1] Ephesian pragmatism, predatory mercantilism, and a generally pluralistic atmosphere (Christianity excepted, of course) that embraced philosophies of no particular distinction or profundity also seem remarkably familiar today.

Ephesus, though, will seem quite foreign to us in other ways. For example, Ephesian politicians normally expended their own money for public works and projects. A letter from the emperor Antoninus Pius (A.D. 138–161) regarding a very prominent and beneficent political figure illustrates this (IEph. 1491).[2] In it we learn that Vedius Antoninus had complained to the emperor about the Ephesians' lack of appreciation for the many buildings he had added to the city. Pius duly chides

---

1. For example, Tib. Claudius Artemidorus, a pancratist (like a kick-boxer) under Nero, received honorary citizenship of Rome, Tralles, Alexandria, and Ephesus, where a statue of him stood (IEph. 1124). Some, like Tib. Claudius Philologus Theseus, victor in (musical?) contests (IEph. 1135), and Tib. Julius Apolaustus, the pantomime (IEph. 2070), received honorary memberships on city councils as well.

2. Throughout this chapter, the following title abbreviations appear: IEph. = *Die Inschriften von Ephesos*, ed. Wankel et al. (Bonn, 1979–84); IMag. = *Die Inschriften von Magnesia am Maenander*, ed. O. Kern (Berlin, 1900); IPriene = *Die Inschriften von Priene*, ed. F. Hiller von Gaertringen (Berlin, 1906); IPrusias = *Die Inschriften von Prusias ad Hypium*, ed. Walter Ameling (Bonn, 1985); ITralles = *Die Inschriften von Tralleius und Nysa*, ed. Fjodor B. Polijakov (Bonn, 1989); Neue Inschriften VIII, IX, X, XI, XII = Knibbe et al.'s *JÖAI* articles in the Bibliography.

the city for failure to provide their benefactor with sufficient distinctions in return. Ephesian public figures were willing to exhaust their fortunes in patriotic generosity, asking for—and sometimes demanding—public honors for themselves and for their families in return.

While this political custom strikes us as foreign, there are other descriptions of first-century Ephesus that will strike us as exceedingly strange. This city, we are told, was "a bastion and bulwark of women's rights"[3] in the midst of a uniformly unfeminist Greco-Roman world.[4] Its renowned state goddess, Artemis Ephesia, is said to have been "a powerful female deity who elevated the status of women,"[5] "a symbol of Women's Liberation"[6] and of "matriarchy."[7] Her cult statue alone—"a multi-mammary grotesque"[8]—is said to attest to a society overshadowed by a runaway fertility cult serviced by multitudes of priestesses, sacred prostitutes, eunuchs, and hermaphrodites.[9] The Amazons, mythical female warriors sometimes regarded as the founders of Ephesus, were symbolic of a general "sex reversal" in this city that engaged in anti-male cult practices.

This "matriarchal" or "feminist" Ephesus would have struck its "patriarchal" Greco-Roman contemporaries as strange also. They knew the Amazon myths from the poets, but many shrugged them off: "The bards tell many lies."[10] Few Greeks took their Amazon myths to mean anything beyond proving how topsy-turvy distant barbarians really were.[11]

---

3. Marcus Barth, *Ephesians 4–6*, Anchor Bible, 2 vols. (Garden City: Doubleday, 1974), 2:661.

4. "For a man to be ruled by a woman is the very height of hubris" (Democritus).

5. Catherine Clark Kroeger, "1 Timothy 2:12—A Classicist's View," in *Women, Authority and the Bible*, ed. A. Mickelsen (Downers Grove: InterVarsity, 1986), 227–28; cf. Edith Specht, "Kulttradition einer weiblichen Gottheit: Beispiel Ephesos," in *Maria, Abbild oder Vorbild?*, ed. H. Röckelein et al. (Tübingen: Edition Diskord, 1990), 41.

6. Marcus Barth, "Traditions in Ephesians," *New Testament Studies* 30 (1984): 16.

7. "Matriarchy" is used with various meanings in Richard Clark Kroeger and Catherine Clark Kroeger, *I Suffer Not a Woman: Rethinking 1 Timothy 2:11–15 in Light of Ancient Evidence* (Grand Rapids: Baker, 1992).

8. Hubert Martin, "Artemis," *ABD*, 1:464; cf. W. K. C. Guthrie, *The Greeks and Their Gods* (Boston: Beacon, 1950), 101.

9. Camden M. Cobern, *New Archeological Discoveries*, 2nd ed. (New York: Funk & Wagnalls, 1917), 465; Sharon Hodgin Gritz, *Paul, Women Teachers, and the Mother Goddess at Ephesus: A Study of 1 Timothy 2:9–15 in Light of the Religious and Cultural Milieu of the First Century* (Lanham, Md.: University Press of America, 1991), 39–40, 116; and Kroegers, *I Suffer Not a Woman*, 93, 196.

10. Plutarch, *Moralia* 16A; cf. Plato, *Respublica* 376E–378E.

11. See Mary Lefkowitz, "Influential Women," in *Images of Women in Antiquity*, ed. A. Cameron and A. Kuhrt (Detroit: Wayne State University Press, 1983), 49; and Lorna Hardwick, "Ancient Amazons—Heroes, Outsiders or Women?" *Greece and Rome* 37 (1990): 14–36 ("The Amazons recur as fringe motifs, emblems of geographical remoteness," p. 33); cf. "Amazones," in *Der Kleine Pauly* (hereafter *Kl. Pauly*), ed. K. Ziegler and W. Sontheimer, 5 vols. (Munich: Deutscher Taschenbuch, 1979); "Amazons," *OCD*.

What may come as a surprise to the reader, though, is that the ancient Ephesians themselves would find this modern portrait of their culture, of Artemis Ephesia, and of her cult as unbelievably strange—in fact, mythical. The "feminist Ephesus" did not exist, even though the idea of it and its constituent elements are well ingrained in modern popular and even some scholarly literature.

What makes the issue of historical background so important is that painting Ephesus as an exotic feminist social-religious culture often serves a popular egalitarian reading of 1 Timothy 2:9–15.[12] For example, Richard and Catherine Kroeger have suggested that "Such a pagan element, based upon sex hostility and reversal of gender roles, may well have found a place in a cult practice among the dissidents in the congregation at Ephesus. . . . If this is the case, the condemnation (i.e., 1 Tim. 2:12) is not directed against women participating in leadership but rather against a monopoly on religious power by women."[13] Hence, in their opinion, Paul required only that *Ephesian* women not teach or exercise authority over men, since they were infected by an anomalous cultural outlook. Paul's words do not relate to women per se.

This essay will not scrutinize today's reconstructions of the Ephesian situation. The trouble would be that the line of argument would be entirely negative. For instance, one way to deny that this city was a bastion of women's rights or that Artemis Ephesia was a fertility deity with eunuchs and sacred prostitutes among her cult personnel is by evaluating the evidence (or lack thereof) adduced by those who maintain the "feminist Ephesus" position. We would find it wanting.[14] But this does not provide the reader with a feel for what Ephesus was truly like, and that is the intention of this essay. When you know the real Ephesus, you find the "feminist Ephesus" unacceptable.

In order to discover the real Ephesus, we must study relevant statements in ancient literature and peruse the extant primary materials. We have, for instance, almost four thousand inscriptions from Ephesus, more than from any other city in the region, and they require careful interpretation. In the end, our reliance on primary materials from Ephesus will let us form our conclusions about the nature of its society and the background situation of 1 Timothy. What was the culture of Ephesus like? Who was in charge? How did the Ephesians worship

12. Ephesus, of course, was the destination of 1 Timothy (1:3), and perhaps an important center for the whole canon; see Eugene E. Lemcio, "Ephesus and the New Testament Canon," *Bulletin of the John Rylands Library* 69 (1986): 210–34.

13. Kroegers, *I Suffer Not a Woman*, 93. Cf. John W. Cooper, *A Cause for Division? Women in Office and the Unity of the Church* (Grand Rapids: Calvin Theological Seminary, 1991), 50.

14. For a critique of *I Suffer Not a Woman* along these lines, see S. M. Baugh, "The Apostle among the Amazons," *Westminster Theological Journal* 56 (1994): 153–71.

their state goddess, Artemis? What was she like? In the process of describing Ephesus in this general fashion, I hope to accomplish a secondary purpose as well: to show that the "feminist Ephesus" construct is not historically plausible. The essay will conclude by addressing some specific issues relating to the situation behind 1 Timothy.

Historical Sketch

Ephesus, along with other colonies, was founded on the west coast of modern Turkey by Greek adventurers roughly around the time of the Israelite judges.[15] The physical setting for ancient Ephesus was highly favorable, especially for commerce. It had a natural harbor for overseas trade, and a royal road up the nearby Maeander River valley connected inland for important eastern passage and trade.[16]

Some myths have it that the Amazons were the original founders of Ephesus (Strabo, *Geog.* 11.5.4; Pausanius 7.4–5). This has been used as evidence of Ephesus's supposed "feminist" character. The Ephesians themselves, however, officially ascribed the foundation of their city to a Greek hero named Androclus. An oracle directed him to found the city at the site where he killed a boar while hunting (Strabo, *Geog.* 14.1.3, 21; Pliny, *H.N.* 5.115). The Ephesians called Androclus "the creator of our city" (IEph. 501) and celebrated the city's foundation annually as "Androclus-day" (IEph. 644).[17]

Ephesus's cultural heritage was Greek. While it possessed the trappings of democracy, it had no grand tradition of equality like Athens, equality among male citizens, that is. What Theodor Mommsen said of

15. Technical overviews are D. Knibbe, "Ephesos: Historisch-epigraphischer Teil," A. Pauly, G. Wissowa, and W. Kroll, *Real-Encyclopädie der Klassichen Altertumwissenschaft* (hereafter *PW* suppl. [1893–], 12:248–97; and D. Knibbe and W. Alzinger, "Ephesos vom Beginn der römischen Herrschaft in Kleinasien bis zum Ende der Principatszeit," *Aufstieg und Niedergang der römischen Welt* (hereafter *ANRW*) (Berlin: Walter de Gruyter, 1980), 2.7.2: 748–830. More popular are D. Knibbe and B. Iplikçioglu, *Ephesos im Spiegel seiner Inschriften* (Vienna: Schindler, 1984); and W. Elliger, *Ephesos: Geschichte einer antiken Weltstadt* (Stuttgart: Kohlhammer, 1985). For a full bibliography, see Richard E. Oster, *A Bibliography of Ancient Ephesus*, ATLABS 19 (Metuchen: Scarecrow, 1987); cf. G. H. R. Horsley, "The Inscriptions of Ephesus and the New Testament," *Novum Testamentum* 34 (1992): 105–68.

16. This was possibly Paul's route when "he passed through the upper regions and arrived at Ephesus" (Acts 19:1); see Stephen Mitchell, *Anatolia* (Oxford: Clarendon, 1993), maps 3 and 7. But compare David French, "Acts and the Roman Roads of Asia Minor," *The Book of Acts in Its First Century Setting: The Book of Acts in Its Graeco-Roman Setting* (Grand Rapids: Eerdmans and Carlisle: Paternoster, 1994), 55–57.

17. Androclus and his boar were also minted on Ephesian coins; see Barclay V. Head, *Historia Numorum: A Manual of Greek Numismatics* (Chicago: Argonaut, 1967; repr. of 1911 ed.), 577.

Asia Minor in general was true of Ephesus specifically: "Asia Minor was just old subject-territory and, under its Persian as under its Hellenic rulers, accustomed to monarchic organization; here less than in Hellas did useless recollections and vague hopes carry men away beyond the limited municipal horizon of the present, and there was not much of this sort to disturb the peaceful enjoyment of such happiness in life as was possible under the existing circumstances."[18] From the time of its capture by King Croesus of Lydia in the sixth century B.C., Ephesus never enjoyed independence from foreign domination. Croesus, Cyrus, Darius, Athens, Sparta, Alexander, Lysimachus, the Seleucids, the Attalids, Mithridates, and finally the Romans had all captured or controlled Ephesus in their turns. The city's political life was dominated by kings, tyrants, satraps, bureaucrats, and proconsuls, but never by radical democrats. Ephesus never adopted an egalitarian democratic ideology that would necessitate feminism or, minimally, the inclusion of women in public offices.[19] Ephesus's mood was pragmatic and politically accommodating. "All is flux" was a famous dictum of the Ephesian philosopher Heraclitus, well expressing the city's adaptability to changing political climates. At the time of Paul, the political climate was Roman—not feminist.

Although Ephesus had suffered terrible economic and political turmoil in the first century B.C., the *pax Augusta* inaugurated a golden age of peace lasting roughly two centuries. Augustus himself, during a brief stop at Ephesus after Actium, confirmed the city's place as the provincial capital. Paul stepped into a city that was well on its way to eclipsing old rivals Miletus, Smyrna, and Pergamum as "the greatest and first metropolis of Asia" (IEph. 22; et al.). With a population somewhere around one hundred thousand, Ephesus eventually was to become one of the largest and most important cities in the empire next to Rome.[20]

18. Theodor Mommsen, *The Provinces of the Roman Empire*, 2 vols. (Chicago: Ares, 1974; repr. of 1909 ed.), 1:354.

19. William Ramsay's work has sometimes been used to impute an indigenous Anatolian matriarchal influence on Ephesus. The idea of matriarchy in Asia Minor finds little support among historians today, and Ramsay himself explicitly says that matriarchy made little headway in the Hellenic cities; see *Cities and Bishoprics of Phrygia* (Oxford: Clarendon, 1895), 94–96; cf. Edwin Yamauchi, "Ramsay's Views on Archaeology in Asia Minor Reviewed," in *The New Testament Student and His Field*, New Testament Student 5, ed. J. Skilton (Phillipsburg, N.J.: Presbyterian & Reformed, 1982), 27–40. On the related issue of matrilinearity, see Baugh, "Apostle among the Amazons," 163–64.

20. Some higher estimates of Ephesus's population (e.g., 200,000+ by T. R. S. Broughton ["Roman Asia Minor," in *An Economic Survey of Ancient Rome*, ed. T. Frank (Baltimore, 1938), 4:812–13] and David Magie [*Roman Rule in Asia Minor*, 2 vols. (hereafter *RRAM*) (Princeton: Princeton University Press, 1950), 1:585; 2:1446, n. 50]) are based on a misreading of an inscription (IEph. 951); cf. Preston Duane Warden and Roger S. Bagnall, "The Forty Thousand Citizens of Ephesus," *Classical Philology* 83 (1988): 220–23.

Political Institutions

The municipal organization of Ephesus had formal resemblance to the Athenian democratic model, with the male citizen body (δῆμος) divided into tribes (φυλαί) comprising the state assembly (ἐκκλησία).[21] The municipal ruling body was the 450-member state council (βουλή), presided over by the secretary of the people (ὁ γραμματεὺς τοῦ δήμου).[22]

There were a number of primary magistrates and civic groups at Ephesus. No women are known to have filled these magistracies at Ephesus in the first century.[23] Furthermore, there were no women's civic groups to compare with the state council, gerousia, or ephebia.

Table 1.1
Male Magistrates of Ephesus

Roman Proconsul	ἀνθύπατος	Supreme de facto governor over all areas of life
Secretary of the People	ὁ γραμματεὺς τοῦ δήμου	Chief civil magistrate of Ephesus
Councilor	βουλευτής	Member of the state council (βουλή)

21. The mob is addressed in Acts 19 as though an ordinary meeting of the ἐκκλησία— "Men, Ephesians" (ἄνδρες Ἐφέσιοι; vv. 35, 39)—recalling that women were technically not citizens of Hellenic *poleis*. See an inscription from Magnesia-on-Maenander, where prayers are offered at a festival of Artemis Leucophryene "for the safety of the city and countryside, *citizens* and *women* and children and all resident aliens" (IMag. 98; emphasis added). Cf. E. L. Hicks, ed., *The Collection of Ancient Greek Inscriptions in the British Museum* (hereafter *IBM*), pt. 3 (Oxford: Clarendon, 1890), 68–71; Dieter Knibbe, *Forschungen in Ephesos. 9.1.1. Der Staatsmarkt. Die Inschriften des Prytaneions. Die Kureteninschriften and sonstige religiöse Texte* (Vienna: Österreichischen Akademie der Wissenschaften, 1981), 107–9; and Guy M. Rogers, "The Assembly of Imperial Ephesos," *Zeitschrift für Papyrologie und Epigraphik* 94 (1992): 224–28.

22. We know the names of scores of these men. From the first century are: Heraclides III (IEph. 14); Tatianus (IEph. 492); Tib. Claudius Aristio (IEph. 234–35, et al.); C. Julius Didymus (Neue Inschriften IX, 120–21); Alexander Memnon, son of Artemidorus (IEph 261); and L. Cusinius (either *episkopos* or grammateus; Barclay V. Head, *Catalogue of the Greek Coins in the British Museum: Ionia* (hereafter *BMC*) (reprint ed. Bologna, 1964), no. 205 and IEph. 659B, 716, etc.). Either Alexander Memnon or L. Cusinius could be the grammateus of Acts 19:35.

23. I am aware that women magistrates in other Asian cities are sometimes highlighted (e.g., Paul Trebilco, *Jewish Communities in Asia Minor* [Cambridge: Cambridge University Press, 1991], 113–24); however, a precise study of the nature and time period of those offices is needed before social and political implications can be drawn from female incumbents. The significant difference between the Ephesian *prytany* and the same office in other cities as discussed below is a case in point (a difference not represented in Trebilco, ibid., 119–21). And the social, political, and religious upheavals of the third century A.D. created a climate in which women might appear in traditionally male roles.

General	στρατηγός	Executive magistrate
Market-Director	ἀγορανόμος	Control of grain supply, economy, and market
Gymnasiarch	γυμνασίαρχος	Oversight of culture and education in gymnasia; financial underwriting (a "liturgy" not a magistracy)

Table 1.2
Male Civic Groups in Ephesus

State Council	βουλή	Chief governmental body with oversight of all public affairs; 450 members
The People, Assembly	ὁ δῆμος ἐκκλησία	Male citizen body that ratified decisions of state council; 1,000–2,000 members
Gerousia	γερουσία	Broad extraconstitutional influence over religion, finances, culture, etc.; 300+ members
Ephebia	ἐφηβεία	Aristocratic cultural youth group (the group for younger boys is παιδές; older youths are νέοι); under an ephebarch and gymnasiarch

City councilors were normally chosen by lot from each tribe for an annual term. Under Roman influence, though, the Ephesian council began to resemble the aristocratic Roman senate, with perpetual, even hereditary terms of office.[24] This is just one example of extensive evidence for the growing influence of Roman cultural and political ideas *(Romanitas)* in Pauline Ephesus, which appears to have been more far-reaching than in Palestine.[25]

24. For an Ephesian councilor who served nineteen consecutive years, see IEph. 1017–35 (under Trajan and Hadrian). Roman officials like Pliny might deliberately limit councilors to "free men from the better class families *(honestorum hominum liberi)* than from the commoners *(plebs)*" *(Epistulae* 10.79). Cf. G. W. Bowersock, *Augustus and the Greek World* (Oxford: Clarendon, 1965), 87–88.

25. Another important indication of acceptance of *Romanitas* is the high incidence of Roman citizenship among Ephesians. For Roman citizens among the Ephesian "fishermen and fishmongers" (IEph. 20), see S. M. Baugh, "Paul and Ephesus: The Apostle among His Contemporaries" (unpubl. Ph.D. diss., University of California, Irvine, 1990), 165–93, 222–25; cf. G. H. R. Horsley, in *New Documents Illustrating Early Christianity* (hereafter *New Docs*), ed. G. H. R. Horsley and S. R. Llewelyn, 6 vols. (Macquarie University, 1981–92), 95–114.

Roman *patria potestas* ("patriarchy"),[26] merged with the Greek institutions of male citizenship and male magistrates, gerousia, ephebia, and gymnasia, did not make for female cultural dominance. Even though women had some public roles at Ephesus, leadership in the political and social spheres was solidly in the hands of exclusively male institutions.[27]

Religious Climate

Although Artemis Ephesia dominated the public religion of her hometown, the Ephesians were ordinary Hellenic polytheists. A full house of Greek deities as well as some imports are in evidence from the temples, altars, and dedications in Ephesus. Familiar names include Aphrodite, Apollo, Asclepius, Athena, Dionysus, Pluto, Poseidon, and Zeus. The latter appears as Zeus Keraunios, Zeus Ktesios, Zeus Polieus, Zeus Melichios, and Zeus Soter.[28] The more esoteric cults include the mysteries of Demeter Karpophoros, private house cults of Dionysus, the public cult of Dionysus "before the city,"[29] and a cult of God Most High ("Theos Hypsistos") whose appellation may or may not have come about through Jewish influence.

Ephesus had been under the control of the Ptolemies earlier, so it is no surprise to find a fairly vigorous cult of Isis and Serapis, even Anubis (IEph. 1231 and 1213), probably revived by Cleopatra's visit to the city in the days of Mark Anthony.[30] Local Anatolian deities were represented at Ephesus by the Phrygian god, Zeus Sabazios, and by the Phrygian mother goddess, Meter. Some worshipers, covering all bases, dedicated their offerings "to all the gods and goddesses" (Neue Inschriften

26. See esp. W. K. Lacey, "Patria Potestas," in *The Family in Ancient Rome*, ed. B. Rawson (Ithaca, N.Y.: Cornell University Press, 1986), 121–44. His thesis: *"[P]atria potestas* was the fundamental institution of the Romans which shaped and directed their world-view" (p. 140).

27. The asiarchs—mentioned in Acts 19:31—were another, especially prominent group of men. Whether this was a priesthood or an honorary title is subject for debate, but the asiarchs' high social status is not. See Kearsley, *New Docs 4*, 46–55; Steven J. Friesen, *Twice Neokoros: Ephesus, Asia, and the Cult of the Flavian Imperial Family* (Leiden: E. J. Brill, 1993), 92–112; and Baugh, "Paul and Ephesus," 132–63, 214–21.

28. Many epigraphical references to the deities at Ephesus are collected in IEph. 1201–71; cf. Dieter Knibbe, "Ephesos—Nicht nur die Stadt der Artemis: die 'anderen' ephesischen Götter," in *Studien zur Religion und Kultur Kleinasiens*, ed. S. Sahin et al. (Leiden: E. J. Brill, 1978), 2:489–503; and, Richard Oster, "Ephesus as a Religious Center under the Principate, I. Paganism before Constantine," *ANRW* 2.18.3 (1990): 1661–1728.

29. See R. Merkelbach, "Die ephesischen Dionysosmysten vor der Stadt," *Zeitschrift für Papyrologie und Epigraphik* 36 (1979): 151–56.

30. See Günther Hölbl, *Zeugnisse ägyptischer Religionsvorstellungen für Ephesos* (Leiden: E. J. Brill, 1978).

VIII, no. 131). At least one scholar believes that another dedication was made "to the Pantheion" in a truly pantheistic sense.[31]

The majority of these deities, even the goddesses, were served by male priests at Ephesus.[32] This is a bit unusual, since "a priestess very commonly officiated for goddesses and a priest for gods" in Greek cults.[33] Certainly "a bastion and bulwark of women's rights" would have had as many priestesses in evidence as in contemporary cities—not fewer as we find at Ephesus.[34]

The Artemisium

Ephesus was not a temple-city like the oracular centers of Claros or Delphi, yet the temple of Artemis dominated the city in many ways, partly by sheer size.[35] The Artemisium was the largest building in the Greek world, about four times larger than the Athenian Parthenon. It boasted 127 massive columns decorated with friezes. Its adornments by some of the most famous painters and sculptors of antiquity made it one of the Seven Wonders of the World (Pliny, *H.N.* 16.213–14; 35.92–93; 36.95–97; Pausanius 6.3.15–16).[36] Hence its fame: "What man is there after all who does not know that the city of the Ephesians is guardian of the temple of the great Artemis?" (Acts 19:35).[37] And its considerable

31. Chr. Börker, "Eine pantheistische Weihung in Ephesos," *Zeitschrift für Papyrologie und Epigraphik* 41 (1981): 181–88.

32. For example: P. Rutelius Bassus Junianus, priest of Demeter Karpophoros (IEph. 1210); Isidorus, son of Apollonis, son of Apollonis, priest of "Karpophoros Earth" (IEph. 902) (apparently different than Demeter Karpophoros; so Walter Burkert, *Greek Religion* [Cambridge, Mass.: Harvard University Press, 1985], 175); C. Sossianus, priest of Isis and Serapis (IEph. 1213); Nic[ius?], priest of Theos Hypsistos (IEph. 1235); Demetrius, son of Myndius, son of Nester, priest of Zeus Keraunios (IEph. 1239); and a few named priests and unnamed priestesses of Dionysus (IEph. 902, 1600–1, et al.). See also priests of civic groups: priests of the council (IEph. 941 and Neue Inschriften XII, no. 22); a priest of the ephebes (IEph. 836); and a priest of the *molpoi* (a guild of musicians) (IEph. 901 and 3317).

33. Burkert, *Greek Religion*, 98.

34. Women served as priestesses in more than forty Athenian cults during the classical era when women's public functions outside the home were scarce; cf. Michael Grant, *A Social History of Greece and Rome* (New York: Charles Scribner's Sons, 1992), 8.

35. The temple did not dominate the city's skyline, though, since it was situated about a mile (2 km) from downtown Ephesus.

36. Cf. Anton Bammer, *Das Heiligtum der Artemis von Ephesos* (Graz, Austria: Akademische, 1984).

37. The cult of Artemis Ephesia was spread throughout Asia Minor and Syria, and was even in Italy: "Whereas the leader of our city, the goddess Artemis, is honored not only in her hometown—which she has caused to be honored more than all cities through her own divinity—among both Greeks as well as barbarians, so that her rites and precincts have been set up everywhere" (IEph. 24B; A.D. 160). Cf. Robert Fleischer, *Artemis von Ephesos und verwandte Kultstatuen aus Anatolien und Syrien* (Leiden: E. J. Brill, 1973).

tourist appeal brought "no small income" to many Ephesians outside the silversmith guild (Acts 19:24–27).

The Artemisium illustrates the intimate connection between the economic and the religious spheres of life at Ephesus, and it was the city's dominant economic power. The temple's influence was especially felt in two areas: banking and land-holding. As a bank and money lender, the Artemisium was "the common treasury of Asia" (Aelius Aristides, *Oratio* 23.24), holding in deposit "not alone money of the Ephesians but also of aliens and of people from all parts of the world, and in some cases states and kings" (Dio Chrysostom, *Oratio* 31.54). As a land-holder, the extant boundary stones show that Artemis owned extensive, rich farmlands in the Cayster River valley. A rough estimate shows her in possession of about 77,000 acres of land, though she may well have owned more lands whose boundary markers have not yet been found.[38]

The Temple Hierarchy

Who held the actual reins of power over the considerable wealth and sway of the Artemisium? We know of sacred guilds that administered Artemis's various resources, but they were probably bureaucratic agencies that followed the policies of someone else.[39] What we find is something entirely expected for a Hellenic city of the imperial era: supreme control over the Artemisium was exercised by civil magistrates with active meddling by Roman governors. There are various ways to substantiate this, but the easiest is with one clear example deriving from the lifetime of Paul. The following is a portion of an edict of the provincial proconsul, Paullus Fabius Persicus, possibly at the personal direction of Claudius himself:

> . . . The temple of Artemis herself—which is an adornment to the whole province because of the magnificence of the building, the antiquity of the worship of the goddess, and the abundance of the incomes granted to the

38. The boundary stone inscriptions are collected in IEph. 3501–12, including a map of the area and the location of the stones; cf. Dieter Knibbe et al., "Der Grundbesitz der ephesischen Artemis im Kaystrostal," *Zeitschrift für Papyrologie und Epigraphik* 33 (1979): 139–46.

39. "The Sacred Rent (or Wage) Office" (IEph. 1577A, 3050, etc.) probably administered leases on temple lands to peasant farmers and larger agricultural concerns. One such concern was represented by another bureau known variously as "Those Engaged in the Taste" (IEph. 728), "The College of the Sacred Tasters" (IEph. 2076), or more fully, "The College of the Sacred Wine Tasters," an association engaged in the production and distribution of wine grown on the sacred soil of Artemis (so *Supplementum epigraphicum Graecum* [hereafter *SEG*] 35, no. 1109). One sacred association of the Artemisium (*hieropoioi*) apparently owned their own land (Neue Inschriften IX, 118–19).

goddess by the Emperor (or, Augustus)—is being deprived of its proper revenues. These had been sufficient for the maintenance and for the adornment of the votive offerings, but they are being diverted for the illegal wants of the leaders of the *Koinon*,[40] according to what they consider will bring them profit. . . . While using the appearance of the divine temple as a pretext, they sell the priesthoods as if at public auction.[41] Indeed, they invite men of every kind to their sale, then they do not select the most suitable men upon whose heads the crown would fittingly be placed. (Instead) they restrict incomes to those who are being consecrated to as (little) as they are willing to accept, in order that they themselves might appropriate as much as possible. (IEph. 17–19; A.D. 44)

This edict shows that the Roman government—and perhaps the emperor personally as *pontifex maximus*[42]—believed it held authority to regulate and oversee religious affairs in Ephesus as in other provincial cities.[43] Furthermore, the Persicus inscription shows that officials in

40. The term κοινόν in the singular normally refers to the provincial League of Asia, while the plural form (κοινά), used elsewhere in this inscription, corresponds to *res publica*, the city-state. Although it is not certain whether these are precisely city or provincial officers, the same city magistrates were the ones who filled the provincial posts, so the distinction is not critical here. Cf. Baugh, "Paul and Ephesus," 159–61.

41. A "donation" for the honor of serving in various priesthoods was common in the Greek world. For instance, in Egypt, a certain priest offered 2,200 drachmas for his temple's prophetic office (A. S. Hunt and C. C. Edgar, *Select Papyri*, LCL, 2 vols. [Cambridge, Mass.: Harvard University Press and William Heinemann, 1932–34], 2, no. 353). But this practice upset Roman sensibilities. They preferred to grant and acquire priesthoods through patronage. Pliny the Younger, for example, was appointed to the college of augurs through imperial patronage, not through payment (*Ep.* 10.13 and 4.8). This confined membership of priesthoods to "people of the right sort," which, of course, is what Persicus had in mind. Perhaps among the "wrong sort" acquiring priesthoods of Artemis were freedmen like Domitian's procurator, Tib. Claudius Clemens, who became a "trustee" (*neopoios*) of the Artemisium (IEph. 853 and 1812). Cf. Magie, *RRAM*, 1:545–46; and esp. 2:1403–4, n. 17.

42. In Greek, ἀρχιερεὺς μέγιστος (IEph. 259B; Claudius).

43. Earlier Augustus had personally limited the boundaries of the asylum area of the Artemisium (Strabo, *Geog.* 14.1.23; Cass. Dio 51.20.6). See also Pliny and Trajan's correspondence for rulings on religious matters in Bithynia (*Ep.* 10.49–50; 68–71); cf. A. N. Sherwin-White, *The Letters of Pliny: A Historical and Social Commentary* (Oxford: Clarendon, 1966), 632, 655–59. Further evidence of Roman oversight of Ephesian religion is as follows: (1) The city petitioned Roman proconsuls for permission (a) to perform mysteries "to Demeter Karpophoros and Thesmophoros and the divine emperors . . . with all sanctity and lawful customs" (IEph. 213; A.D. 88–89); and (b) to carry on festivals throughout the month of Artemision in honor of Artemis (IEph. 24; A.D. 162–64). (2) The municipality and temple establishment placed themselves under the patronage of individual Romans: "Lucius Antonius son of Marcus (a brother of Mark Anthony) . . . patron (πάτρων) and benefactor of Artemis and of the city" (IEph. 614A; ca. 49 B.C.); and the same for Marcus Messalla Corvinus, a prominent figure under Augustus (Neue Inschriften XII, no. 18). Cf. R. P. Saller, *Personal Patronage under the Early Empire* (Cambridge: Cambridge University Press, 1982); and Bowersock, *Augustus and the Greek World*, 12ff.

local government had direct control over access to the Artemisium's priesthood. The wedding between civil government officials and religious affairs was normal for Hellenic cities, where "a magistrate was usually a priest as a part of his official functions."[44]

If Ephesus truly "stood as a bastion of feminine supremacy in religion,"[45] we would expect to find either priestesses or other women controlling the resources of the Artemisium and appointments to its offices. Instead, Ephesian religious affairs were governed by the Roman and municipal authorities who were decidedly male.

Table 1.3
Male Religious Groups in Ephesus

Priest of Artemis	ἱερεὺς Ἀρτέμιδος	Probably cultic duties and financial underwriting (not the same as the megabyzos)
Kouretes	κουρῆτες	Broad oversight over cult of Artemis and of Hestia Boulaia; important cultic duties; 6–9 members annually
Neopoios	νεοποιός (νεοποιής)	Oversight of Artemisium building and furnishings
Essene	ἐσσήν	Annual priesthood requiring cultic purity
Various bureaus and groups of the Artemisium		The rent office, sacred wine tasters, sacred victors, hierophants, etc.
Megabyzos	Μεγάβυζος	Obsolete eunuch priest of the Artemisium
Prytanis	πρύτανις	Priesthood of Hestia Boulaia in Prytaneion (a few girls and women also served)
High Priest (of Asia) Asiarch (?)	ὁ ἀρχιερεὺς (τῆς Ασίας) ἀσιάρχης	Financial upkeep of imperial cult; ceremonial duties at festivals; sometimes called "*neocoros*" of the imperial cult (uncertain whether "asiarch" was synonymous with "high priest of Asia")

44. "Priests," *OCD*; cf. Burkert, *Greek Religion*, 95–98. In Acts 19:35 the grammateus mentions that the city (i.e., its magistrates) was "*neocoros* of the great goddess" (cf. IEph. 647). "Neocoros" refers to the individual or group charged with the oversight of a cult; cf. R. A. Kearsley, *New Docs 6*, 203–6.

45. Kroegers, *I Suffer Not a Woman*, 54.

As implied in the Persicus edict, the "auctioning" of priesthoods of Artemis concerned "men" (ἄνθρωποι) who served as "priests" (ἱερεῖς) (IEph. 18C.8 and 12). Although these terms could be used generically, other inscriptions name men who served as "priests of Artemis,"[46] so these were not necessarily priestesses. The financial costs and perquisites implied in the Persicus inscription are the only details we have for the character of the male priests of the goddess.

The next group of sacred officers, the κουρῆτες, was "doubtlessly the most important cult group connected to the temple of Artemis."[47] Strabo the geographer provides a helpful description of the kouretes' leadership in the annual, ritual reenactment of the birth of Artemis Ephesia:

> Above the grove [Ortygia] lies Mt. Solmissus, where, it is said, the Curetes (kouretes) stationed themselves, and with the din of their arms frightened Hera out of her wits when she was jealously spying on Leto, and when they helped Leto to conceal from Hera the birth of her children. There are several temples in the place. . . . A general festival is held there annually; and by a certain custom the youths (neoi) vie for honour, particularly in the splendour of their banquets there. At that time, also, a special college (ἀρχεῖον, "magistracy") of the Curetes (kouretes) holds symposiums and performs certain mystic sacrifices. (*Geog.* 14.1.20; LCL trans.)[48]

The epigraphical remains regarding the kouretes are extensive. We know that early in the reign of Augustus their headquarters was moved to the prytaneion probably from the Artemisium.[49] The names of the six to nine annual kouretes were inscribed there each year during the im-

46. C. Julius Atticus was "priest of Artemis Soteira (and) of the family of Caesar" (IEph. 1265), Apollonius Politicus was "the priest of Artemis" who dedicated a local altar (Neue Inschriften IX, 120–21), and Servilius Bassus was "(priest) of Artemis" under Augustus (IEph. 4337). An imperial freedman under Nero, C. Stertinius Orpex (whose daughter was a priestess of Artemis), says that he donated five thousand denarii "to the council of the Ephesians and to the priests" (IEph. 4123). Also, a "priest of Artemis" figures prominently in Achilles Tatius's second-century novel when the story's venue shifts to Ephesus ("Leucippe and Clitophon," Books 7–8).

47. Ellinger, *Ephesos*, 127; cf. Knibbe, *Kureteninschriften* and the brief treatment by R. A. Kearsley in *New Docs 6*, 196–202.

48. In the myth of Artemis's birth, Hera, wife of Zeus, tried to destroy Leto's children, the twins Artemis and Apollo. Their birthplace was believed by most of the Greek world to be on Delos, called "Ortygia" in earlier days, but the Ephesians claimed that it was in their mountain grove of that name (Tacitus, *Ann.* 3.61); cf. "Ortygia," *Kl. Pauly*.

49. The prytaneion is the building housing the state cult of Hestia and the "prytany" (see below). The move of the kouretes may indicate the consolidation of control over the affairs of the Artemisium by municipal powers through Roman influence (cf. Kearsley, *New Docs 6*, 197). Their close alliance with the municipality explains why Strabo calls their office a "magistracy," even though they retained priestly functions in the birthday festival.

perial period, and over fifty of these lists are extant (IEph. 1001–57, et al.). Two important facts emerge from these lists. First, the kouretes (and their assistants) were frequently also city-councilors, illustrating the close integration of the civic and religious realms at Ephesus as was common in Greco-Roman cultures. Second, the kouretes were men.[50]

Hence, the following modern interpretation of the kouretes as priestesses epitomizes the kind of problematic historical imagination encountered in the interpretations of Ephesus as a feminist culture:

> In Ephesus women assumed the role of the man-slaying Amazons who had founded the cult of Artemis of Ephesus. . . . The female dancers at the temple of the Ephesian Artemis clashed their arms, so lethal weapons were part of the priestesses' religious accoutrements. There are reasons to suspect that the dances may have contained a simulated attack on males, especially as they were performed with spears. . . . They would surely have inspired terror; and this, Strabo tells us, was one of the purposes of the dance.[51]

These "female dancers" (kouretes) were men, and the goddess Hera was the one to be scared off in the ritual reenactment.

Another group associated with the Artemisium were the *neopoioi*, who functioned something like a board of trustees for temple property (IEph. 27, 1570–90b, 2212, etc.).[52] We know that the neopoioi held office for a term, since an aorist participle form of the word (νεοποιήσας) appears, and that the office involved significant financial commitment since many neopoioi claimed that they were "voluntary" and served "generously."[53]

50. For example, here is one of the lists: "In the prytany of Tib. Claudius Tib. f. Quirina Romulus the emperor-loyal priest for life, the pious, emperor-loyal kouretes, all city-councilors (βουλευταί) were: M. Pompeius Damonicus; Tib. Claudius Capito; C. Numicius Peregrinus; Tib. Claudius Claudianus; Alexander, son of Alexander, the ephebarch; Ephesius son of Aristonicus. The sacred-assistants were: P. Cor(nelius) Aristo, [victim-inspector and city-councilor]; Myndicius, hierophant and city-councilor; Epikrates, sacred-herald; Atticus, incense-bearer; Trophimus, flute-player at the drink-offering" (IEph. 1020; A.D. 100/3).

51. Kroegers, *I Suffer Not a Woman*, 186–87.

52. Since the discovery of an inscription mentioning a first-century neopoios named Demetrius (IEph. 1578A), it has been debated whether this might be the silversmith of Acts 19. A first-century silversmith, M. Antonius Hermias, served as neopoios (IEph. 2212), so it remains possible, though not proven. See Horsley, *New Docs 4*, 7–10, 127–29.

53. For instance: "The loyal C. Mindius Hegymenus, who served as *decemprimus*, ephebarch with distinction, harbor-master, superintendent of education, and as voluntary neopoios piously and generously, the father of Mindia Stratonike Hegymene, high priestess of Asia of the temples in Ephesus and *theoros* of the Great Olympiad, and of Mindia Soteris Agrippine, priestess of lady Artemis, the grandfather of a sacred herald . . . [broken off]" (Neue Inschriften IX, 125). The decemprimus (δεκάπρωτος) was probably a financial officer of the Artemisium; cf. *SEG* 38, no. 1181.

The sacred office of *essene* is of interest to New Testament scholars for its Qumran associations.[54] In the pre-Roman era, essenes appeared alongside the neopoioi as those charged with inscribing decrees of enfranchisement of new citizens in the Artemisium. In the imperial period, however, the Ephesian essenes held an annual priesthood with duties in cultic rites requiring chastity (even if married) and other kinds of ritual purity during their term of office (Pausanius 8.13.1). The purity requirement is signified on the inscriptions by the phrase "completed my term as essene *purely* (ἀγνῶς)," and the financial obligations of office is indicated by their having served "generously."[55]

There were a number of other minor guilds and groups associated with the Artemisium that do not need elaboration here.[56] Suffice it to say that the men who filled these posts and the other major offices discussed were fully involved in the civic life of Ephesus. Many of them discharged a variety of sacred and civil offices during their lifetimes or served subsequent years in the same offices.[57]

In other treatments of the Artemis hierarchy, one figure frequently draws primary, indeed, sometimes sole attention: the *megabyzos*. This eunuch priest has fired the imagination of modern interpreters like no other.[58] The simple fact, however, is that this priesthood was obsolete by Paul's day; there were no more megabyzoi.[59] Hence, to speak of the megabyzos in connection with Pauline Ephesus is anachronistic.

54. See Hicks, *IBM*, 3:85; A. H. Jones, *Essenes: The Elect of Israel and the Priests of Artemis* (New York: University Press of America, 1985); and J. Kampen, "A Reconsideration of the Name 'Essene,'" *Hebrew Union College Annual* 57 (1986): 61–81, esp. pp. 68–74.

55. For example: "To Good Fortune. I give thanks to you, Lady Artemis. C. Scaptius Frontinus, neopoios, city councilor, along with my wife, Herennia Autronia. I completed a term as essene (ἐσσηνεύσας) purely and piously. The drink offering was performed by Theopompos III (great-grandson) of Menecrates, the votary" (IEph. 1578B; first or second century A.D.); and, "In the year of the chief staff-bearer, M. Aurelius Poseidonius. I give thanks to you Lady Artemis. Aur. Niconianus Eucarpus son of Agathemerus, voluntary neopoios, chrysophorus, member of the gerousia, and gymnasiarch of the gerousia, in that I piously and generously fulfilled two terms as essene" (Neue Inschriften IX, 120).

56. For example, sacred-victors (ἱερονεῖκαι) of the games in honor of Artemis were supported after their victories as "votaries" (ἱεροί) of the goddess (IEph. 18.22 and 17.46–50) and may also have been called "crown-bearers" (χρυσοφόροι). Cf. Hicks, *IBM*, 3:85–87; and Oster, "Ephesus as a Religious Center," 1722.

57. For example: "The most sacred association of neopoioi of our lady, the goddess Artemis, have honored the loyal Cornelius Gamus, high-councilor, general, sheriff, neopoios, decemprimus, twice secretary (of the people), chrysophorus, superintendent of education (*paidonomon*) . . . " [broken off] (Neue Inschriften IX, 121–22); and, "I give you thanks, Lady Artemis. Metrodorus Damas, Jr., grandson of Alexas, Teïos tribe, Eurypompios division; I completed a term as neopoios piously and [two as es]sene, (I dedicate this) with my three children, and [my w]ife, and brother" (IEph. 1588).

58. The Kroegers connect the megabyzos with possible ritual castration in the Christian community of 1 Tim. 2 (*I Suffer Not a Woman*, 94).

59. Richard Oster attributes the disappearance of the megabyzos to the rise of Roman hegemony at Ephesus ("Ephesus as a Religious Center," 1721–22). Strabo, in the late first

The discussion of sacred offices so far has shown that the cult hierarchy of Artemis Ephesia was securely under the control of the male political establishment of Ephesus. And many of the local civil magistrates themselves filled the priesthoods. There is nothing surprising
about this; it was typical of Hellenic cults and cultures. Hence, to maintain that "the primary religious power [in Ephesus] lay with women by
the first century c.e."[60] runs counter to the clear and abundant evidence
we have briefly reviewed.

Artemis Ephesia

A survey of some New Testament reference works on Artemis of Ephesus shows a consensus that she was "not the virgin huntress of Graeco-
Roman tradition, but the many-breasted Asian mother-goddess, the
symbol of fertility."[61] There are three interrelated components to this
statement: (1) Artemis Ephesia was not the virgin huntress of Greco-
Roman tradition; (2) (because) the adornments on her cult statues represent breasts; (3) (instead,) Artemis of Ephesus was a mother or fertility goddess. Although these seem to be well-entrenched opinions, they
run counter to the judgment of specialists in Ephesian studies and
should consequently be rethought. I will challenge each *seriatim*.

The character of the classical Hellenic Artemis (Diana to the Romans) is presented in this early hymn: "I sing of Artemis, whose shafts
are of gold, who cheers on the hounds, the pure maiden, shooter of
stags, who delights in archery, own sister to Apollo. . . . (After the hunt)
she hangs up her curved bow and her arrows, and heads and leads the
dances, gracefully arrayed (along with the Muses and Graces)" (*Homeric Hymns* 27; LCL trans.). Artemis was the ever-virgin consort of wild

century b.c., speaks of the megabyzos as something from the past: "[The Ephesians]
used to have (εἶχον) eunuch priests, whom they would call (ἐκάλουν) 'Megabyzoi.' They
were ever looking elsewhere for people worthy of such a high position (προστασία),
and they used to be held (ἦγον) in high honor. It was necessary (ἐχρῆν) for virgins to
serve with them. Nowadays, some of their customary practices are preserved, and others less so" (*Geog.* 14.1.23). Note that "megabyzos" does not appear on any of the
roughly four thousand inscriptions from Ephesus. The only epigraphical reference to
this figure occurs in two connected honorary inscriptions from Priene from 334/3 b.c.
(IPriene 3 and 231).

60. Kroegers, *I Suffer Not a Woman*, 71, 196.

61. J. B. Prichard, ed., *The Harper Atlas of the Bible* (New York: Harper & Row, 1987),
175. See also L. R. Taylor, "Artemis of Ephesus," in *The Beginnings of Christianity*, ed.
F. Foakes Jackson and K. Lake (London: Macmillan, 1933), 5:253; H. Martin, "Artemis,"
ABD, 1:464–65; and D. Wheaton, "Diana," *NBD*, 311–12. Cf. Lynn LiDonnici, "The Images
of Artemis Ephesia and Greco-Roman Worship: A Reconsideration," *Harvard Theological
Review* 85 (1992): 389–415.

forest nymphs, who spurned marriage and relations with men. Her devotees, like priggish Hippolytus, were distinguished by perfect chastity
(Euripides, *Hippolytus*). Should they lose their virtue—even innocently
like Callisto—they were summarily banished from her presence as devotees defiled (Ovid, *Met.* 2.409–507). An even worse fate awaited unfor-
tunate ones like Actaeon, who accidently came upon Artemis bathing:
he was turned into a stag and torn limb from limb by his own hounds
(Ovid, *Met.* 3.138–255). A wild huntress, remote and unpredictable, Artemis loved the chase and the bow; even though she was mistress of animals and helper in childbirth, one of her swift shafts might cause the
sudden and inexplicable death of a maiden.

Some writers on the early history of Greek religion believe that Artemis originated in Asia Minor and that her role in childbirth points back
to an origin as the Anatolian mother goddess.[62] This notion, of course,
underlies modern opinions about Artemis Ephesia's identification as a
mother or fertility goddess in Paul's day. But Artemis's origin was long
forgotten even by the classical period. Already in the earliest literature
Artemis was "the virgin who delights in arrows" (*Homeric Hymns* 9),
"the unbroken virgin" (*Odyssey* 6.109), and "the mistress of the beasts"
(*Iliad* 21.470), but never a mother or confused with Aphrodite. "Whatever the roots of her fertility connections, the dominant conception of
Artemis in the classical period is that of the virgin huntress."[63]

Richard Oster, who has worked extensively on Artemis and Ephesus,
maintains that Artemis Ephesia herself conformed to this general
Greco-Roman conception of Artemis-Diana and rejects the fertility associations for this goddess because of "the deafening silence from all
the primary sources. None of the extant myths point in this direction,
neither do the significant epithets of the goddess."[64]

The myths of Artemis Ephesia all refer to her as the classical "fair-
child of Leto (sired) from Zeus" (IEph. 1383) and twin sister of Apollo,[65]
or as the virginal guardian of maidenhood and of chastity.[66] As we saw
earlier, the special priesthood of essenes maintained sexual purity dur-

62. But compare Louise Bruit Zaidman and Pauline Schmitt Pantel (*Religion in the
Ancient Greek City*, trans. P. Cartledge [Cambridge: Cambridge University Press, 1992]: 5),
who challenge this interpretation of Artemis and the "origins-theory" methodology behind it.

63. Mark P. O. Morford and Robert J. Lenardon, *Classical Mythology*, 4th ed. (New
York: Longman, 1991), 182; see esp. pp. 173–84. Cf. "Artemis" in *Kl. Pauly* and *OCD*; and
Burkert, *Greek Religion*, 149–52.

64. Oster, "Ephesus as a Religious Center," 1725–26; cf. his "The Ephesian Artemis as
an Opponent of Early Christianity," *Jahrbuch für Antike und Christentum* 19 (1976): 28;
and Paul Trebilco, "Asia," in *The Book of Acts in Its Graeco-Roman Setting*, 316–36.

65. See Leto and the nativity of Artemis depicted on Ephesian coins (e.g., *BMC* no.
374) and in Strabo (*Geog.* 14.1.20); cf. Oster, "Ephesus as a Religious Center," 1711–12.

66. Achilles Tatius, *Clitophon and Leucippe* 8.11–14.

ing their terms of service for "the pure goddess,"[67] "the most-holy (ἁγι-ωτάτη) Artemis" (e.g., IEph. 617 and 624).

The most significant evidence of Artemis Ephesia's virgin identity comes, again, from the epigraphical remains, the public records whereby the Ephesians displayed their conceptualization of their state goddess before the world. A lengthy record of a second-century A.D. oracle gives Artemis Ephesia's epithets in classic, Homeric form and terms.[68] She is "the virgin" (line 14; παρθένον), the "renowned, vigilant maiden" (line 12), and "Artemis the pure" (line 16). As the goddess who watches over childbirth, she is the "midwife of birth and grower of mortals" and the "giver of fruit" (lines 3–4). And as huntress she is "Artemis with beautiful quiver" (line 2), the "arrow-pourer" (line 11; ἰοχέαιρα),[69] the "irresistible straight-shooter" (line 11).[70]

On the second point, the "breasts" on the cult statues, at the very least one must concede Robert Fleischer's conclusion from his exhaustive study of the representations of Artemis Ephesia: "Regarding the meaning of the 'breasts' it is still not possible today to advance beyond mere speculation."[71] More pointedly, William Ramsay noted long ago that "They were not intended, however, to represent breasts, for no nipple was indicated."[72] (They also begin well below the breast area on most

67. ἡ καθαρὰ θεός from Tatius, *Clitophon*, 8.8. In the same passage, Tatius's priest of the "virgin" (παρθένος) goddess is accused of defiling his priesthood by allowing illicit sex in the Artemisium's precincts. See also Pseudo-Heraclitus, who interpreted the (pre-Pauline) Ephesian custom of having a eunuch as priest of Artemis (the megabyzos) because of fear "lest a man as a priest service her virginity!" (David R. Worley, trans., "Epistle 9," in *The Cynic Epistles*, SBLSBS 12, ed. A. Malherbe [Atlanta: Scholars Press, 1977], 213).

68. Neue Inschriften XII, no. 25; cf. Fritz Graf, "An Oracle against Pestilence from a Western Anatolian Town," *Zeitschrift für Papyrologie und Epigraphik* 92 (1992): 267–79.

69. A poetic epithet found in Homer and the Homeric Hymns (above); cf. Liddell-Scott-Jones, *Greek-English Lexicon*.

70. In the novel by Xenophon of Ephesus, the Ephesian heroine dresses in a fawnskin hunting costume complete with quiver and arrows. In consequence, "Ephesians would reverence her as Artemis when they saw her in the sacred precincts" (*Ephesiaca* 1.3; probably 2nd cent. A.D.).

71. Fleischer, *Artemis von Ephesos*, 87. Cf. Fleischer, "Artemis von Ephesos und Verwandte Kultstatuen aus Anatolien und Syrien Supplement," in *Studien zur Religion und Kultur Kleinasiens*, ed. S. Sahin et al. (Leiden: E. J. Brill, 1978), 324–31; and A. Hill, "Ancient Art and Artemis: Toward Explaining the Polymastic Nature of the Figurine," *Journal of the Ancient Near Eastern Society* 21 (1992): 91–94.

Fleischer covers all interpretations of the "breasts" to date, observing that the breast interpretation did not originate from pagan worshipers of Artemis but from secondary Christian writers Minucius Felix and Jerome. Other interpretations include pendants from a necklace, sacred grapes, bee eggs, and scrota of sacrificed bulls (!); cf. Fleischer, *Artemis von Ephesos*, 74–88. In favor of the "grape thesis," there is an interesting painting of Bacchus covered with large grapes at Pompeii; cf. T. Feder, *Great Treasures of Pompeii and Herculaneum* (New York: Abbeville, 1978), 14–15.

72. *Asian Elements in Greek Civilisation* (Chicago: Ares, 1976; repr. of 1927 ed.), 82. Ramsay took the objects to be bee eggs.

representations.) And confirmation that they are not breasts comes
from the fact that very similar ornamentation appears on Anatolian re-
liefs of Zeus and on a statuette of Cybele below her breasts, which are
discernable under her gown.[73]

We should also take into account that a statue of a classically Hellenic Artemis was found in an Ephesian home and that a similar cult
statue of Artemis Ephesia with bow and torches is evidenced from the
oracle inscription mentioned above, which "has an iconography radically different from what we know about the famous statue of Ephesian
Artemis . . . [it is] a statue of a more common type."[74] That the Ephesians had no trouble associating the deity symbolized by the exotic cult
statue as the classical Artemis is illustrated by coins with the head of the
maiden huntress with bow and quiver on one side and the "polymastic"
cult statue on the other.[75]

Since "to write history on the basis of iconographic sources alone, is
a risky business that can lead only to the most dubious conclusions"[76]
we must rely more upon the myths, epithets, and descriptions of Artemis Ephesia to discover how the ancients conceived of her. The ornaments on her representations cannot establish Artemis Ephesia as a fertility or mother goddess without corroborating evidence.

Finally, there should be no need to belabor point number three (Artemis as a fertility goddess) if we have presented sufficient evidence
that her ornaments were not fertility symbols (breasts) and that she was
otherwise identified with the typical Hellenic Artemis in contemporary
Ephesian sources. There is simply no evidence from Artemis Ephesia's
cult practices to substantiate her as a fertility or mother goddess. Instead, what we do know of her worship shows it to have been a typical
Hellenic state cult, with "feasts," "festivals," and "public sacrifices"
(IEph. 24), banquets (IEph. 951; Strabo, *Geog.* 14.1.20), processions
(IEph. 1577, 26–37, and 221), and contests of athletes, actors, and musicians at the "Great Artemisia" and other sacred games in her honor

73. Fleischer, *Artemis von Ephesos*, plates 58, 138–41; cf. LiDonnici, "Images of Artemis," figs. 2–3.

74. Graf, "Oracle against Pestilence," 269–70. For the classical statue, see Anton Bammer et al., *Führer durch das archäologische Museum in Selçuk-Ephesos* (Vienna: Öster-
reichisches Archäologisches Institut, 1974), photo 9. For torches of classical Artemis, see
Pausanius, 8.37.1 (Arkadia).

75. Stefan Karwiese, "Ephesos: Numismatischer Teil," *PW Suppl.* 12.311. Karwiese
references several other types: "griech(ische) Artemis m(it) Bogen u(nd) Köcher," "jagende
Artemis," kneeling stags, torches, etc. (ibid., 307ff.); cf. Head, *Historia Numorum*, 571–77.
One coin from the third century A.D. has "Artemis of the Ephesians" riding a car drawn by
stags; see Peter Robert Franke, *Kleinasien zur Römerzeit: Griechisches Leben im Spiegel der
Münzen* (Munich: C. H. Beck, 1968), no. 355; cf. nos. 350–51 and 353.

76. Stella Georgoudi, "Creating a Myth of Matriarchy," in *A History of Women in the
West*, ed. P. Pantel (Cambridge: Belknap/Harvard University Press, 1992): 1:460.

(e.g., IEph. 1081–1160).[77] Fertility and orgiastic rituals in the Greco-Roman world were much different.[78]

None of this implies that the ancient Ephesians were uniform in their theological conceptions, that they lacked a syncretistic spirit, or that they rejected the worship of fertility deities out of some higher religious principles. Nor was Ephesian paganism necessarily as innocent as the inscriptions portray; certainly, the obsession with magic at Ephesus exposes the demonic side of its religion (Acts 19:13–19).[79] But these things are common elsewhere too; the Ephesians were little different in their religious conceptions from inhabitants of other Pauline cities.

The Ephesians did worship fertility goddesses (Demeter, Gē, and Meter), but so did most of their pagan contemporaries. Furthermore, it cannot be shown that worship of such deities, or of any female deity, translated into societal status, rights, or power for women in ancient societies. To say that it did at Ephesus because of the centrality of the worship of Artemis Ephesia is sheer speculation that runs counter to the facts. One would have to say the same thing about Athens and their cult of Athena Polias, which is often used as a paradigm for a thoroughly patriarchal society.

We have presented only males in politics and religion to this point, and we have seen them filling the principal positions. So far, the primary sources have forced grave doubts on the "feminist Ephesus" thesis, and this essay has challenged particularly the modern interpretation of Artemis as a fertility or mother deity who sponsored the religious or social superiority of women over men at Ephesus. However, we have not yet discussed Ephesian women. What were their civic roles? Since some did play a part in Ephesian public life, we must now give them due attention. But first, the problems that this particular subject poses to the scholar of ancient history need to be mentioned.

77. See, for example, the procession in honor of Artemis Ephesia described by Xenophon of Ephesus; "The Ephesian Tale," G. Anderson, trans., in *Collected Ancient Greek Novels*, ed. B. P. Reardon (Berkeley: University of California Press, 1989), 128–69. Cf. I. Ringwood, "Festivals of Ephesus," *American Journal of Archaeology* 76, no. 1 (1972): 17–22. It has been said that the cult of Artemis Ephesia was a mystery religion in the technical sense fulfilled only by women (hence, a fertility cult); so Kroegers, *I Suffer Not a Woman*, 97–98, 186–88, et al. The term μυστήρια does occur on Ephesian inscriptions, but it refers to rituals depicting the nativity of Artemis (involving the male kouretes; see above) according to Oster, "Ephesus as a Religious Center," 1711–13; Kearsley, *New Docs 6*, 196–202; and Rogers, *Sacred Identity*, 81. And men did "fulfill the mysteries" at Ephesus as well as young girls and women (IEph. 26, 1069, and Neue Inschriften XII, no. 6).

78. For example, see the worship of Cybele in Juvenal, *Satire* 6.512–20; 2.82–99. There is, by the way, scant evidence for the worship of Cybele at Ephesus; cf. Oster, "Ephesus as a Religious Center," 1688.

79. Cf. Clinton E. Arnold, *Ephesians: Power and Magic. The Concept of Power in Ephesians in Light of Its Historical Setting*, SNTSM 63 (Cambridge: Cambridge University Press, 1989).

Women in Antiquity

The secondary works on women of antiquity understandably focus on either classical Athens or imperial Rome, which makes our task more difficult. For example, legal prerogatives of women in Rome are frequently imputed to women in the free Greek city-states, which had their own long-standing laws and traditions (developing *Romanitas* in the provinces notwithstanding).[80] Furthermore, changes in women's legal status are often used to posit a rise in their social status[81] even though there is no necessary correlation between the two.

A further condition that should limit blanket statements on women is the sharp distinction between cities like Ephesus and their rural possessions. Life was much different in the outlying hamlets and villages than in the cities, and the rural people easily comprised 75 percent to 80 percent of the total population in antiquity.[82] And of the metropolitan population, perhaps as many as one-third or more were slaves who lacked any sort of legal rights or social position.[83] Even if freed, slaves often remained in a subordinate role in the *oikos* closely resembling their former service.[84]

In societies with at best a small middle class in the modern sense and with a minuscule urban elite, any assertion about "women's rights" is relevant for only a tiny fraction of all ancient women. Few had the leisure and social position to profit from legal rights or social openings, even if available. We will, therefore, proceed cautiously from evidence that is notoriously inadequate, often only partly understood, and self-contradictory at times.[85]

80. Cf. Jane F. Gardner, *Women in Roman Law and Society* (Bloomington: Indiana University Press, 1991).

81. For example, Everett Ferguson, *Backgrounds of Early Christianity,* 2nd ed. (Grand Rapids: Eerdmans, 1993), 72; and Gritz, *Paul, Women Teachers,* 16–18. Compare Eva Contarella, *Pandora's Daughters* (Baltimore: Johns Hopkins University Press, 1987), 140–41. Cf. Ramsay MacMullen, "Woman in Public in the Roman Empire," *Historia* 29 (1980): 208–18.

82. See, for example, Apuleius, *Metamorphoses,* and Longus, "Daphnis and Cloe" for somewhat idealized portraits of Greek rural life in the imperial period. Cf. Fergus Millar, "The World of the *Golden Ass,*" *Journal of Roman Studies* 71 (1981): 63–75; and Ramsay MacMullen, *Roman Social Relations 50 B.C. to A.D. 284* (New Haven: Yale, 1974), 1–56.

83. Galen estimates that one-third of second-century Pergamum's population were slaves; see Géza Alföldy, *The Social History of Rome* (London: Croom Helm, 1985), 137. In first-century Ephesus, even some slaves owned slaves to perform their service (IEph. 18.18–22).

84. Freed slaves remaining in the *oikos* is illustrated by their inclusion in family grave plots: "I desire that my slaves, freedmen, and slave girls be placed in this tomb" (IEph. 2414). Cf. "Freigelassene," *Kl. Pauly;* "Freedmen," *OCD;* and Thomas Wiedemann, *Greek and Roman Slavery* (Baltimore: Johns Hopkins University Press, 1981), 3–4, 52–56.

85. For example, Plutarch gives contradictory views of Spartan women within one essay: They were famous for ruling over their men, yet one Spartan woman said: "When I

One firm starting point has already been established from our discussion so far: men filled Ephesian magistracies and its most prominent social positions. This alone rules out the kind of feminism sometimes conferred on Ephesus. In addition, we have blaring silence regarding feminism from curious explorers like Strabo and Pliny the Elder in their comments on Ephesus.[86] They give no hint whatsoever that women dominated this city.

And it is not as though the ancients would not have recognized a feminist society. They sometimes spoke about (fanciful) gynecocrats like the Amazons, who were supposed to rule foreign lands in distant times; yet with the notice that, "What I have to say will appear, on account of its fabulous nature to resemble tales from mythology (μύθοι)" (Diod. Sic. 2.44.3; cf. 2.46.6). In such stories of "people among whom women possessed sovereignty" (ἔθνους . . . γυναικοκρατουμένου—whence English "gynecocracy") (Diod. Sic. 2.45.1), only the women were involved in "manly military prowess," magistracies, and the affairs of state. Husbands were consigned to spinning and weaving—litmus tasks for dutiful Greek wives—and other domestic chores, including the care of children (e.g., Diod. Sic. 1.27.2; 2.44.1–5; 3.53.1–4). Family roles in Ephesus were not like this, however.

Are we correspondingly left with the position that "The opinion Thucydides imputes to Pericles reflects the ancient world's prevailing view of women: the less said about them the better"?[87] Were Ephesian women locked in their homes by jealous and severe patriarchs? And is it correct to say that: "Old-fashioned women proved their modesty by going out as little as possible and never showing themselves in public without a partial veil"?[88]

It is true that women appear only rarely in the epigraphical remains from Ephesus. Normally the city's patrons do not mention their wives at all; if they do, it is something like: "P. Hordeonius Lollianus with wife" (IEph. 20). Wives do occasionally appear by name on Ephesian

---

was a child, I learned obedience to my father . . . and since I became a wife, now I obey my husband" (*Lacaenarum apophthegmata* [*Mor.* 240E and 242B]). Which was the real Spartan woman? The ruler, the ruled, or a *tertia quis*?

For similar cautions, see Hugo Montgomery, "Women and Status in the Greco-Roman World," *Studia theologica* 43 (1989): 115–24; and Averil Cameron, "'Neither Male Nor Female,'" *Greece and Rome* 27 (1980): 60–68.

86. Not to mention Achilles Tatius, Aelius Aristides, Dio Chrysostom, Diodorus Siculus, Herodotus, Pausanius, Plutarch, and Xenophon of Ephesus.

87. Pauline Schmitt Pantel, "Representations of Women," in *A History of Women*, 1:2; cf. Thucydides 2.44; Plutarch in *De mulierum virtutes* (*Mor.* 242E–F).

88. Paul Veyne, "The Roman Empire," in *A History of Private Life: From Pagan Rome to Byzantium, I*, ed. P. Veyne (Cambridge, Mass.: Belknap/Harvard University Press, 1987), 73. On veils, see Richard Oster, "When Men Wore Veils to Worship: The Historical Context of 1 Corinthians 11.4," *New Testament Studies* 34 (1988): 481–505.

stones, although frequently as models of classical female virtues, particularly "modesty" or "prudence" (the term that appears in 1 Tim. 2:9, 15).[89] For example, Laevia Paula was given this eulogy at her funeral procession: "The state council and people crown Laevia L. f. Paula who lived a modest and decorous life (σώφρονα καὶ κόσμιον ζήσασαν βίον)" (IEph. 614B; A.D. 16–37). It is clear from comparing her memorial with her husband's—M. Antonius Albus who was "the patron (προστάτης) of the temple of Artemis and of the city" (IEph. 614C)—that Laevia was honored because of her husband's benefactions, not for her own public services. She did not act as head of their oikos.[90]

Nevertheless, Ephesian women and girls do appear in some official capacities, not just as the honorably mentioned wives of patriarchs and patrons. Evidence to this effect picks up in the first century A.D., so we cannot trace it to a long-standing emphasis on a "feminine principle" connected to Amazons, Ephesian culture, or Artemis Ephesia. Upon examination, we find a few first-century women filling one or more of four offices: priestess of Artemis, *kosmeteira*, *prytanis*, and high priestess of Asia.

Table 1.4
Female Priesthoods in Ephesus

Priestess of Artemis	ἱερεία Ἀρτέμιδος	Cultic duties in processions; financial underwriting of cult; some were young girls

89. σωφροσύνη. Also: "good judgment," "moderation," "self-control," "Esp. as a feminine virtue *decency, chastity*" (BAGD and LSJ). Sometimes seen as part of a New Testament "code-of-conduct"; see David C. Verner, *The Household of God: The Social World of the Pastoral Epistles*, SBLDS 71 (Chico, Calif.: Scholars Press, 1983), 134–39; cf. Hermann von Lips, "Die Haustafel als 'Topos' im Rahmen der urchristlichen Paränese," *New Testament Studies* 40 (1994): 261–80.

90. An even more pointed illustration of the value placed on female "modesty" at Ephesus is demonstrated in this honorary inscription of unknown date: "(Heraclides Didymus) . . . [unknown office] of Artemis and was benefactor of the people because of his personal, universal excellence, his piety toward Artemis, his acumen and trustworthiness in learning, and his goodwill toward the people. [Ammion, daughter of Perigenus,] wife of Heraclides Didymus son of Menis (was honored) because of her personal modesty (σωφροσύνη) and because of the goodwill of her husband, Heraclides, toward the demos" (IEph. 683A; lacunae supplied from IEph. 683B). It is explicitly stated that Ammion received honorable mention because of her husband's public benefactions; her own praise consists of the stock expression of "modesty."

See also a grave inscription from Prusias-on-Hypius (Bithynia), where: "Aur(elia) Chrestiniane Rufina, known as Himeris, was the modest and husband-honoring wife (ἡ σώφρων καὶ φίλανδρος γυνή) of the silversmith Aur(elius) Socratianos Pasikrates, she lived a decorous life (κοσμίως) for 31 years" (IPrusias 89). The editor calls the phrase in question "Eine typische Formulierung für eine Frau" and cites other examples.

Kosmeteira	κοσμήτειρα	Responsible for adornment of cult statue of Artemis for festival (?); often the priestess of Artemis also
Prytanis	πρύτανις	Priesthood of Hestia Boulaia in Prytaneion; financial underwriting of cult; some were young girls, but most prytaneis were male
High Priestess of Asia	ἀρχιερεία Ἀσίας	Financial upkeep of imperial cult; cultic duties probably focused on divinized empresses; only two known in Ephesus from the late first century

A first-century kouretes list serves as an example of relevant evidence (though it is rare that one woman filled all three offices): "In the prytany of Vedia Marcia, the daughter of Pu[blius], priestess (of Artemis) and high priestess of Asia" (IEph. 1017; A.D. 93–100). Let us discuss each office in turn (though combining the Artemis priestess and kosmeteira).[91]

Priestesses of Artemis

It should come as no surprise to find women serving as priestesses at Ephesus. In fact, women held a variety of priesthoods and unofficial functions in state cults throughout the Greco-Roman world.[92] As mentioned earlier, the ancients thought it especially fitting for a priestess to serve goddesses in the same way that sacrifices of female animals were normally offered to female deities. Furthermore, Greek women regularly participated in a variety of ways in state cults regardless of the sex

91. A few Ephesians served as priestesses of Leto, Athena, and other gods (e.g., IEph. 4107 and Neue Inschriften IX, 142–43); cf. honors for a Magnesian woman who was "priestess also of Demeter in Ephesus" (IMag. 158). Women also appear as "envoys" (θεωροί) to the Ephesian "Olympic games" (e.g., IEph. 891–96). The *theōros*, often a priestess, represented the state's matrons at the sacred games as at Olympia (Pausanias, 2.20.8–9); cf. H. Engelmann, "Zu Inschriften aus Ephesos," *Zeitschrift für Papyrologie und Epigraphik* 26 (1977): 154–55.

There is also some evidence for women as benefactresses of public works, although after the first century A.D.; cf. G. M. Rogers, "Constructions of Women at Ephesus," *Zeitschrift für Papyrologie und Epigraphik* 90 (1992): 215–23.

92. See Mary Lefkowitz and Maureen Fant, eds., *Women's Life in Greece and Rome: A Source Book in Translation* (Baltimore: Johns Hopkins University Press, 1982), 113–27, 249–62; Ross Kraemer, *Maenads, Martyrs, Matrons, Monastics: A Sourcebook on Women's Religions in the Greco-Roman World* (Philadelphia: Fortress, 1988), 11–38, 211–17; cf. Louise Bruit Zaidman, "Pandora's Daughters and Rituals in Grecian Cities," in *A History of Women*, 338–76; John Scheid, "The Religious Roles of Roman Women," ibid., 377–408.

of the honoree. Women might garland[93] or lustrate sacrificial victims, play musical instruments,[94] sing, shout a distinct cry (ὀλολυγή), chant, dance, pour libations, prepare sacred garments or sacrificial foods, bear water or sacred objects in processions, prophesy at the oracles, and so on.[95]

Who were the priestesses of Artemis of Ephesus? What do we know about them? As the example of Vedia Marcia illustrates, most of the priestesses had Roman names, suggesting that they were members of the municipal elite; perhaps some were even daughters of Roman immigrants.[96]

Vedia is identified as the "daughter of Pu[blius]," but not as the wife of anyone. In fact, many of the priestesses named on the inscriptions are identified only by the names of one or both parents or by their ancestors, leaving husbands unmentioned.[97] This is important, since most Ephesian women are identified as the "wife of so-and-so." "What's your husband's name?" (Aristophanes, *Thesmophoriazusae* 619) was the normal way to identify a married woman in the Greek world. Therefore Vedia Marcia was not (yet?) married.

What should we make of this? Another priestess of Artemis, Ulpia Euodia Mudiane, daughter of Mudianus and Euodia, says that she "performed the mysteries and made all expenses *through my parents*" (IEph. 989; emphasis added). This priestess of Artemis and others like her were unmarried girls.[98] Since Greek girls usually married soon after pu-

---

93. The στέμματα in Acts 14:13.

94. See Johannes Quasten, *Music and Worship in Pagan and Christian Antiquity*, trans. B. Ramsey (Washington, D.C.: National Association of Pastoral Musicians, 1983), 1–31; esp. p. 17, where two female flutists and two veiled girls appear on the pedestal of a statuette of Artemis Ephesia in Rome. Quasten interprets the scene as an incense offering.

95. "Whereas inequality between the sexes was the rule in the political sphere, it appears that honors and responsibilities in the religious sphere were divided according to some other principle. Priestesses seem to have had the same rights and duties as priests" (Zaidman, "Pandora's Daughters," 373).

Also, women alone performed certain mystic rituals in the Thesmophoria festival celebrated in many Hellenic cities, including Ephesus. See the parody by Aristophanes (*Thesmophoriazusae*); cf. "Thesmophoria," *Kl. Pauly*; Marcel Detienne, "The Violence of Wellborn Ladies: Women in the Thesmophoria," in *The Cuisine of Sacrifice among the Greeks*, ed. M. Detienne and J.-P. Vernant (Chicago: University of Chicago Press, 1989), 129–47; and Burkert, *Greek Religion*, 242–46.

96. An inscription of Trajanic date was dedicated: *favisori civitatis Ephesiorum qui in statario negotiantur*, "To the patron of the Ephesian citizenry who conduct business in the slave market" (IEph. 646). These were Roman businessmen who possessed local citizenship also.

97. For priestesses of Artemis named by their parents and ancestors, see, for example, IEph. 492; 508; 980–989A; 3059; 3072.

98. IEph. 3072 (ca. A.D. 270) is a lengthy memorial for "the most-missed daughter" of Vedius Servilius Gaius who similarly "fulfilled the mysteries through her father Gaius." It is not certain whether she was a prytanis (below) or priestess of Artemis (especially

berty, these priestesses of the "virgin" Artemis Ephesia must have been about fourteen years old or even younger (some Greek girls were married at age twelve).[99]

What were the duties of the priestesses of Artemis, especially given that some were young girls? Although our knowledge of their cultic responsibilities is sketchy and somewhat conjectural, they unquestionably did not engage in sacred prostitution.[100] These were the maiden daughters (and wives?) of the wealthy elite who served their goddess "circumspectly" (ἱεροπρεπῶς; IEph. 987–88), "piously and with decorum" (εὐσεβῶς καὶ κοσμίως; IEph. 3059), and "worthily of the goddess and of her family" (Neue Inschriften XIII, no. 160).[101] The whole idea is absurd for the priestesses of Artemis, "the unbroken virgin."[102]

We can say with some confidence, though, that (as with other priesthoods in this period) monetary obligations were paramount for Artemis's priestesses. We saw already that the parents of the priestess Ulpia Euodia Mudiane provided the requisite funds for her. Adding more details, two first-century (?) priestesses, Vipsania Olympias and her

---

since the Artemisium was sacked by raiding Goths only a few years earlier if the date is accurate). The prytanis and gymnasiarch Ploutarchos inscribed a prayer to Hestia and Artemis on behalf of his children, "priestesses of Artemis" (IEph. 1068).

99. That such young girls could serve as priestesses of Artemis Ephesia fits Plutarch's comparison of her priestesses with the Roman vestal virgins (*Moralia* 795D–E). Along with this, one broken inscription of a priestess of Artemis mentions that she came from a line of ancestors who served in the "virgin-office" (ἐκ παρθενῶν[ος]; IEph. 990).

For possible married priestesses, see Auphidia Quintilia, "priestess (of Artemis) and high priestess (of Asia) of the temples in Ephesus," who paid for an honorary statue of her husband, "Tib. Claudius Aelius Crispus the asiarch, agonothete of the great Ephesian (games), secretary of the people, secretary of the state council, and all other liturgies" (IEph 637). We know that the priestesses Kallinoe and Hordeonia Paulina had sons (IEph. 615A; 981, cf. 690), but we cannot tell whether they had served in the temple before their marriage or afterward.

Achilles Tatius says: "From ancient days this temple [the Artemisium] had been forbidden to free women who were not virgins. Only men and virgins were permitted here. If a non-virgin woman passed inside, the penalty was death" (7.13) (J. Winkler, trans., in *Collected Ancient Greek Novels*, 267). There is some doubt about whether Tatius had firsthand knowledge of Ephesus though.

100. Compare n. 8.

101. At the very least, most priestesses had Roman names and were presumably the daughters of Roman citizens. There were strict penalties for prostitution under Roman law for them; see Gardner, *Women in Roman Law*, 127–34, 250–53.

102. While sacred prostitution is sometimes proposed, say, in Aphrodite's cult at Corinth ("Prostitution," *Kl. Pauly* [4.1192]), it is a disputed question; see Burkert, *Greek Religion*, 158, 408, n. 9; cf. 108–9. In any case, there is no ancient evidence for sacred prostitution at Ephesus whatsoever, even though a (secular) brothel has been excavated there; cf. Otto Meinardus, "The Alleged Advertisement for the Ephesian Lupanar," *Wiener Studien* 7 (1973): 244–48.

(adopted?) sister Vipsania Polla, "wreathed the temple and all its precincts in the days of the goddess' manifestations, making the public sacrifices and the distributions (of money) to the council and gerousia" (IEph. 987–88). Another priestess "(made) all the distributions of her priesthood" (IEph. 997) while the priestess Flavia Chrysanthe "fulfilled the myster[ies] generously" (Neue Inschriften IX, 123). The requisite donations and generosity for Artemis's priestesses were apparently set by the state council itself, since another stone reads: "(name lost) served as priestess of Artemis piously and generously . . . and gave 5,000 denarii to the city in accordance with the state council's measure" (Neue Inschriften XI, no. 8, 176; ca. A.D. 165). We may suppose that at least part of the definition of "pious" service as priestess was serving "generously."

Another of the priestesses' duties beyond financial underwriting of the cult is suggested by the associated title, *kosmeteira* ("adorner"), often held concurrently by the priestess (IEph. 892, 983–84, 989, etc.). The etymology of this title suggests something to do with adorning the cult statue of Artemis with clothing and ornaments, which was common in the Greek world and clearly evidenced for Artemis Ephesia (IEph. 2).[103] The role of the priestess and kosmeteira may have centered on providing sacred adornments for Artemis similar to the role of the girls and priestesses, who made and presented an ornate new robe *(peplos)* to Athena during the Athenian Panathenaia.[104]

The priestesses of Artemis Ephesia fit the general picture of women's participation in Greco-Roman cults. These were sometimes the young daughters of municipal elites whose financial contributions to the cult festivals were important aspects of their sacred service. The fact that these were sometimes prepubescent girls makes the priestesses of Artemis Ephesia particularly unlikely material from which to posit a gynecocratic society. Their duties, beyond financial obligations, would have been necessarily ceremonial ones, perhaps connected with sacred clothing, rather than ones that evidence women "as prime movers and mediators in religion" at Ephesus.[105]

---

103. Also: "When Fl(avius) Perigenes was prytanis, Vedia Papiane was priestess of Athena for life, T. Fl(avius) Julianus was secretary of the people, when the fullers and whiteners of the goddess Artemis were in charge, (the following) boys and girls (παῖδες καὶ παρθένοι) presented the adornment (τὸν κόσμον) to the goddess . . . " (there follows a list naming eight boys, no girls) (Neue Inschriften IX, 142–43). Cf. F. Sokolowski, "A New Testimony on the Cult of Artemis of Ephesus," *Harvard Theological Review* 58 (1965): 427–31.

104. "Panathenaia," in *Kl. Pauly* and *OCD*.

105. Kroegers, *I Suffer Not a Woman*, 70.

Prytanis

"I give thanks to Mistress Hestia and to all the gods," wrote the *prytanis* Aurelia Juliane, daughter of Paparion, "for they returned me safe and sound to my parents" (IEph. 1066). In other Greek states, the prytany was a high-ranking executive magistracy of the state council, often the office whose annual incumbent's name dated state documents.[106] The pre-imperial Ephesian prytany possibly had this eponymous, magisterial character (cf. IEph. 9), but not by the time Aurelia Juliane and other females served as prytaneis; the Ephesian office had changed.[107]

For some reason, after the reign of Augustus when the new prytaneion was built, the Ephesian prytany became a subordinate priesthood of Hestia-of-the-Council (Hestia Boulaia), the flame-goddess of the hearth. In a Greek oikos, keeping the hearth-fire burning was an important task, and worship of Hestia as the eternal flame symbolized the family's continuity, health, and dependence on the gods for its basic needs, among which fire was the most important.[108] The cult of Hestia in the city's prytaneion was simply an extrapolation from the oikos: "The fire cult, then, proceeding from a necessary task in daily life, became a symbol for political unity embracing numerous families. . . . This cult of Hestia was thus a clear indication that the whole city was actually a single, big family."[109]

106. I.e., the "eponymous" office. See the series: Robert K. Sherk, "Eponymous Officials of Greek Cities I," *Zeitschrift für Papyrologie und Epigraphik* 83 (1990): 249–88; "Eponymous . . . II," *Zeitschrift für Papyrologie und Epigraphik* 84 (1990): 231–95; "Eponymous . . . III," *Zeitschrift für Papyrologie und Epigraphik* 88 (1991): 225–60; "Eponymous . . . IV," *Zeitschrift für Papyrologie und Epigraphik* 93 (1992): 223–72; "Eponymous . . . V," *Zeitschrift für Papyrologie und Epigraphik* 96 (1993): 267–95. On the Greek prytany, see "Prytanen," *Kl. Pauly* ("erscheinen P. als Höchstmagistrate vieler Städte an der W.-Küste Kleinasiens"; 4.1206); "Prytaneis" in *OCD*; A. H. M. Jones, *The Greek City* (Oxford: Clarendon, 1940), 178–79.

107. The main witnesses of women who served as prytanis come from the annual lists of kouretes dated by the eponymous prytaneis inscribed in the prytaneion. The prytaneis are collated in Knibbe, *Kureteninschriften*, 162–64; and his "Neue Kuretenliste," 125–27. There are fifty-four men and twelve women prytaneis from the first to third centuries A.D., but only two women are from the first century A.D. No women are attested as prytaneis on earlier inscriptions.

108. Symbolized in Greek mythology when Prometheus tricked Zeus by clandestinely giving fire to men and raising them above the brutes. In wrathful response, Zeus created a "beautiful, evil" (καλὸν κακόν) woman (Pandora) (Hesiod, *Theogonia* 562–612). Hestia herself was represented as "immortal flame" and "ever-maiden" (ἀειπάρθενος) (IEph. 1063–64) and corresponds to the Roman Vesta. Cf. Oster, "Ephesus as a Religious Center," 1688–91.

109. Reinhold Merkelbach, "Der Kult der Hestia im Prytaneion der Griechischen Städte," *Zeitschrift für Papyrologie und Epigraphik* 37 (1980): 77–92; quote from p. 79; cf. Knibbe, *Kureteninschriften*, 101–5.

In the Greek oikos, a young girl tended the hearth-fire, so it was natural for Hestia Boulaia to be served by a girl at the city's hearth as well. This is precisely the case with Aurelia Juliane, who was "returned to her parents" after her term of office. Like some of the priestesses of Artemis, some prytaneis were prepubescent girl-priestesses whose wealthy families acquired the honor for their daughters.[110]

The specific duties of the Ephesian prytany in the imperial era primarily involved significant monetary expenditures. The clearest evidence of this is a long inscription from the late second or early third century A.D. summarizing an "ancestral law" regulating the prytanis's duties (IEph. 10).[111] The cultic duties were lighting the altar fires, making incense and herb offerings, and participating in animal sacrifices (daily), paeans, processions, and night festivals. The inscription explicitly says that the prytanis paid the bill "out of his private resources."[112]

Even if some female prytaneis were married, we must conclude that the prytany had no magisterial powers during the period when females served as prytaneis, though a high honor for a prytanis and her family. Would a prepubescent girl—or boy for that matter—be given magisterial responsibilities today?[113] For the same reasons, tenure in this office

110. Cf. Merkelbach, "Kult der Hestia," 80. One epigraphical example reads: "[Broken—see editors' note for reconstruction from IEph. 987] . . . (a female) performed the public sacrifices and likewise made the distributions [to the council] and to the gerousia from the sacrifices and to the temple household and to the sacred-victors of games for Artemis, [expended?] her private d[enarii?] on account of the generosity (τὰς φιλοδοξίας) of her father for the prytany and [gymnasi]archy and all the other phil[anthropic. . . .]" (Neue Inschriften XII, no. 21). This girl-prytanis and gymnasiarch may never have set foot in a gymnasium; cf. Waldo E. Sweet, *Sport and Recreation in Ancient Greece* (New York: Oxford University Press, 1987), 134–44. In IEph. 650, a mother "undertook the prytany on behalf of her son from her funds"; the prytanis was either dead or too young to serve himself (cf. IEph. 4339).

111. Translated with brief comments by A. L. Connolly in *New Docs 4*, 106–7.

112. The regulations of IEph. 10 put the prytanis's activities under the oversight of a hierophant, who ensured that all was done according to "ancestral custom" (πάτριος νόμος). (He received "the head, tongue, and hide" from sacrificial animals as his due portion.) The inscription specified a fine for the negligent prytanis; "the kouretes and the hierophant are to make exaction for failure to attend to each particular point as specified."

113. Furthermore, the prytany was no longer always the eponymous office at Ephesus outside the kouretes inscriptions; many in the Christian era are dated by the terms of office of the provincial proconsul or the secretary of the people. For example: "[To Artemis Ephesia] and to the Emperor Caesar Augustus and to the neocorate people of the Ephesians, when P. Calvisius Ruso was proconsul. Erected by Claudia Trophime daughter of Philippos and Melissa, priestess and prytanis, when Tib. Cl(audius) Aristio the asiarch was secretary (of the people), restored when J[ul]ius Titian[us] was secretary of the people" (IEph. 508; A.D. 92/93). Kearsley mistakenly says that the female prytanis here is "the official by whose term the erection of a statue in a public place is dated" (*New Docs 6*, 26). Claudia Trophime is the donor of the statue (of Domitia or Domitian?); the eponymous officers are the proconsul and grammateus.

by girls cannot be viewed as a sign of a "women's rights" ideology. It shows rather that the city was willing to expand its base of individuals who would underwrite certain civic expenses in exchange for honors and priesthoods.[114]

High Priestess of Asia

The final official capacity in which we find women serving at Ephesus is as high priestesses of Asia, connected with the Roman imperial cult. This office in particular has been used as a sign of the advancement of women's social status in the province.[115] We will delve into this priest-hood only briefly, because, in the first place, its history and character have been fully explored in easily accessible works on the imperial cult in Asia Minor.[116] Second, the high priestesses of Asia represent nothing new; women held various priesthoods from the earliest times in the Greco-Roman state cults and particularly in earlier ruler cults honoring Hellenistic queens.[117]

The cult for the female personification of Roman power, the goddess Roma, is traceable in Asia to about 200 B.C. The early forms of this cult were municipal establishments under the oversight of a magistrate who served as "priest of Roma" at an altar or sacred precinct.[118] After Augus-tus allowed the provincial league *(koinon)* of Asia to establish a temple

114. In IEph. 1064, the prytanis Tullia spent her own funds lavishly. Similarly an im-perial freedman under Augustus, C. Julius Nicephorus, contributed heavily to games and sacrifices at Ephesus. His generosity probably explains how someone of former servile status could become a "prytanis for life" (IEph. 859 and 859A).

115. For example: "Especially in Asia Minor did women display public activity . . . and several of them obtained the highest priesthood of Asia—perhaps the greatest honor that could be paid to anyone" (James Donaldson, quoted in Ben Witherington, *Women in the Earliest Churches* [Cambridge: Cambridge University Press, 1988], 14, and in Kroegers, *I Suffer Not a Woman*, 93). The ranking of priesthoods implied by Donaldson's phrase "highest priesthood of Asia" is misleading. There were no other priesthoods of the pro-vincial imperial cult, and these priests had no *ex officio* role in other cults.

116. S. R. F. Price, *Rituals and Power: The Roman Imperial Cult in Asia Minor* (Cam-bridge: Cambridge University Press, 1984); and S. Friesen, *Twice Neokoros*; cf. H. Engel-mann, "Zum Kaiserkult in Ephesos," *Zeitschrift für Papyrologie und Epigraphik* 97 (1993): 279–89.

117. For instance, Queen Laodice III, wife of Antiochus III, received a cult in grati-tude for her establishment of dowries for the daughters of poor citizens of Iasos (ca. 196 B.C.). The cult was served by an unmarried "priestess of Aphrodite Laodice" and included "a procession on the queen's birthday and sacrifices by all the brides and bridegrooms to the queen" (in Price, *Rituals and Power*, 30).

118. For example, see IEph. 9 for a name-list of about thirty Ephesian priests of Roma from ca. 51–17 B.C. State cults for individual Romans are also known. For instance, see a dedication for Titus Peducaeus Canax from Nero's reign (IEph. 702). Among his other offices Canax was "priest of Rome and of Publius Servilius Isauricus." The cult of

for Roma at Pergamum in 29 B.C. (Cassius Dio 51.20.6–8; Tacitus, *Ann.* 4.37), the cult became a provincial affair with priests participating in (and funding) regular sacrifices, festivals, and games.

Women (sometimes girls) held early priesthoods in honor of the wives and mothers of Roman rulers.[119] However, the earliest, single reference to a provincial high priestess of Asia dates to the reign of Nero, though the evidence for this early date is very tenuous.[120] At Ephesus, the earliest high priestess dates to Domitian (though male provincial priests are found there earlier), and only two high priestesses can be dated to the first century.[121] There were apparently no high priestesses in Ephesus until twenty-five to thirty years after 1 Timothy was written, making them slightly anachronistic as an institution for this period.[122]

The service of provincial high priestesses probably arose to accommodate the worship of the divinized empresses like Domitia, wife of Domitian, and "Sabina, the divine Augusta, wife of the Emperor (Hadrian)" (IEph. 278).[123] Hence, the female high priesthood was analogous to the private priestesses of Hellenistic queens or of Livia Augusta, and it fits the general pattern of Greek religion for female divinities to be served ordinarily by a female priesthood.

The high priestesses of Asia probably did nothing out of the ordinary. Like the high priests, their most important function was financial;

Isauricus, who was an exceptionally beneficent provincial governor (46–44 B.C.), extended into the second century A.D. at Ephesus.

The title "high priest (of Roma and Augustus)" came into use at the beginning of the first century and "high priest of Asia" a few decades later. See the lists of high priests, high priestesses, and asiarchs in Friesen, *Twice Neocoros*, 172–208; and Margarete Rossner, "Asiarchen und Archiereis Asia," *Studii Clasice* 16 (1974): 112–42.

119. For instance, these brothers and young sister (?) served the imperial family at Ephesus in the reign of Tiberius: "So then the following are priests for life with double-shares (of sacrificial meat) and exception from duties: [Servilius] Bassus himself [priest] of Artemis; Servilia Secunda (priestess) of the Augustan Demeter Karpophoros; and (Servilius) Proclus (priest) of the sons of Drusus Caesar the new Dioscuri" (IEph. 4337). (Livia Augusta, wife of Augustus and mother of Tiberius, is given divine rank by association with Demeter, although her official divinization was not decreed until the reign of Claudius; cf. Price, *Rituals and Power*, 63–64. And the Dioscuri were Castor and Polydeuces, mythological twins of Zeus. Twins were born to Drusus, son of Tiberius, and Livilla about A.D. 19 [Tacitus, *Ann.* 2.84]).

120. See Friesen, *Twice Neokoros*, 85–88.

121. Vedia Marcia (IEph. 1017; see above) and Julia Lydia Laterane, wife of "the *princeps* of the Ephesians" (Pliny, *Ep.* 6.31) and high priest of Asia, Tib. Claudius Aristio (IEph. 424A, et al.). Friesen lists six high priestesses for the first century A.D. throughout the province (compared to dozens of high priests). His total is 29 high priestesses covering roughly a 150-year span compared with well over 100 high priests (and an equally high number of asiarchs); see *Twice Neocoros*, 172–208.

122. Dating 1 Timothy to the second half of Nero's reign; cf. D. Carson, D. Moo, and L. Morris, *An Introduction to the New Testament* (Grand Rapids: Zondervan, 1992), 372–73.

123. Cf. Friesen, *Twice Neocoros*, 81–89.

someone had to underwrite the sacrifices, banquets, games, buildings, and other elements of the imperial cult.[124] "The council and people honored Claudia Ammion, the wife of the high priest P. Gavius Capito, who was appointed high priestess of Asia, because of both her own and her husband's acts of generosity (φιλοδοξίας) to the city" (IEph. 681; first or second century A.D.).[125] Unlike the male high priests who had political functions in the provincial league, the high priestesses of Asia had no governmental role in the koinon.[126]

To find women as high priestesses of Asia does not necessarily signal a shift of views on the familial roles of women in Asia or in Ephesus. This is witnessed by one Aelia Ammia from Phrygia, who served as "high priestess of the greatest temples in Ephesus." Among her chief virtues were her "humility and devotion to her husband" (σωφροσύνη τε καὶ φιλανδρία).[127] The few high priestesses of Asia simply demonstrate that some of the daughters and wives of the municipal elite moved in provincial circles and held priesthoods in that connection. This is not surprising in light of the "powerful international network of marriage ties and alliances" among some of these municipal elites in Asia Minor.[128]

In sum, priesthoods in various cults (especially where female divinities were concerned) were held by the daughters and wives of some of the wealthy families in Ephesus under the general oversight of male provincial and municipal authorities. This was the practice throughout the Greek world as well as in Ephesus. Specifically, that women—and

124. As an example for high priests: "The council [and people] honored, T. Flavi[us Montanus] . . . high[priest of Asia of the temple i]n Ephesus of the koinon of Asia . . . he completed the theater and dedicated (it) during his high priesthood, he sponsored (gladiatorial) single-combats and hunts, he also sp[onsored] a banquet for the citizens and gave 3 den(arii) to each" (IEph. 2061; ca. A.D. 102–116). The high priests and priestesses had ceremonial privileges at the cult events, of course—something like the grand marshal of a modern parade. Cf. Price, *Ritual and Power*, 101–32, 188–91, 207–33 *et passim*.

125. The punctuation here is probably correct: the honorary inscription, not the high priesthood itself, was given to Claudia because of the benefactions. See also Tata of Aphrodisias "who, as priestess of the imperial cult a second time, twice supplied oil for athletes in hand-bottles" (trans. in Kraemer, *Maenads*, 216).

126. See Jürgen Deininger, *Die Provinziallandtage der Römischen Kaiserzeit* (Munich: C. H. Beck, 1965), 18; and Friesen, *Twice Neocoros*, 89–92. One important duty of the provincial delegates was to send deputations to Rome to bring charges of misgovernment against proconsuls; cf. P. A. Brunt, "Charges of Provincial Maladministration under the Early Principate," *Historia* 10 (1961): 189–227.

127. Cf. 1 Tim. 2:9, 15; Titus 2:4. Ammia's inscription is given in Kearsley, *New Docs* 6, 26–27; but her conclusion from this evidence is a bit odd: "[S]ome women stepped beyond the conventions of social anonymity and domestic fidelity" [sic].

128. Richard D. Sullivan, "Priesthoods of the Eastern Dynastic Aristocracy," in *Studien zur Religion und Kultur Kleinasiens*, ed. S. Sahin et al. (Leiden: E. J. Brill, 1978), 2:914–39.

young girls—served in priesthoods, though considered an honor,[129] had no demonstrable correlation with "emancipation" or domination in social, political, or religious affairs at Ephesus or elsewhere.[130]

Women and Education

Discussion of women from the Ephesian aristocracy brings up the question of women's cultural opportunities and the teaching of 1 Timothy 2:12. One egalitarian interpretation of this verse states that since Paul regularly supported the ordained teaching ministry of women, his prohibition must have been aimed simply at the *unlearned* women of Ephesus. After all, women in antiquity "were less likely to be educated than men."[131] This line of reasoning, however, requires us to accept a number of problematic assumptions and is hardly convincing.

Ephesus was "a center of philosophical and rhetorical studies" (Philostratus, *Vitae Sophistarum* 8.8),[132] and it possessed a well-known medical college in its center for the Muses. When modern analysts say that women were "uneducated" in antiquity, they usually mean that they were not in schools like this.[133] It is true that women do not appear as the sophists, rhetors, teachers, philosophers, doctors, and their disciples in ancient sources from Ephesus.[134] Although the extant evidence

129. For example, the fact that both men and women occasionally refer to their ancestry from priestesses as a sign of noble descent is a sign of the priesthood's honorary value (e.g., IEph. 810, 933, 994, and 4336).

130. "We should not be too quick to equate service to ancient deities with power and authority. . . . Women's service as priestesses and other cult functionaries in classical Greece, particularly in the service of goddesses who themselves functioned as paradigms for proper women, provides one example. There is little evidence that such priesthoods extended the scope of women's public activities beyond the specific cultic context to the larger political, economic, and social spheres, even when we acknowledge that the very delineation of the religious from other spheres of human activity is a modern conception" (Ross Kraemer, *Her Share of the Blessings: Women's Religions among Pagans, Jews, and Christians in the Greco-Roman World* [New York: Oxford University Press, 1992], 90).

131. Craig S. Keener, *Paul, Women and Wives: Marriage and Women's Ministry in the Letters of Paul* (Peabody, Mass.: Hendrickson, 1992), 83 (on 1 Cor. 14:34–35; see pp. 107–13 for similar reasoning for 1 Tim. 2).

132. Ephesus shook with "a chorus of rhetoricians and their noisy applause" according to Tacitus (*Dialogus de Oratoribus* 15.3).

133. To say that the women were disqualified from teaching in the Christian church merely because they did not attend specialized schools in rhetoric or philosophy claims too much. Paul specifically rejected the devices of the sophists and rhetoricians as the essential component of his own preaching (1 Cor. 1:17; 2:1–2; etc.), and no such qualifications were expected for male teachers and elders (1 Tim. 3:1–7; Titus 1:5–9).

134. They are: "T(ib.) Claudius Flavianus Dionysius rhetor" (IEph. 426; 3047; *VS* 1.22); T. Flavius Damianus (IEph. 672a–b, 676a, 678a, 735, 811, 2100, 3029, 3051, 3080–81), "a most illustrious man," prominent building donor, and city councillor (*VS* 2.23); Hadrianus of Tyre, "the sophist" (IEph. 1539); P. Hordeonius Lollianus (IEph. 20), the sophist who

is not very extensive, it nevertheless forces the admission that women teachers were not integral to Ephesian society.[135]

However, to say that Ephesian women were *uneducated* because they did not appear in "graduate schools" of philosophy, rhetoric, and medicine is misleading. Few people in antiquity advanced in their formal education beyond today's elementary school levels, including men like Socrates, Sophocles, and Herodotus.[136] And there were other forms of education in which upper-class women participated at Ephesus, particularly private lectures in salons. For instance, false teachers mentioned in the Pastorals taught women in this venue: "They are the kind who worm their way into *homes* and gain control over weak-willed women" (2 Tim. 3:6; NIV; emphasis added).[137]

Because women's education in antiquity usually took place privately, we get only a glimpse of it here and there. As for women's literacy, daughters of the upper classes needed some level of education for their duties in managing large households.[138] And though they were not commonly found in fields like philosophy, women did read and write literature and poetry during this period.[139]

"was the first to be appointed to the chair of rhetoric at Athens" (*VS* 1.23), whose daughter was a priestess of Artemis (IEph. 984); Ofellius Laetus, a Platonic philosopher (IEph. 3901); (?)ius Secundinus of Tralles, "the platonic philosopher" (IEph. 4340); L. Vevius Severus, "the teacher" (IEph. 611); Soterus of Athens, known by his disciples as the "Chief Sophist" (IEph. 1548), but as a mere "plaything of the Greeks" in Philostratus's opinion (*VS* 2.23). Note that the list of μαθηταί of Soterus are all males (IEph. 1548). See Neue Inschriften VIII, 149–50 for an inscribed philosophical diatribe originating from an Ephesian school; ibid., 136–40 discusses sophists' tax exemptions. Cf. G. W. Bowersock, *Greek Sophists in the Roman Empire* (Oxford: Clarendon, 1969), and Broughton, *RAM*, 853–55.

All doctors named on Ephesian stones are male; for instance, Tib. Claudius Demostratus Caelianus, asiarch, grammateus, prytanis, and priest of Asclepius (IEph. 278; 643; 719; et al.); cf. IEph. 1162, 2304, and 4101A; and Broughton, *RAM*, 851–53.

135. Obviously, the feminist Ephesus construct falters again at this point.

136. See H. I. Marrou, *Education in Antiquity*, 76. Contrast, for example, Keener, *Paul, Women and Wives*, 97, n. 66.

137. "The private house seems to have been the most popular place for philosophers and sophists to hold their classes" (Stanley Stowers, "Social Status, Public Speaking and Private Teaching: The Circumstances of Paul's Preaching Activity," *Novum Testamentum* 26 [1984]: 66). A wall-painting of Socrates in a first-century Ephesian home may mark the house as a lecture salon. The mural appears on the cover of a Penguin volume of Plato (*Early Socratic Dialogues*, ed. T. Saunders). There was also a "auditorium" at Ephesus for public lectures (IEph. 3009); cf. C. J. Hemer, "Audeitorion," *Tyndale Bulletin* 24 (1973): 128. For the "school of Tyrannus" of Acts 19:9, see Baugh, "Paul and Ephesus," 120–25.

138. See William V. Harris, *Ancient Literacy* (Cambridge, Mass.: Harvard University Press, 1989), 252; cf. Susan Guettel Cole, "Could Greek Women Read and Write?" in *Reflections of Women in Antiquity*, ed. H. Foley (New York: Gordon & Breach Science, 1981), 219–45.

139. For example, Telesilla of Argos (Plutarch, *Mor.* 245C–F); cf. women poets in Lefkowitz and Fant, *Women's Life*, 4–10. Samuel Dill's classic work is still helpful for Roman women here: *Roman Society from Nero to Marcus Aurelius* (London: Macmillan, 1905), 79–80.

While women's literary works were usually designed for private consumption and are therefore lost for the most part, there are exceptions from Ephesus. For instance, we have several extant tributes to Hestia from female prytaneis.[140] Two poetic epigrams for Hestia ("sweetest of gods . . . ever-streaming light") in particular are said to have been written by the first-century prytanis Claudia herself (IEph. 1062 [both epigrams]). These show that some upper-class Ephesian girls and women were among the known female devotees of literature in the Greek world.

We can assume, then, from the foregoing that some female members of the Pauline church were at least literate and possibly had a modicum of formal or informal learning. The elaborate coiffures, jewelry, and clothing mentioned in 1 Timothy 2:9 and the warning to the rich in 1 Timothy 6:17–18 show clearly that there were wealthy women in the Ephesian congregation. At least some of these women were educated, a few, possibly, highly accomplished in letters or poetry.[141] Indeed, Paul probably knew Ephesian women who privately sat at the feet of teachers like Hymenaeus and Philetus, who were "ever learning, but never able to enter into knowledge of the truth" (2 Tim. 2:17; 3:7). Hence, I cannot agree that there were no literate or educated women in the church of 1 Timothy so that women would *eo ipso* be disqualified from teaching there.

Hairstyles and Romanitas

There was an increasing permeation of Roman culture in Ephesus during the first century. Interestingly enough, we may possibly see its effects in 1 Timothy 2 itself. Although Paul's exhortation for women to "adorn themselves with modesty and humility (σωφροσύνη)" (1 Tim. 2:9) fits the expectations of either Greek or Roman society, the adornment of the hair "with braids and gold or with pearls" (cf. 1 Pet. 3:3) fits a new trend originating in Rome.

Greek hairstyles for women during this period were for the most part simple affairs: hair was parted in the middle, pinned simply in the back

140. We possess the thanksgiving dedication from the girl-prytanis Aurelia Juliane (IEph. 1066; see above), though we can only suppose that it was actually written by her. It is not particularly inspired and follows standard lines. We also have two dedicatory prayers of the prytanis Tullia (see below), which are metrical with distinctly poetic vocabulary (IEph. 1063–64). See Dill (*Roman Society*, 80) for a reference to "Balbilla, a friend of the wife of Hadrian" who wrote Greek verses on the Colossus of Memnon. This is Julia Balbilla, the Ephesian (?) granddaughter of Tib. Claudius Balbillus, an Ephesian who served as prefect of Egypt and was probably Nero's court astrologer (Suetonius, *Nero* 36; IEph. 3041–42), founding the Balbilleia games at Ephesus; cf. *PW Suppl.* 5:59–60.

141. In light of Acts 19:19, these *litterae* may have included works on magic and spells.

or held in place with a scarf or headband. Roman coiffures were similar until the principate. The women of the imperial household originated new styles; by the Trajanic period they had developed into elaborate curls, braids, high wigs, pins, and hair ornaments that were quickly copied by the well-to-do throughout the empire: "See the tall edifice rise up on her head in serried tiers and storeys!" (Juvenal, *Satire* 6). One can even date representations of women by the increasing complexity of hair fashions.[142]

If Roman styles seem a bit too far away to affect Ephesian fashions, consider that portraits of reigning empresses often appeared on coins minted in Ephesus and other Asian cities and that they had prominent statues in both public and private places.[143] Portraits of provincial women from the era show that the imperial coiffures were copied in Ephesus and the other cities of Asia.[144]

Paul's injunction regarding elaborate hairstyles reflects the increasing influence of Rome at Ephesus during the third quarter of the first century A.D. And his skeptical response to this trend was due to his judgment that simplicity and modesty in dress befit pious women rather than external extravagance.[145] Furthermore, his reaction to women's imitation of the latest hairstyles is understandable since it was quite a new trend, really begun only a decade or so before, and it carried connotations of imperial luxury and the infamous licentiousness of women like Messalina and Poppaea.[146] Today, it is the equivalent of warning Christians away from imitation of styles set by promiscuous pop singers or actresses.

142. See J. J. Pollitt in *The Oxford History of Classical Art*, ed. J. Boardman (Oxford: Oxford University Press, 1993), 247, no. 242. See photos no. 89, 92, 94–95, 116A, 126, 130, 132, et al. for Greek women shown on coins, vases, and statuary, and plate xxii, no. 325A for a gold hair ornament with sapphires and pearls from a later period. Cf. "Haartracht. Haarschmuck," *Kl. Pauly*.

143. For example, a portrait of Livia (with a somewhat elaborate hairstyle) was found in a private dwelling in Ephesus; see Maria Aurenhammer, "Römische Porträts aus Ephesos: Neue Funde aus dem Hanghaus 2," *Jahreshefte des Österreichschen Archäologischen Institutes in Wien* 54 (1983): Beiblatt, 105–12 (photos 1–3). See also Jale Inan and Elisabeth Rosenbaum, *Roman and Early Byzantine Portrait Sculpture in Asia Minor* (London: British Academy, 1966) for Asian portraits of Livia (plate VII), Octavia (plate VIII—very elaborate coiffure), and Agrippina the elder and younger (plates XI–XII).

144. For instance, the portrait of an Ephesian woman mirrors the hairstyle of Octavia and Livia (cp. Inan and Rosenbaum, *Roman and Early Byzantine Portrait Sculpture*, plate LXXXI, no. 140 and plates VII-VIII, nos. 11–12 and the remarks on p. 123). See plate LXIV, no. 109 for another provincial woman with the same style.

145. For men, Paul's equivalent exhortation was to avoid obsession with "body-sculpting" in gymnasia in place of piety (1 Tim. 4:8).

146. "Elaborate hairdressing and makeup were part of the self-presentation for the better-class whores" (i.e., "loose-living society ladies" as described by Juvenal [*Satire 6*]) (Gardner, *Women in Roman Law*, 251).

Summary and Conclusions

Ephesus was in most ways a typical Hellenic society. It was a burgeon-ing trade and commercial center somewhat like Corinth, though unlike Corinth (reconstituted as a Roman colony[147]) Ephesus's Greek roots were well preserved in its political and cultural institutions. The state council, gerousia, gymnasia, and religious hierarchies (including priestesses) were typically Hellenic.

Ephesus was also the center of Roman administration for the prov-ince, meaning that a Roman proconsul, like P. Fabius Persicus in Paul's day, might well give direction to its municipal government and reli-gious affairs. Various pieces of evidence show that the city increasingly accepted Roman culture. For instance, the rising incidence of Roman names and Roman citizenship among Ephesians, the transformation of the democratic state council into an aristocratic senate, the enthusias-tic advancement of the imperial cult, and even the elaborate hairstyles referred to in 1 Timothy 2 attest to inroads of *Romanitas* at Ephesus.

Paul's injunctions throughout 1 Timothy 2:9–15, then, are not tem-porary measures in a unique social setting. Ephesus's society and reli-gion—even the cult of Artemis Ephesia—shared typical features with many other contemporary Greco-Roman cities. Ephesus was thor-oughly Greek in background and character, yet influence of *Romanitas* is clearly discerned. Hence, we have every reason to expect Paul to apply the restriction of women from teaching and exercising official rule over a man to "every place" (v. 8).

Furthermore, there is no reason to suspect that the Christian women of Ephesus would regard Paul's exhortation to modesty and humility as unusual or necessarily unpalatable, even if they had earlier served as priestesses in pagan cults. As we saw, some of these elite girls and women were praised for their "modesty" and "devotion-to-husband." If they were to have read Plutarch's advice to a bride *(Coniugalia prae-cepta)*—and we believe that at least some Ephesian women were able and had the leisure to read such works—they would have encountered injunctions similar to Paul's on extravagance, modesty, and silence (*Mor.* 142C–D; 145A–B).

Indeed, Paul actually seems a bit more "liberal" than Plutarch, since the latter wants a virtuous wife to be hidden away when not accompa-nied by her husband and advises her not to make her own friends but to be content with her husband's (*Mor.* 139C; 140D). Paul positively opens the road to learning to all women by enjoining them to learn in the church. Furthermore, Paul does not tell women to remain clois-

147. Cf. D. W. J. Gill, "Corinth: A Roman Colony in Achaea [sic]," *Biblische Zeitschrift* 37 (1993): 259–64.

tered at home but to exercise their gifts in the practice of public good works and especially in the discipleship of younger women (1 Tim. 5:9–10; Titus 2:4–5; etc.).

Even though Paul's first readers could not have read Plutarch—he was only a boy then—many of the inscriptions about first- and second-century women in Ephesus draw attention to their "modesty" and domestic fidelity in accordance with traditional Greco-Roman expectations for women. And there is explicit evidence that Ephesian women embraced this role in the person of Tullia. This young girl, after serving as prytanis, thanked Hestia with two metrical inscriptions (implying some degree of education). In the first she prays that "since she immaculately completed her obligations of patronage (προστασία), so grant children to her . . . because of (her) unimpeachable modesty (σωφρο-σύνη) and wisdom" (IEph. 1063). This is hardly clamoring for women's rights by an Amazon-inspired female magistrate.

If this chapter has added anything concrete to this volume's discussion of 1 Timothy 2:9–15, it is that exegetical treatments can proceed with the assumption that Ephesus was not a unique society in its era. Specifically, it was not a feminist society as we read today in statements on 1 Timothy 2:12–13 like this:

> In a religious environment saturated with the "feminine principle" due to the Artemis cult, attitudes of female exaltation or superiority existed. Verse 13 attempts to correct such an emphasis. Also the myths of Cybele and Attis from which the Ephesian Artemis sprang emphasized the creation of the goddess first, then her male consort. Paul could be affirming the historical truthfulness of the biblical narratives to expose the fiction-based nature of the *Magna Mater* myths.[148]

The claims and assumptions here are a thorough misrepresentation of ancient Ephesus and of Artemis Ephesia. On the other hand, I do not intend to imply that the religious environment of Ephesus was "saturated with a 'masculine principle'" (whatever that might be). We have seen women given honors, public recognition, and religious functions at Ephesus within the general rubric of Roman and municipal magistrates' oversight. There is no evidence of Ephesian denigration of women per se.

Furthermore, the reader should be warned that some contemporary discussions of women in antiquity are so influenced by modern biases they cannot appreciate and accurately describe the character and dynamics of the situation then. Ancient women's role in the home is frequently referred to today as "confinement"—a prejudicial term—and

---

148. Sharon Hodgin Gritz, "The Role of Women in the Church," in *The People of God: Essays on the Believers' Church* (Nashville: Broadman, 1991), 308.

thus ignores a woman's sometimes extensive authority and management over domestic affairs.[149] Not very long ago, an American authoress could say, "Ma and her girls were Americans, *above doing men's work*."[150] Perhaps ancient women held a similar opinion. They may not have held public office or taught, not because it was forbidden by domineering men, but because they did not care to. They had their own spheres of influence.[151]

There is still work to be done to allow ancient women to speak for themselves as much as our limited sources allow. But the important points relevant to 1 Timothy may be considered as adequately attested in the sources reported here. These sources by their very nature refer to predominantly upper-class people. But there is good evidence that at least some women from such elite circles were part of the Ephesian congregation.[152]

In the course of our discussion, we have seen Ephesian girls and women in traditional Greco-Roman roles. Aristocratic women participated alongside their husbands as managers of sometimes extensive households:[153] "This memorial and the outlying area belongs to Pomponia Faustina, kosmeteira of Artemis (inherited) from her forebears,[154] and to Menander her husband. Myrrachis, Nico, and the rest of Menander's freedmen care for the tomb" (IEph. 1655). Ephesian women's official functions were expressed almost entirely in the sacred priesthoods. Most, though, whose names would never be inscribed on stone, were much like women encountered anywhere else at the time: wives, mothers, and midwives; farmers, fullers, and fishmongers; scullery maids, bar-girls, and prostitutes; mediums, fortune-

149. See, for example, the varied and challenging responsibilities outlined for a fourteen-year-old Greek bride (Xenophon, *Oeconomicus*, Book 7). See also the many areas of expertise of the homemaker in Prov. 31.

150. Laura Ingalls Wilder, *The Long Winter* (New York: HarperCollins, 1971; 1st ed. 1940), 4; emphasis added.

151. See esp. David Cohen, "Seclusion, Separation, and the Status of Women in Classical Athens," *Greece and Rome* 36 (1989): 3–15.

152. Gerd Theissen's seminal conclusions on the varied social strata represented in the Corinthian church can be maintained for Ephesus also. This was one of the main conclusions of my "Paul and Ephesus" (e.g., p. 202). See Theissen, "Soziale Schichtung in der korinthischen Gemeinde," *Zeitschrift für die neutestamentliche Wissenschaft* 65 (1974): 232–72; translated as "Social Stratification in the Corinthian Community," in *The Social Setting of Pauline Christianity* (Philadelphia: Fortress, 1982), 69–119. Cf. Alan Padgett, "Wealthy Women at Ephesus: 1 Timothy 2:8–15 in Social Context," *Interpretation* 41 (1987): 19–31 (although I cannot agree with his exegesis of the target passage).

153. The "slope-house" *(Hanghaus)* complex of Ephesus is a distinctly rich archaeological find. Originating in the first century A.D., the connected, multistoried private dwellings measure as much as 3,000 square feet each, and contain rich frescoes and other works of art, peristyle courtyards, and indoor plumbing. Cf. Elliger, *Ephesos*, 71–78.

154. Was the tomb inherited or the office of kosmeteira?

tellers, and slaves. These women hardly had time for Amazonian phantasies.

In 1 Timothy 2, after reminding the wealthy women of Ephesus in particular about true piety in contrast to outward show, Paul anticipates that such women might misunderstand their inherited, worldly privileges to imply that they could step outside their divinely ordered role in the new covenant community. He points them instead to their distinct, profound, and significant roles in the church. And Paul's teaching on distinctly feminine virtues would have resonated with the ideals of their culture through the light of general revelation: "A woman's particular virtue is modesty (σωφροσύνη), for by it she is enabled to honor and love her husband" (Phintys, daughter of Callicrates, a Pythagorean philosopher).[155]

---

155. From book 4 of Joannes Stobaeus's anthology accessed through the *Thesaurus Linguae Graecae* of University of California, Irvine.

2

A Certain Kind of Letter:
The Genre of 1 Timothy

T. David Gordon

One often hears that Paul's prohibition against women teaching is inapplicable today since he wrote 1 Timothy to address a specific situation in the church at Ephesus. Such a statement raises the question of the normativity of instructions given to a church facing a particular set of circumstances. Is it the case that the attempt to impose the command in 1 Timothy 2:12 violates the genre and character of 1 Timothy? It is not the purpose of this chapter to deal with the various grammatical or lexical issues raised in 1 Timothy 2. Those matters are discussed by other contributors. The present chapter seeks to determine the genre of 1 Timothy in order to provide a general literary framework for the interpretation of 1 Timothy 2.

The Authorship of the Pastorals

Arguably, the question of who wrote the Pastoral Epistles (1 and 2 Timothy; Titus) has a significant bearing on how we are to interpret their message. Some may hold that the explicit claim that Paul wrote the letter at the beginning of each of the Pastorals settles the issue by itself (cf. 1 Tim. 1:1; 2 Tim. 1:1; Titus 1:1). Others have argued that pseudonymity (i.e., the practice of writing a literary work under a pseudonym, or false name) was an accepted literary convention during the New Testament period.[1]

---

1. For a defense of pseudonymity, see Kurt Aland, "The Problem of Anonymity and Pseudonymity in the Christian Literature of the First Two Centuries," *Journal of Theological Studies* 12 (1961): 39–49; David G. Meade, *Pseudonymity and Canon: An Investigation*

The question is not merely whether pseudonymity as such was current during the New Testament period—it was, as numerous pseudonymous Gospels, Acts, and Apocalypses testify. The question is not even merely whether pseudonymity was a phenomenon used for the epistolary genre—though that clearly is important, as the discussion below will show. The question is ultimately whether a pseudonymous letter would have been acceptable within the Christian canon, that is, whether the church would have accepted a pseudonymous epistle as authoritative and inspired even though she knew that the purported author of a New Testament letter was not the real author.

The case cannot be fully argued here; a few remarks must suffice. First, there is very little, if any, evidence for pseudonymous epistles during the New Testament period.[2] Second, while pseudepigraphy itself was certainly current during the time the New Testament was written, it is very doubtful whether a pseudepigraphical work would have been acceptable within the canon of the Christian Scriptures.[3] Third, the arguments commonly advanced against the Pauline authorship of the Pastorals—differences in theology and style from the accepted Pauline Epistles and difficulties fitting the Pastorals into the chronological framework of the Book of Acts—are not genuine obstacles to authenticity.[4] A different subject matter (the ordering of churches with a view toward the postapostolic era) and perhaps the use of amanuenses are arguably sufficient to account for different emphases (though not theological contradictions) and vocabulary in the Pastorals.[5] For these

---

into the Relationship of Authorship and Authority in Jewish and Earliest Christian Tradition (Grand Rapids: Eerdmans, 1987), esp. 118–39; and Richard Bauckham, "Pseudo-Apostolic Letters," Journal of Biblical Literature 107 (1988): 469–94; for a defense of authenticity, especially in epistolary literature, see Donald Guthrie, New Testament Introduction, rev. ed. (Downers Grove: InterVarsity, 1990), 607–49, 1011–28; and D. A. Carson, Douglas J. Moo, and Leon Morris, An Introduction to the New Testament (Grand Rapids: Zondervan, 1992), 367–71.

2. See Carson, Moo, and Morris, Introduction, 367–71.

3. Cf. Grant R. Osborne, The Hermeneutical Spiral: A Comprehensive Introduction to Biblical Interpretation (Downers Grove: InterVarsity, 1991), 257.

4. For recent defenses of the authenticity of the Pastoral Epistles, see Luke T. Johnson, The Writings of the New Testament: An Interpretation (Philadelphia: Fortress, 1986), 381–407; E. Earle Ellis, "Pseudonymity and Canonicity of New Testament Documents," in Worship, Theology and Ministry in the Early Church: Essays in Honor of Ralph P. Martin, ed. M. J. Wilkins and T. Paige, JSNTSS 87 (Sheffield: JSOT, 1992), 212–24.

5. For efforts to investigate the differences in vocabulary between the Pastorals and the undisputed Pauline epistles, see Kenneth Grayston and G. Herdan, "The Authorship of the Pastorals in the Light of Statistical Linguistics," New Testament Studies 6 (1959): 1–15; P. F. Johnson, "The Use of Statistics in the Analysis of the Characteristics of Pauline Writing," New Testament Studies 20 (1973): 92–100; and J. A. Libby, "A Proposed Methodology and Preliminary Data on Statistically Elucidating the Authorship of the Pastoral Epistles" (M.Div. thesis, Denver Seminary, 1987).

reasons, all the contributors of the present volume accept the Pauline authorship of the Pastorals and presuppose it in their argument.

What difference does it make whether Paul wrote 1 Timothy? To begin with, Paul's apostolic authority is bound up with his instructions, in the present case for a woman not to teach or to have authority over a man (1 Tim. 2:12).[6] Whether the "I" of "I do not permit" in 1 Timothy 2:12 is the apostle Paul or a later pseudepigraphical author really *does* matter, since Paul was given a unique salvation-historical role in the establishment of the early church (cf., e.g., Eph. 3:1–10, or the second half of the Book of Acts).[7] Moreover, once the name of the author is acknowledged as fictional, the purported setting, date, and other circumstances are also subject to this acknowledgment, so that it would become increasingly difficult to determine the actual message of a given passage in the Pastorals with certainty. Nevertheless, the fact remains that 1 Timothy, whether pseudonymous or not, is part of the Christian canon, so that the instructions found in it (including 2:9–15) remain authoritative for the ordering of the church.

The Issue of Genre

To discuss the genre of a work is to discuss its nature. If that nature is common to other works, all the better. But a discussion of the genre of a given biblical book does not depend on the presence of works of a similar nature. By talking of the genre of 1 Timothy, we are therefore not necessarily implying that the Pastoral Epistles are instances of a well-established literary genre in the ancient world. While it is helpful to locate given biblical books, or portions thereof, within well-known categories of literature, it is important to recognize that some biblical books, such as the Gospels, are unique in certain respects.

In the following essay, we will first discuss the occasional nature of epistles in general, then the distinctive nature of the Pastoral Epistles,

6. Cf. William W. Klein, Craig L. Blomberg, and Robert L. Hubbard Jr., *Introduction to Biblical Interpretation* (Dallas: Word, 1993), 354: "Authorship can make quite a difference in how one interprets, say, 1 Tim. 2:8–15. For various reasons many scholars deny that Paul could have written the Pastorals. Instead, they view these three letters as the product of a disciple of Paul a generation later who wrote when the Church was becoming more institutionalized and chauvinistic. By that time, Christians had allegedly lost sight of the totally egalitarian positions of Jesus and Paul (cf. esp. Gal. 3:28) and were lapsing back into the bad habits of the surrounding culture. Such a view, then, allows Christians to disregard the prohibitions in 1 Tim. 2:12 against women teaching or having authority over men in church."

7. The dichotomy erected by Meade, *Pseudonymity and Canon*, 139, who asserts "that in the Pastorals, attribution is primarily an assertion of authoritative tradition, not of literary origins," is therefore invalid.

and finally the more precise question of the normative value of 1 Timothy 2 for today.

The Occasional Nature of the Epistolary Genre

Students of the New Testament commonly, and rightly, refer to the occasional character of the New Testament epistles, reminding us that the various letters were written for specific reasons and to specific locations.[8] Even when a letter is "circular," such as the Ephesian letter, its circular nature is part of its author's intention.

The particular occasion for which a letter is written is significant both for interpreting and for applying that letter. In some situations, the occasion of a given letter might be such as to render some of its particular requirements nonapplicable to other situations. For example, Paul's request that Timothy bring his cloak from Troas (2 Tim. 4:13) does not oblige anyone other than Timothy, since the occasion of this request was Timothy's impending visit to Paul. The occasional nature of the New Testament epistles need not imply, however, that there remains of necessity no application of particular instructions for those whose situation is different.[9]

When and if the particular instructions or exhortations are grounded in some theological or ethical norm or rationale, as opposed to some purely practical or local exigency, such as Paul's need for a cloak from Troas, then the norm continues to inform other situations. Thus, the norms that inform each occasion must be determined as well as the occasion itself. This determination of the informing norm enables us to make applications to other situations. It is interpretively dangerous to observe only the occasion without also observing the norms by which that occasion is informed.[10] This matter is of such importance that we

8. Cf. Gordon D. Fee and Douglas Stuart, *How to Read the Bible for All Its Worth* (Grand Rapids: Zondervan, 1982), 45–46; Klein, Blomberg, and Hubbard, *Introduction to Biblical Interpretation*, 352–53.

9. Contra the suggestion made by some that the occasional nature of epistles makes them virtually inapplicable to other, different situations. This tendency can be observed in Gordon D. Fee, "Reflections on Church Order in the Pastoral Epistles, with Further Reflections on the Hermeneutics of *ad hoc* Documents," *Journal of the Evangelical Theological Society* 28 (1985): 142–48. More satisfying are the nine questions proposed by Klein et al., *Interpretation*, 411–21, who rightly indicate that theological norms may be implicit as well as explicit, and that such norms, if genuinely implicit, are obligatory. Of course, Paul's instructions in 1 Tim. 2:11–12 are explicit.

10. As a parade example of such an error one might recall Bultmann's arguments about 1 Corinthians 15. Bultmann's Paul did not really believe in a bodily resurrection. However, his debate with the (alleged) gnostics drove him to make the kind of statements contained in 1 Corinthians 15. For Bultmann, Paul's epistles are explicable exclusively in terms of the occasion. There are effectively no theological norms that inform the situation.

might find it useful to consider several examples of informing norms in Paul's letters, particularly in the Pastoral Epistles.

The argument in 1 Corinthians 14 about the unintelligibility of tongues, which renders them nonedifying to the hearers (whether they are also unedifying to the speakers is a debate we need not enter here), is relevant to the Protestant insistence that worship be conducted in the vernacular language. The norms beneath these instructions are, first, that gifts are given to edify, and second, that unintelligible forms of communication are not edifying. The instructions in 1 Corinthians 14 that limit the number of those who pray or prophesy are likewise based upon a norm, that is, that God is not a God of confusion but a God of peace (v. 33). For this reason everything should be done "decently and in good order" (v. 40).

The various Pauline instructions regarding food (Romans 14; 1 Corinthians 8; 1 Tim. 4:3–5) deal with food offered to idols as well as with religious scruples about food. In each situation, the norms are the same: that God has made all that exists, and that therefore an item of food is clean, if it can be received in good conscience and with thanksgiving to God the Creator. Nevertheless, love is more important than liberty. It is never appropriate to exercise personal freedom at the expense of the spiritual welfare of another person.

Paul gives instructions regarding the enrollment of widows for diaconal relief in 1 Timothy 5. While only widows are referred to in this text, the norm behind it is the Old Testament discussion of God as a defender of the orphan and widow, the father of the fatherless. Thus these instructions are also rightly invoked when there is a discussion of any destitute individual enrolled for diaconal assistance in the church.[11]

Apart from these instances, a closer look at 1 Timothy reveals that Paul frequently states general norms in the course of a discussion that applies these norms to the specific occasion at hand. In these cases, it would of course be wrong to deny the general applicability of norms merely because Paul applies them to specific circumstances in the epistle at hand. Instances of this pattern in 1 Timothy include the following:

- Paul's exhortation to men to pray in a certain manner (2:8)
- the need for women to wear modest clothing and to "clothe themselves" ultimately with good works (2:9–10)
- the entire discussion of qualifications for overseers and deacons (3:1–13; cf. v. 15)
- the claim that everything created by God is good and that nothing is to be rejected if it is received with thanksgiving (4:4–5)

---

11. Indeed, in our particular culture, with its insurance and retirement plans, often the last person to need financial assistance is a widow!

- the categorical assertion that believers ought to provide for members of their own family (5:8) in the context of 5:1–16

In all these instances, Paul, while applying general norms to specific circumstances, nevertheless affirms certain norms to be of general validity, transcending the particular occasion. Moreover, he considers Scripture itself to be normative (cf. 2 Tim. 2:15; 3:16–17), making it the basis for further general norms.

Finally, 1 Timothy also includes significant teaching on theology, Christology, grace, ethics, and other matters that were clearly focused on the epistolary situation while not being limited by it. The following instances found in 1 Timothy may serve as examples of such teaching, which even "progressive" interpreters of 1 Timothy 2 accept as transcending to the epistle's occasion:

- Christ Jesus came into the world to save sinners (1:15)
- God desires all people to be saved (2:4)
- there is one God, and one mediator between God and people, the man Jesus Christ, who gave his life as a ransom for all (2:5–6)
- the christological hymn in 3:16 (cf. 2 Tim. 2:11–13)
- the theological and christological affirmations made in 6:13–16

If these teachings are considered to be addressed to, and yet to transcend, the original occasion, it may be asked why not consider other injunctions legitimate that, while being written to a particular audience, are founded on general norms that likewise transcend the immediate context? If the ad hoc nature of New Testament literature, and epistles in particular, is carried to an improper extreme, much commonly recognized, exceedingly valuable theological, christological, and ethical teaching would be forfeited, not merely passages such as 1 Timothy 2:12.

In each of these examples, we discover that norms and occasions converge. Paul's letters consist largely of his application of norms to particular occasions. The importance of this practice for the interpretation of our text lies in the fact that Paul's comments may not be dismissed as unapplicable to our situation merely because our situation is different. The norms by which Paul addressed one occasion are still norms, and may be germane to other situations as well. More specifically, Paul's instructions regarding women may not be dismissed on the (alleged) ground that Ephesian women were unruly or heretics.

Even if there were evidence available to defend such speculation (but see chapter 1), this evidence would not by itself remove the text from consideration for the application to our present situation, *if* Paul supplied an informing norm in the text. Therefore, even if modern women were all well ordered and orthodox, and even if the Ephesian women had all been unruly or even heretical, the norm that informed Paul's situation would still be normative in our situation.

A proper understanding of the occasional nature of apostolic letters is very significant for interpretion as well as application. If specific occasions are not addressed by the application of norms, then the interpretive value of letters written to such situations is restricted to situations that are largely identical. If, on the other hand, specific occasions are addressed normatively, then the interpretive value of letters written to such situations is not so restricted. The norms themselves are valuable and potentially useful in many other situations.

The Distinctive Genre of the Pastorals

Like other New Testament letters, the Pastoral Epistles consist of the application of norms to specific occasions. Are there any distinctive traits to these letters that require distinctive interpretive or applicatory considerations?

The Pastoral Epistles are the only New Testament writings that are expressly written with the purpose of providing instructions for ordering churches at the close of the apostolic era. The very apostle who had established churches and provided for their continued oversight, doctrinal purity, and worship, now gives instructions to his co-workers regarding the organization of churches in subsequent generations. The norms and principles he himself had observed in the ordering of his churches, Paul makes explicit to his colleagues so that they, too, might order their churches correctly.

Thus Paul writes to Titus: "For this reason I left you in Crete, that you might set in order what remains, and appoint elders in every city as I directed you" (1:5). Similarly, he addresses Timothy as follows: "I am writing these things to you, hoping to come to you before long; but in case I am delayed, I write so that you may know how one ought to conduct himself in the household of God, which is the church of the living God, the pillar and support of the truth" (1 Tim. 3:14–15).

Having indicated such a purpose, it is not surprising that the content of the Pastoral Letters includes the following:

- instructions regarding the duties and qualifications of officeholders (1 Tim. 3:1–13; 5:1–2; 2 Tim. 2:1–26; 4:1–5; Titus 1:5–9; 2:1–15; 3:1–11)
- instructions regarding the enrolling of qualified widows for diaconal assistance (1 Tim. 5:3–16)
- instructions regarding public prayer (1 Tim. 2:1–15)

- instructions regarding remuneration of the ministers of the Word (1 Tim. 5:17–19)
- instructions regarding the suppression of heresy (1 Tim. 1:3–7; 2 Tim. 4:3–4; Titus 1:10–11)

For our purposes, the significance of recognizing this particular nature of the Pastoral Letters is fairly evident. These letters contain norms that are especially germane to the issues of life in the church, the "household of God." The instructions in these letters, far from being primarily of local significance, are significant wherever there is concern for the proper ordering of God's house. Indeed, as instructions given to postapostolic ministers, the instructions contained in the Pastoral Epistles are particularly germane to other postapostolic churches.[12]

Norms Applied to a Specific Situation: 1 Timothy 2:11–15

Paul describes the general occasion for writing 1 Timothy in 1:3–4: "As I urged you upon my departure for Macedonia, remain on at Ephesus, in order that you may instruct certain men not to teach strange doctrines, nor to pay attention to myths and endless genealogies, which give rise to mere speculation rather than furthering the administration of God which is by faith." One important function of the letter appears therefore to be Paul's correction of errors in the instructional ministry of the Ephesian church.

However, while the refutation of false teachers and their teachings features prominently especially in chapters 1 and 4, the epistle also includes many instructions that need not necessarily have been caused by false teaching but may merely reflect Paul's general effort to provide apostolic teaching for the ordering of the church in Ephesus and, by extension, for churches in the late and postapostolic era in general (cf. chaps. 2, 3, and 5).[13]

---

12. Indeed, we might note in this regard that the Pastoral Epistles are perhaps more germane to our situation than any of the other letters. The other letters are written to churches that were often ordered by apostles, and may contain instructions unique to that circumstance in the history of redemption. By contrast, the Pastoral Letters are written to churches manifestly not ordered by apostles but by postapostolic ministers.

13. This is not to say that aspects of chap. 2, for example, may not refer to false teachings to which the Ephesian church was exposed. Cf., e.g., the suggestion by Adolf Schlatter, *The Church in the New Testament Period*, trans. Paul P. Levertoff (London: SPCK, 1955), 255, that it was against the gnostic tendency of substituting a false asceticism for marriage that "Paul coined the powerful slogan that woman is saved by child-bearing, not by refusing to become a mother (1 Tim 2.15)." I am indebted for this reference to Andreas Köstenberger.

In fact, 1 Timothy 2:1–3:16 appears to form a unit introduced by the statement, "First of all, then" (2:1), and concluded by the phrase, "I write so that you may know how one ought to conduct himself in the household of God" (3:15), followed by a "common confession."[14] In this section, Paul addresses behavior and roles for men and women during times of congregational teaching and worship (2:1–15) and the qualifications for officeholders (3:1–13). The division between chapters 2 and 3 may obscure the important coherence between the end of chapter 2 and the beginning of chapter 3. What is especially noteworthy is that the injunction that an overseer must be the husband of one wife (however interpreted) in 3:2 presupposes that only men are eligible for this church office, thus confirming and building on the command in 2:12.

Besides the issues of proper behavior and roles in the church, Paul addresses a number of other matters of abiding concern: the enrollment of widows by the church (5:3–16); the proper manner of handling accusations against elders in the church (5:17–22); the duties of believing slaves (6:1–2); and warnings to the rich (6:17–19). Note, then, that the situation at Ephesus, far from being unusual, finds Paul addressing the very matters that were of enduring concern in all the churches (cf., e.g., Acts 2:42; 14:23).

It is crucial to note the causal relation of verses 13 and 14 to the preceding verses.[15] Paul grounds his comments in a reality that exists outside of Ephesus: "For Adam was formed first, then Eve; and Adam was not deceived, but the woman was deceived and became a transgressor."

This is sufficient reason to recognize that some enduring principle is applied to this specific situation. The convergence of norm and occasion that we expect to find in Paul's letters is *expressly* communicated in the present passage. There is a command, and there is a norm, and these are connected by a causal particle (γάρ).

The specific "norm" Paul uses to address the situation in Ephesus is grounded in the entire created and fallen order, not merely the Ephesian context. Some have suggested that in the redeemed state in Christ these matters are no longer valid, since they address the human condition after the fall but before the provision of redemption in Christ. We would argue, however, that if redemption resolved the matter, Paul

14. Cf. Martin Dibelius and Hans Conzelmann, *The Pastoral Epistles*, Hermeneia (Philadelphia: Fortress, 1972), 35. Contra Gordon D. Fee, *1 & 2 Timothy, Titus*, NIBC (Peabody, Mass.: Hendrickson, 1988), 61–77, who depreciates the function of οὖν in 2:1 as marking a new section and consequently interprets virtually every detail in 2:1–15 as refuting heresies along the lines of 1:3–4.

15. When a command or other instruction is given in paraenetic material, it is highly unlikely that the expression γάρ is to be taken in any other way than causal. Contra Philip B. Payne, "Libertarian Women in Ephesus: A Response to Douglas J. Moo's Article '1 Timothy 2:11–15: Meaning and Significance,'" *Trinity Journal* 2, n.s. (1981): 175–77.

would never have given these instructions to the community of the redeemed. Moreover, Paul's first argument (i.e., that Adam was created first) has to do with creation, not the fall. Paul understood the norms touching upon creation *and* the fall to be germane to the situation at Ephesus. The temporal priority of the man in creation and the temporal priority of the woman in the fall *together* are the ground for a woman not to teach or to exercise authority over a man.[16]

At any rate, it is ultimately irrelevant whether we discover the Ephesian women to have been the least or the most unruly in the entire Mediterranean area, unless the norm being applied to that situation were the norm of orderliness. If the norm applied were the norm of order, as in the case of 1 Corinthians 14, then the relative unruliness of the Ephesian women would be significant. If these women were disorderly, and if Paul were addressing that disorder in terms of the norm of order, then our application of the passage would be essentially identical to our application of 1 Corinthians 14. But this is not the case. Paul does not refer to God's being a God of peace.

Rather, Paul points to Adam and Eve, noting specifically the order in which they were created (i.e., the man first) and which of them was deceived first (i.e., the woman). On *this* ground he does not permit a woman to teach or have authority over a man.

Similarly, it is irrelevant whether we are able to discover that the Ephesian women were teaching the heresy referred to in 1:3–4. Eve did not teach heresy, or even teach at all, and the fact that Adam was created before her has nothing to do with teaching of any kind. The norm that Paul applies to this situation is therefore not limited to circumstances in which heresy is being taught.

To clarify the matter, let us consider what has taken place in the discussion of 1 Timothy 2, with special focus on the matter of occasion and norm. Some have determined that the Ephesian *occasion* was characterized by unruly or heterodox women. Consequently, Paul would have urged these women to be silent and not to teach or to have any authority over men *because* in their situation this would be *disorderly* or *heretical*. Thus people have debated the merits of the evidence for and against unruly or heretical women as though this were ultimately decisive for the interpretation of the present passage. But the relevance of that evidence depends entirely upon the assumption that the *norm* being applied is that of *orderliness* or *orthodoxy*.

16. It is not my purpose here to explain Paul's theological reasoning fully, but rather to establish that Paul provides a theological rationale, however we understand it. See the more extensive treatment of the pertinent issues by T. Schreiner in chap. 5 of this book. Cf. also D. J. Moo, "What Does It Mean Not to Teach or Have Authority over Men?" in *Recovering Biblical Manhood and Womanhood*, ed. John Piper and Wayne Grudem (Wheaton: Crossway, 1991), 190–91.

Paul, however, not only says nothing about orderliness or orthodoxy, but provides a completely different norm to the situation at hand, that is, the norm of the temporal priority of Adam's creation and Eve's deception. Paul considers his command regarding a woman's silence to be the proper application of Adam's priority in creation and Eve's "priority" in the fall.

We might very well disagree with Paul (if our view of Scripture so permitted—mine does not), or we may very well find his reasoning opaque, but we cannot honestly change the norm he applies to his situation on such grounds.

Concluding Observations

As with all occasional letters, there are norms beneath many of the specific instructions. Beneath the specific requirement that a woman not teach or exercise authority over a man in the church is the norm of the proper relations between man and woman in the created and fallen sphere. Paul's arguments are grounded in principles touching upon creation and the fall and are thus germane to the creation prior to its consummated state. As with all Pastoral Letters, the instructions regarding life in the postapostolic church are especially germane to our setting, which is postapostolic as well.

3

A Difficult Word:
αὐθεντέω in 1 Timothy 2:12

H. Scott Baldwin

The total vocabulary of the New Testament is a little over 5,400 words. With a knowledge of only 170 of the most frequently used words, the student of biblical Greek is able to recognize more than 70 percent of all the words in the Greek New Testament. With a vocabulary of 500 Greek words, a person can read the New Testament without great difficulty. However, for careful study and exegesis of the text, a problem arises with those words that appear only once in the New Testament. These hapax legomena present a problem for both the reader and the scholar. The reader discovers that to learn every word in the New Testament, nearly 2000 hapax legomena must be memorized. It is a formidable task to learn so many words so infrequently encountered in the text! But for the scholar, hapax legomena can present an even greater challenge. Since language usage is the key to understanding the meaning of a word, how does the New Testament scholar determine the meaning of words that appear only once in the New Testament or even the whole Bible? Often context reveals the basic sense of a word. If the general flow of the text is understood, usually the meaning of the word will be evident. Occasionally, however, the context may make several different meanings for a hapax legomenon seem appropriate or at least possible. The scholar must then turn to sources outside the New Testament and evaluate other uses of the word to narrow the meaning. Such is the case with αὐθεντέω, which appears in 1 Timothy 2:12.

First Timothy 2:12 declares, "I permit no woman to teach or αὐθεντεῖν a man." What Paul intends to say by use of the word αὐθεντεῖν is debated. The various definitions proposed result in surprisingly different interpretations of the verse. Thus, a careful analysis of the term is warranted. Since αὐθεντεῖν is a New Testament hapax legomenon the exegete must investigate extrabiblical materials to assist in analyzing Paul's meaning. Often turning to sources outside the New Testament can be as easy as consulting one of the standard New Testament or ancient Greek lexicons. However, in the case of the word αὐθεντέω, it is evident that many lexicons do not provide as thorough or comprehensive an explanation of the term as we might desire. A precise consensus as to the meaning of the word has not been achieved among well-known lexicographers. (Table 3.1 provides a summary of the conclusions of several modern lexicons.)

Partly because of the uncertainty in the lexicons, partly because of theological and practical concerns, scholars have recently undertaken to study afresh this difficult word. There have been five significant word studies in the past fifteen years on the origin and meaning of αὐθεντέω. Some insight has been gained from each. However, methodological or technological shortcomings have limited the extent to which each has been able to contribute to a satisfactory resolution of the meaning of the term.

Table 3.1
αὐθεντέω in Modern Lexicographers

Sophocles[a]	1. to be in power, to have authority over 2. to be the originator of anything 3. to compel 4. mid: to be in force
Preisigke[b]	1. beherrschen (= to rule, control, dominate) 2. verfügungsberechtigt sein (= to have legitimate authority to dispose of something) 3. Herr sein, fest auftreten (= to be master, to act confidently)[c]
Lampe[d]	1. hold sovereign authority, act with authority 2. possess authority over 3. assume authority, act on one's own authority 4. be primarily responsible for, instigate, authorize
Moulton and Milligan[e]	1. from the word "master, autocrat"[f]
LSJ[g]	1. to have full power or authority over 2. to commit murder
Mayser[h]	1. Herr sein, fest auftreten (= to be master, to act confidently)
BAGD[i]	1. have authority over, domineer[j]

Louw and Nida[k]	1. to control in a domineering manner—'to control, to domineer'
DGE[l]	1. tener autoridad sobre andros [como algo prohibido a la mujer] (= to have authority over a male [as something prohibited to a woman])

a. E. A. Sophocles, *Greek Lexicon of the Roman and Byzantine Periods (from B.C. 146 to A.D. 110)* (New York: Scribner's, 1887), ad loc.

b. Friedrich Preisigke, *Wörterbuch der griechischen Papyrusurkunden* (Berlin: Erben, 1925), ad loc.

c. These English renderings are those of *The Oxford-Duden German Dictionary* (Oxford: Clarendon, 1990).

d. G. W. H. Lampe, *Patristic Greek Lexicon* (Oxford: Clarendon, 1961), ad loc.

e. J. H. Mouton and G. Milligan, *The Vocabulary of the Greek New Testament* (Grand Rapids: Eerdmans, 1963), ad loc.

f. This is found under the heading αὐθεντέω. However, Moulton and Milligan begin their article with a discussion of the noun and cite only one instance of the verb.

g. Liddell, Scott, Jones, and McKenzie, *Greek English Lexicon* (Oxford: Clarendon, 1968), ad loc.

h. Edwin Mayser, *Grammatik der griechischen Papyri aus der Ptolemäerzeit, Band 1* (Berlin: de Gruyter, 1970), ad loc.

i. W. Bauer, W. F. Arndt, F. W. Gingrich, and F. W. Danker, *A Greek-English Lexicon of the New Testament*, 2d ed. (Chicago: University of Chicago Press, 1979), ad loc.

j. It is interesting to note that the use of the term "domineer" appeared somewhere between the fifth edition of Walter Bauer's *Griechisch-Deutsches Wörterbuch* (Berlin: Töpelmann, 1958) and the English adaption and translation by BAGD. The negative term "domineer" became included perhaps mistakenly in the definition for αὐθεντέω. Bauer's German rendering, "herrschen über jemand," does not of necessity demand the negative "domineer" but merely "rule over" or "have absolute sway over."

k. J. P. Louw and E. A. Nida, eds., *Greek-English Lexicon of the New Testament*, 2d ed. (New York: United Bible Societies, 1989), 474.

l. F. Adrados, ed., *Diccionario Griego-Español* (Madrid: Consejo Superior de Investigaciones Cientificas, Instituto Filologia, 1991), ad loc.

In 1979 Catherine Kroeger asserted that αὐθεντέω was an erotic term whose essential meaning was "to thrust oneself."[1] Further, she asserted that the word was associated with fertility practices. Three years later, Carroll Osburn convincingly demonstrated that Kroeger's position was "more curious than substantive."[2] Osburn went on to make his own case for the meaning of αὐθεντέω: "to dominate or domineer." George Knight III produced a very careful and detailed study of αὐθεντέω.[3] He

1. C. C. Kroeger, "Ancient Heresies and a Strange Greek Verb," *Reformed Journal* 29 (1979): 12–15.

2. Carroll Osburn, "ΑΥΘΕΝΤΕΩ (1 Timothy 2:12)," *Restoration Quarterly* 25 (1982): 1–12. See also A. J. Panning, "ΑΥΘΕΝΤΕΙΝ—A Word Study," *Wisconsin Lutheran Quarterly* 78 (1981): 185–91, who also takes issue with C. Kroeger's *Reformed Journal* article.

3. G. W. Knight III, "ΑΥΘΕΝΤΕΩ in Reference to Women in 1 Timothy 2.12," *New Testament Studies* 30 (1984): 143–57.

concluded that the translation of the KJV ("to usurp authority") was "evidently erroneous" and that "The RSV, NAB, NIV and The Translator's Testament have caught the essence of the meaning of αὐθεντέω and present probably the most satisfactory rendering with their phrase 'to have authority.'" However, Knight's work, though exactingly executed, was not comprehensive enough to resolve the debate since it focused on a very limited database.

Leland Wilshire remedied this deficiency in his study.[4] Using the computer database of the *Thesaurus Linguae Graecae*, Wilshire was able to identify "314 or so references to αὐθεντέω and its cognates." Wilshire concluded that

> the 314 literary citations of the TLG computer (plus the pertinent references in BAGD analyzed by Knight along with others in the papyri) may be of help in understanding the meaning of 1 Tim 2.12. Sometime during the spread of koine, the word αὐθεντέω went beyond the predominant Attic meaning connecting it with murder and suicide and into the broader concept of criminal behavior. It also began to take on the additional meanings of "to exercise authority/power/rights" which became firmly established in the Greek Patristic writers to mean "exercise authority."[5]

Wilshire came to no solid conclusion with respect to the definition of αὐθεντέω in this article. However, he seemed to indicate a notion of "exercising authority" should be associated with the term.[6] In a later clarifying article, Wilshire offered "instigating violence" as the best definition and averred that it was not until the time of the patristic fathers that the meaning "exercise authority" appeared.[7]

Recently, Richard and Catherine Kroeger have published an extensive study of αὐθεντέω as part of their treatise on 1 Timothy 2:12.[8] They conclude that αὐθεντέω has "a wide range of meanings." Among them are "(1) to begin something, to be responsible for a condition or action, (2) to rule, to dominate, (3) to usurp power or rights from another, (4) to claim ownership, sovereignty, or authorship." In particular, they find αὐθεντέω "has implications of killing, beginning, and copulating." Spe-

---

4. L. E. Wilshire, "The TLG Computer and Further Reference to ΑΥΘΕΝΤΕΩ in 1 Timothy 2.12," *New Testament Studies* 34 (1988): 120–34.

5. Ibid., 131.

6. His whole series of questions about 1 Timothy 2, ending with the question "Does not the extended passage in 1 Timothy argue that the concept of 'authority' is under consideration?" gives evidence of this. See ibid., 130–31.

7. L. E. Wilshire, "1 Timothy 2:12 Revisited: A Reply to Paul W. Barnett and Timothy J. Harris," *Evangelical Quarterly* 65 (1993): 53.

8. R. C. Kroeger and C. C. Kroeger, *I Suffer Not a Woman: Rethinking 1 Timothy 2:12 in Light of Ancient Evidence* (Grand Rapids: Baker, 1992), 84–104, 185–88.

cifically they prefer that 1 Timothy 2:12 be taken to mean "proclaim oneself author of man."

Looking over the results of these studies, it seems their effect has been to make the real meaning of αὐθεντέω more obscure than ever! The purpose of this chapter is to provide a thorough lexical study of αὐθεντέω. This will allow us to identify the most probable meaning of the verb in 1 Timothy 2:12 and give us data to critique the contributions of other scholars. This will also provide the basis for syntactical and exegetical evaluation of 1 Timothy 2:12 in the chapters that follow. Specifically, (1) we will suggest a satisfactory method for analyzing αὐθεντέω. This may give us a clue why scholars have reached widely differing conclusions about the meaning of the verb. (2) We will present an English summary of every currently known instance of the use of the verb in ancient Greek literature (see appendix 2, section I). Full citations in Greek and English with a summary can also be found in appendix 2, section III, which allow the specialist to verify the accuracy of our conclusions. (3) We will provide an analysis of all this material, which is summarized in table 3.2. (4) Finally, we draw conclusions concerning the possible meanings of the word in 1 Timothy 2.

The Limitations of Word Studies

Before we begin, it is important to recognize the limitations of lexical studies. Following the older linguistic theories of the nineteenth century, there was a strong presumption that word studies would yield the meaning of a word with indisputable certainty. Newer linguistical investigations have brought this assumption under suspicion. Ferdinand de Saussure noted that in language, "tout se tient" ("all things hold together"). That is, language must be viewed as an interconnected system wherein the *context* provides the clues to the meaning of the words used.[9]

This principle has important implications. On the one hand, the competent user of a language can contextualize most anything. Every competent English speaker knows that "raise" may have several very distinct meanings: "to raise the flag," "to raise corn in Nebraska," "to raise children." Our ability to contextualize alerts us to the fact that by

9. The reverse side was also acknowledged by Saussure: While any individual speaker has his or her immediate and intended use of the language, there is an overall pattern of how language is used in sum or aggregate. The personal use of language Saussure calls *la parole* and the widespread pattern he titles *la langue*. *La langue* must exist or no one could ever communicate with another and society would lapse into linguistic solipsism. One *can* talk about what "English speakers" say, not merely what "an English speaker" says.

"raise" we do not mean "nurture the flag," "hoist corn," or "plant and water children."

On the other hand, no word has a meaning value of zero, that is, no word is an entirely blank check, able to mean anything we choose depending on the context in which we choose to put it. Linguist Rudolf Carnap's sentence "Pirots karulize elatically!"[10] is perfect according to normal English syntax. Yet it means nothing at all because the three words have no known meanings from any other context. Linguist Roland Barthes points out that speech is not an act of pure creativity. (If it were, we would understand in what way the pirots are karulizing!) Rather, a speaker uses and combines what is already in the language to accomplish his or her ends.[11]

At the same time, speakers can use words in unusual or unique ways. This occurs regularly with metaphors or in poetry. Consider the following scene: "The caravan navigated the last stretch of sandy waste, piloting their sulking and knock-kneed ships safely into the harbor of the oasis." It is precisely because "ship" and "camel" have distinctive meanings that the unexpected substitution of one word for the other gives metaphor its memorable quality. But no reputable word study should conclude from such a use as this, for example, that one legitimate meaning of "ship" must be "camel."

All this places three very practical limitations on word studies:

1. Lexical studies (properly conducted) are nothing more than summaries of contemporaneous uses of the word under consideration. Lexis is not a prescription of what a word must mean nor an absolute proscription of what a word cannot mean in a given context. Rather, it is a *description* of what people who use the word normally mean to indicate by its use.

2. No lexical study is a 100 percent guarantee that a word has a specific meaning in any given passage. The presence of poetics, metaphor, or the specialized use of a word by a subculture unknown to the lexicographer prohibits such certainty. However, when the semantic range of a word is established across a wide spectrum of language use, the burden of proof lies on the exegete to show why

---

10. Rudolf Carnap, *The Logical Syntax of Language* (London: Kegan, 1937), 2.

11. "The combinative aspect of speech is, of course, of capital importance, for it implies that speech is constituted by the recurrence of identical signs: it is because the signs are repeated in successive discourses [with different speakers] and within one and the same discourse (although they are combined in accordance with the diversity of various people's speech) that each sign becomes an element of the language; and it is because speech is essentially a combinative activity that it corresponds to an individual act and not to pure creation." See Roland Barthes, *Elements of Semiology*, trans. A. Lavers and C. Smith (New York: Hill & Wang, 1968), 15.

in this particular case the normal and well-attested usage should not be taken as the meaning in the passage at hand.[12]

3. Understanding the meaning of a word in a specific context is a trial-and-error process. This process goes through the following steps: (a) We have a preunderstanding of the word based on its use in other contexts. This is the dictionary meaning (or denotation) we carry around in our heads or lexicons. (b) We attempt to apply the denotation to the present context. (c) We then check to see if the resulting sentence makes sense using this meaning. (d_1) If it does, we search for the precise nuance of the word in the context at hand. (d_2) If it does not, we investigate why not. We may ask questions such as, Is the word misspelt? Is there a denotation to the word we did not know about? Is the writer using metaphor?

Limitation #3 will become particularly important to us in subsequent chapters after we have the results of our study of αὐθεντέω in hand.

Methodology of Word Studies

Any formal attempt to discover the meaning of αὐθεντέω must be based on sound methodology. In particular, in analyzing αὐθεντέω confusion has arisen when some scholars have failed to distinguish the verbal forms from the noun forms of the word. Further, failure to analyze the data by genre and date has resulted in unwarranted assertions. These difficulties have led to faulty conclusions in some of the word studies mentioned above.

The methodology employed in this study (separating verb and noun) is justified for several reasons. First, there are numerous examples in Greek where the verbal form does not correspond to all the meanings of the noun.[13] We cannot uncritically assume αὐθεντέω is exactly equivalent to "be an αὐθέντης" in every one of its senses. Our driving principle must be how people actually use language, not some theory about the origin of this or that word (etymology). Second, this methodology (separating verb and noun) is the same methodology employed by all recent lexicographers. Third, we have precedent to separate verb and noun forms—particularly in the case of αὐθεντέω—from the ancient

---

12. The same must be said where a word appears in different places with distinct meanings. If one meaning is obviously appropriate to the context under investigation, and the other meaning clearly inappropriate, the entire burden of proof is upon the exegete to show why the appropriate meaning should not be adopted.

13. Compare λογίζομαι/λόγος, δύναμαι/δύναμις, παρακαλέω/παράκλητος, ἐπιστατέω/ἐπιστάτης, δεσποτέω/δεσπότης.

lexicographer Hesychius.[14] Finally, though the verb αὐθεντέω is relatively rare,[15] the eighty-two references presented in this study are believed to be adequate to evaluate the meaning of the verb.[16] This argument has more weight in light of the fact that the material presented
here is an attempt to provide an exhaustive list of the ancient uses of the
verbal form known to scholars to date.[17] For these reasons we shall confine our study to the verbal form alone.

Results and Analysis of the Study

All currently known occurrences of the verb αὐθεντέω are given in appendix 2.[18] In analyzing this material, it becomes evident that the one

14. Hesychius of Alexandria (5th cent. A.D.) noted in his lexicon:

αὐθεντεῖν· ἐχουσιάζειν
αὐθέντης· ἐχουσιαστής. αὐτόχειρ, φονεύς

Or, to render this in English,

αὐθεντεῖν = to exercise authority
αὐθέντης = person in authority, doer of a thing/one who kills himself, murderer

Hesychius is only known to us in a 15th cent. A.D. manuscript and the work is known
to have suffered redaction in many places. Therefore, it is not useful as a primary source
for our purposes. However, at the very least it corroborates the distinction between verb
and noun that I have highlighted here. See entries A 8259/60 of *Hesychii Alexandrini Lexicon*, vol. 1, ed. Kurt Latte (Hauniae, 1953), 279.

15. The Greek corpus includes at a minimum some 60 million words of text (*Thesaurus Linguae Graecae Newsletter* 20 [May 1992]: 3) when the known edited papyri are included. The verb αὐθεντέω appears about 110 times.

16. Compare the number of citations found in other lexicographers: Lampe (30),
BAGD (12), Sophocles (11), and LSJ (4), including citations of 1 Tim. 2:12.

17. There are two exceptions to this. Among the church fathers we find direct quotation of 1 Tim. 2:12 appearing more than twenty times. Obviously such quotation offers
little lexical help in understanding the meaning of αὐθεντέω and therefore has not been
considered. There are also ten uses of the verbal αὐθεντέω in four separate recensions of
the *Alexander Romance*. While this "history" of Alexander the Great is believed to have
been written by a certain pseudo-Callisthenes around A.D. 300, it is not at all clear to what
century we should date the texts at hand. Michael Grant, *Greek and Latin Authors* (New
York: Wilson, 1980), 81, asserts the "work is only available in editions of the later Roman
Empire." But the citations in question are Middle Greek and appear to come from the late
Byzantine MSS mentioned by A. P. Kazhdan, *The Oxford Dictionary of Byzantium*, vol. 1
(Oxford: Oxford University Press, 1991), 58. Thus, they lie beyond the period of consid-
eration for this study.

18. This material was gathered by computer searches of two CD-ROMs: (1) *Greek
Documentary CD-ROM (#6)*. This includes documentary papyri (as well as ostraca) prepared by Duke University with the help of the University of Michigan, and Greek Inscriptions prepared at Cornell, Ohio State, and the Institute for Advanced Study. This CD-ROM
is published by The Packard Humanities Institute, Los Altos, Calif. (CD-ROM #6 contains
more than 130 editions of papyri, including major collections such as BGU, POxy, PLond,
PFamTebt, etc.); and (2) *Thesaurus Linguae Graecae CD-ROM #D* prepared by the Univer-

unifying concept is that of *authority*. Four outworkings of authority are reflected in the distinct meanings of the verb. Table 3.2 gives a summary of the meanings of αὐθεντέω for quick reference.

Table 3.2
The Meaning of αὐθεντέω

1. To rule, to reign sovereignly
2. To control, to dominate
    a. to compel, to influence someone/thing
    b. middle voice: to be in effect, to have legal standing
    c. hyperbolically: to domineer/play the tyrant
    d. to grant authorization
3. To act independently
    a. to assume authority over
    b. to exercise one's own jurisdiction
    c. to flout the authority of
4. To be primarily responsible for or to instigate something
5. To commit a murder[a]

a. Unattested before the 10th cent. A.D., see below.

Meaning 1, "to rule, to reign sovereignly," reflects unhindered authority to act based on inherent or divine right. Its thirteen uses are intransitive (simply, "I rule"). Philodemus uses it of officials, that is, of those who have authority by right of office. Chrysostom uses it of both humanity and deity. The church fathers use it frequently of members of the Godhead.

Meaning 2, "to control, to dominate,"[19] reflects authority from the standpoint of actually having control or ability to dominate an object.

---

sity of California, Irvine. Searches were conducted using "IBYCUS," a proprietary PC system of the Packard Humanities Institute. However, both CD-ROMs can be read as well on standard IBM 80386 or Mackintosh-based computers (using standard CD-ROM player with serial port connections) if appropriate software is obtained from one of several vendors. Searches were conducted to find all occurrences of αὐθεντέω (αυθεντ-, ηυθεντ-). The results of these searches were then collated with the results of manual searches of published lexicographers, ancient and modern, including those listed in table 3.1.

19. This should not be confused with "domineer." The distinction between domineer and dominate becomes an important one in the exegesis of 1 Timothy 2. Therefore, the two terms should not be taken as interchangeable. *The Compact Oxford Dictionary of the English Language* (Oxford: Oxford University Press, 1971), ad loc. gives the meaning of "to dominate," a transitive verb, as "to bear rule over, to have a commanding influence on, to master." By connotation this is a negative term in some instances when used as a description of human relationships, but not necessarily so. In contrast "domineer" is defined as an intransitive verb meaning "to rule or govern arbitrarily or despotically. . . . to exercise authority in an overbearing manner." Therefore, dominate and domineer are not synonyms unless it is shown that the domination is considered improper.

It may be used in this sense either transitively or intransitively. Ptolemy writes that Saturn dominates Mercury and the moon. Didymus the Blind reports on the practice of his church, saying that women pray and prophesy just as Mary did. But though Mary did these things, she did not write Scripture so as not to exercise control over men. This meaning may imply a kind of control that can be employed in the legitimate exercise of an office.[20] This, also, apparently is the meaning Origen found for αὐθεντέω in 1 Timothy.[21]

Meaning 2a, "to compel, to influence someone/thing," is to seek to exercise authority and/or possibly gain the ability to exercise authority/control. Athanasius employs this sense when speaking of the activity of the Holy Spirit. Chrysostom uses it of Jesus, who can compel dead bodies to rise. Ammonius uses it of the apostles, who write letters that compel obedience. These are clearly positive examples. However, the three remaining examples probably should not be understood to prove a negative meaning for αὐθεντέω in and of themselves. That is, they may not indicate "coercion" in its worst sense. In *BGU 1208* the influence the writer exercises on the boatman is viewed as achieving positive results and even the boatman gets his "full fare." In the other two cases, though the results of the act are negative (the fall, the crucifixion), we cannot say more than that the context indicates a negative connotation. There is not sufficient warrant to postulate a new meaning such as "tyrannize" or "coerce." To the contrary, Chrysostom says that Eve "exercised authority once *wrongly*" (ηὐθέντησεν ἅπαξ κακῶς). The implication obviously is that Chrysostom could not make the negative force felt without the addition of κακῶς, and therefore, he did not regard the verb αὐθεντέω as negative in itself. Malalas's use is somewhat different: though the Jews pressured Pilate, influencing his decision, it cannot be said that they usurped his position or coerced his complicity in Jesus' death, as if Rome were subservient to Jerusalem. But at the very least we must say that "compel" is the intended meaning, if not something stronger.

Meaning 2b, "to be in effect, to have legal standing," occurs with the use of the middle voice. It is exceedingly rare, occurring only three of eighty-two times. Hippolytus uses it to describe legal authority of a master over a slave. It is also found twice in the *Chronicon Paschale*

20. The Lexicon of Hesychius agrees with this assessment. Under the entry for ἡγεῖτο, the imperfect of ἡγέομαι, "I lead," Hesychius defines this with "ηὐθέντει, ἦρχεν," from αὐθεντέω and ἄρχω respectively. See Hesychius, entry H 49.

21. Origen (died c. A.D. 253), in what may be the earliest extant commentary on 1 Tim. 2:12, cites the verse and then appears to go on to define αὐθεντεῖν with the words ἡγεμόνα γίνεσθαι τῷ [τοῦ ἀνδρός], "be a ruler [over a man] in speaking." See p. 42 of the text quoted in C. Jenkins, "Documents: Origen on I Corinthians," *Journal of Theological Studies* 10 (1909): 29–51.

with respect to a decree becoming authoritative at a certain point in time.

Meaning 2c, "to domineer/play the tyrant," is substantiated by only a single case. From the context it is clear that Parker's translation ("do not act the despot") for αὐθέντει is correct. This is the sole unambiguous instance I have found where αὐθέντεω is plainly intended to convey the negative meaning "tyrannize." In this unique usage Chrysostom has apparently transformed "exercise sole authority" into "play the tyrant."[22]

Meaning 2d, "to grant authorization," is found in the letters of Marcian and Pulcheria to Leo of Rome. The idea is that Leo has control and can say "yes" or "no" to a calling of a synod or council. Athanasius tells us that Christ did not rain fire down on Sodom of himself, but that the Father authorized it.

Meaning 3, "to act independently," carries the idea of being one's own authority. This meaning appears eight times. The idea is not intrinsically negative. As George Knight has pointed out, it does not mean in-and-of-itself "usurp authority."[23] While in *PLond 1708* Psates has apparently acted on his own authority to cheat his siblings, and Chrysostom says we should not seek "to have our own way." Chrysostom also has Jesus say that he does not need to rebuild the temple of his own body by command of the Father, but "exercises his own authority in the matter."

Meaning 3a, "to assume authority over," is a positive term that appears to imply that one moves forward to fill the leadership role. In *BGU 103* the request is that the bishop "assume authority" over the matter and resolve a domestic squabble. The term appears to be used as an equivalent of the colloquial phrase, "step up to the plate," or "take charge."

Meaning 3b, "to exercise one's own jurisdiction," is a negative term. It refers to a condition that results when one has arrogated to himself or herself the judgments or authority belonging to another. In this it is like "usurp." However, "usurp" refers to the *action* of wrongfully appropriating or supplanting, while αὐθέντεω refers to the *state* in which one is when he or she has achieved independent jurisdiction. Thus, the word is used three times to speak of an underlord who carries out an execution that ought to have been sanctioned by the king. It is used of other officials who release prisoners, lighten tribute, or convene assem-

22. Parker's choice of "despot" illustrates a closely related phenomenon in English: "despot = sole ruler" which by repeated hyperbole has become "despot = tyrant."

23. This investigation employs many sources from the church of early centuries A.D., where the concept of "independence" is one that would not have found whole-hearted acceptance. Submission to authority, not independence, was one of the driving values of the early church. So several of the examples given are in a context where the author undoubtedly intends the word to carry negative connotations.

blies without full authorization. The word is always used in this sense intransitively.[24] If the text has been properly reconstructed, the infinitive αὐθεντεῖν appears as a definition of αὐτοδικεῖν in Moeris's second-century A.D. lexicon. There he seems to indicate that the Attic αὐτοδικέω, "having independent jurisdiction," can be rendered by the Hellenistic αὐθεντέω.

Meaning 3c, "to flout authority," is found three times. John Malalas uses αὐθεντέω transitively with this to indicate the army has "sidestepped" the authority of the senate and, on its own, has selected an emperor. The same phrase as that used by Malalas is also found in the tenth-century work *About Strategy* with a similar sense.

Meaning 4, "to be primarily responsible for or instigate something," has been erroneously taken by the Kroegers[25] to mean "to be the organic origin of something" with a sense analogous to γεννάω or τίκτω.[26] However, a close examination of the five occurrences of αὐθεντέω with this meaning shows they are closer to the meaning recognized by Lampe, "to instigate." In two of the five uses αὐθεντέω is directly paralleled in the text by the verb προΐστημι, "to be the leader, to direct, to be the ringleader."[27]

What is significant is that the sometimes asserted meaning, "to murder" (5), is not substantiated for any period even remotely close to the period of the writing of the New Testament. The available evidence shows this meaning to appear indisputably only once, and that only in the tenth century A.D.[28] This occurrence is in a Byzantine scholarly note on a play by Aeschylus (d. 456 B.C.). It is essential to note that this occurrence is found in an Atticising work. That is, it is a work intentionally carried out in imitation of the style of classical Greek, which predates the Koine of the New Testament by several hundred years.

Much confusion as to the existence of the meaning "to murder" has arisen by failing to distinguish between the verb αὐθεντέω and the noun form αὐθέντης. The noun is attested to mean, among other things, "murderer." Our assertion that αὐθεντέω as a verb did not mean "to murder" in the koine at any time remotely contemporaneous with the New Testament is corroborated by the evidence of two ancient lex-

24. Hesychius provides a confirming note here in his definition of αὐτοδικεῖ (see entry A 8049). He says, αὐτοδικεῖ = αὐθεντεῖ ὅταν αὐτὸς λέγῃ. That is, "he has independent jurisdiction = αὐθεντεῖ, when he speaks himself/on his own authority."

25. Kroegers, *I Suffer Not a Woman*, chap. 9.

26. BAGD records the figurative and symbolic use of these two terms in the sense of "being the origin of something."

27. A similar parallel of προΐστημι and αὐθεντέω is found in Hesychius at the entry for αὐτάντας. There we read, ὁ προεστώς τινος πράγματος, καὶ αὐθεντῶν. That is, "The one who is in charge and in command of some matter." See entry A 8367.

28. It must be noted that the scholion in question appears in a tenth-century manuscript. Many scholars believe the scholion itself may be centuries older.

icons. Hesychius in the fifth century A.D. as noted above[29] only assigns the meaning of ἐξουσιάζειν to αὐθεντεῖν, though he says αὐθέντης may mean "murderer." The Suda, a tenth-century A.D. lexicon, provides more information. It acknowledges that some use αὐθέντης to mean "murderer." The Suda records that αὐθέντης simply indicates αὐτόχειρ, which the Suda takes to mean, "one who does a thing by his own hand," or perhaps "murderer." The verb αὐθεντήσαντα, it says, means κύριος γενόμενος, "having become lord over." It then goes on to explain the word by the action of King Mithridates (the VI), who ordered murder to be done by letter but did not bear the sword himself. So then we see that even in the fifth century A.D., αὐθεντέω (the verb) carried the idea of authority/responsibility. Evidently, only much later was it connected in some way with the idea of "murder" and even then it did not mean that exclusively nor was it used to mean such by all speakers of Greek.[30]

An objection might be raised by those concerned with the etymology of Greek. Analogous to words like δεσπότης/δεσποτέω, ἐπιστάτης/ἐπιστατέω, ὑπηρέτης/ὑπηρετέω, is not the noun αὐθέντης the origin of the verb αὐθεντέω? Therefore, should not all the meanings of the noun apply to the verb? In logic classes, perhaps. In the real world the case is not so simple. If, for instance, there were a single common spelling arising from different roots with different meanings, as some etymologists claim is the case with αὐθέντης,[31] then the formulation, αὐθέντης → αὐθεντέω, would not necessarily be true for each and every meaning of αὐθέντης. But whatever the origin of the words, neither δεσπότης,

29. See n. 14.

30. Dr. Al Wolters, who very kindly reviewed this article before publication (all errors, of course, remain my sole responsibility), challenged me on this point in a private letter urging, "Even this is to concede too much, in my opinion." Then, referring to the Scholion on *Aeschylus* he writes, "The verb *authenteō* is attested only once in the meaning 'to murder,' and this anomalous use is best explained as a case of hypercorrection by an Atticist pedant, based on the noun *authentēs* meaning 'murderer' in Attic usage." If Dr. Wolters' analysis is correct, and it very well may be, then the tenth-century scholion, the sole certain use of αὐθεντέω to mean "murder," is not a "development" at all, but an anachronism harkening back to classical Greek. Therefore the reference in the Suda must mean "be responsible for," not "be responsible for a murder."

31. Etymologists themselves do not agree on the origin of αὐθεντέω. The Suda offers a creative, but what can only be taken as fanciful, etymology for the word. Moulton and Milligan, 91, report, "The history of this word has been satisfactorily cleared up by P. Kretschmer," and go on to explain that αὐθέντης comes by haplology (the dropping out of a letter) from αὐτοθέντης whose root is θείνω, "to murder, to slay." On the other hand, αὐθέντης meaning "master" or "ruler" comes from αὐτ-ἕντης whose root sense is ἀνύω, "to accomplish." Thus through homography two widely divergent meanings share a common spelling, but not a common origin. P. Chantraine, *Dictionnaire étymologique de la langue Grecque*, vol. 1 (Paris: Klincksieck, 1968), 139, while acknowledging the possibility of two roots disagrees: "Moins vraisemblable encore est l'idée de Kretschmer selon qui deux mots . . . se seraient confondus."

ἐπιστάτης, nor αὐθέντης share all the meanings of their co-ordinate verbs by the simple addition of "to be a. . . ." From even these limited examples, the principle is evident, once again, that it is language *use*, not etymology, which determines the meaning of words.

A final observation may be made from the data of table 3.3. There appears among these data only limited historical development of the meaning of αὐθεντέω across fourteen centuries. The use of the word by Christian sources certainly brought it into a whole new sphere of application with respect to God and Christ. However, the same meanings apparently existed throughout the entire period. It is possible that some of the meanings 2 through 4 *may* have developed after the New Testament period, but the data are scanty enough that we can have no certainty. The data available, however, provide clear indication that the meaning "murder" was foreign to the usage of the New Testament period. The widely understood meanings of αὐθεντέω were based on the idea of the possession or exercise of authority.

Table 3.3
Chronological Distribution
of Various Meanings of αὐθεντέω

1. To rule, to reign sovereignly
   [1st cent. B.C.] Philodemus
   [A.D. 325] Eusebius
   [c. A.D. 390] Chrysostom
   [6th cent. A.D.] Romanus Melodus

2. To control, to dominate
   [2nd cent. A.D.] Ptolemy
   [c. A.D. 390] Chrysostom
   [A.D. 790] Second Council of Nicea
   [12th cent. A.D.] Michael Glycas

2a. To compel, to influence
   [27 B.C.] BGU 1208
   [A.D. 390] Chrysostom
   [A.D. 690] Joannes Malalas

2b. Middle: to be in effect, to have legal standing
   [A.D. 235] Hippolytus
   [7th cent. A.D.] Chronicon Paschale
2c. Uniquely: to domineer
   [c. A.D. 390] Chrysostom

2d. To grant authorization
   [c. A.D. 350] Athanasius

[A.D. 451] Marcian
[d. A.D. 638] Sophronius

3. To act independently
[c. A.D. 390] Chrysostom
[5th cent. A.D.] Ammonius Alexandrius
[6th cent. A.D.] PLond 1708

3a. To assume authority over
[c. A.D. 390] Chrysostom
[6th–7th cent. A.D.] BGU 103
[9th cent. A.D.] Photius

3b. To exercise one's own jurisdiction
[2nd cent. A.D.] Moeris
[A.D. 450] Olympiodorus
[9th cent. A.D.] Photius
[13th–14th cent. A.D.] Thomas Magister

3c. To flout the authority of
[c. A.D. 690] John Malalas
[10th cent. A.D.] Constantine VII

4. To be primarily responsible for, to instigate
[c. A.D. 325] Eusebius
[A.D. 449] Leo I
[10th cent. A.D.] Scholia on Homer

5. To commit a murder
[10th cent. A.D.] Scholia on Aeschylus

Conclusions

With respect to αὐθεντέω in 1 Timothy 2:12 and the meanings identified in table 3.2, it may be concluded:

1. The root meaning involves the concept of authority.
2. The context of 1 Timothy 2 appears to make meaning 1, "to rule, to reign sovereignly," impermissible.
3. Meanings 2 or 2a, "to control, to dominate" or "to compel, to influence someone," are entirely possible.
4. Meaning 2c, "to play the tyrant," could only correspond to Chrysostom's unique usage if the context could be shown to intend the same clear use of hyperbole, and the context does not seem to do that.

5. Noting that αὐθεντεῖν in 1 Timothy 2:12 is transitive, a translation of "assume authority over" (i.e., meaning 3a) could be appropriate, while 3 or 3b, which are intransitive, would not. If a negative meaning were intended, meaning 3c, "to flout the authority of," could be possible.
6. It is difficult to imagine how meaning 2d, "to grant authorization," or meaning 4, "to instigate," could make sense in 1 Timothy.
7. Meaning 5 appears to be impermissible on chronological grounds.
8. Further syntactical/contextual studies of 1 Timothy are required to decide with certainty among meanings 2, 2a, 3a, and 3c.

We have come a long way in our understanding of the meaning of αὐθεντέω as it was used by speakers of koine Greek. We have even been able to narrow down the range of meanings that might be appropriate in 1 Timothy 2:12. But before we can enter into the trial-and-error process of identifying the meaning of αὐθεντέω in that verse (which we will do in chapter 5) we must examine the difficult sentence structure of 1 Timothy 2:12 in the next chapter.

4

A Complex Sentence Structure in 1 Timothy 2:12

Andreas J. Köstenberger

The issue of word meanings has been explored in chapter 3. We learned that although each word has a range of possible meanings, certain meanings are outside this range. As we now proceed to determine the meaning of αὐθεντεῖν within its specific context, we can expect to be able to narrow its possible meanings to its probable meaning in 1 Timothy 2:12. This, in turn, will prepare the way for the exegesis of the verse in the following chapter.

The Significance of Syntactical Background Studies for the Interpretation of 1 Timothy 2:12

The passage reads as follows: "I do not permit a woman to teach or have authority over a man" (or, in the original Greek, διδάσκειν δὲ γυναικὶ οὐκ ἐπιτρέπω οὐδὲ αὐθεντεῖν ἀνδρός, ἀλλ᾽ εἶναι ἐν ἡσυχίᾳ). The syntactical pattern found in 1 Timothy 2:12 can be laid out as follows:

- a negated finite verb ("I do not permit," οὐκ ἐπιτρέπω)
- governing a (preceding) infinitive ("to teach," διδάσκειν)
- which is connected by the coordinating conjunction οὐδέ ("or")
- with a second infinitive ("to have authority," αὐθεντεῖν);
- this phrase is then contrasted with the adversative ἀλλά ("but")
- and yet another infinitive ("to be in quietness," εἶναι ἐν ἡσυχίᾳ).[1]

---

1. A study of preceding infinitives in the Pauline literature indicates that it is hard to find any consistent significance. Cf. the nineteen instances of preceding infinitives in the

Or, in other words, the pattern is:

(1) a negated finite verb + (2) infinitive + (3) οὐδέ + infinitive + (4) ἀλλά + infinitive[2]

The need for syntactical background studies to understand 1 Timothy 2:12 has been recognized by P. B. Payne and D. J. Moo, who engaged in a detailed exchange on the syntactical significance of οὐδέ in the verse. Payne argued that οὐδέ connects the two infinitives διδάσκειν and αὐθεντεῖν "in order to convey a single coherent idea," that is, as a hendiadys, so that the passage should be rendered as follows: "I do not permit a woman to teach in a domineering manner."[3] Moo disputed this notion as firmly as Payne asserted it, arguing that, while οὐδέ "certainly usually joins 'two *closely related* items,'" it does not usually join together words that restate the same thing or that are mutually interpreting."[4] Moo concluded that, while teaching and having authority are closely related, "they are nonetheless distinct," referring also to 1 Timothy 3:2, 4–5 and 5:17, where these two concepts are distinguished.[5]

Indeed, Payne's study is subject to improvement at several points. First, Payne studies only Paul. A more comprehensive study of the uses of οὐδέ in the whole New Testament is needed, if for no other reason than that the Pauline authorship of the Pastorals, including 1 Timothy, remains in dispute. Second, Payne studies all the occurrences of οὐδέ in Paul, even where it joins nouns, not verbs. It would seem desirable to sharpen the focus by studying the passages where οὐδέ joins verbs.[6]

Pauline writings: Rom. 7:18; 8:8; 1 Cor. 7:36; 14:35; 15:50; 2 Cor. 8:10; 11:30; 12:1; Gal. 4:9, 17; Phil. 1:12; 2 Thess. 1:3; 1 Tim. 2:12; 3:5; 5:11, 25; 6:7, 16; 2 Tim. 2:13. At any rate, the central thesis of this essay is not affected by whether the first infinitive precedes or follows the negated finite verb. Likewise, the presence or absence of the final element (i.e., a contrasting third infinitive) does not materially affect our thesis.

2. This final element (ἀλλά + infinitive) may not always be found.

3. P. B. Payne, "οὐδέ in 1 Timothy 2:12," paper read at the 1986 annual meeting of the Evangelical Theological Society, 10.

4. D. J. Moo, "What Does It Mean Not to Teach or Have Authority over Men? 1 Timothy 2:11–15," in *Recovering Biblical Manhood and Womanhood—A Response to Evangelical Feminism,* ed. J. Piper and W. Grudem (Wheaton: Crossway, 1991), 187.

5. Ibid.

6. Note that preliminary studies of οὐδέ linking nouns yielded results similar to those in the present study of οὐδέ linking verbs. The imprecision of Payne's work is also characteristic of the study by R. C. and C. C. Kroeger, *I Suffer Not a Woman: Rethinking 1 Timothy 2:11–15 in Light of Ancient Evidence* (Grand Rapids: Baker, 1991), 83–84, 189–92, whose examples are either passages in which οὐδέ joins two nouns or in which the word is not οὐδέ but οὐδέν. The Kroegers' suggestion that αὐθεντεῖν in 1 Tim. 2:12 may be an "infinitive of indirect discourse" must be rejected since they do not provide a single example of an infinitive of indirect discourse following οὐδέ in the New Testament or elsewhere.

Third, Payne does not consider uses of μηδέ in Paul or elsewhere in the New Testament. Only seven instances remain where Paul uses οὐδέ to connect verbs (1 Cor. 15:50; 2 Cor. 7:12; Gal. 1:17; 4:14; Phil. 2:16; 2 Thess. 3:8; 1 Tim. 6:16). However, references including μηδέ in writings traditionally attributed to Paul provide eight further examples alone (Rom. 9:11, 16b; 14:21; 2 Cor. 4:2; Col. 2:21; 2 Thess. 2:2; 1 Tim. 1:3–4; 6:17). Notably, two of these, 1 Timothy 1:3–4 and 6:17, occur in the same letter. Fourth, Payne already starts with the assumption that αὐθεντεῖν means "domineer." However, that is the very thing that needs to be established, not asserted. What is called for is an inductive study of all the instances of οὐδέ joining verbs, both in the New Testament and in extrabiblical Greek literature. This investigation will distill the database for understanding the syntax of 1 Timothy 2:12 with implications for the meaning of αὐθεντεῖν.

Fifth, since Payne presupposes that αὐθεντεῖν means "domineer," he concludes that "teach" and "domineer" by themselves are conceptually too far apart to be joined by οὐδέ (which usually joins closely related terms) in a coordinating manner. Thus, Payne views the second term joined by οὐδέ in 1 Timothy 2:12, αὐθεντεῖν, as subordinate to the first, διδάσκειν. But if αὐθεντεῖν were to mean "to have authority" rather than "to domineer," it would be quite closely related to διδάσκειν, "to teach." In that case, consistent with Payne's own observations on how οὐδέ generally functions, οὐδέ could well link the two closely related terms, "to teach" and "to have authority," in a coordinating fashion. Payne's argument is circular, and his conclusion is unduly predetermined by his presupposition regarding the meaning of αὐθεντεῖν. Sixth, Payne's terminology is ambiguous when he calls two terms "closely related." He seems to use this terminology in the sense of "essentially one" so that he can conclude that in 1 Timothy 2:12 "οὐδέ joins together two elements in order to convey a single coherent idea." However, as will be shown below, two terms can be "closely related" and yet be distinct. For example, Matthew 6:20 refers to heaven "where thieves neither break in nor steal." While "breaking in" and "stealing" are sequentially related and may be seen as components of essentially one event, burglary, the two activities are not so closely related as to lose their own distinctness. The burglar first breaks in and then steals.

Seventh, Payne is inconsistent in his use of terminology regarding his categories of the usage of οὐδέ. On page 1, he terms his second category "those which specify with greater clarity the meaning of one word or phrase by conjoining it with another word or phrase." Yet in his conclusion on page 10, he calls the same category "οὐδέ joins together two elements in order to convey a single coherent idea." From the beginning of his paper until the end, Payne has subtly shifted from one definition of his crucial category to another. While his definition on page 1 allows for terms to be closely related and yet distinct, Payne's categorization on page 10 unduly narrows his earlier definition so that now closely related yet distinct terms seem excluded. Eighth, on page 10 Payne notes translations that render αὐθεντεῖν with "domineer" or similarly negative connotations. He fails to observe, however, that neither the NASB, RSV, nor NIV renders the term with a negative connotation. The NASB has "exercise authority"; the NIV and RSV translate αὐθεντεῖν with "to have authority."

We may summarize the argument thus far. Two methodological paths have been taken to identify the proper rendering of 1 Timothy 2:12: word studies and syntactical studies. The rarity of the use of αὐθεντεῖν and other limitations make word studies of only limited value for the present problem. The major syntactical study on the passage is subject to some significant improvements. Therefore, a fresh study of New Testament syntactical parallels to 1 Timothy 2:12 needs to be undertaken.[7] Furthermore, extrabiblical Greek literature from the period preceding or contemporary with the New Testament should be consulted to supplement the study of syntactical parallels to 1 Timothy 2:12.

Syntactical Parallels to 1 Timothy 2:12 in the New Testament

Strictly speaking, there is only one close syntactical parallel to 1 Timothy 2:12 in the New Testament, Acts 16:21, where the same construction, a negated finite verb + infinitive + οὐδέ + infinitive, is found.[8] How-

---

7. A few constraints should be noted. Although the subject of this chapter is *syntactical* background studies, the conclusions drawn from the syntax as found in 1 Tim. 2:12 will involve *semantic* judgments (especially in the two patterns of the usage of οὐδέ that will be identified). There are also other syntactical (as well as semantic) issues raised by 1 Tim. 2:12 that will not be dealt with in this study, such as the question of whether or not ἀνδρός should be read with both διδάσκειν and αὐθεντεῖν or exactly how the ἀλλά-clause at the end of v. 12 relates to the preceding clause and which verb should be supplied there. Even the verbal aspect or verb tense of the verbs involved will not be dealt with at this stage of the investigation since, as will become evident, the major thesis of this essay is not materially affected by the aspect or tense of the verbs.

8. This syntactical pattern is not necessarily always found in this particular chronological order. For example, in 1 Tim. 2:12, the first infinitive precedes the negated finite verb so that the order there is (2), (1), (3), and (4). A study of preceding infinitives in the Pauline literature, however, indicates that it is hard to find any consistent significance in preceding rather than following infinitives. Cf. the nineteen instances of preceding infinitives in the Pauline writings, Rom. 7:18; 8:8; 1 Cor. 7:36; 14:35; 15:50; 2 Cor. 8:10; 11:30; 12:1; Gal. 4:9, 17; Phil. 1:12; 2 Thess. 1:3; 1 Tim. 2:12; 3:5; 5:11, 25; 6:7, 16; 2 Tim. 2:13. Either way, the central thesis of this essay is not affected by whether the first infinitive precedes or follows the negated finite verb. Likewise, the presence or absence of element (4) does not substantially affect the thesis of this essay.

ever, if one allows for verbal forms other than infinitives to be linked by οὐδέ, fifty-two further passages can be identified. These can be grouped into two patterns of the usage of οὐδέ:

- Pattern #1: two activities or concepts are viewed positively in and of themselves, but their exercise is prohibited or their existence denied due to circumstances or conditions adduced in the context.
- Pattern #2: two activities or concepts are viewed negatively and consequently their exercise is prohibited or their existence denied or to be avoided.

In both patterns, the conjunction οὐδέ coordinates activities of the same order, that is, activities that are either both viewed positively or negatively by the writer or speaker.

Pattern #1, the prohibition or denial of two activities or concepts that are otherwise viewed positively, is found in the following New Testament passages: Matthew 6:26=Luke 12:24; Matthew 6:28=Luke 12:27; Matthew 7:6, 18; 10:14=cf. Mark 6:11; Matthew 13:13; 22:46; 23:13; Mark 8:17; 13:15; Luke 6:44; 17:23; 18:4; John 14:17; Acts 4:18; 9:9; 16:21; 17:24–25; 21:21; Romans 9:11, 16; 14:21; 1 Corinthians 15:50; Galatians 1:16–17; Colossians 2:21; 1 Timothy 2:12; 6:16; Hebrews 10:8; 1 John 3:6; and Revelation 12:8.

Pattern #2, the prohibition or denial of two activities that are both viewed negatively, can be seen in Matthew 6:20=Luke 12:33; Matthew 12:19; Luke 3:14; John 4:15; 14:27; Acts 2:27; 2 Corinthians 4:2; 7:12; Galatians 4:14; Philippians 2:16; 2 Thessalonians 2:2; 3:7–8; 1 Timothy 1:3–4; 6:17; Hebrews 12:5; 13:5; 1 Peter 2:22; 3:14; and Revelation 7:16. Overall, there are thirty-three examples of the first and twenty of the second pattern in the New Testament (see table 4.1).

Table 4.1
Patterns of the Usage of οὐδέ in the New Testament

Pattern #1: Two activities or concepts are viewed positively in and of themselves, but their exercise is prohibited or their existence denied due to circumstances or conditions adduced in the context.

Matt. 6:26	οὐ σπείρουσιν (sow)	οὐδὲ θερίζουσιν (harvest) οὐδὲ συνάγουσιν εἰς ἀπο- θήκας (gather into barns)
Matt. 6:28	οὐ κοπιῶσιν (labor)	οὐδὲ νήθουσιν (spin)
Matt. 7:6	Μὴ δῶτε (give)	μηδὲ βάλητε (throw)
Matt. 7:18	οὐ δύναται ποιεῖν (can yield)	οὐδὲ ποιεῖν (yield)*

Matt. 10:14	μὴ δέξηται (receive)	μηδὲ ἀκούσῃ (listen)
Matt. 13:13	οὐκ ἀκούουσιν (hear)	οὐδὲ συνίουσιν (understand)
Matt. 22:46	οὐδεὶς ἐδύνατο ἀποκριθῆναι (could answer)	οὐδὲ ἐτόλμησέν ἐπερωτῆσαι (dared to ask)
Matt. 23:13	οὐκ εἰσέρχεσθε (enter)	οὐδὲ ἀφίετε εἰσελθεῖν (permit to enter)
Mark 6:11	μὴ δέξηται (receive)	μηδὲ ἀκούσωσιν (listen; cf. Matt. 10:14)**
Mark 8:17	οὔπω νοεῖτε (understand)	οὐδὲ συνίετε (understand)
Mark 13:15	μὴ καταβάτω (go down)	μηδὲ εἰσελθάτω (enter)
Luke 6:44	οὐ συλλέγουσιν (pick)	οὐδὲ τρυγῶσιν (gather)
Luke 12:24	οὐ σπείρουσιν (sow)	οὐδὲ θερίζουσιν (harvest; cf. Matt. 6:26)
Luke 12:27	οὐ κοπιᾷ (labor)	οὐδὲ νήθει (spin; cf. Matt. 6:28)
Luke 17:23	μὴ ἀπέλθητε (depart)	μηδὲ διώξητε (follow)
Luke 18:4	οὐ φοβοῦμαι (fear [God])	οὐδὲ ἐντρέπομαι (care [about man])
John 14:17	οὐ θεωρεῖ (behold)	οὐδὲ γινώσκει(know)
Acts 4:18	μὴ φθέγγεσθαι (speak)	μηδὲ διδάσκειν (teach)
Acts 9:9	οὐκ ἔφαγεν (eat)	οὐδὲ ἔπιεν (drink)
Acts 16:21	οὐκ ἔξεστιν παραδέχεσθαι (accept)	οὐδὲ ποιεῖν (practice)
Acts 17:24–25	οὐκ κατοικεῖ (dwell)	οὐδὲ θεραπεύεται (be served)
Acts 21:21	μὴ περιτέμνειν (circumcise)	μηδὲ περιπατεῖν (walk [in customs])
Rom. 9:11	μήπω γεννηθέντων (born)	μηδὲ πραξάντων (done)
Rom. 9:16	οὐ τοῦ θέλοντος (wishing)	οὐδὲ τοῦ τρέχοντος (running)
Rom. 14:21	μὴ φαγεῖν (eat)	μηδὲ πιεῖν (drink)
1 Cor. 15:50	κληρονομῆσαι οὐ δύναται (can inherit)	οὐδὲ κληρονομεῖ (inherit)*
Gal. 1:16–17	οὐ προσανεθέμην (consult)	οὐδὲ ἀνῆλθον (go up)
Col. 2:21	μὴ ἅψῃ (touch)	μηδὲ γεύσῃ μηδὲ θίγῃς (taste, handle)
1 Tim. 2:12	διδάσκειν οὐκ ἐπιτρέπω (teach)	οὐδὲ αὐθεντεῖν ἀνδρός (have authority over a man)

1 Tim. 6:16	εἶδεν οὐδείς (see)	οὐδὲ ἰδεῖν δύναται (can see)
Heb. 10:8	οὐκ ἠθέλησας (desire)	οὐδὲ εὐδόκησας (be well-pleased)
1 John 3:6	οὐχ ἑώρακεν (see)	οὐδὲ ἔγνωκεν (know)
Rev. 12:8	οὐκ ἴσχυσεν (prevail)	οὐδὲ τόπος εὑρέθη (place be found)*

Pattern #2: Two activities or concepts are viewed negatively and consequently their exercise is prohibited or their existence is to be denied or they are to be avoided.

Matt. 6:20	οὐ διορύσσουσιν (break in)	οὐδὲ κλέπτουσιν (steal)
Matt. 12:19	οὐκ ἐρίσει (quarrel)	οὐδὲ κραυγάσει (cry out)
Luke 3:14	μηδένα διασείσητε (extort money)	μηδὲ συκοφαντήσητε (accuse falsely)
Luke 12:33	κλέπτης οὐκ ἐγγίζει (thief come near)	οὐδὲ διαφθείρει (destroy; cf. Matt. 6:20)*
John 4:15	μὴ διψῶ (thirst)	μηδὲ διέρχωμαι ἀντλεῖν (come to draw)
John 14:27	μὴ ταρασσέσθω (let be troubled)	μηδὲ δειλιάτω (be afraid)
Acts 2:27	οὐκ ἐγκαταλείψεις (abandon)	οὐδὲ δώσεις ἰδεῖν διαφθοράν (give to see decay)
2 Cor. 4:2	μὴ περιπατοῦντες ἐν πανουργίᾳ (walk in deceit)	μηδὲ δολοῦντες (distort)
2 Cor. 7:12	οὐκ ἕνεκεν τοῦ ἀδικήσαντος (the wrongdoer)	οὐδὲ ἕνεκεν τοῦ ἀδικηθέντος (the injured party)
Gal. 4:14	οὐκ ἐξουθενήσατε (treat with contempt)	οὐδὲ ἐξεπτύσατε (scorn)
Phil. 2:16	οὐκ εἰς κενὸν ἔδραμον (run in vain)	οὐδὲ εἰς κενὸν ἐκοπίασα (labor in vain)
2 Thess. 2:2	μὴ σαλευθῆναι (become unsettled)	μηδὲ θροεῖσθαι (become alarmed)
2 Thess. 3:7–8	οὐκ ἠτακτήσαμεν (be idle)	οὐδὲ ἐφάγομεν (eat another's food)
1 Tim. 1:3–4	μὴ ἑτεροδιδασκαλεῖν (teach error)	μηδὲ προσέχειν μύθοις (pay attention to myths)
1 Tim. 6:17	μὴ ὑψηλοφρονεῖν (be arrogant)	μηδὲ ἠλπικέναι ἐπὶ πλούτου (put hope in wealth)

Heb. 12:5	μὴ ὀλιγώρει (despise)	μηδὲ ἐκλύου (consider lightly)
Heb. 13:5	οὐ μή ἀνῶ (leave)	οὐδ' οὐ μή ἐγκαταλίπω (forsake)
1 Pet. 2:22	ἁμαρτίαν οὐκ ἐποίησεν (commit sin)	οὐδὲ εὑρέθη δόλος (deceit be found)*
1 Pet. 3:14	μὴ φοβηθῆτε (be afraid)	μηδὲ ταραχθῆτε (be disturbed)
Rev. 7:16	οὐ πεινάσουσιν (hunger)	οὐδὲ διψήσουσιν (thirst)

*=change of subject; **=change from sing. to pl. verb form.

The first pattern can be illustrated by a few examples. In Acts 16:21, the closest syntactical parallel to 1 Timothy 2:12 in the New Testament, the two terms in the infinitive, παραδέχεσθαι and ποιεῖν, are conceptual parallels. "Accepting" and "practicing" do not carry negative connotations in and of themselves. However, due to circumstances indicated in the context, "being Romans," the exercise of these otherwise legitimate activities is considered "not lawful." In Acts 4:18 Luke reports that the authorities, because of their antagonism to Christ, forbid the early church to speak and teach in the name of Jesus (two activities that carry no negative connotations in and of themselves). In Acts 21:21 Paul is told that there are reports that he forbids Jews living among Gentiles to carry out two activities viewed positively by the speakers, circumcising their children and living according to Jewish customs. In Galatians 1:16–17 Paul insists that, upon his conversion, he did not immediately consult with others nor go up to Jerusalem, two activities that are not intrinsically viewed negatively, to underscore that he had been divinely commissioned. And in Colossians 2:21 the writer quotes the maxim "Do not touch, do not taste, do not handle," as the (legalistic) prohibition of activities not viewed negatively in and of themselves.

The following examples are instances of the second pattern, the prohibition or denial of two activities that are viewed negatively by the writer or speaker. In John 4:15 the Samaritan woman expresses her desire to avoid two things she views negatively, thirsting and having to come to the well to draw water. In Philippians 2:16 Paul states that he wants to avoid two activities he views negatively, running in vain and laboring in vain. In 2 Thessalonians 3:7–8 Paul denies that, at his previous visit, he had engaged in two activities that he views negatively, being idle and eating another's food. A passage in the epistle under consideration, 1 Timothy 1:3–4, indicates the instruction to Timothy to command certain ones to avoid two activities the author views negatively, teaching error and holding to myths and endless genealogies.

Later in the same epistle, in 6:17, one finds the instruction to Timothy to command the rich in his congregation to avoid two things viewed negatively by the writer, being arrogant and setting their hope on the uncertainty of riches.

These examples set forth the New Testament evidence that οὐδέ joins terms that denote activities that are either both viewed positively or negatively by the writer or speaker. The implication of this observation for 1 Timothy 2:12 is that there are only two acceptable ways of rendering that passage: (1) "I do not permit a woman to teach [error] or to domineer over a man," or (2) "I do not permit a woman to teach or to exercise authority over a man." In the first instance, both "teaching error" and "domineering a man" would be viewed negatively by the writer. In the latter case, both "teaching" and "exercising authority" would be viewed positively in and of themselves, yet for reasons to be gleaned from the context the writer does not permit these.

Before deciding on one of the two patterns for 1 Timothy 2:12, a preliminary clarification needs to be made. A distinction should be drawn, especially in the first scenario, between the fact that two activities or concepts are viewed positively in and of themselves, and their prohibition due to circumstances. In the case of 1 Timothy 2:12, the writer's "I do not permit" has apparently at times been taken to mean that he views the two activities, διδάσκειν and αὐθεντεῖν, themselves negatively, in the sense of "teaching in a domineering way," or the like. However, one should keep in mind that it is possible for the writer to evaluate negatively the exercise of activities he generally views positively, due to certain circumstances, without tainting the two terms themselves.

For example, I may tell my pregnant wife that I do not want her to drive alone or be on the road at night. There is nothing wrong with driving alone or being on the road at night. It is just that, under the circumstances, my wife's pregnancy, I prefer for her not to engage in these activities. Or you may tell your child not to climb a ladder or to go near a cliff. There is nothing wrong with climbing a ladder or even going near a cliff. It is just that, since you fear for your children's safety, you do not permit them to engage in two activities that are otherwise viewed as permissible. In short, it remains a legitimate possibility for a writer to deny someone for certain reasons the exercise of activities he otherwise views positively.

In the light of this clarification, 1 Timothy 2:12 could legitimately be seen as an example of the first pattern, that is, the denial of two activities that are viewed positively in and of themselves, under contextually adduced circumstances. That this is indeed the case is strongly suggested by the use of the term διδάσκειν, which is consistently viewed positively in the New Testament, including the Pastorals, when used absolutely, that is, unaccompanied by contextual qualifiers such as those denoting the content of someone's teaching.[9]

The Kroegers' claim that "If the context of 1 Timothy 2:12 is neutral and refers only to the activity of teaching rather than to its positive or negative content, then it is the only time that διδάσκειν is so used in the Pastorals" is contradicted by passages like the following:

- 1 Timothy 4:11: Παράγελλε ταῦτα καὶ δίδασκε ("Command and teach these things")
- 1 Timothy 6:2: Ταῦτα δίδασκε καὶ παρακάλει ("Teach and encourage these things")
- 2 Timothy 2:2: Ταῦτα παράθου πιστοῖς ἀνθρώποις οἵτινες ἱκανοι ἔσονται καὶ ἑτέρους διδάξαι ("Pass on these things to faithful individuals who will be able to teach others also")[10]

In each case, διδάσκειν is clearly viewed positively by the writer and is linked with activities such as encouraging, exhorting, and the passing on of apostolic tradition. And when the Kroegers contend that "the verb here [i.e., in 1 Tim. 2:12] forbids women to teach a wrong doctrine, just as 1 Timothy 1:3–4 and Titus 1:9–14 also forbid false teaching," it must be asserted that in 1 Timothy 1:3–4 it is ἑτεροδιδάσκαλειν, not διδάσκειν, which is used, while in Titus 1:9–14 there is ample contextual indication that false teaching is in view, a feature that is absent from the context of 1 Timothy 2:12.[11]

It should further be noted that the effort to make αὐθεντεῖν subordinate to διδάσκειν so that it in effect functions as an adverb and to give it a negative connotation, as in "to teach in a domineering way," is contradicted by the fact that οὐδέ does not function as a subordinating but as a coordinating conjunction. Neither the syntactical parallels in the New Testament nor the extrabiblical parallels lend support to the contention that the second term linked by οὐδέ modifies the first term ad-

9. This is one major reason why, after screening less close syntactical parallels, this study will proceed to search extrabiblical Greek literature for more exact parallels involving, as in 1 Tim. 2:12, two infinitives governed by a negated finite verb. The fact that, strictly speaking, there is only one close syntactical parallel to 1 Tim. 2:12 in the New Testament does not mean that New Testament passages in which a negated finite verb governs two verb forms other than infinitives are without value for identifying general patterns of the usage of οὐδέ. Rather, the New Testament allows one to identify a basic pattern of the usage of οὐδέ that can then be tested and refined by resorting to extrabiblical Greek literature. This is the approach followed in the present study.

10. Cf. especially 1 Tim. 4:11; 6:2; and 2 Tim. 2:2; in contrast to ἑτεροδιδάσκαλειν, which is found in 1 Tim. 1:3–4 and 6:3.

11. Cf. Kroegers, *I Suffer Not a Woman*, 81. See also Payne, "οὐδέ," 6–8, who argues that teaching is an activity viewed positively in and of itself in the New Testament and in Paul.

verbially. And while "teaching" and "exercising authority" may well be perceived jointly in 1 Timothy 2:12, these concepts do not blend to the extent that they become one concept in which the two constituent elements are no longer distinguishable.

Since, therefore, the term διδάσκειν is used absolutely in the New Testament for an activity that is viewed positively in and of itself, and since οὐδέ coordinates terms that are either both viewed positively or negatively, αὐθεντεῖν should be seen as denoting an activity that is viewed positively in and of itself as well. Thus, 1 Timothy 2:12 is an instance of the first pattern, in which the exercise of two activities is prohibited or the existence of two concepts is denied by the writer due to special considerations.[12]

The immediate context of the passage, 1 Timothy 2:11, supports this conclusion. Framed by the inclusio of ἡσυχία at the beginning of verse 11 and at the end of verse 12, there are two corresponding pairs of terms: "learning" in verse 11 corresponds to "teaching" in verse 12, and "full submission" in verse 11 relates to "having authority" in verse 12. The writer first expresses his desire for a woman to learn in full submission. Conversely, he then registers his prohibition of the opposite, a woman's teaching or being in authority over a man. He closes by reiterating his desire for a woman to learn in submission. "Learning" and "teaching," "full submission" and "having authority" are contrasted, the former terms being viewed positively in the case of women, the latter ones negatively. Thus, syntax and context join in suggesting that 1 Timothy 2:12 be rendered as "I do not permit a woman to teach or to have authority over a man."

Syntactical Parallels to 1 Timothy 2:12 in Extrabiblical Literature

The study of syntactical parallels to 1 Timothy 2:12 in the New Testament yielded significant insights. Two patterns of the use of οὐδέ were identified, both consisting of coordinated expressions of the same order. However, since the New Testament contains only one exact syntactical parallel where οὐδέ links two *infinitives* governed by a negated finite verb, it seems desirable to extend the scope of this investigation to extrabiblical Greek literature preceding or contemporary with the New Testament era.

The IBYCUS system, a computer program with the capability of searching virtually all of the extant ancient Greek literature, has enabled the researcher to study all Greek literature directly relevant for

12. Cf. Kroegers, *I Suffer Not a Woman*, 81.

the study of the syntax used in 1 Timothy 2:12 (i.e., literature from the third century B.C. until the end of the first century A.D.)—the LXX, the papyri and inscriptions available on the Ibycus, and all the extant works of Polybius, Dionysius Halicarnassensis, Diodorus Siculus, Josephus, Philo, and Plutarch.

Forty-eight syntactical parallels to 1 Timothy 2:12 in extrabiblical Greek literature were found: five in the LXX, two in inscriptions, six in Polybius, three in Dionysius Halicarnassensis, two in Diodorus Siculus, nine in Josephus, one in Philo, and twenty in Plutarch. Plutarch accounts for almost half of the references, Josephus and Polybius together provide another third. Following is a list of syntactical parallels to 1 Timothy 2:12:

LXX

1. 1 Macc. 15:14: καὶ ἐκύκλωσεν τὴν πόλιν, καὶ τὰ πλοῖα ἀπὸ θαλάσσης συνῆψαν, καὶ ἔθλιβε τὴν πόλιν ἀπὸ τῆς γῆς και τῆς θαλάσσης, καὶ (1) οὐκ εἴασεν οὐδένα (2) ἐκπορεύεσθαι (3) οὐδὲ εἰσπορεύεσθαι. "He surrounded the city, and the ships joined battle from the sea; he pressed the city hard from land and sea, and (1) permitted no one (2) to leave (3) or enter it."[13]

2. Sir. 18:6: (1) οὐκ ἔστιν (2) ἐλαττῶσαι (3) οὐδὲ προσθεῖναι, καὶ οὐκ ἔστιν ἐξιχνιάσαι τὰ θαυμάσια τοῦ κυρίου. "[Who can measure his majestic power? And who can fully recount his mercies?] (1) It is not possible (2) to diminish (3) or increase them, nor is it possible to trace the wonders of the Lord."

3. Isa. 42:24b: οὐχὶ ὁ θεός, ᾧ ἡμάρτοσαν αὐτῷκαὶ (1) οὐκ ἐβούλοντο ἐν ταῖς ὁδοῖς αὐτοῦ (2) πορεύεσθαι (3) οὐδὲ ἀκούειν τοῦ νόμου αὐτοῦ; "[Who gave Jacob up for spoil, and Israel to plunderers?] Was it not God, against whom they have sinned, and in whose ways (1) they were not willing (2) to walk, and whose law (3) they did not obey?"

4. Ezek. 44:13: καὶ (1) οὐκ ἐγγιοῦσι πρός με τοῦ (2) ἱερατεύειν μοι (3) οὐδὲ τοῦ προσάγειν πρὸς τὰ ἅγια υἱων τοῦ Ισραηλ οὐδὲ πρὸς τὰ ἅγια τῶν ἁγίων μου καὶ λήμψονται ἀτιμίαν αὐτῶν ἐν τῇ πλανήσει, ᾗ ἐπλανήθησαν. "And (1) they shall not come near to Me (2) to serve as a priest to Me, (3) nor come near to any of the holy things of the sons of Israel, nor to the holiest of my holy things; but they shall bear their dishonor in their shame by which they have deceived."

5. DanTh. 5:8: καὶ εἰσεπορεύοντο πάντες οἱ σοφοὶ τοῦ βασιλέως καὶ (1) οὐκ ἠδύναντο τὴν γραφὴν (2) ἀναγνῶναι (3) οὐδὲ τὴν σύγκρισιν γν-

---

13. Translations for texts 1, 2, and 5 are taken from Bruce M. Metzger, *The Apocrypha of the Old Testament* (New York: Oxford University Press, 1977); translations for texts 3, 4, and 7 are my own; and translations for texts 8–48 are taken from the Loeb Classical Library series.

ὡρίσαι τῷ βασιλεῖ. "Then all the king's wise men came in, but (1) they could not (2) read the inscription (3) [n]or make known its interpretation to the king."

Inscriptions

6. Attica.IG II(2).11589 (third century B.C.): . . . (1) οὐκ ἄνσχετο (2) δῶρα δέχεσθαι (3) οὐδὲ κλύειν ἱκέτου Τισαμενοῖο πατρός. ". . . (1) he did not stand up (2) to receive gifts (3) nor to give ear to the suppliant, Tisamenoios the father."

7. PZenPestm.21 (246 B.C.): Νίκων δὲ ὁ κρινόμενος πρὸς Ἀντίπατρον (1) οὐκ ἔφατο (2) εἰληφέναι τὸ παιδάριον παρ᾽ αὐτῶν (3) οὐδὲ ἔχειν αὐτὸ παρευρέσει οὐδεμιᾷ. "Nikon the judge (1) did not say to Antipater (2) to take the boy from them (3) nor to hold him under any pretense."

Polybius (202–120 B.C.)

8. *Hist.* 2.56.10: (1) δεῖ τοιγαροῦν οὐκ (2) ἐκπλήττειν τὸν συγγραφέα τερατευόμενον διὰ τῆς ἱστορίας τοὺς ἐντυγχάνοντας (3) οὐδὲ τοὺς ἐνδεχομένους λόγους ζητεῖν καὶ τὰ παρεπόμενα τοῖς ὑποκειμένοις ἐξαριθμεῖσθαι, καθάπερ οἱ τραγῳδιογράφοι, τῶν δὲ πραχθέντων καὶ ῥηθέντων κατ᾽ ἀλήθειαν αὐτῶν μνημονεύειν πάμπαν, κἂν πάνυ μέτρια τυγχάνωσιν ὄντα. "A historical author (1) should not (2) try to thrill his readers by such exaggerated pictures, (3) nor should he, like a tragic poet, try to imagine the probable utterances of his characters or reckon up all the consequences probably incidental to the occurrences with which he deals, but simply record what really happened and what really was said, however commonplace."

9. *Hist.* 5.10.5: (1) οὐ γὰρ ἐπ᾽ ἀπωλείᾳ δεῖ καὶ ἀφανισμῷ τοῖς ἀγνοήσασι (2) πολεμεῖν τοὺς ἀγαθοὺς ἄνδρας, ἀλλ᾽ ἐπὶ διορθώσει καὶ μεταθέσει τῶν ἡμαρτημέων, (3) αὐδὲ συναναιρεῖν τὰ μηδὲν ἀδικοῦντα τοῖς ἠδικηκόσιν, ἀλλὰ συσσῴζειν μᾶλλον καὶ συνεξαιρεῖσθαι τοῖς ἀνοιτίοις τοὺς δοκοῦντας ἀδικεῖν. "For good men (1) should not (2) make war on wrong-doers with the object of destroying and exterminating them, but with that of correcting and reforming their errors, (3) nor should they involve the guiltless in the fate of the guilty, (4) but rather extend to those whom they think guilty the mercy and deliverance they offer to the innocent."

10. *Hist.* 6.15.8: . . . τούτους (1) οὐ δύνανται (2) χειρίζειν, ὡς πρέπει, ποτὲ δὲ τὸ παράπαν (3) οὐδὲ συντελεῖν . . . "[For the processions they call triumphs, in which the generals bring the actual spectacle of their achievements before the eyes of their fellow-citizens,] (1) cannot (2) be properly organized and sometimes even cannot (3) be held at all, [unless the senate consents and provides the requisite funds.]"

11. *Hist.* 30.5.8.4–6: . . . (1) οὐκ ἐβούλοντο (2) συνδυάζειν (3) οὐδὲ προκαταλαμβάνειν σφᾶς αὐτοὺς ὅρκοις καὶ συνθήκαις, (4) ἀλλ᾿ ἀκέραιοι διαμένοντες κερδαίνειν τὰς ἐξ ἑκάστων ἐλπίδας. "[As they wished none of the kings and princes to despair of gaining their help and alliance,] (1) they did not desire (2) to run in harness with Rome (3) and engage themselves by oaths and treaties, (4) but preferred to remain unembarrassed and able to reap profit from any quarter."

12. *Hist.* 30.24.2.3–4: . . . (1) οὐ δοκοῦσι δὲ (2) γινώσκεσθαι παρὰ τοῖς ἀπαντῶσιν (3) οὐδὲ συνορᾶσθαι διότι λέλυνται σαφῶς, ἐὰν μή τι παράλογον ποιῶσι καὶ τῶν ἄλλων ἐξηλλαγμένον. "The inhabitants of Peraea were like slaves unexpectedly released from their fetters, who, unable to believe the truth, take longer steps than their natural ones] and (1) fancy that those they meet will (2) not know (3) and see for certain that they are free unless they behave in some strange way and differently from other men."

13. *Hist.* 31.12.5–6: . . . τὴν δὲ σύγκλητον (1) οὐ τολμήσειν ἔτι (2) βοηθεῖν (3) οὐδὲ συνεπισχύειν τοῖς περὶ τὸν Λυσίαν τοιαῦτα διεργασαμένοις. "For the Syrians would at once transfer the crown to him, even if he appeared accompanied only by a single slave,] while the senate (1) would not go so far as (2) to help (3) and support Lysias after his conduct."

Dionysius Halicarnassensis (first century B.C.)

14. *De Thucydide* 7.13–15: Θουκυδίδῃ δὲ τῷ προελομένῳ μίαν ὑπόθεσιν, ᾗ παρεγίνετο αὐτός, (1) οὐκ ἥρμοττεν (2) ἐγκαταμίσγειν τῇ διηγήσει τὰς θεατρικὰς γοητείας (3) οὐδὲ πρὸς τὴν ἀπάτην ἁρμόττεσθαι τῶν ἀναγνωσομένων, ἣν ἐκεῖναι πεφύκασι φέρειν αἱ συντάξεις, (4) ἀλλὰ πρὸς τὴν ὠφέλειαν. "Thucydides, however, chose a single episode in which he personally participated: (1) it was therefore inappropriate for him (2) to adulterate his narrative with entertaining fantasies (3) or to arrange it in a way which would confuse his readers, as his predecessors' compositions would naturally do. His purpose was to benefit his readers."

15. *Antiqu. Rom.* 10.12.3–5: . . . ἢ ὡς (1) οὐ δεῖ (2) κοινωνεῖν (3) οὐδὲ παρεῖναι τῇ ζητήσει τοὺς ἀνειληφότας τὴν τοῦ δήμου ἀρχήν. ". . . or that the magistrates of the populace (1) ought not (2) to take part in or (3) be present at the inquiry."

16. *De Comp. Verb.* 23:2–5: (1) οὐ ζητεῖ καθ᾿ ἓν ἕκαστον ὄνομα ἐκ περιφανείας (2) ὁρᾶσθαι (3) οὐδὲ ἐν ἕδρᾳ πάντα βεβηκέναι πλατείᾳ τε καὶ ἀσφαλεῖ οὐδὲ μακροὺς τοὺς μεταξὺ αὐτῶν εἶναι χρόνους. "[The polished style of composition, which I placed second in order, has the following character.] (1) It does not intend each word (2) to be viewed from all sides, (3) nor that every word shall stand on a

broad, firm base, nor that the intervals of time between them shall be long."

Diodorus Siculus (c. 40 b.c.)

17. *Bibl. Hist.* 3.30.2.8–9: (1) οὐ χρὴ δὲ (2) θαυμάζειν (3) οὐδὲ ἀπιστεῖν τοῖς λεγομένοις, πολλὰ τούτων παραδοξότερα κατὰ πᾶσαν τὴν οἰκουμένην γεγονότα διὰ τῆς ἀληθοῦς ἱστορίας παρειληφότας. "(1) Nor is there any occasion (2) to be surprised at this statement (3) or to distrust it, since we have learned through trustworthy history of many things more astonishing than this which have taken place throughout all the inhabited world."

18. *Bibl. Hist.* 3.37.9.1–4: διόπερ τηλικούτου μεγέθους ὄφεως εἰς ὄψιν κοινὴν κατηντηκότος (1) οὐκ ἄξιον (2) ἀπιστεῖν τοῖς Αἰθίοψιν (3) οὐδὲ μῦθον ὑπολαμβάνειν τὸ θρυλούμενον ὑπ' αὐτῶν. "Consequently, in view of the fact that a snake of so great a size has been exposed to the public gaze, (1) it is not fair (2) to doubt the word of the Ethiopians (3) or to assume that the report which they circulated far and wide was a mere fiction."

Josephus (a.d. 37–100)

19. *Ap.* 2.6.1–3: (1) ἔστι μὲν οὖν οὐ ῥᾴδιον αὐτοῦ (2) διελθεῖν τὸν λόγον (3) οὐδὲ σαφῶς γνῶναι τί λέγειν βούλεται. "His argument (1) is difficult (2) to summarize and his meaning (3) to grasp."

20. *Ap.* 2.212.1–2: (1) οὐ γὰρ ἐᾷ τὴν γῆν αὐτῶν (2) πυρπολεῖν (3) οὐδὲ τέμνειν ἥμερα δένδρα, ἀλλὰ καὶ σκυλεύειν ἀπείρηκεν τοὺς ἐν τῇ μάχῃ πεσόντας καὶ τῶν αἰχμαλώτων προυνόησ. "(1) He does not allow us (2) to burn up their country (3) or to cut down their fruit trees, and forbids even the spoiling of fallen combatants."

21. *BJ* 5.199.3–5: κατὰ γὰρ τὰς ἄλλας (1) οὐκ ἐξῆν (2) παρελθεῖν γυναιξίν, ἀλλ' (3) οὐδὲ κατὰ τὴν σφετέραν ὑπερβῆναι τὸ διατείχισμα. "For women (1) were not permitted (2) to enter by the others (3) nor yet to pass by way of their own gate beyond the partition wall."

22. *Ant.* 2.116.3–5: ὡς (1) οὐ προσῆκε μὲν αὐτὸν περὶ τἀδελφοῦ (2) δεδιέναι (3) οὐδὲ τὰ μὴ δεινὰ δι' ὑποψίας λαμβάνειν . . . "[Judas, ever of a hardy nature, frankly told him] that (1) he ought not (2) to be alarmed for their brother (3) nor harbour suspicions of dangers that did not exist."

23. *Ant.* 6.20.3–5: (1) οὐκ (2) ἐπιθυμεῖν ἐλευθερίας (1) δεῖ μόνον, ἀλλὰ καὶ ποιεῖν δι' ὧν ἂν ἔλθοι πρὸς ὑμᾶς, (3) οὐδὲ βούλεσθαι μὲν ἀπηλλάχθαι δεσποτῶν ἐπιμένειν δὲ πράττοντας ἐξ ὧν οὗτοι διαμενοῦσιν. ". . . (1) ye ought not to be content (2) to yearn for liberty, but should do also the deeds whereby ye may attain it, (3) nor merely long to be rid of your masters, while continuing so to act that they shall remain so."

24. *Ant.* 6.344.5–6: . . . (1) οὐκ ἔγνω (2) φυγεῖν αὐτὸν (3) οὐδὲ φιλοψυχήσας προδοῦναι μὲν τοὺς οἰκείους τοῖς πολεμίοις καθυβρίσαι δὲ τὸ τῆς βασιλείας ἀξίωμα, ἀλλά . . . "[For he, although he knew of what was to come and his impending death, which the prophet had foretold,] yet (1) determined not (2) to flee from it (3) or, by clinging to life, to betray his people to the enemy and dishonour the dignity of kingship; instead. . ."

25. *Ant.* 7.127.1–3: Τοῦτο τὸ πταῖσμα τοὺς Ἀμμανίτας (1) οὐκ ἔπεισεν (2) ἠρεμεῖν (3) οὐδὲ μαθόντας τοὺς κρείττονας ἡσυχίαν ἄγειν, (4) ἀλλὰ πέμψαντες πρὸς Χαλαμάν . . . "This defeat (1) did not persuade the Ammanites (2) to remain quiet (3) or to keep the peace in the knowledge that their enemy was superior. (4) Instead they sent to Chalamas."

26. *Ant.* 14.346.1–3: ὁ δὲ Ὑρκανὸν (2) ἀπολιπεῖν (1) οὐκ ἠξίου (3) οὐδὲ παρακινδυνεύειν τἀδελφῷ. "Phasael, however, (1) did not think it right (2) to desert Hyrcanus (3) or to endanger his brother."

27. *Ant.* 15.165.3–4: ὁ μὲν γὰρ Ὑρκανὸς ἐπιεικείᾳ τρόπου καὶ τότε καὶ τὸν ἄλλον χρόνον (1) οὐκ ἠξίου (2) πολυπραγμονεῖν (3) οὐδὲ νεωτέρων ἅπτεσθαι. "Now Hyrcanus because of his mild character (1) did not choose either then or at any other time (2) to take part in public affairs (3) or start a revolution."[14]

Philo (ca. 25 B.C.–A.D. 40)

28. *Posterity and Exile of Cain* 84.5–7: (1) οὐ γὰρ (2) ἀναπτῆναι, θησίν, εἰς οὐρανὸν (3) οὐδὲ πέραν θαλάσσης ἀφικέσθαι (1) δεῖ κατὰ ζήτησιν τοῦ καλοῦ. "'For (1) it is not necessary,' he says, (2) 'to fly up into heaven, (3) nor to get beyond the sea in searching for what is good.'"

Plutarch (A.D. 40–120)

29. *Rom.* 9.2.4–5: ὅτι γὰρ (1) οὐκ ἠξίουν οἱ τὴν Ἄλβην οἰκοῦντες (2) ἀναμιγνύναι τοὺς ἀποστάτας ἑαυτοῖς (3) οὐδὲ προσδέχεσθαι πολίτας . . . "For that the residents of Alba (1) would not consent (2) to give the fugitives the privilege of intermarriage with them, (3) nor even receive them as fellow citizens [is clear]."

30. *Cor.* 27.4.1: τὰ γὰρ ἄλλα πάντα λυμαινόμενος καὶ διαφθείρων, τοὺς ἐκείνων ἀγροὺς ἰσχυρῶς ἐφύλαττε, καὶ (1) οὐκ εἴα (2) κακουργεῖν (3) οὐδὲ λαμβάνειν ἐξ ἐκείνων οὐδέν. "For while he maltreated and destroyed everything else, he kept a vigorous watch over the lands of the patricians, and (1) would not suffer anyone (2) to hurt them (3) or take anything from them."

---

14. Note that "to take part in public affairs" is not as neutral as this translation might suggest. Cf. Liddell and Scott, 1442: πολυπραγματέω: "mostly in bad sense, to be a meddlesome, inquisitive busybody; esp. meddle in state affairs, intrigue."

31. *Tim.* 37.2.1: ὧν Λαφυστίου μὲν αὐτὸν πρός τινα δίκην κατεγγυῶντος (1) οὐκ εἴα (2) θορυβεῖν (3) οὐδὲ κωλύειν τοὺς πολίτας. "Of these, Laphystius once tried to make him give surety that he would appear at a certain trial, and Timoleon (1) would not suffer the citizens (2) to stop the man (3) by their turbulent disapproval [lit.: nor to prevent him]."

32. *Comp. Arist. et Cat.* 4.2.1: (1) οὐ γὰρ ἔστι (2) πράττειν μεγάλα φροντίζοντα μικρῶν, (3) οὐδὲ πολλοῖς δεομένοις βοηθεῖν πολλῶν αὐτὸν δεόμενον. "(1) It is impossible for a man (2) to do great things when his thoughts are busy with little things; (3) nor can he aid the many who are in need when he himself is in need of many things."

33. *Pyrrh.* 33.6.4: σπασάμενον γὰρ τὸ ξίφος ἢ κλίναντα λόγχην (1) οὐκ ἦν (2) ἀναλαβεῖν (3) οὐδὲ καταθέσθαι πάλιν, ἀλλ᾽ ἐχώρει δι᾽ ὧν ἔτυχε τὰ τοιαῦτα πάντα, καὶ περιπίπτοντες ἀλλήλοις ἔθνησκον. "For when a man had drawn his sword or poised his spear, (1) he could not (2) recover (3) or sheathe his weapon again, but it would pass through those who stood in its way, and so they died from one another's blows."

34. *Ages.* 32.3.3–4: ἐπεὶ δὲ φιλοτιμούμενος ὁ Ἐπαμεινώνδας ἐν τῇ πόλει μάχην συνάψαι καὶ στῆσαι τρόπαιον (1) οὐκ ἴσχυσεν (2) ἐξαγαγεῖν (3) οὐδὲ προκαλέσασθαι τὸν Ἀγησίλαον, ἐκεῖνος μὲν ἀναζεύξας πάλιν ἐπόρθει τὴν χώραν. "Epaminondas was ambitious to join battle in the city and set up a trophy of victory there, but since (1) he could (2) neither force (3) nor tempt Agesilaus out of his positions, he withdrew and began to ravage the country."

35. *Quom. Adul.* 64.E.7–8: Ὁρᾷς τὸν πίθηκον; (1) οὐ δύναται τὴν οἰκίαν (2) φυλάττειν ὡς ὁ κύων, (3) οὐδὲ βαστάζειν ὡς ὁ ἵππος, οὐδ᾽ ἀροῦν τὴν γῆν ὡς οἱ βόες. "You must have noticed the ape. (1) He cannot (2) guard the house like the dog, (3) nor carry a load like the horse, nor plow the land like oxen."

36. *Cons. ad Apoll.* 115.E.3.: ἀνθρώποις δὲ πάμπαν (1) οὐκ ἔστι (2) γενέσθαι τὸ πάντων ἄριστον (3) οὐδὲ μετασχεῖν τῆς τοῦ βελτίστου φύσεως (ἄριστον γὰρ πᾶσι καὶ πάσαις τὸ μὴ γενέσθαι). "But for men (1) it is utterly impossible (2) that they should obtain the best thing of all, (3) or even have any share in its nature (for the best thing for all men and women is not to be born)."

37. *Reg. et Imp. Apopht.* 185.A.2: πρὸς δὲ τοὺς θαυμάζοντας τὴν μεταβολὴν ἔλεγεν ὡς (1) "οὐκ ἐᾷ με (2) καθεύδειν (3) οὐδὲ ῥαθυμεῖν τὸ Μιλτιάδου πρόπαιον." "[Themistocles while yet in his youth abandoned himself to wine and women. But after Miltiades, commanding the Athenian army, had overcome the barbarians at Marathon, never again was it possible to encounter Themistocles misconducting himself.] To those who expressed their amazement at the change in him, he said that 'the trophy of Miltiades (1) does not allow me (2) to sleep (3) or to be indolent.'"

38. *Act. Rom. et Graec.* 269.D.8–9: (1) οὐ δεῖ δὲ τῶν ἡμερῶν τὸν ἀκριβέσ-
τατον ἀριθμὸν (2) διώκειν (3) οὐδὲ τὸ παρ᾽ ὀλίγον ουκοφαντεῖν . . .
"But (1) we must not (2) follow out the most exact calculation of
the number of days (3) nor cast aspersions on approximate reckon-
ing [since even now, when astronomy has made so much progress,
the irregularity of the moon's movements is still beyond the skill of
mathematicians, and continues to elude their calculations]."

39. *Act. Rom. et Graec.* 273.E.9–10: Διὰ τί τοῖς μὴ στρατευομένοις μὲν
ἐν στρατοπέδῳ δ᾽ ἄλλως ἀναστρεφομένοις (1) οὐκ ἐξῆν ἄνδρα (2)
βαλεῖν πολέμιον (3) οὐδὲ τρῶσαι; "Why were men who were not
regularly enlisted, but merely tarrying in the camp, (1) not allowed
(2) to throw missiles at the enemy (3) or to wound them?"

40. *Act. Rom. et Graec.* 291.B.3–4: Διὰ τί τοῖς ἱερεῦσι τούτοις ἀρχὴν (1)
οὐκ ἐφεῖτο (2) λαβεῖν (3) οὐδὲ μετελθεῖν; "Why were these priests
(1) not allowed (2) to hold office (3) nor to solicit it?"

41. *De E Apud Delph.* 385.A.9: . . . (1) οὐκ ἦν εὐπρεπὲς (2) παράγειν (3)
οὐδὲ παραιτεῖσθαι. "[On many other occasions when the subject
had been brought up in the school I had quietly turned aside from
it and passed it over, but recently I was unexpectedly discovered
by my sons in an animated discussion with some strangers,
whom, since they purposed to leave Delphi immediately,] (1) it
was not seemly (2) to try to divert from the subject, nor was it
seemly for me (3) to ask to be excused from the discussion [for
they were altogether eager to hear something about it]."

42. *De Def. Orac.* 426.B.1: (1) οὐ γὰρ ὡς σμήνους ἡγεμόνας δεῖ (2) ποιεῖν
ἀνεξόδους (3) οὐδὲ φρουρεῖν συγκλείσαντας τῇ ὕλῃ μᾶλλον δὲ συμ-
φράξαντας. "[Yet such an organization is altogether appropriate
for the gods.] For (1) we must not (2) make them unable to go out,
like the queens in a hive of bees, (3) nor keep them imprisoned by
enclosing them with matter, or rather fencing them about with it."

43. *De Tranqu. Anim.* 474.A.12: (1) οὐ δεῖ τοῖς ἑτέροις (2) ἐξαθυμεῖν (3)
οὐδ᾽ ἀπαγορεύειν. "(1) We should not (2) be disheartened (3) or de-
spondent in adversity [but like musicians who achieve harmony
by consistently deadening bad music with better and encompass-
ing the bad with the good, we should make the blending of our life
harmonious and conformable to our own nature]."

44. *De Tranqu. Anim.* 475.D.3: ὅθεν (1) οὐ δεῖ παντάπασιν (2) ἐκ-
ταπεινοῦν (3) οὐδὲ καταβάλλειν τὴν φύσιν . . . "Therefore (1) we
should not altogether (2) debase (3) and depreciate Nature [in the
belief that she has nothing strong, stable, and beyond the reach of
Fortune, but, on the contrary, . . . we should face the future un-
daunted and confident.]"

45. *Quaest. Conviv.* 706.D.5: ἐρῶντι μὲν γὰρ πολυτελοῦς (1) οὐκ ἔστι
τὴν Πηνελόπην (2) προσαγαγεῖν (3) οὐδὲ συνοικίσαι τὴν Πάνθειαν.

"If a man has a passion for a costly harlot, (1) we cannot (2) bring Penelope on stage, (3) nor marry Pantheia to him [but it is possible to take a man who is enjoying mimes and tunes and lyrics that are bad art and bad taste, and lead him back to Euripides and Pindar and Menander, "washing the brine from the ears with the clear fresh water of reason," in Plato's words]."

46. *Quaest. Conviv.* 711.E.3: ὥσθ᾽ ὁ οἶνος ἡμᾶς (2) ἀδικεῖν (1) οὐκ ἔοικεν (3) οὐδὲ κρατεῖν. "The wine (1) seems not (2) to be harming us (3) or getting the best of us."

47. *Aetia Phys.* 918.B.4: . . . ἡ δ᾽ ἄγαν περίψυξις πηγνύουσα τὰς ὀσμὰς (1) οὐκ ἐᾷ (2) ῥεῖν (3) οὐδὲ κινεῖν τὴν αἴσθησιν; "[Why is ground that has become dewy unfavorable for hunting so long as the cold lasts? . . . A spoor does this when there is warmth to free and release it gently] whereas excessive chill freezes the scents and (1) does not allow them (2) to flow (3) and affect [i.e., move] our perception."

48. *Brut. Rat.* 990.A.11: . . . καὶ (1) οὐκ ἐᾷ (2) θιγεῖν (3) οὐδὲ λυπῆσαι τὴν γεῦσιν ἀλλὰ διαβάλλει καὶ κατηγορεῖ τὴν φαυλότητα πρὶν ἢ βλαβῆναι. "[It (our sense of smell) admits what is proper, rejects what is alien] and (1) will not let it (2) touch (3) or give pain to the taste, but informs on and denounces what is bad before any harm is done."

Confirming the earlier study of the use of οὐδέ in the New Testament, these instances suggest that the construction "negated finite verb + infinitive + οὐδέ + infinitive" is used to link two infinitives denoting concepts or activities that are either both viewed positively or negatively by the writer. The same two patterns of the usage of οὐδέ are found: pattern #1, where two activities or concepts are viewed positively in and of themselves, but where their exercise is prohibited or their existence denied due to circumstances or conditions adduced in the context; and pattern #2, where two activities or concepts are viewed negatively and where consequently their exercise is prohibited or their existence denied or to be avoided. Table 4.2 documents these two patterns.

Table 4.2
Patterns of the Usage of οὐδέ in Ancient Greek Literature

Pattern #1: Two activities or concepts are viewed positively in and of themselves, but their exercise is prohibited or their existence denied due to circumstances or conditions adduced in the context.

1. LXX: 1 Macc. 15:14	ἐκπορεύεσθαι (leave)	εἰσπορεύεσθαι (enter)
2. LXX: Sir. 18:6	ἐλαττῶσαι (diminish)	προσθεῖναι (increase)
3. LXX: Isa. 42:24b	πορεύεσθαι (walk)	ἀκούειν (obey)

4. LXX: Ezek. 44:13 — ἱερατεύειν (serve as priest) — προσάγειν (come near)

5. LXX: DanTh 5:8 — ἀναγνῶναι (read) — γνωρίσαι (make known)

6. Inscr.: Attica — δέχεσθαι (receive gifts) — κλύειν (give ear to supplication)

10. Polyb., *Hist.* 6.15 — χειρίζειν (be organized) — συντελεῖν (be held at all)

12. Polyb., *Hist.* 30.24 — γινώσκεσθαι (know) — συνορᾶσθαι (see)

13. Polyb., *Hist.* 31.12 — βοηθεῖν (help) — συνεπισχύειν (support)

15. D. Hal., *Ant. R.* 10.12 — κοινωνεῖν (take part in) — παρεῖναι (be present at)

19. Jos., *Ap.* 2.6.1–3 — διελθεῖν (discern) — γνῶναι (know)

21. Jos., *B. J.* 5.199 — παρελθεῖν (enter) — ὑπερβῆναι (pass by)

23. Jos., *Ant.* 6.20 — ἐπιθυμεῖν (yearn for) — βούλεσθαι (want)*

25. Jos., *Ant.* 7.127 — ἠρεμεῖν (remain quiet) — ἡσυχίαν ἄγειν (keep quiet)

28. Philo, *Post.* 84.5 — ἀναπτῆναι (fly up) — ἀφικέσθαι (go beyond)*

29. Plut., *Rom.* 9.2 — ἀναμιγνύναι (intermarry) — προσδέχεσθαι (receive as citizen)

32. Plut., *Comp.* 4.2 — πράττειν (do great things) — βοηθεῖν (help)

33. Plut., *Pyrrh.* 33.6 — ἀναλαβεῖν (take again) — καταθέσθαι (sheathe again)

35. Plut., *Adul.* 64.E — φυλάττειν (guard) — βαστάζειν (carry)

36. Plut., *Apoll.* 115.E — γενέσθαι (obtain) — μετασχεῖν (have a share)

38. Plut., *Act.* 269.D — διώκειν (follow) — συκοφαντεῖν (approximate)

40. Plut., *Act.* 291.B — λαβεῖν (hold office) — μετελθεῖν (solicit office)

45. Plut., *Conv.* 706.D — προσαγαγεῖν (bring on stage) — συνοικίσαι (marry)

47. Plut., *Phys.* 918.B — ῥεῖν (flow) — κινεῖν (move)

Pattern #2: Two activities or concepts are viewed negatively and consequently their exercise is prohibited or their existence is denied or they are to be avoided.

7. Inscr.: PZenPestm.	εἰληφέναι (take away)	ἔχειν (hold in pretense)
8. Polyb., *Hist.* 2.56	ἐκπλήττειν (thrill)	ζητεῖν (seek to imagine)
9. Polyb., *Hist.* 5.10.5	πολεμεῖν (make war)	συναναιρεῖν (involve guiltless)
11. Polyb., *Hist.* 30.5	συνδυάζειν (run in harness)	προκαταλαμβάνειν (engage)
14. D. Hal., *Thuc.* 7.13	ἐγκαταμίσγειν (adulterate)	ἁρμόττεσθαι (confuse)
16. D. Hal., *De Comp.* 23	ὁρᾶσθαι (be viewed)	βεβηκέναι (stand)
17. Diod. Sic., *B.H.* 3.30	θαυμάζειν (be surprised)	ἀπιστεῖν (distrust)
18. Diod. Sic., *B.H.* 3.37	ἀπιστεῖν (doubt)	ὑπολαμβάνειν (view as fictional)
20. Jos., *Ap.* 2.212.1	πυρπολεῖν (burn)	τέμνειν (cut down)
22. Jos., *Ant.* 2.116	δεδίεναι (be alarmed)	λαμβάνειν (harbor suspicions)
24. Jos., *Ant.* 6.344	φυγεῖν (flee)	προδοῦναι (betray)
26. Jos., *Ant.* 14.346	ἀπολιπεῖν (desert)	παρακινδυνεύειν (endanger)*
27. Jos., *Ant.* 15.165	πολυπραγμονεῖν (intrigue)	ἅπτεσθαι (start a revolution)
30. Plut., *Cor.* 27.4	κακουργεῖν (hurt)	λαμβάνειν (take from)
31. Plut., *Tim.* 37.2	θορυβεῖν (stop)	κωλύειν (hinder)
34. Plut., *Ages.* 32.3	ἐξαγαγεῖν (force)	προκαλέσασθαι (tempt)
37. Plut., *Apoph.* 185.A	καθεύδειν (sleep)	ῥαθυμεῖν (be idle)
39. Plut., *Act.* 273.E	βαλεῖν (throw missiles)	τρῶσαι (wound)
41. Plut., *De E* 385.A	παράγειν (try to divert)	παραιτεῖσθαι (be excused)
42. Plut., *Orac.* 426.B	ποιεῖν ἀνεξόδους (make unable)	φρουρεῖν (keep imprisoned)
43. Plut., *Tran.* 474.A	ἐξαθυμεῖν (be disheartened)	ἀπαγορεύειν (be despondent)

44. Plut., *Tran.* 475.D	ἐκταπεινοῦν (debase)	καταβάλλειν (depreciate)
46. Plut., *Conv.* 711.E	ἀδικεῖν (harm)	κρατεῖν (get the best of)*
48. Plut., *Brut.* 990.A	θιγεῖν (touch)	λυπῆσαι (give pain to)

*=preceding infinitive.

Again, we may consider a few examples of each pattern. Pattern #1 can be illustrated by the following instances. Polybius writes (#10) that victory processions cannot be properly organized or sometimes be held at all unless the senate consents and provides the requisite funds. While "organize" and "hold" are both viewed positively in and of themselves by the writer, Polybius indicates that the holding of these processions is not possible unless certain conditions are met: the senate's consent and the requisition of appropriate funds. At another occasion (#13) Polybius writes that "the senate would not go so far as to help or support Lysias after his conduct." Again, the writer views the two activities (here synonyms), "helping" and "supporting," positively in and of themselves, but the help is denied because of Lysias's (unacceptable) conduct. Josephus writes (#23) that "you ought not to be content to yearn for liberty . . . nor merely long to be rid of your masters." While the writer views his readers' yearning for liberty and their longing to be rid of their masters positively in and of themselves, he indicates in the context why these longings by themselves are insufficient unless accompanied by action and change in behavior.

A few examples of pattern #2 show instances where two activities or concepts are both viewed negatively by the writer and where consequently their exercise is prohibited or their existence is denied or to be avoided. An inscription (#7) indicates that a judge ordered Antipater not "to take the boy from them or to hold him under any pretense." Clearly both activities, taking the boy away from them as well as holding him under any pretense, are viewed negatively by the judge, who consequently denies the exercise of these activities. Josephus writes (#27) that "Hyrcanus because of his mild character did not choose . . . to meddle in state affairs or start a revolution." "Meddling in state affairs" and "starting a revolution" are both viewed negatively by the writer, who asserts that it was Hyrcanus's "mild character" that kept him from engaging in these undesirable activities. In a writing by Plutarch (#46, note the preceding infinitive), the existence of two negative effects of wine is denied: "The wine seems not to be harming us or getting the best of us."

Conclusion

In analogy to the observations made in the study of New Testament syntactical parallels to 1 Timothy 2:12 above, the following conclusions may be drawn.[15] The implication of the identified patterns of the usage of οὐδέ for 1 Timothy 2:12 is that the activities denoted by the two infinitives διδάσκειν and αὐθεντεῖν will either both be viewed positively or negatively by the writer. That is, the passage should either be rendered, "I do not permit a woman to teach [error] or to usurp a man's authority," or "I do not permit a woman to teach or to have (or exercise) authority over a man."

The meaning of διδάσκειν in 1 Timothy 2:12 is therefore an important preliminary issue in determining the meaning of αὐθεντεῖν. As was argued above, διδάσκειν, when used absolutely, always in the New Testament denotes an activity that is viewed positively by the writer, to be rendered "to teach" (cf. esp. 1 Tim. 4:11; 6:2; 2 Tim. 2:2). If the writer had intended to give the term a negative connotation in 1 Timothy 2:12, he would in all likelihood have used the term ἑτεροδιδασκαλεῖν (as in 1 Tim. 1:3; 6:3) or some other contextual qualifier specifying the (inappropriate or heretical) content of the teaching (as in Titus 1:11).

Since then the first part of 1 Timothy 2:12 reads "But I do not permit a woman to teach" and the coordinating conjunction οὐδέ requires the second activity to be viewed correspondingly by the writer, αὐθεντεῖν should be regarded as viewed positively as well and be rendered "to have (or exercise) authority," and not "to flout the authority of" or "to domineer."

---

15. The primary thesis that this chapter seeks to establish is that the two concepts connected by οὐδέ are both viewed either positively or negatively. The following subcategories of this basic pattern may be identified: (1) synonymous concepts: Matt. 7:18; Mark 8:17; John 14:27; Acts 2:27; 1 Cor. 15:50; Gal. 4:14; Phil. 2:16; 2 Thess. 2:2; 1 Tim. 6:16; Heb. 10:8; 12:5; 13:5; 1 Pet. 3:14; (2) conceptual parallels: Matt. 6:28 = Luke 12:27; Matt. 7:6; 10:14 = Mark 6:11; Matt. 12:19; Luke 3:14; 6:44; 18:4; John 14:17; Acts 4:18; 17:24–25; Rom. 9:16; 2 Cor. 4:2; Col. 2:21; 2 Thess. 3:7–8; 1 Pet. 2:22; 1 John 3:6; Rev. 12:8; (3) complementary concepts: Acts 9:9; Rom. 14:21; 2 Cor. 7:12; Rev. 7:16; (4) sequential concepts: Matt. 6:20, 26 = Luke 12:24; Matt. 13:13; Mark 13:15; Luke 12:33; 17:23; John 4:15; Rom. 9:11; (5) ascensive concepts: Matt. 22:46; Acts 16:21; (6) specific to general or general to specific: (a) specific to general: Acts 21:21; 1 Tim. 2:12; (b) general to specific: Gal. 1:16–17; 1 Tim. 1:3–4; 6:17. Note that there may be some overlap among these categories so that they should not be understood to be totally mutually exclusive but rather as indicating the most likely emphasis on the relationship between the two concepts linked by οὐδέ.

5

An Interpretation of 1 Timothy 2:9–15: A Dialogue with Scholarship

Thomas R. Schreiner

The role of women in the church is probably the most emotionally charged issue in American evangelicalism today. I have been in public forums where the question has been debated, and the tension in the room is palpable. It is particularly difficult when I lecture on the issue at a seminary, for there are always women in the class who feel called to serve as pastors. To have a professor question the legitimacy of this call in a public setting is, to say the least, emotionally agonizing for women who feel called to pastor.[1] It also smacks of a public attack on a minority group since in my classes men usually outnumber women. Most of these women students have already been subjected somewhere in their journey to insensitive and cruel comments by men. Thus, the public examination of the issue by a professor who holds to the historic view can be almost unbearable.[2] Those of us who support the historic view on this question must bend over backwards to love those with whom we disagree, and to assure them that we still hope and pray that God will bless their ministries, even though we believe that it is a mistake for women to take on a pastoral role.

1. I would make a distinction between a call to the ministry and a call to be a pastor/overseer/elder. Women attend seminary because they are called to the former, but some misinterpret their call in terms of being called to the latter.

2. I have attempted to use positive terms for both positions. The position that sees no ministry limitations for women will be called the progressive view, while the view that argues that women should not serve as pastors/elders/overseers will be called the historic view. People on both sides of the debate may object to these terms. They are not intended to settle the debate in any way. They are used because labels such as conservative/traditional or liberal/radical often obscure the real issues.

In fact, I desired to believe that there are no limitations for women in ministry and that every ministry position is open to them.[3] When studying at Fuller Seminary, I read many articles on the whole question, hoping that I could be exegetically convinced that all ministry offices should be opened to women. Upon reading the articles, though, I remained intellectually and exegetically unconvinced of the plausibility of the "new" interpretations of the controversial passages. Indeed, reading the progressive interpretations persuaded me that the historic view was true, since the former involved strained interpretations of the "problem" passages. I remember saying to a friend of mine, who is a New Testament scholar, "I would like to believe the position you hold. But it seems as if you have to leap over the evidence of the text to espouse such a position." He replied, "Tom, you are right. Take that leap. Take that leap." Leaping over the evidence is precisely what I am unwilling to do.

Thus, I remain intellectually and exegetically unconvinced that the progressive position is tenable. There are many social pressures today, especially in academic circles, to retreat from the historic view. Some evangelical institutions will not even consider hiring a scholar who holds the historic view, even though they allow diverse positions on baptism, eschatology, church government, or how the inspiration of Scripture should be defined. This policy is usually unwritten, but those who are familiar with the schools in question know that they exclude a priori scholars who believe in or espouse the historic view. Evidently, they feel the text is so clear and that the historic position is so unjust that it must not even be represented on the faculty, despite the fact that it has been the majority position throughout church history.

Many who are unfamiliar with the biblical text, or have not engaged in much exegesis of the relevant passages (and this includes many pastors, unfortunately!) surrender the historic view rather easily.[4] To many the historic position seems unloving and discriminatory, and the general atmosphere of our society encourages people to liberate themselves from traditional views. American culture often lauds those who discard conventional positions and brands those who advocate "new" positions as courageous, creative, and thoughtful. On the other hand, those who hold the historic view are considered to be temperamentally

---

3. Some defenders of the historic view have said that my emotions and desires should conform to God's will on the role of women, and thus I should not wish that the situation were different from God's intention. This is probably correct. But I am telling my story here, which includes desires that have not always been in accord with God's will.

4. I am *not* saying that all those who hold a different position than I are unfamiliar with the biblical text. Obviously, many fine scholars disagree with the historic position on exegetical grounds. My point is that many who have a shallow understanding of the biblical text are departing from the historic view for reasons other than exegetical ones.

contentious, narrow, and perhaps even psychologically hampered. These latter qualities are doubtless true of some (but not all!) who support the historic view, and yet it does not follow that the historic view is thereby falsified. The truth or falsity of both views must be established by an intensive exegesis of the biblical text.

Even though more and more people are temperamentally inclined to assume that the progressive position is correct, it will be argued in this essay that the recent interpretations of 1 Timothy 2:9–15 in defense of the progressive position are exegetically unpersuasive. The burden of my essay will be to interact with this recent research and to set forth reasons for questioning its validity.[5] Those scholars who embrace the feminist position, such as Paul Jewett, but argue that Paul was wrong or inconsistent in 1 Timothy 2, are exegetically more straightforward and intellectually more convincing than those who contend that Paul did not actually intend to restrict women teaching men in 1 Timothy 2.[6]

The Life Setting for the Text

One of the central planks for the progressive view is the occasional nature of 1 Timothy. Too often, it is argued, scholars have seen 1 Timothy as a manual of church structure, so that the directives given are under-

5. In this essay I interact mainly with "biblical" progressives instead of "radical" feminists, for the latter tend to agree with my exegesis of 1 Tim. 2:11–15 but critique it as patriarchal. For the most notable contribution from the radical feminist position see Elizabeth Schüssler Fiorenza, *In Memory of Her: A Feminist Theological Reconstruction of Christian Origins* (New York: Crossroad, 1985). I am grateful to Philip H. Towner for allowing me to see his helpful unpublished essay ("Feminist Approaches to the New Testament: 1 Timothy 2:8–15 as a Test Case") in which he has briefly surveyed and analyzed the contributions of radical and biblical feminists to the interpretation of 1 Tim. 2:8–15.

6. Paul K. Jewett, *Man as Male and Female* (Grand Rapids: Eerdmans, 1975), 112–13, 119. Surprisingly, Clarence Boomsma (*Male and Female, One in Christ: New Testament Teaching on Women in Office* [Grand Rapids: Baker, 1993], 53–82) argues that even though Paul's exegesis of the Genesis text in 1 Timothy 2 is flawed in that it does not represent the intended meaning of the text of Genesis, it was appropriate for the particular situation addressed in 1 Timothy. Thus, he claims (p. 58) that even though Paul's "argument from Genesis 2 is without support in the text," one should not conclude that Paul was in error or uninspired. He "rightly" misinterpreted (!) the text of Genesis in order to correct an abuse by the women addressed in 1 Timothy 2. Boomsma concludes, therefore, that 1 Tim. 2:11–15 rightly interpreted does not prohibit women from serving in church office today. It is hard to imagine how Paul's argumentation in 1 Timothy 2 has any integrity if Boomsma is correct. Boomsma's exegesis is a creative (but hardly convincing!) attempt to circumvent the meaning of the text. His exegesis is illustrative of the lengths to which scholars will go to sustain their presuppositions. Albert Wolters (*Calvin Theological Journal* 29 [1994]: 278–85) in a brilliant and kind review dismantles Boomsma's thesis, showing that it squares neither with the text of 1 Tim. 2:11–15 nor with logic.

stood to be permanently binding on all churches.[7] What has not been sufficiently appreciated is that the Pastoral Epistles are addressed to specific situations; particularly they are aimed against false teaching that was imperiling the churches.[8] Thus, the letters should not be understood as timeless marching orders for the church but must be interpreted in light of the specific circumstances that occasioned them.

The emphasis on the specific situation and occasion of the letters is salutary. The Pastoral Epistles are not doctrinal treatises that float free from the circumstances that called them forth. In the case of 1 Timothy it is clear that the letter is written to counteract false teaching (1:3–11, 18–20; 4:1–10; 5:11–15; 6:3–10, 20–21). Indeed, the transition between 1 Timothy 1:18–20 and 2:1 indicated by "therefore" (οὖν) shows that the following instructions relate to the charge to resist false teaching (cf. 1 Tim. 1:3, 18).[9] The entire letter is designed to correct the abuses introduced by the heretics into the community.

Having said this, we must be careful not to conclude from the occasional nature of the letter that 1 Timothy has no application to the church today. It would be a grave mistake to argue as follows:

1. First Timothy was written to counteract a specific situation in the life of the church.
2. Nothing written to a specific situation is normative for the church today.
3. Therefore, 1 Timothy contains no directives for the church today.

If we were to claim that documents written to specific situations are not applicable to the church today, then the rest of the New Testament would not be applicable to us either, since it is probable that all New Testament books were addressed to particular communities facing special circumstances. Universal principles are tucked into books written to respond to specific circumstances.

Of course, careful scholars who favor the progressive view do not argue that the directives in 1 Timothy are inapplicable merely because

7. See, e.g., Stephen B. Clark, *Man and Woman in Christ* (Ann Arbor: Servant, 1980), 192.

8. This view is commonplace now. See especially Gordon D. Fee, *1 and 2 Timothy, Titus* (NIBC; Peabody, Mass.: Hendrickson, 1988), 1–31; idem, *Gospel and Spirit* (Peabody, Mass.: Hendrickson, 1991), 54–55; Philip H. Towner, *The Goal of Our Instruction* (JSNTSup 34; Sheffield: JSOT Press, 1989), 21–45; Sharon Hodgin Gritz, *Paul, Women Teachers, and the Mother Goddess at Ephesus* (Lanham: University Press of America, 1991), 31–49, 105–16; Richard Clark Kroeger and Catherine Clark Kroeger, *I Suffer Not a Woman: Rethinking 1 Timothy 2:11–15 in Light of Ancient Evidence* (Grand Rapids: Baker, 1992), *passim*; Ben Witherington III, *Women in the Earliest Churches* (SNTSMS 58; Cambridge: Cambridge University Press, 1988), 118.

9. So Fee, *1 Timothy*, 60–61.

of the life situation that called them forth. They rightly insist that the specific life setting of the letter must inform our interpretation and application of specific passages. Thus, we must probe to see whether Paul's admonitions to women in 1 Timothy 2:9–15 are temporary directives due to the impact of the false teachers. Can we show that Paul prohibited women from teaching men solely on the grounds of the false teaching afflicting the Ephesian church? The progressive view is not established merely by saying that the proscription on women teaching men emerged because of the impact that the false teachers had on women. There is little doubt that the heretics had an influence on the women in the community (cf. 1 Tim. 5:11–15; 2 Tim. 3:6–7), and it is likely that the issues of women's adornment and teaching arose as a consequence of the adversaries' leverage.[10] Nonetheless, Paul may have responded to these specific problems with a general principle that is universally applicable. Whether he does in fact appeal to a universal principle and what that principle is must be established by an interpretation of the verses in question.

Naturally, if one could show that the prohibition against women teaching men were explicable solely on the grounds of the false teaching and its specific features, then the progressive position would be greatly strengthened. For instance, Richard and Catherine Kroeger set forth the features of the heresy in amazing detail, seeing it as an amalgamation of Jewish-gnostic traditions and Ephesian devotion to Artemis.[11] They argue that the false teachers proclaimed the priority of Eve over Adam and that Eve enlightened Adam with her teaching. Paul's words on Adam being created first and Eve's deception were intended to counterbalance the adversaries' exaltation of Eve. If this reconstruction is accurate, then the thesis that Paul's instruction contains temporary restraints on women is enhanced.[12] Unfortunately, the Kroegers' reconstruction is riddled with methodological errors. They nod in the direction of saying that the heresy is "proto-gnostic," but consistently appeal to later sources to establish the contours of the heresy.[13] The

10. Contra Susan T. Foh, *Women and the Word of God* (Grand Rapids: Baker, 1979), 122–23.

11. Kroegers, *I Suffer Not a Woman*, esp. 42–43, 50–52, 59–66, 70–74, 105–13. Cf. also Mark D. Roberts, "Woman Shall Be Saved: A Closer Look at 1 Timothy 2:15," *TSF Bulletin* 5 (1981): 5; Ronald W. Pierce, "Evangelicals and Gender Roles in the 1990s: 1 Tim 2:8–15: A Test Case," *Journal of the Evangelical Theological Society* 36 (1993): 347–48, 353.

12. For a thorough analysis and refutation of the view that Ephesus was influenced by an early form of feminism, see S. M. Baugh's essay in this volume.

13. Bruce Barron ("Putting Women in Their Place: 1 Timothy 2 and Evangelical Views of Women in Church Leadership," *Journal of the Evangelical Theological Society* 33 [1990]: 451–59) makes the same mistake of reconstructing the heresy on the basis of second-century gnosticism. To read into the text (p. 454) that Eve was the heroine for the false teachers can only be substantiated by appealing to second-century writings. That

lack of historical rigor, if I can say this kindly, is nothing less than astonishing.[14] They have clearly not grasped how one should apply the
historical method in discerning the nature of false teaching in the
Pauline letters.[15]

The work of Sharon Gritz is much more restrained and sober than
that of the Kroegers, though there are similarities in terms of her conclusions.[16] She posits that the restriction on women teaching men was
due to the infiltration of the cult of the mother goddess, Artemis, in
Ephesus.[17] Even if her case were established, this would hardly prove
that the restriction on women was limited to the particular situation,
for Paul could be giving a universal principle that was precipitated by
special circumstances. The central weakness of Gritz's work, however,
is that she nowhere provides any kind of in-depth argument for the influence of the Artemis cult in 1 Timothy. She records the presence of
such a cult in Ephesus and then simply assumes that it functions as the
background to the letter. To say that sexual impurity (1 Tim. 5:11–14)
and greed (1 Tim. 6:3–5) are signs of the Artemis cult is scarcely persuasive![18] Many religious and nonreligious movements are plagued with
these problems. Gritz needs to show that the devotion to myths and genealogies (1 Tim. 1:3–4), the Jewish law (1 Tim. 1:6–11), asceticism
(1 Tim. 4:3–4), and knowledge (1 Tim. 6:20–21) indicate that the problem was specifically with the Artemis cult.

Many scholars who reconstruct the situation behind the Pastorals
should pay greater heed to the fragmentary nature of the evidence.[19]
Robert Karris observes that "it seems extremely difficult to infer from

---

this was a plank of the adversaries' teaching is scarcely clear from 1 Timothy itself. Even
if one sees the opponents as gnostic in some sense, Werner G. Kümmel (*Introduction to
the New Testament,* 17th ed. [Nashville: Abingdon, 1975], 379) rightly remarks, "there is
then not the slightest occasion, just because the false teachers who are being opposed are
Gnostics, to link them up with the great Gnostic systems of the second century."

14. For three devastating reviews of the Kroegers' work, see Robert W. Yarbrough, "I
Suffer Not a Woman: A Review Essay," *Presbyterion* 18 (1992): 25–33; Albert Wolters, "Re-
view: *I Suffer Not a Woman,*" *Calvin Theological Journal* 28 (1993): 208–13; S. M. Baugh,
"The Apostle among the Amazons," *Westminster Theological Journal* 56 (1994): 153–71.

15. See, e.g., John M. G. Barclay, "Mirror-Reading a Polemical Letter: Galatians as a
Test Case," *Journal for the Study of the New Testament* 31 (1987): 73–93.

16. Gritz, *Mother Goddess,* 11–49, 105–16; cf. also Philip B. Payne, "Libertarian
Women in Ephesus: A Response to Douglas J. Moo's Article, '1 Timothy 2:11–15: Meaning
and Significance,'" *Trinity Journal* 2 (1981): 182.

17. Baugh in his essay in this volume indicates that the evidence is lacking that Artemis was identified as a mother goddess. If she was identified as such, this occurred about
a millennium before the New Testament was written and was forgotten by Paul's day.

18. Gritz, *Mother Goddess,* 114–16.

19. So Douglas J. Moo, "What Does It Mean Not to Teach or Have Authority over
Men? 1 Timothy 2:11–15," in *Recovering Biblical Manhood and Womanhood,* ed. J. Piper
and W. Grudem (Wheaton: Crossway, 1991), 180–81.

the polemic the nature of the opponents' teaching."[20] He concludes that "The author of the Pastorals is quite tight-lipped about the teachings of his opponents."[21] Perhaps Karris is too pessimistic about our ability to delineate the heresy, but some scholars are far too confident about their ability to reconstruct the life setting in some detail.

A more promising and cautious approach has been proposed by Philip Towner.[22] He suggests that the problem in the Pastoral Epistles was a form of overrealized eschatology, which is analogous in many respects to a similar phenomenon in 1 Corinthians.[23] The belief that the resurrection had already occurred (2 Tim. 2:18; cf. 1 Tim. 1:20) was not a denial of resurrection altogether, but signals that the opponents believed in a spiritual resurrection with Christ.[24] Such overrealized eschatology could also explain their food prohibitions and dim view of marriage (1 Tim. 4:1–3). Perhaps it could also account for the emancipation of women from previous norms (1 Tim. 2:9–15; cf. 1 Cor. 11:2–16; 14:33b–36). Towner's reconstruction is only a possibility. While it certainly does not answer all our questions, it has the virtue of being a reconstruction that does not depend on second-century evidence.[25] In addition, the nature of the false teaching is gleaned from the evidence of the Pastoral Epistles themselves. By contrast, those who see the Artemis cult as prominent appeal to a movement that is not mentioned or even clearly implied in the Pastoral Epistles.

Whatever the specific features of the heresy, firm evidence is lacking that the priority or superiority of Eve played any part in the false teaching. Nor is it clear that 1 Timothy 5:13 demonstrates that women were *teaching* the heresy.[26] Paul does not say that "they were *teaching* things that were not fitting," but that "they were *speaking* things that were not fitting."[27] It is scarcely clear in this context (although it cannot be dismissed as a possibility) that Paul is responding to false teaching as he

20. Robert J. Karris, "The Background and Significance of the Polemic of the Pastoral Epistles," *Journal of Biblical Literature* 92 (1973): 550.

21. Ibid., 562. Incidentally, I do not find Karris's own suggestion, that the author used the typical polemic of the philosophers against the sophists, persuasive.

22. Towner, *Goal of Our Instruction*, 21–45.

23. See Anthony C. Thiselton, "Realized Eschatology at Corinth," *New Testament Studies* 24 (1978): 510–26.

24. For a similar suggestion, see William L. Lane, "1 Tim. iv. 1–3: An Early Instance of Over-Realized Eschatology?" *New Testament Studies* 11 (1965): 164–67.

25. Depending on later evidence also mars J. Massingberd Ford's suggestion that the heresy was an early form of Montanism; see "A Note on Proto-Montanism in the Pastoral Epistles," *New Testament Studies* 17 (1970–71): 338–46.

26. Contra Fee, *Gospel and Spirit*, 55; Witherington, *Women*, 118. Nor does the description of the heresy as "profane and old-womanish myths" (1 Tim. 4:7) imply that the false teachers were women; contra Roberts, "1 Timothy 2:15," 5.

27. The Greek word used is λαλέω, not διδάσκω.

does in other texts (e.g., 1 Tim. 1:3–11; 4:1–5; 6:3–10). The false teachers specifically named in the Pastorals are all men (1 Tim. 1:20; 2 Tim. 2:17–18; cf. 2 Tim. 4:14), and women are portrayed as being influenced by the heresy (1 Tim. 5:11–15; 2 Tim. 3:5–9) rather than as being its purveyors.[28] Towner is probably correct in concluding that an emancipation movement among women was a side-effect rather than a specific goal of the teaching of the agitators.[29] Perhaps women began to engage in teaching because they had fallen prey to an overrealized eschatology.[30] They may have believed that the resurrection had already occurred (2 Tim. 2:18) and thus the distinctions between men and women were erased since the new age had dawned. In any case, the suggestion that women were prohibited from teaching because they were mainly responsible for the false teaching cannot be substantiated from the text. Even if some women were spreading the heresy (which is uncertain but possible), an explanation is still needed as to why Paul proscribes only women from teaching. Since men are specifically named as purveyors of the heresy, would it not make more sense if Paul forbade all false teaching by both men and women? A prohibition against women alone seems to be reasonable only if *all* the women in Ephesus were duped by the false teaching. This latter state of affairs is quite unlikely, and the probable presence of Priscilla in Ephesus (2 Tim. 4:19) also stands against it.

A Word on the Near Context

The first chapter of 1 Timothy demonstrates that the letter is a response to false teaching. In 2:1–7 Paul emphasizes that God's desire is for all, including kings and other governing authorities, to be saved. Perhaps the adversaries used their myths and genealogies to argue that salvation was not possible for some people. Thus, Paul employs his apostolic authority (2:7) to pronounce upon God's universal purpose and intention in sending Christ as a ransom for all. Thereby believers are enjoined to pray for the salvation of all people.

A new section opens with verse 8, but the word "therefore" (οὖν) shows an intimate connection with verses 1–7. The link between the two sections is strengthened when we observe that Paul calls on the men to pray (v. 8), presumably for the salvation of all those referred to in verses 1–7.[31] Perhaps the anger and disputing that are forbidden in

---

28. Cf. Towner, *Goal of Our Instruction*, 26, 39–40.

29. Ibid., 39–40.

30. Cf. Philip H. Towner, *1–2 Timothy & Titus* (IVPNTCS; Downers Grove: InterVarsity, 1994), 75–76.

31. The contrast between ἄνδρας in v. 8 and γυναῖκες in v. 9 shows that the former refers to males, not females.

verse 8 were precipitated by the teaching of the agitators, which caused the church to veer away from its purpose of praying for the salvation of unbelievers.[32] The words "I want" (βούλομαι) do not merely express Paul's personal opinion and preference for prayer and the avoidance of anger. Indeed, they immediately follow verse 7, which is a powerful defense of Paul's apostolic authority. Thus, they express an authoritative command to pray.[33]

When Paul calls on men to pray "in every place" (ἐν παντὶ τόπῳ), this is probably a reference to house churches.[34] Thus, the directives here relate to a public church meeting when believers are gathered together.[35] Perhaps the words "in every place" refer to all churches everywhere, not just those in Ephesus (cf. Mal. 1:11; 1 Cor. 1:2).[36] In any case, a public worship context is still in view, whether the reference is to house churches in Ephesus or to all churches everywhere. These observations on the public nature of the praying in verse 8 are significant, for verses 9–15 are also directed to public assemblies. This is clear in verses 11–12, where women are prohibited from teaching or exercising authority over men. George Knight questions whether verses 9–10 are limited to public meetings since wearing appropriate clothing and good works are necessary at all times, not just in worship services.[37] Knight correctly observes that proper clothing and good works extend beyond worship services, but Paul's exhortations on suitable attire probably stem from indecorous adornment being worn at public meet-

32. Cf. Alan Padgett, "Wealthy Women at Ephesus: I Timothy 2:8–15 in Social Context," *Interpretation* 41 (1987): 22.

33. So Donald Guthrie, *The Pastoral Epistles* (TNTC; Grand Rapids: Eerdmans, 1957), 73–74; J. N. D. Kelly, *A Commentary on the Pastoral Epistles* (Grand Rapids: Baker, 1963), 65; Ceslaus Spîcq, *Saint Paul les épîtres pastorales*, 2 vols., 4th ed. (EBib; Paris: J. Gabalda, 1969), 371–72; Norbert Brox, *Die Pastoralbriefe*, 4th ed. (RNT; Regensburg: F. Pustet, 1969), 130; Martin Dibelius and Hans Conzelmann, *The Pastoral Epistles* (Hermeneia; Philadelphia: Fortress, 1972), 75; Jürgen Roloff, *Der erste Brief an Timotheus* (EKK; Zürich: Benziger, 1988), 130; George W. Knight III, *The Pastoral Epistles* (NIGTC; Grand Rapids: Eerdmans, 1992), 128; Gottlob Schrenk, *TDNT*, 1:632.

34. Fee, *1 and 2 Timothy*, 70; Knight, *Pastoral Epistles*, 128; Padgett, "Wealthy Women," 22; Douglas J. Moo, "I Timothy 2:11–15: Meaning and Significance," *Trinity Journal* 1 (1980): 62; Witherington, *Women*, 119.

35. C. K. Barrett, *The Pastoral Epistles* (The New Clarendon Bible; Oxford: Clarendon, 1963), 54; Robert D. Culver, "A Traditional View: Let Your Women Keep Silence," in *Women in Ministry: Four Views*, ed. B. Clouse and R. G. Clouse (Downers Grove: InterVarsity, 1989), 34.

36. Walter Lock, *A Critical and Exegetical Commentary on the Pastoral Epistles* (ICC; Edinburgh: T. & T. Clark, 1936), 30; Craig S. Keener, *Paul, Women and Wives: Marriage and Women's Ministry in the Letters of Paul* (Peabody: Hendrickson, 1992), 123, n. 19; Towner, *Goal of Our Instruction*, 205–6; Paul W. Barnett, "Wives and Women's Ministry (1 Timothy 2:11–15)," *Evangelical Quarterly* 61 (1989): 225, 236; Steve Moyter, "Expounding 1 Timothy 2:8–15," *Vox Evangelica* 24 (1994): 92.

37. Knight, *Pastoral Epistles*, 130–31.

ings. The call to do good works is probably occasioned by an improper focus on adornment in the gatherings of the community, even though the works extend beyond church meetings. If the above observations are correct, there is no need to see a shift away from public worship in verses 9–10.[38]

Women's Adornment in 1 Timothy 2:9–10

The text is ambiguous regarding the connection between verses 8 and 9. Is Paul saying, "Likewise I want the women to pray with respectable adornment," or "Likewise I want the women to adorn themselves with respectable adornment"? Some scholars favor the idea that the infinitive "to pray" (προσεύχεσθαι) follows the implied verb "I want."[39] In support of this is the "likewise" (ὡσαύτως) linking verses 8 and 9. Just as Paul wants the men to pray in a certain manner (i.e., "lifting up holy hands without wrath and disputing"), so too he wants the women to pray with respectable deportment. It is more likely, however, that the infinitive "to adorn" (κοσμεῖν) completes the implied verb "I want."[40] The word "likewise" is a loose transition and does not indicate that the exact same activities are in mind (cf. 1 Tim. 3:8, 11; 5:25; Titus 2:3, 6). The connection between verse 8 and verses 9–15, then, is as follows: In verse 8 Paul considers the problem men have when gathered for public worship (anger and disputing in prayer), while in verses 9–15 two issues that have cropped up with the women in public gatherings (adornment and teaching men) are addressed. One should not conclude from the call to men to pray and women to adorn themselves properly that only men should pray in worship or that they should take the spiritual leadership in worship.[41] First Corinthians 11:5 clarifies that women are allowed to participate by praying in public meetings.[42]

38. Cf. Gritz, *Mother Goddess*, 126; Keener, *Women's Ministry*, 103; Kelly, *Pastoral Epistles*, 66; Moo, "1 Timothy 2:11–15," 63; Roloff, *Timotheus*, 132.

39. Barrett, *Pastoral Epistles*, 55; Mary Evans, *Woman in the Bible* (Downers Grove: InterVarsity, 1983), 101; Gritz, *Mother Goddess*, 126; Gottfried Holtz, *Die Pastoralbriefe* (THKNT; Berlin: Evangelische Verlagsanstalt, 1972), 65–66; Keener, *Women's Ministry*, 102; David M. Scholer, "1 Timothy 2:9–15 and the Place of Women in the Church's Ministry," in *Women, Authority and the Bible*, ed. A. Mickelsen (Downers Grove: InterVarsity, 1986), 200–201; Barnett, "1 Timothy 2:11–15," 227–28; Witherington, *Women*, 263, n. 203.

40. So Foh, *Women and the Word of God*, 122; Knight, *Pastoral Epistles*, 132; Moo, "1 Timothy 2:11–15," 63; Roloff, *Timotheus*, 126; Towner, *Goal of Our Instruction*, 207; Brox, *Pastoralbriefe*, 132.

41. Contra Culver, "Traditional View," 35; and Clark, *Man and Woman*, 194, respectively.

42. Rightly Towner, *Goal of Our Instruction*, 207–8.

What is meant by the word γυναῖκας in verse 9 and throughout the rest of this passage? Does it refer to women in general, or more specifically to wives? If it refers to wives both here and in subsequent verses, then women are not forbidden from teaching publicly in church. They are merely prohibited from teaching and exercising authority over their husbands. The idea that wives rather than women in general are the referent has been argued at some length by Gordon Hugenberger.[43] He contends that a reference to women and men in general is not demanded in writing to the church, for Peter in a text (1 Pet. 3:1–7) which is quite similar to 1 Timothy 2:9–15 only refers to husbands and wives. Moreover, appropriate dress for women (v. 9), good works (v. 10), and child-rearing (v. 15) apply outside worship contexts. He thinks public worship is not necessarily in view, for the phrase "every place" does not refer to public meetings in 1 Corinthians 1:2 and 1 Thessalonians 1:8, and a public context is not needed for lifting one's hands in prayer. In addition, elsewhere in Paul the terms γυνή and ἀνήρ usually refer to wives and husbands, not women and men in general. Further, he asserts that the parallels between Titus 2:4–5 and 1 Peter 3:1–7 are crucial for establishing the referent in 1 Timothy 2. In fact, Hugenberger thinks that the extensive verbal and conceptual parallels between 1 Timothy 2 and 1 Peter 3 "must be determinative for our exegesis" of 1 Timothy 2.[44] He believes that it is unthinkable that no discussion of the family would occur in 1 Timothy.

The burden of Hugenberger's argument is that parallel texts show that Paul refers to husbands and wives in 1 Timothy 2:8–15. He especially leans on the parallels between 1 Timothy 2:8–15 and 1 Peter 3:1–7, seeing the latter as "determinative" for the meaning of the former. However, the texts hardly correspond in every respect, despite some impressive parallels. For instance, the 1 Peter text refers to *nonbelieving* husbands (3:1).[45] And in 3:7 husbands are addressed in terms of their specific responsibilities to their wives (cf. Eph. 5:25–30, 33; Col. 3:19). No admonition for husbands regarding their relationship with their wives is present in 1 Timothy 2. Finally, it is obvious that Peter has husbands and wives in view in 1 Peter 3 since he says "wives should be subject to *their own* (ἰδίοις) husbands" (v. 1; cf. v. 5). It is precisely this kind of clarifying evidence that 1 Timothy 2:8–15 lacks, with the result that most scholars detect a reference to men and women in general.

43. Gordon P. Hugenberger, "Women in Church Office: Hermeneutics or Exegesis? A Survey of Approaches to 1 Tim 2:8–15," *Journal of the Evangelical Theological Society* 35 (1992): 341–60. For a similar view, see Gritz, *Mother Goddess*, 125, 131, 133, 135, 136, 140; N. J. Hommes, "Let Women Be Silent in Church," *Calvin Theological Journal* 4 (1969): 13–14, 19–20; cf. Barnett, "1 Timothy 2:11–15," 232–33.

44. Hugenberger, "Women in Church Office," 355.

45. So Timothy J. Harris, "Why Did Paul Mention Eve's Deception? A Critique of P. W. Barnett's Interpretation of 1 Timothy 2," *Evangelical Quarterly* 62 (1990): 336.

It is hardly impressive to say that elsewhere γυνή and ἀνήρ refer to husbands and wives since in those texts a reference to husbands and wives is indicated plainly in the context, and such passages are not even debated with respect to this issue.[46] Some examples will illustrate how clear the evidence is: "the married woman" (ἡ ὕπανδρος γυνή, Rom. 7:2); "each man should have his own wife" (τὴν ἑαυτοῦ γυναῖκα, 1 Cor. 7:2); "to the married" (τοῖς γεγαμηκόσιν, 1 Cor. 7:10); "if any brother has a wife" (ἀδελφὸς γυναῖκα ἔχει, 1 Cor. 7:12); "her husband" (ὁ ἀνήρ αὐτῆς, 1 Cor. 7:39); "Let them ask their own husbands at home" (τοὺς ἰδίους ἄνδρας, 1 Cor. 14:35);[47] "I betrothed you to one husband" (2 Cor. 11:2); "More are the children of the desolate one than of the one having a husband" (Gal. 4:27); "Wives being subject to their own husbands" (αἱ γυναῖκες τοῖς ἰδίοις ἀνδράσιν, Eph. 5:22); "husband of one wife" (1 Tim. 3:2; cf. 1 Tim. 3:12; 5:9; Titus 1:6); "instruct the young women to be lovers of their husbands (φιλάνδρους) . . . being subject to their own husbands" (τοῖς ἰδίοις ἀνδράσιν, Titus 2:5). By way of contrast, the lack of such qualifications in 1 Corinthians 11:2–16 shows that Paul is not referring to just husbands and wives, but to men and women in general. In Colossians 3:18–19 Paul could conceivably be referring to men and women in general, but the context (the next pericope deals with relations between parents and children, 3:20–21) and the call to "love your wives" (3:19) reveal that husbands and wives are in view. The very lack of such specificity in 1 Timothy 2:8–15 has rightly led most commentators to see a reference to men and women in general. Hugenberger demands that the Pauline usage elsewhere must obtain here, but he fails to notice the significant contextual differences between these other texts and 1 Timothy 2 and ends up imposing these other texts on the interpretation of 1 Timothy 2.[48]

Hugenberger's observations on the general applicability of appropriate dress, good works, and child-rearing (better child-bearing) are apropos. And yet they call into question the thesis that only wives are

46. I could cite more examples from most of these texts, but provide only one example from each so as not to prolong the point and bore the reader unduly. Greek is cited only insofar as it is necessary to make the point.

47. But the reference to women in 1 Cor. 14:34 is not just to wives. See D. A. Carson, "'Silent in the Churches': On the Role of Women in 1 Corinthians 14:33b–36," in *Recovering Biblical Manhood and Womanhood,* ed. J. Piper and W. Grudem (Wheaton: Crossway, 1991), 151.

48. Hugenberger ("Women in Church Office," 353) is correct, strictly speaking, in saying that the Greek article or possessive pronoun is not necessary for a reference to husbands and wives. Even though an article or possessive pronoun is not demanded, the lack of such and the generality of the context have persuaded most scholars that Paul is speaking of men and women in general. What Hugenberger fails to appreciate is that Paul provides no determinative clues (as he does in all the texts referring to husbands and wives) that husbands and wives are intended.

being addressed, for it is quite improbable that Paul would be concerned about the adornment of wives but not the dress of single women.[49] Issues of adornment were probably occasioned by dress at public worship, even if they extend beyond that sphere.[50] The flow of thought of 1 Timothy as a whole commends a public setting. False teachers are threatening the church, and Timothy is charged to stem the tide of their influence. First Timothy 2:8–15 is succeeded by an exhortation to appoint overseers and deacons in the church (1 Tim. 3:1–13), and both are offices that relate to public ministry in the church. The Pauline instructions are designed to make the church a bulwark against the false teaching (1 Tim. 3:14–15). Indeed, Paul immediately returns to the threat of false teaching and the need to resist it (1 Tim. 4).[51] It seems improbable, contrary to Hugenberger, that Paul would insert teaching on husbands and wives at home in the midst of his polemic against false teachers.[52] I conclude with most commentators that a reference to husbands and wives in 1 Timothy 2:8–15 is quite improbable.[53] Instructions are given instead regarding proper behavior for men and women in public meetings of the church.

Advocates of the progressive view often raise the issue of women's adornment in discussions about the legitimacy of women teaching men. For example, Alvera Mickelsen says, "Those who believe that verse 12 forever bars all women of all time from teaching or having authority over men usually ignore the commands in the other six verses in this section. This is a classic case of 'selective literalism.' If this passage is universal for all Christian women of all time, then no woman should ever wear pearls or gold (including wedding rings) or have braided hair or expensive clothing."[54] David Scholer argues that in the culture of

49. So Ben Wiebe, "Two Texts on Women (1 Tim 2:11–15; Gal 3:26–29): A Test of Interpretation," *Horizons in Biblical Theology* 16 (1994): 57.

50. And Hugenberger's thesis is improbable if "in every place" (v. 8) refers to public meetings, and thus he cites parallel texts to question the worship context here. But what makes a public worship context likely is not only the words "in every place," but also the activity occurring there: prayer (v. 8) and teaching (vv. 11–12).

51. If Paul wanted to discuss the relationship between husbands and wives, he probably would have linked it with his advice to slaves in 1 Tim. 6:1–2 (cf. Eph. 5:22–6:9; Col. 3:18–4:1).

52. In addition, Hugenberger's evidence is not decisive. First Cor. 1:2 probably refers to public Christian meetings (see Gordon D. Fee, *The First Epistle to the Corinthians* [NICNT; Grand Rapids: Eerdmans, 1987], 34), while 1 Thess. 1:8 and 2 Cor. 2:14 have a wider reference. The context is decisive for the particular interpretation of the phrase.

53. E.g., Ronald Y. K. Fung, "Ministry in the New Testament," in *The Church in the Bible and in the World*, ed. D. A. Carson (Grand Rapids: Baker, 1987), 200–201; Moo, "1 Timothy 2:11–15," 63–64; Towner, *Goal of Our Instruction*, 212; Witherington, *Women*, 119.

54. Alvera Mickelsen, "An Egalitarian View: There Is Neither Male Nor Female in Christ," in *Women in Ministry: Four Views*, ed. B. Clouse and R. G. Clouse (Downers Grove: InterVarsity, 1989), 201.

Paul's day proper adornment for women was linked to submission to husbands.[55] He insists that women's adornment (vv. 9–10) must be applied in the same way as the prohibitions against women teaching (vv. 11–12).[56] One cannot legitimately claim that the latter is normative whereas the former is culturally relative. Those who prohibit women from teaching men should, to be consistent, also forbid the wearing of any jewelry by women. Neither can they escape, he reasons, by saying that submission is the principle that undergirds the wearing of appropriate attire, so that the wearing of jewelry is permitted as long as one has a submissive spirit. Suitable adornment and submission are inextricably linked, and one cannot surrender the former and maintain the latter. Scholer concludes that a careful interpretation of the text in its historical-cultural setting neither proscribes a woman from wearing jewelry nor from teaching men, but that those who uphold the historic view have inconsistently enforced the proscription on teaching men while ignoring the verses on proper adornment.[57]

The questions raised by these scholars are crucial and will be addressed in my explanation of these verses. We begin, though, by noting what the verses actually say. Paul calls upon the women to "adorn themselves with respectable deportment" (v. 9). The word καταστολῇ (deportment) probably refers to both suitable clothing and suitable behavior.[58] The rest of verses 9–10 elaborates on proper deportment. It consists of modesty and discretion with respect to dress instead of enticing and ostentatious clothing. Attire that is immodest and lacking in mature judgment includes braiding the hair, gold, pearls, and expensive clothing. Women who profess godliness should focus on good works rather than outward adornment.

Precisely what is Paul's intention here? Scholer and others rightly conclude that a proscription of all jewelry on the basis of these verses alone can fall into the error of excessive literalism. We should not rule out too quickly, though, the possibility that we have ignored these verses because they indict our culture. Nonetheless, we have an important clue to Paul's intention in the words "expensive clothing" (ἱματισμῷ

55. David Scholler (sic), "Women's Adornment: Some Historical and Hermeneutical Observations on the New Testament Passages," *Daughters of Sarah* 6 (1980): 3–6; idem, "1 Timothy 2:9–15," 200–202; cf. Fee, *Gospel and Spirit*, 57–58, 61; Keener, *Women's Ministry*, 103–7; Clark, *Man and Woman*, 194; Moo, "What Does It Mean?" 181–82.

56. So also Payne, "Libertarian Women," 189–90; Gordon D. Fee, "Reflections on Church Order in the Pastoral Epistles, with Further Reflection on the Hermeneutics of *Ad Hoc* Documents," *Journal of the Evangelical Theological Society* 28 (1985): 150.

57. For Scholer's interpretation of the text as a whole, see "1 Timothy 2:9–15," 193–219.

58. So Dibelius and Conzelmann, *Pastoral Epistles*, 45–46; Gritz, *Mother Goddess*, 126; Guthrie, *Pastoral Epistles*, 74; Knight, *Pastoral Epistles*, 133; Moo, "1 Timothy 2:11–15," 63; contra Lock (*Pastoral Epistles*, 31), who sees only a reference to dress.

πολυτελεῖ).[59] The proscription is not against all wearing of clothing, but luxurious adornment, an excessive devotion to beautiful and splendid attire.[60] The similar text in 1 Peter 3:3 supports this interpretation, for read literally it prohibits all wearing of clothing, which is scarcely Peter's intention. The words on clothing provide help in understanding the instructions on braids, gold, and pearls. Paul's purpose is probably not to ban these altogether, but to warn against expensive and extravagant preoccupation with one's appearance. James Hurley suggests that the command is directed against the elaborate hair styles that were worn by fashionable women and wealthy courtesans.[61] Probably the plaiting of hair with gold is indicted since braiding hair was common, enhancing the thesis that what is being forbidden is an excessive devotion to outward adornment.[62] In the Greco-Roman world a polemic against ostentation of wealth was common (Juvenal, *Satires*, 6.352–65, 6.457–73; Plutarch, *Mor.* 142ab). And the wearing of jewelry was not absolutely forbidden in Judaism (Gen. 24:22; Exod. 35:22; *b. Šhab.* 64b; *Jos. As.* 18:6).[63] In conclusion, the text does not rule out all wearing of jewelry by women but forbids ostentation and luxury in adornment.[64]

It is also likely that these words on adornment contain a polemic against seductive and enticing clothing.[65] This is suggested by the words "modesty and discretion" (αἰδοῦς καὶ σωφροσύνης, v. 9). In both Jewish and Greco-Roman literature sexual seductiveness is linked with extravagant adornment (*T. Reub.* 5:1–5; *T. Jud.* 12:3; *Test. Jos.* 9:5; *1 Enoch* 8:1–2; Judith 10:3–4; Rev. 17:4; 18:16).[66] We can draw, then,

59. The Kroegers' suggestion (*I Suffer Not a Woman*, 74–75) that the women may have been disrobing during worship based on a fresco in Pompeii with Dionysian worshipers doing such is an example of mirror-reading and parallelomania at its worst.

60. So Barnett, "1 Timothy 2:9–15," 226, 228; Clark, *Man and Woman*, 194; Culver, "Traditional View," 35; Susan T. Foh, "A Male Leadership View: The Head of the Woman Is the Man," in *Women in Ministry: Four Views*, ed. B. Clouse and R. G. Clouse (Downers Grove: InterVarsity, 1989), 80; Gritz, *Mother Goddess*, 127; Guthrie, *Pastoral Epistles*, 75; Keener, *Women's Ministry*, 103; Knight, *Pastoral Epistles*, 135; Moo, "What Does It Mean?" 182; Thomas C. Oden, *First and Second Timothy and Titus* (Louisville: John Knox, 1989), 94; Padgett, "Wealthy Women," 23; Scholer, "1 Timothy 2:9–15," 201–2; Witherington, *Women*, 119–20.

61. James B. Hurley, *Man and Woman in Biblical Perspective* (Grand Rapids: Zondervan, 1981), 199.

62. So Keener, *Women's Ministry*, 105; cf. Knight, *Pastoral Epistles*, 135.

63. See Keener, *Women's Ministry*, 103–4.

64. Motyer ("Expounding 1 Timothy," 94) suggests Paul speaks against the self-assertiveness of women.

65. Keener, *Women's Ministry*, 103–6; Knight, *Pastoral Epistles*, 135–36; Moo, "What Does It Mean?" 182; Scholer, "1 Timothy 2:9–15," 201–2; idem, "Women's Adornment," 6; Oden, *First Timothy*, 95; Towner, *Goal of Our Instruction*, 208; Witherington, *Women*, 119–20; Gritz, *Mother Goddess*, 126–27. Gritz, without warrant, takes this as evidence of the influence of the Artemis cult.

66. For citations from Greco-Roman literature, see Scholer, "Women's Adornment," 4–5.

two principles from these verses. Not only is extravagant and ostentatious adornment prohibited but also clothing that is seductive and enticing.[67] These words are desperately needed in our culture, for materialism and sexual seductiveness with respect to adornment still plague us. Of course, this text applies to men as well as to women, for if men devote too much money and attention to clothing or dress seductively, they fall under the same indictment.[68]

We have already noted that some scholars argue that suitable clothing was linked with submission to one's husband in Paul's day. Scholer, in particular, cites a number of texts to support this view.[69] Nonetheless, that these two themes are wedded to the extent that Scholer argues is unpersuasive. In 1 Peter 3:1–6, for instance, the two themes are found side by side, but it goes beyond the evidence of the text to say that submission is expressed by one's attire. In the other texts that Scholer cites the vice that is specified with regard to the women is unchastity, not insubordination or lack of submission.[70] The devotion to and the honor of the husband demanded probably relate to faithfulness to the married bed rather than submission.[71] In any case, not a word is said about lack of submission in 1 Timothy 2:9–10, and thus reading this theme into the text is questionable.

For the sake of argument, though, we will assume for a moment that Scholer and others are correct about suitable adornment being tied to submission. Even if this is the case, it does not logically follow that the principle of submission must be jettisoned if one does not literally apply the words regarding proper attire. Of course, the principle regarding suitable adornment needs to be taken seriously today, for the instructions on adornment prohibit ostentation and seductiveness in clothing. However, *if* such adornment were banned by Paul for the sole reason that it expressed lack of submission, then it seems that the principle informing the commands could be retained in our culture without requiring the first-century cultural expression of that principle. No one

67. Pierce ("Gender Roles," 352) may be correct in suggesting that humility is enjoined here, but his view that humility is the "primary focus" of not only this text but all the texts relating to leadership in 1 Timothy is mistaken. Although the women in Ephesus may have been conducting themselves in inappropriate ways because of pride, 1 Tim. 2:9–15 does not specifically pinpoint lack of humility as the problem. Nor does the passage on the appointment of elders and deacons (1 Tim. 3:1–13) highlight pride as the central issue for leaders. I am not denying that pride may have been an issue for leaders in 1 Timothy, but Pierce has not established that it is the *primary* one, nor has he provided any evidence that it was particularly a problem for women.

68. So Keener, *Women's Ministry*, 107.

69. Scholer, "Women's Adornment," 3–6.

70. Cf. ibid., 4–5.

71. I am not denying that submission was expected by these authors. I am only questioning whether this submission was regularly associated with adornment.

in our culture would believe that a woman wearing jewelry or a wedding band was declaring her independence from a man. In fact, wearing a wedding band is often taken to mean just the opposite. In our culture such adornment would not communicate lack of submission. Submission to one's husband would be expressed in other ways.

Scholer's conclusion that a principial application of the biblical text would be illegitimate is unconvincing. We rightly apply the principle from other biblical texts without requiring the literal practice that communicated the principle in Paul's day. For instance, we are not *required* to drink wine for stomach aches today (1 Tim. 5:23), but the principle behind Paul's admonition still applies to us. We should use an antacid or some other medicine when suffering from stomach problems. So too, in American culture we do not typically express our affection with a holy kiss (1 Cor. 16:20). We should not conclude from this that we *must* greet one another with a holy kiss. Nor should we argue that if we do not literally practice the holy kiss, then this verse is inapplicable to us. The principle is that we should greet one another with warm affection, and in our culture that may be expressed by a warm handshake or a hug. In our culture, therefore, the admonitions in verses 9–10 contain the principle that women should not dress ostentatiously or seductively. The intention of the text is not to ban the wearing of all jewelry. This raises, of course, the question as to how the principle in verses 11–12 should be applied today. Perhaps the principle undergirding those verses is not violated if women teach men today. Such an application of these verses is certainly possible, and thus we must interpret those verses carefully to see what the principle is.

Should a Woman Teach or Exercise Authority over a Man?

Virtually every word in verses 11–12 is disputed. Thus, I will attempt to construct my argument piece by piece, although it is impossible to interpret the parts without appealing to the whole, and so other issues must be broached in the midst of the analysis of individual elements as well. Verse 11 is translated as follows: "A woman should learn silently with all submission." The singular "woman" (γυνή) is generic, and thus should not be limited to an individual woman. The alternation from the plural "women" in verses 9–10 to the singular "woman" in verses 11–12 reveals that the latter is generic and all women are included.[72]

Paul enjoins all women to learn (μανθανέτω). It has often been pointed out that this represents an advance over some traditions in Ju-

---

72. We will see in our discussion of v. 15 below that a similar phenomenon is present.

daism where women were forbidden from learning.[73] The exhortation implies a belief in the intellectual capability of women and their ability to profit from instruction and education. Certainly those of the historic position should also encourage women to grow in their knowledge of the Scriptures. Philip Payne says that the injunction for women to learn is the only command in this text.[74] It will be argued, however, when we analyze the verb "I permit" (ἐπιτρέπω) that this observation is linguistically naive, even if it is rhetorically impressive. The injunction to learn, many aver, implies that the women could teach after they learn. Therefore, it is claimed that the only reason for the prohibition on women teachers was lack of education or the influence of the false teachers.[75]

Several things need to be said in response to the above observations. Even though progressives are right in detecting a commendation of women learning in verse 11, the thrust of the command is obscured in their exegesis by abstracting the imperative verb from the rest of the sentence. Paul does not merely say, "Women must learn!" He says, "Women must learn silently and with all submission." The focus of the command is not on women learning, but *the manner* and *mode* of their learning.[76] Progressives are correct in seeing a commendation of women learning, for the propriety of women learning is implied in the use of the imperative verb. But Paul's main concern is the way they learn, that is, silently and with all submissiveness. An illustration might help. If I were to say to my son, "You must drive the car carefully and wisely," the sentence assumes that driving the car is permissible and suitable for my son. Nonetheless, the focus of my instruction is not on permission to drive the car; that is assumed. What I am mainly concerned about is the *manner* in which he drives it. Similarly, that women should learn is undoubtedly commended, and yet the central concern is the manner in which they learn.

73. Barnett, "1 Timothy 2:11–15," 229; Foh, *Women and the Word of God*, 124; Gritz, *Mother Goddess*, 128; Hurley, *Man and Woman*, 200; Oden, *First Timothy*, 96; Ben Witherington III, *Women in the Ministry of Jesus* (SNTSMS 51; Cambridge: Cambridge University Press, 1984), 6–10; Towner, *Goal of Our Instruction*, 313–14, n. 78. As Towner points out, this calls into question Jewett's view that Paul's instructions here simply reflect a rabbinic worldview (see n. 6). On the other hand, Hugenberger ("Women in Church Office," 349) wisely warns against overly simplistic versions of what the rabbis taught.

74. Philip B. Payne, "Part II: The Interpretation of 1 Timothy 2:11–15: A Surrejoinder," in *What Does the Scripture Teach about the Ordination of Women?* (Minneapolis, unpublished paper, 1986), 96.

75. Gilbert Bilezikian, *Beyond Sex Roles* (Grand Rapids: Baker, 1985), 179; Evans, *Woman in the Bible*, 101; Keener, *Women's Ministry*, 107–8, 112; Padgett, "Wealthy Women," 24; Payne, "Surrejoinder," 97, 99; Aída D. B. Spencer, "Eve at Ephesus," *Journal of the Evangelical Theological Society* 17 (1974): 218–19.

76. So Hurley, *Man and Woman*, 201; Moo, "1 Timothy 2:11–15," 64; "What Does It Mean?" 183; Witherington, *Women*, 263, n. 207.

Neither is it convincing to say that permission to learn implies that women can teach once they have sufficient learning. Such exegesis overlooks what we have just pointed out, namely, that the command does not concentrate on the fact that women should learn but the manner in which they should do so. Moreover, Paul could have easily said in verse 12, "But I do not permit a woman to teach a man until she is sufficiently educated." Instead, verse 12 says that women cannot teach or exercise authority over men. Progressives read out of the injunction to learn, permission to teach, but verse 12 prohibits this very activity.[77]

The two adverbial phrases in verse 12 regarding the mode in which women should learn should be noted. First, Paul says they should learn "silently" (ἐν ἡσυχίᾳ). Most scholars today argue that this word does not actually mean "silence" here, but refers to a quiet demeanor and spirit that is peaceable instead of argumentative.[78] The use of the same word in 1 Timothy 2:2 supports this thesis, for there absolute silence is not intended but a gentle and quiet demeanor. The parallel text in 1 Peter 3:4 also inclines us in the same direction, since the "gentle and quiet spirit" of the wife in the home can scarcely involve absolute silence! In addition, if Paul wanted to communicate absolute silence, he could have used the noun σιγή (silence) rather than ἡσυχία (quietness). The resolution of this question is not of prime importance for the debate before us, for the meaning of the text is not drastically changed either way. A quiet, respectful demeanor when learning would certainly be in accord with Paul's instructions in verse 11. Though either meaning is possible here, "silently" is to be preferred, on the basis of the context of verse 12.[79] There women are proscribed from teaching and exercising authority over men; instead, they are εἶναι ἐν ἡσυχίᾳ (to be silent). The most natural antonym to teaching in this context is "silence." Of course, ἡσυχία (quietness) does not invariably refer to silence in other contexts. However, the word-group does bear the meaning "silence" in some texts (e.g., Luke 14:4; Acts 22:2). Thus, the question comes down to what the word means in this specific context. It is not compelling to say that Paul would have used σιγή (silence) if silence were intended. This observation smacks of an older word study ap-

---

77. Cf. Moo, "What Does It Mean?" 184.

78. Barnett, "1 Timothy 2:11–15," 229; Clark, *Man and Woman*, 195; Evans, *Woman in the Bible*, 101; Fee, *1 Timothy*, 84; Gritz, *Mother Goddess*, 129; Holtz, *Die Pastoralbriefe*, 69; Keener, *Women's Ministry*, 108; Payne, "Libertarian Women," 169–70; Witherington, *Women*, 120; Wiebe, "1 Tim 2:11–15," 58; Motyer, "Expounding 1 Timothy," 93–95.

79. So Fung, "Ministry," 197–98; Knight, *Pastoral Epistles*, 139; Moo, "1 Timothy 2:11–15," 64; idem, "The Interpretation of 1 Timothy 2:11–15: A Rejoinder," *Trinity Journal* 2 (1981): 199; idem, "What Does It Mean?" 183; Towner, *Goal of Our Instruction*, 212–13.

proach in which there was a fund of words, each bearing meanings distinct from one another. Instead, the words σιγή and ἡσυχία overlap in some respects, and therefore we must decide from the context which meaning is intended.

Second, women should learn ἐν πάσῃ ὑποταγῇ (in all submission). Probably the word "all" has an elative sense, meaning "with entire submissiveness."[80] To what are the women to be submissive? It has been suggested that women are to be submissive to God,[81] the congregation in general,[82] sound teaching,[83] the contemporary social structure,[84] or the women's teachers.[85] We are aided in answering this question by the parallels between verses 11 and 12. Verses 11 and 12 constitute an inclusio; verse 11 begins with "in silence" and verse 12 concludes with "in silence." The permission for women to "learn" is contrasted with the proscription for them "to teach," while "all submissiveness" is paired with "not exercising authority over a man." The submission in view, then, is likely to men, since verse 12 bans women from exercising authority over men. Yet the context of verse 12 (more on this below) suggests that the submission of all women to all men is not in view, for not all men taught and had authority when the church gathered. Thus, we should not separate submission from what is taught from submission to those who taught it. Women were to learn with entire submissiveness from the men who had authority in the church and manifested that authority through their teaching.[86]

The δέ introducing verse 12 is a mild adversative that clarifies more precisely the command in verse 11.[87] The two verses are closely tied together, and perhaps even chiastic.[88] The phrase ἐν ἡσυχίᾳ (in silence)

80. Roloff, *Timotheus*, 135, n. 125.

81. Oden, *First Timothy*, 97.

82. Evans, *Woman in the Bible*, 101.

83. Gritz, *Mother Goddess*, 130; Andrew C. Perriman, "What Eve Did, What Women Shouldn't Do: The Meaning of ΑΥΘΕΝΤΕΩ in 1 Timothy 2:12," *Tyndale Bulletin* 44 (1993): 131.

84. Towner, *Goal of Our Instruction*, 214.

85. Padgett, "Wealthy Women," 24.

86. So Barnett, "1 Timothy 2:11–15," 230; Dibelius and Conzelmann, *Pastoral Epistles*, 47; Fung, "Ministry," 198; Knight, *Pastoral Epistles*, 139; Moo, "1 Timothy 2:11–15," 64; idem, "What Does It Mean?" 183; Roloff, *Timotheus*, 135.

87. Spencer's view ("Eve at Ephesus," 219) that the δέ is a signal to the church that the prohibition in v. 12 is temporary since it contradicts v. 11 is quite arbitrary; rightly Evans, *Woman in the Bible*, 102.

88. Cf. Fung, "Ministry," 336, n. 186; Moo, "1 Timothy 2:11–15," 64; Barnett, "1 Timothy 2:11–15," 228–29; Harris, "Eve's Deception," 340; Witherington, *Women*, 120. I question whether there is a chiasm here because then the idea of exercising authority should have preceded teaching. Instead, the two verses are closely related, with an inclusio binding them together. Another problem with seeing a chiasm is that the scholars cited above do not agree on the chiastic arrangement.

introduces verse 11 and concludes verse 12, and thus functions as an in-clusio for these verses. "Women should learn in silence" (ἐν ἡσυχίᾳ μαν-θανέτω, v. 11), but are not permitted "to teach" (διδάσκειν, v. 12).[89] They are to learn "in all submission" (ἐν πάσῃ ὑποταγῇ, v. 11), but are not "to exercise authority over men" (αὐθεντεῖν ἀνδρός, v. 12). These corre-spondences and antitheses between verses 11 and 12 indicate that An-drew Perriman's view that verse 12 is parenthetical is unconvincing.[90] Verse 12 follows on the heels of verse 11 and clarifies its meaning. Miss-ing the relationship between verses 11 and 12 has the consequence of vitiating Perriman's exegesis of this text, since his interpretation de-pends on this analysis.

The verb "I do not permit" (ἐπιτρέπω, v. 12) has been the subject of some controversy. It is often said that the verb reflects only a temporary prohibition. Scholars appeal to the verbal form being a present active indicative first singular, concluding from this that Paul is not permit-ting women to teach or exercise authority over men *for a restricted pe-riod of time*.[91] It is also claimed that the intrinsic meaning of ἐπιτρέπω demonstrates that a temporary prohibition is intended, for the verb elsewhere never indicates a universally applicable command. Indeed, as noted above, some even capitalize on the form being indicative, and state that the only imperative in the text is in verse 11.

This latter point should be taken up first, for it is extraordinarily mis-leading and betrays a wooden view of Greek by implying that one can only have commands if the imperative mood is used. On the contrary, Paul often uses present indicatives in cases where the context reveals a command is intended. For instance, the call to pray for all people in 1 Timothy 2:1 is introduced by a present indicative (παρακαλῶ, I ex-hort; cf. Rom. 12:1; 1 Cor. 1:10; Eph. 4:1; Phil. 4:2; 2 Tim. 1:6). So, too, the directive for men to pray without wrath and disputing is introduced by a present indicative (βούλομαι, I want, 1 Tim. 2:8; cf. 1 Tim. 5:14; Titus 3:8). The assertion that verse 11 contains the only command in the text, therefore, can hardly be taken seriously.

But does the present active indicative first singular form reflect a temporary prohibition, or is it merely Paul's personal opinion? Once

89. Roloff (*Timotheus*, 138) rightly observes that learning silently with all submissive-ness (v. 11) is opposed to teaching in v. 12.

90. Perriman, "What Eve Did," 129–30, 139–40. Perriman says that the shift from the imperative μανθανέτω to the indicative ἐπιτρέπω indicates the parenthetic nature of v. 12. His argument falters because he fails to see that an indicative may introduce a command. Nor is there any evidence that Perriman has considered the close relationship between vv. 11 and 12 (see n. 88) in his study.

91. Bilezikian, *Beyond Sex Roles*, 180; Fee, *1 Timothy*, 72; Kroegers, *I Suffer Not a Woman*, 83; Oden, *First Timothy*, 97–98; Padgett, "Wealthy Women," 25; Payne, "Libertar-ian Women," 170–72; idem, "Surrejoinder," 97, 100–101; Roberts, "1 Timothy 2:15," 5; Witherington, *Women*, 120–21; Wiebe, "1 Tim 2:11–15," 59.

again, the answer is negative on both counts.[92] Numerous injunctions are given by Paul in the present active indicative first singular that are universal commands. For instance, the command to present one's body to God as a living and holy sacrifice is introduced with a present active indicative first singular (παρακαλῶ, I exhort, Rom. 12:1), and it is obviously a universally applicable command. In many other instances such universal commands exist with present active indicatives in the first person (e.g., Rom. 15:30; 16:17; 1 Cor. 1:10; 4:16; 7:10; 2 Cor. 10:1; Eph. 4:1; Phil 4:2; 1 Thess. 4:1, 10; 5:14; 2 Thess. 3:6, 12; 1 Tim. 2:1, 8; 5:14; 2 Tim. 1:6; Titus 3:8). The point is not that the present active indicative first person form in 1 Timothy 2:12 *proves* that the command is universal and for all time. My point is more modest. Those who appeal to the form of the word as if it established the temporary nature of the prohibition transcend the evidence. The form does no such thing, and such a thesis must be established on other grounds.

More promising, on first glance, is the contention that ἐπιτρέπω contains the idea of a temporary limitation by virtue of its intrinsic meaning. That the verb may relate to a specific situation is obvious in a number of contexts (Matt. 8:21 par.; Mark 5:13 par.; John 19:38; Acts 21:39, 40; 26:1; 27:3; 28:16). Nonetheless, the argument is again dubious. The specificity of the situation is plain not from the verb itself but from the context in which it occurs. For instance, in Matthew 8:21 we know that the request for permission to bury one's father before following Jesus relates to a specific situation that will not last forever. But this is scarcely explicable from the verb ἐπιτρέπω itself; we know this because one can only bury one's father once.[93] In other contexts ἐπιτρέπω is not necessarily limited to a specific situation (cf. 1 Cor. 14:34; 16:7; Heb. 6:3; Ign. *Eph.* 10:3; *1 Clem.* 1:3; *Ant.* 20:267). Whether what is permitted or forbidden is universal cannot be determined by the tense of the verb, nor its intrinsic meaning. It is the context in which the verb occurs that is decisive. If I say to my daughter, "You are not permitted to drive the car one hundred miles per hour," it is obvious (or should be!) that this is a universal prohibition. But if I say, "You are not permitted to go into the street," it is also plain that this is a temporary restriction given to a young girl of two years of age who is not yet able to handle herself safely in the street. In conclusion, the mere presence of the word ἐπιτρέπω cannot be used to establish the temporary nature of the restriction, nor can it establish that we have a universal principle for all

92. See Moo, "1 Timothy 2:11–15," 65; idem, "Rejoinder," 199–200; idem, "What Does It Mean?" 185.

93. It should also be noted that most of the examples cited have the aorist tense, while 1 Tim. 2:12 has the present tense (cf. 1 Cor. 14:34). Too much weight should not be assigned to this argument, though, for the aorist tense has too often been said to refer to once-for-all action.

time.[94] Only the context can resolve that question, and verse 12 alone does not contain sufficient evidence to answer it, although it will be argued below that verse 13 establishes that the prohibition is a universal one.

Two things are forbidden for a woman: teaching and exercising authority over a man. The emphatic position of "to teach" at the beginning of verse 12 does not show that the verse is a parenthesis.[95] Instead, Paul emphasizes that although women are permitted to learn, they cannot teach. Teaching here involves the authoritative and public transmission of tradition about Christ and the Scriptures (1 Cor. 12:28–29; Eph. 4:11; 1 Tim. 2:7; 2 Tim. 3:16; James 3:1).[96] It is clear from the rest of the Pastoral Epistles that the teaching in view is the public transmission of authoritative material (cf. 1 Tim. 4:13, 16; 6:2; 2 Tim. 4:2; Titus 2:7). The elders in particular are to labor in teaching (1 Tim. 5:17), so that they can refute the false teachers who advance their heresy (1 Tim. 1:3, 10; 4:1; 6:3; 2 Tim. 4:3; Titus 1:9, 11). It is crucial that the correct teaching and the apostolic deposit are passed on to the next generation (2 Tim. 1:12, 14; 2:2).

The prohibition against women teaching is not absolute, and it is probably given because some women were teaching both men and women when the church assembled.[97] The object of the infinitive "to

94. Rightly Scholer, "1 Timothy 2:9–15," 203, n. 28.

95. Contra Perriman, "What Eve Did," 130.

96. Contra Witherington, *Women*, 121. Rightly Fung, "Ministry," 198; H. Greeven, "Propheten, Lehrer, Vorsteher bei Paulus," *Zeitschrift für die neutestamentliche Wissenschaft* 44 (1952–53): 19–23; Clark, *Man and Woman*, 196; Moo, "1 Timothy 2:11–15," 65–66; idem, "What Does It Mean?" 185–86; Towner, *Goal of Our Instruction*, 215; Robert L. Saucy, "Women's Prohibition to Teach Men: An Investigation into Its Meaning and Contemporary Application," *Journal of the Evangelical Theological Society* 37 (1994): 86–91. Hommes ("Let Women Be Silent," 7–13) misunderstands the nature of teaching by comparing it to mutual discussion. Pierce ("Gender Roles," 349) argues that New Testament teaching was more authoritative, involving a master-discipleship role not practiced today. He observes that teaching today is understood as the imparting of information. This last observation reveals the weakness of much modern biblical teaching. More than the impartation of information should be occurring, since mind and heart should not be so rigidly separated. Pierce overplays the master-disciple dimension of the elder/overseer, but in any case Paul believed that such elders and overseers were *necessary* for the life of the churches in his day (cf. Acts 14:23; 20:17, 28; Phil. 1:1; 1 Tim. 3:1–7; 5:17, 19; Titus 1:5–9). Elders as leaders in local churches were apparently common during New Testament times (Acts 15:2, 4, 6, 22, 23; 16:14; 21:18; James 5:14; 1 Pet. 5:1, 5). I see no reason not to have the same pattern today.

97. Rightly Foh, *Women and the Word of God*, 125; idem, "Male Headship," 81; Fung, "Ministry," 198; Knight, *Pastoral Epistles*, 140; Moo, "Rejoinder," 201; Saucy, "Women's Prohibition," 79–97. Holtz (*Pastoralbriefe*, 69) correctly observes that the object "man" shows that not all teaching or exercise of authority is prohibited. Thus, Harris's ("Eve's Deception," 342) claim that there are no qualifications in this text given regarding women teaching is mistaken. The context also shows that public meetings are in view, and it is legitimate to consult (although not impose) other texts to construct the boundaries of the commands given here. Of course, how to apply this instruction in practical situations is not always easy. See Saucy, "Women's Prohibition," 79–97.

teach" (διδάσκειν) is "man" (ἀνδρός), indicating that women teaching men is what is forbidden.[98] The distance between the two infinitives is exaggerated by those who think that ἀνδρός is not also the object of διδάσκειν. Those who advocate the progressive position point out that Timothy was taught by his mother and grandmother (2 Tim. 1:5; 3:15); that Priscilla and Aquila taught Apollos (Acts 18:26); that women are permitted to teach elsewhere (Titus 2:3); and that all believers are to teach one another (Col. 3:16).[99] But those who hold to the historic view do not doubt that women can teach children or other women. It should be noted that Titus 2:3–4 speaks specifically of women teaching other women, and thus the appeal to women teaching here hardly violates what Paul says in 1 Timothy 2:12. Neither does the private teaching of Apollos by Priscilla and Aquila contradict what is said here, for this is profoundly different from the public and authoritative teaching in view in the Pastoral Epistles. Colossians 3:16 (cf. 1 Cor. 14:26) could be taken to say that women can teach men publicly and officially. But the teaching described there is the mutual instruction that occurs among all the members of the body. Unfortunately, some churches ban women from even doing this, although it is plainly in accord with Scripture. Yet this is quite different from the authoritative transmission of tradition that Paul has in mind in the Pastoral Epistles. Such authoritative teaching is usually a function of the elders/overseers (1 Tim. 3:2; 5:17), and it is likely that Paul is thinking of them here.[100] Thus, women are proscribed from functioning as elders/overseers, but Knight also correctly observes that they are prohibited from the function of public and authoritative teaching of men by this verse as well.[101]

98. Ἀνδρός is the object of both infinitives (Knight, *Pastoral Epistles*, 142; Moo, "Rejoinder," 202; idem, "What Does It Mean?" 186; contra Payne, "Libertarian Women," 175; Fung, "Ministry," 198–99). The singular ἀνδρός scarcely shows that a single man is in view (Perriman, "What Eve Did," 142; Payne, "Surrejoinder," 104). The word is used generically, just as γυνή is.

99. Bilezikian, *Beyond Sex Roles*, 176–78; Payne, "Libertarian Women," 173–74; idem, "Surrejoinder," 102–4; Scholer, "1 Timothy 2:9–15," 206–7.

100. Barnett, "1 Timothy 2:11–15," 230–31; Clark, *Man and Woman*, 199; Foh, "Male Headship," 81; Brox, *Pastoralbriefe*, 134; Moo, "Rejoinder," 212. Contra Fee, *Gospel and Spirit*, 63; Harris, "Eve's Deception," 341. Harris correctly says that the prohibition involves function, not merely office. Nonetheless, 1 Tim. 3:2 and Titus 1:9 suggest that all elders had to have the ability to teach, although some invested more time in teaching (1 Tim. 5:17). Padgett ("Wealthy Women," 25) argues that deacons functioned as teachers. Contra Padgett, the evidence that those appointed in Acts 6 were deacons is uncertain. Even if they were, the text does not establish that teaching was a requirement for deacons. It is telling that being apt to teach, which is required for elders (1 Tim. 3:2; 5:17; Titus 1:9), is not mentioned with respect to deacons.

101. Knight, *Pastoral Epistles*, 141–42. For discussion regarding practical application to today, see Saucy, "Women's Prohibition," 79–97. The comments made here would be contested by Walter Liefeld ("Women and the Nature of Ministry," *Journal of the Evangeli-*

A more powerful objection against the historic position is the assertion that prophecy is just as authoritative as teaching (1 Cor. 12:28; Eph. 2:20; 4:11).[102] Since it is clear that women could prophesy in the public assembly (Acts 2:17–18; 21:9; 1 Cor. 11:5), therefore, it is concluded they should also be permitted to teach. In response, Wayne Grudem has distinguished prophecy and teaching, saying that the latter is based on the apostolic deposit for the church and is more authoritative. Prophecy involves spontaneous revelations in which truth is mixed with error so that the content of the prophecies needs to be sifted.[103] The nonauthoritative nature of New Testament prophecy explains, according to Grudem, why women can prophesy but not teach. Grudem's understanding of New Testament prophecy would explain why women could prophesy but not teach, for the nature and authority of prophecy are quite different from teaching.[104] Even if Grudem is incorrect regarding the nonauthoritative character of New Testament prophecy, the gifts of prophecy and teaching are still distinct.[105] Prophecy is more vertical in nature, while teaching is more horizontal; the former involves spontaneous revelation and in that sense is more charismatic. Prophecy applies to specific situations, and is less tied to the consciousness of the individual than teaching. Moreover, 1 Corinthians 11:2–16 shows that women with the prophetic gift should exercise it in such a

---

cal *Theological Society* 30 [1987]: 49–61; idem, "A Plural Ministry View: Your Sons and Your Daughters Shall Prophesy," in *Women in Ministry: Four Views*, ed. A. Mickelsen [Downers Grove: InterVarsity, 1989], 127–53), for apparently he does not think that any authoritative offices should be present in the church. I cannot discuss this issue here, but it seems plain to me from Acts 11:30; 14:23; 15:2, 4, 6, 22, 23; 16:4; 20:17, 28; 21:18; Phil. 1:1; 1 Tim. 3:1–13; 5:17, 19; Titus 1:5–9; James 5:14; 1 Pet. 5:1–5 that the offices of elder/overseer and deacon existed in the early church. For critiques of Liefeld, see Culver, "Traditional View," 154–59 and Foh, 162 in *Women in Ministry: Four Views*. For a recent defense of the importance of church office, see T. David Gordon, "'Equipping' Ministry in Ephesians 4?" *Journal of the Evangelical Theological Society* 37 (1994): 69–78.

102. Fee, *Gospel and Spirit*, 63; Gritz, *Mother Goddess*, 132; Payne, "Libertarian Women," 184; idem, "Surrejoinder," 102; Scholer, "1 Timothy 2:9–15," 207; James G. Sigountos and Myron Shank, "Public Roles for Women in the Pauline Church: A Reappraisal of the Evidence," *Journal of the Evangelical Theological Society* 26 (1983): 285–86.

103. Wayne Grudem, "Prophecy—Yes, But Teaching—No: Paul's Consistent Advocacy of Women's Participation without Governing Authority," *Journal of the Evangelical Theological Society* 30 (1987): 11–23.

104. I endorsed Grudem's view previously. See Thomas R. Schreiner, "The Valuable Ministries of Women in the Context of Male Leadership," in *Recovering Biblical Manhood and Womanhood*, ed. J. Piper and W. Grudem (Wheaton: Crossway, 1991), 217.

105. Cf. Barnett "1 Timothy 2:11–15," 233; Moo, "1 Timothy 2:11–15," 75; idem, "Rejoinder," 206–7; Gerhard Friedrich, *TDNT*, 6:854; David Hill, *New Testament Prophecy* (Atlanta: John Knox, 1979), 131–33; Karl H. Rengstorf, *TDNT*, 2:158; Greeven, "Propheten," 29–30; Towner, *Goal of Our Instruction*, 215. Sigountos and Shank ("Public Roles," 285–86) disagree with this distinction, even though some of the evidence they adduce actually supports it (289–90). Their contention, that teaching was disallowed in the Greco-Roman world for cultural reasons while prophecy was permissible, is unpersuasive.

way that they do not subvert male leadership.[106] This does not mean
that the prophecies given by women are any less authoritative than
those of men. It does signal that the gift of prophecy can be exercised
by women without overturning male headship, whereas 1 Timothy
2:11–15 demonstrates that women cannot teach men without doing so.

Not only does Paul forbid women to teach men, but he also says that
they should "not exercise authority over" (αὐθεντεῖν) them. The debate
over the meaning of αὐθεντεῖν has been vigorous. The meaning "exercise authority" is most likely.[107] In particular, Henry Scott Baldwin has
pointed out that the verb must be separated from the noun in construct-
ing the definition of the term.[108] Moreover, the near context also suggests that αὐθεντεῖν means "exercise authority," for it functions as the
antonym to "all submissiveness" in verse 11.[109] Catherine Kroeger proposed the interpretation "engage in fertility practices" for the verb in
1979,[110] but the evidence for this meaning was virtually nonexistent,
and her interpretation has not gained acceptance.[111] The Kroegers have
recently suggested that the sentence should read, "I do not allow a
woman to teach nor to proclaim herself the author or originator of a
man."[112] This suggestion is faring little better than the first one, and
shows no signs of gaining any adherents.[113] Leland Wilshire's 1988

106. See my "Head Coverings, Prophecies and the Trinity: 1 Corinthians 11:2–16," in
Recovering Biblical Manhood and Womanhood, ed. J. Piper and W. Grudem (Wheaton:
Crossway, 1991), 124–39. Keener (*Women's Ministry*, 244–45) misunderstood my discussion on the nature of the Old Testament prophecy practiced by Deborah, Huldah, and
other women. I did not argue ("Ministries of Women," 216–17) that their prophecies were
less authoritative, but that they exercised their prophetic gift in such a way that they did
not subvert male leadership.

107. Henry Scott Baldwin's article in this volume; George W. Knight III, "ΑΥΘΕΝΤΕΩ
in Reference to Women in 1 Timothy 2.12," *New Testament Studies* 30 (1984): 143–57; Leland E. Wilshire, "The TLG Computer and Further Reference to ΑΥΘΕΝΤΕΩ in 1 Timothy
2.12," *New Testament Studies* 34 (1988): 120–34; A. J. Panning, "ΑΥΘΕΝΤΕΙΝ—A Word
Study," *Wisconsin Lutheran Quarterly* 78 (1981): 185–91; Moo, "1 Timothy 2:11–15," 66–
67; Gritz, *Mother Goddess*, 134; Barnett, "1 Timothy 2:11–15," 231–32; Padgett, "Wealthy
Women," 25; Fung, "Ministry," 198.

108. See his essay in this volume; cf. also Wolters, "Review: *I Suffer Not*," 211;
Yarbrough, "Review," 28.

109. Knight, "ΑΥΘΕΝΤΕΩ," 152.

110. Catherine C. Kroeger, "Ancient Heresies and a Strange Greek Verb," *Reformed
Journal* 29 (1979): 12–15.

111. Cf. Gritz, *Mother Goddess*, 134; Moo, "1 Timothy 2:11–15," 67; Carroll D. Osburn,
"ΑΥΘΕΝΤΕΩ (1 Timothy 2:12)," *Restoration Quarterly* 25 (1982): 1–8; Panning, "ΑΥΘΕΝ-
ΤΕΙΝ," 185–91.

112. Kroegers, *I Suffer Not a Woman*, 103.

113. For criticisms, see Perriman, "What Eve Did," 132–34; Leland E. Wilshire, "1
Timothy 2:12 Revisited: A Reply to Paul W. Barnett and Timothy J. Harris," *Evangelical
Quarterly* 65 (1993): 54; Wolters, "Review: *I Suffer Not*," 210–11. Payne ("Surrejoinder,"
108–10) lists five different possible meanings for the verb, but the very variety of his proposals suggests the implausibility of his suggestions. In addition, most of his proposals

study led most scholars to believe that he was adopting the meaning "exercise authority" as the most probable in 1 Timothy 2:12.[114] He complains in a recent article that Paul Barnett wrongly read this conclusion out of his work.[115] If there is any deficiency here, it lies with Wilshire rather than Barnett, for a number of scholars have understood Wilshire's 1988 article this way.[116] Now Wilshire suggests that the meaning in 1 Timothy 2:12 is "instigate violence."[117] This latter suggestion is flawed.[118] Even in the first article he failed to distinguish between the meaning of the noun and the verb. In the latter study Wilshire speculates that the problem with women was violence or conflict, but the text gives no indication that women were actually involved in such. Indeed, verse 8 says it was the men who were involved in arguing and disputation, whereas Wilshire concludes that the problem of disputing and arguing Paul limits to the men in verse 8 was actually the main problem with the women! Nor does Wilshire's view explain how the alleged prohibition against violence is related to teaching, and thus his proposal makes little sense in context. Perhaps I can be forgiven for thinking that the evidence actually leads to the conclusion Wilshire seemed to suggest in 1988, but his preference is for another translation, and this led him to write an article that lacked the same high quality as his 1988 piece.[119]

---

assign a negative meaning to the infinitive "to teach," which I will argue below is mistaken.

114. Wilshire, "ΑΥΘΕΝΤΕΩ," 120–34.

115. Wilshire, "Reply," 44.

116. For scholars who interpreted Wilshire this way, see Barnett, "1 Timothy 2:11–15," 231–32; Moo, "What Does It Mean?" 497, n. 18; Wolters, "Review: *I Suffer Not*," 211. Perriman ("What Eve Did," 134–35) rightly observes that the meaning "exercise authority" was the drift of Wilshire's essay despite his protests. In his later article Wilshire ("Reply," 50) says that αὐθεντεῖν meant "authority" only in the second and third centuries. But in his previous article (Wilshire, "ΑΥΘΕΝΤΕΩ," 130) he said, "But there are, however, a series of citations immediately *before*, *during*, and after the time of Paul where some sort of meaning connected with 'authority' is found for the word αὐθεντέω" (italics mine). After I had written the above comments, Paul W. Barnett ("*Authentein* Once More: A Response to L. E. Wilshire," *Evangelical Quarterly* 66 [1994]: 159–62) published an article in which he justifies his interpretation of the first Wilshire article along lines similar to what I have argued here.

117. Wilshire, "Reply," 43–55.

118. So Perriman, "What Eve Did," 136; Barnett, "Response," 161–62.

119. Perriman's own suggestion ("What Eve Did," 136–41) is that αὐθεντεῖν means the "active wielding of influence," so that the emphasis is on the taking of authority. He compares this to Eve's actions influencing Adam with the result that he transgressed. So, too, women teachers who are uneducated should not take authoritative action because they will lead men into sin. The problems with Perriman's analysis are numerous. His interpretation depends on v. 12 being parenthetical, which is dubious. The nuance he assigns to αὐθεντεῖν is not justified contextually, for he does not adequately explain the correlation between "teach" and "exercise authority." Moreover, Köstenberger (see his essay in this volume and my discussion below) has shown that both infinitives are to be construed

Some scholars have said that αὐθεντεῖν cannot mean "exercise authority" because Paul would have used the more common ἐξουσιάζειν (to exercise authority), κυριεύειν (to exercise authority), or ἔχειν ἐξουσίαν (to have authority) if he had wanted to communicate this idea.[120] They claim that the hapax legomenon αὐθεντεῖν reveals that a distinct meaning is in view. This argument is not as convincing as it might appear. Ἀυθεντεῖν and ἐξουσιάζειν have overlapping semantic fields. A review of Baldwin's data (see appendix 2) shows the two words are used synonymously in at least eight different contexts. The expression "have authority" (ἔχειν ἐξουσίαν) does not convey the same meaning as "exercise authority," since it focuses on possession of authority instead of use (cf. Rom. 9:21; 1 Cor. 7:37; 9:4, 5, 6; 11:10; 2 Thess. 3:9). And one might get the impression that Paul frequently uses the verbs ἐξουσιάζω and κυριεύω for "exercise authority," but he uses the former only three times (1 Cor. 6:12; 7:4, [twice]),[121] and the latter on six occasions (Rom. 6:9, 14; 7:1; 14:9; 2 Cor. 1:24; 1 Tim. 6:15). The significance statistically of selecting αὐθεντεῖν instead of ἐξουσιάζειν or κυριεύειν, therefore, is almost certainly overrated. Moreover, ἐξουσιάζω has a clearly negative sense in Luke 22:25 but a positive one in 1 Corinthians 7:4. Thus, one cannot say that Paul had to use this verb to indicate a positive use of authority. What indicates a positive or negative use of authority is the context.[122] The verb κυριεύω is hardly a better choice. When used of God or Christ it has a positive meaning (Rom. 14:9; 1 Tim. 6:15), but elsewhere in Paul it bears a negative meaning (Rom. 6:9, 14; 7:1; 2 Cor. 1:24; cf. Luke 22:25). If Paul had wanted to communicate a positive meaning of exercising authority, the verb κυριεύω would not qualify as a better candidate than αὐθεντέω. Neither ἐξουσιάζω nor κυριεύω necessarily includes a positive concept of exercising authority. Whether the authority is positive or negative is contextually determined. Too much has been made, therefore, of a distinct verb being used in 1 Timothy 2:12. Surely, we need to investigate carefully the meaning of the term in extrabiblical literature, so that the semantic

---

positively in this context. Perriman imports into this text the idea that women were prohibited from teaching because of ignorance or lack of education, but these are not stated or implied.

120. Perriman, "What Eve Did," 135; Kroegers, *I Suffer Not a Woman*, 84; Mickelsen, "Egalitarian View," 202; Scholer, "1 Timothy 2:9–15," 205; Towner, *Goal of Our Instruction*, 216; Wiebe, "1 Tim 2:11–15," 59–60.

121. So Moo, "What Does It Mean?" 186.

122. Andreas J. Köstenberger ("Gender Passages in the NT: Hermeneutical Fallacies Critiqued," *Westminster Theological Journal* 56 [1994]: 264–67) observes that scholars on both sides have attempted to assign exclusive meanings to words, in the case of αὐθεντεῖν either positive or negative, on the basis of extrabiblical literature. Köstenberger correctly comments that these studies are helpful in establishing the semantic range of a word, but they cannot definitively establish the meaning of a term in a specific context.

range of the term is known, and it is instructive that in most cases αὐθεντέω has a positive meaning along the lines of "exercise authority." Nonetheless, in context αὐθεντεῖν could have a negative meaning. We should not rule out the possibility that the context will incline us toward the meaning "domineer" or "play the tyrant" rather than "exercise authority."[123] But we shall see shortly that the definition "exercise authority" is constrained by the context.

The relationship between the two infinitives "to teach" and "to exercise authority" should also be explored. Philip Payne has argued that these two infinitives joined by the word "neither" (οὐδέ) communicate a single coherent idea.[124] Andreas Köstenberger, in a wide-ranging and impressive study of both biblical and extrabiblical literature, demonstrates that Payne's database was too small and that he misinterpreted the evidence.[125] The two ideas are closely related, but two different injunctions are intended.[126] Women are forbidden both to teach and to exercise authority over men. Köstenberger's study also reveals that in constructions with οὐδέ either both items proscribed are viewed negatively or positively. Thus, the verse either means "I do not permit a woman to teach falsely or domineer over a man" or "I do not permit a woman to teach or exercise authority over a man." The latter option is demanded, for there is no evidence here that the infinitive διδάσκειν should be rendered "to teach falsely."[127] If Paul had wanted to communicate that the teaching prohibited was false teaching, then he would have used the verb ἑτεροδιδασκαλέω (I teach false doctrine), which he uses to convey this very idea in 1 Timothy 1:3 and 6:3; or he would have given some other clear contextual clue (like an object clause or an adverb) to indicate that the teaching in view is false teaching. The verb διδάσκω (I teach) has a positive sense elsewhere in the Pastoral Epistles (1 Tim. 4:11; 6:2; 2 Tim.

123. In favor of "domineer," see Fee, *1 Timothy*, 73; Harris, "Eve's Deception," 42; Keener, *Women's Ministry*, 109; Osburn, "ΑΥΘΕΝΤΕΩ," 1–12; Payne, "Libertarian Women," 175; Towner, *Goal of Our Instruction*, 215–16; Witherington, *Women*, 121–22; Boomsma, *Male and Female*, 71–72; Motyer, "Expounding 1 Timothy," 95–96.

124. Payne, "Surrejoinder," 104–8; cf. Boomsma, *Male and Female*, 72–73; Motyer, "Expounding 1 Timothy," 96. Even though Hurley (*Man and Woman*, 201) and Saucy ("Women's Prohibition," 90) have a very different view of the interpretation of the text, they affirm that there are not two distinct commands here.

125. See his chapter in this volume.

126. So also Gritz, *Mother Goddess*, 131; Moo, "1 Timothy 2:11–15," 68; Fung, "Ministry," 199. Fung's suggestion that "nor is she to exercise authority over men" is parenthetical is not persuasive. The Kroegers' suggestion (*I Suffer Not a Woman*, 37–38, 79–80, 189–92), which they ultimately back away from, that οὐδέ and the words that follow may introduce the object of the infinitive διδάσκειν is, if I can put it kindly, fantastic. They did not pay heed to remarks of Walter L. Liefeld (in his response to Catherine Kroeger in *Women, Authority and the Bible*, ed. A. Mickelsen [Downers Grove: InterVarsity, 1986], 246) on this question.

127. So also Gritz, *Mother Goddess*, 134–35.

2:2). The only exception is Titus 1:11, where the context clarifies that false teaching is the object. But no indication is given in the text that false teaching is what is proscribed for women,[128] and thus the verse should be translated as follows, "But I do not permit a woman to teach a man or to exercise authority over a man, but [I want her] to be silent."

The Reason for the Prohibition

Why does Paul command women to learn silently and submissively and forbid them from teaching or exercising authority over men? The reason is provided in verse 13: "For Adam was formed first, then Eve." The second creation account from Genesis 2:4–25 is clearly the text Paul has in mind, for there we find the narrative of Adam being created before Eve.[129] The use of the word "form" (πλάσσω; cf. Gen. 2:7, 8, 15, 19) instead of ποιέω (make; cf. Gen. 1:26–27) also indicates that the reference is to the second creation account in Genesis. The proscription on women teaching men, then, does not stem from the fall and cannot be ascribed to the curse. Paul appeals to the created order, the good and perfect world God has made, to justify the ban on women teaching men.[130] Gordon Fee has recently seemed to suggest that Paul is not appealing to the created order here,[131] but his objections fly in the face of the clear meaning of the text. The created order is invoked; the question is whether this constitutes verses 11–12 as a universal principle.

Those who adhere to the progressive position argue that the γάρ (for) introducing verses 13–14 does not give *reasons* why women should not teach; instead, *illustrations* or *examples* are provided of what happens when women falsely teach men.[132] This understanding of the γάρ is sin-

---

128. Contra the Kroegers, *I Suffer Not a Woman*, 60, 81; rightly Wolters, "Review: *I Suffer Not*," 210. It is surprising that they still maintain this view because Liefeld in his response to Catherine Kroeger (in *Women*, 245) rightly protested that διδάσκειν did not mean "to teach error."

129. J. L. Houlden (*The Pastoral Epistles: I and II Timothy, Titus* [TPINTC; Philadelphia: Trinity Press International, 1976], 71) is mistaken, therefore, in saying that 1 Tim. 2:13 represents contemporary Jewish exegesis of Gen. 3:16–19. Genesis 3 is appealed to in v. 14, not v. 13.

130. So Barnett, "1 Timothy 2:11–15," 234; Barrett, *Pastoral Epistles*, 56; Clark, *Man and Woman*, 191; Culver, "Traditional View," 36; Foh, *Women and the Word of God*, 127; idem, "Male Headship," 82; Fung, "Ministry," 201; Hurley, *Man and Woman*, 205; Joachim Jeremias, *Die Briefe an Timotheus und Titus* (NTD; Göttingen: Vandenhoeck & Ruprecht, 1968), 19; Knight, *Pastoral Epistles*, 142–43; Moo, "1 Timothy 2:11–15," 68; idem, "Rejoinder," 203; idem, "What Does It Mean?" 190–91; Roloff, *Timotheus*, 138.

131. Fee, *Gospel and Spirit*, 61–62.

132. Gritz, *Mother Goddess*, 136; Mickelsen, "Egalitarian View," 203; Padgett, "Wealthy Women," 25; Payne, "Libertarian Women," 176; idem, "Surrejoinder," 111; Scholer, "1 Timothy 2:9–15," 208; Witherington, *Women*, 122.

gularly unconvincing. When Paul gives a command elsewhere in the Pastoral Epistles, the γάρ that follows almost invariably states the reason for the command (1 Tim. 4:7–8, 16; 5:4, 11, 15, 18; 2 Tim. 1:6–7; 2:7, 16; 3:5–6; 4:3, 5–6, 9–10, 11, 15; Titus 3:1–3, 9, 12).[133] So, too, a command is given in verses 11–12 and the reasons for the command are enunciated in verses 13–14.[134] Frankly, this is just what we would expect since even in ordinary speech reasons often follow commands. The implausibility of the progressive view is sealed when we begin to probe how verse 13 functions as an example. Alan Padgett interprets the verse in a highly allegorical manner to yield an illustrative sense, even though such an allegory is scarcely apparent in the text.[135] Padgett says that the text is typological; Eve functions as a type of the rich Ephesian women and Adam as a type of the teachers. Thus, the teachers, like Adam, are formed first in the spiritual sense of being older in the faith and possessing a more accurate understanding of the Old Testament. This is certainly a creative reading of the text, but it does not qualify as serious exegesis. Rather, such an approach is reminiscent of Philo's allegories on the Old Testament.

The historic view has the virtue of adopting the simplest reading of the text. Paul maintains that the Genesis narrative gives a reason why women should not teach men, namely, Adam was created first and then Eve. In other words, when Paul read Genesis 2, he concluded that the order in which Adam and Eve were created signalled an important difference in the role of men and women. Thus, he inferred from the order of creation in Genesis 2 that women should not teach or exercise authority over men. It is customary nowadays for evangelical scholars to claim that a distinction between the roles of men and women cannot be justified from Genesis.[136] But many remain unpersuaded by their exegesis because it seems quite apparent both from 1 Timothy 2:13 and 1 Corinthians 11:8–9 that Paul interpreted Genesis 2 to posit legitimate role differences between men and women.[137] A difference in role or function does not imply that women are inferior to men.[138] The Son will

133. See esp. the evidence Moo ("Rejoinder," 202–3) has marshalled in support of this thesis.

134. Contra Fee (*1 Timothy*, 73) evidence is lacking that the reasons provided in vv. 13–14 support vv. 9–10 as well as vv. 11–12.

135. Padgett, "Wealthy Women," 26–27; cf. Perriman, "What Eve Did," 140. For a more restrained use of typology, see Wiebe, "1 Tim 2:11–15," 60–61.

136. E.g., Bilezikian, *Beyond Sex Roles*, 258–59; Keener, *Women's Ministry*, 116; Kroegers, *I Suffer Not a Woman*, 18.

137. On 1 Cor. 11:8–9, see my comments in "Head Coverings," 133–34.

138. Contra Robert Falconer, "1 Timothy 2:14–15: Interpretive Notes," *Journal of Biblical Literature* 60 (1941): 375; A. T. Hanson, *The Pastoral Epistles* (NCB; Grand Rapids: Eerdmans, 1982), 73; Brox, *Pastoralbriefe*, 134–35; Spîcq, *Epîtres pastorales*, 380; Holtz, *Pastoralbriefe*, 70; Houlden, *Pastoral Epistles*, 65; Kelly, *Pastoral Epistles*, 68.

submit to the Father (1 Cor. 15:28), and yet he is equal to the Father in essence, dignity, and personhood.[139] It is a modern, democratic, Western notion that diverse functions suggest distinctions in worth between men and women. Paul believed that men and women were equal in personhood, dignity, and value but also taught that women had a distinct role from men.

Progressives back away from verse 13 because it calls into question the exegetical edifice they have built to justify women teaching men. For example, Mary Evans says that the relevance of verse 13 for verse 12 is unclear, and that verse 13 merely introduces the next verse about Eve.[140] Gordon Fee asserts that the verse is not central to Paul's argument.[141] Timothy Harris says that the verse "is difficult to understand on any reading."[142] Craig Keener thinks that the argument here is hard to fathom.[143] David Scholer protests that the text is unclear, and that Paul cites selectively from Genesis.[144] Steve Motyer says that logic and justice are nullified if the historic position of verses 13–14 is accepted.[145] It seems that unclarity is in the eye of the beholder, for the thrust of the verse has been deemed quite clear in the history of the church. The creation of Adam first gives a reason why men should be the authoritative teachers in the church. James Hurley notes that the reasoning would not be obscure to people of Paul's time, for they were quite familiar with primogeniture.[146] Even progressives acknowledge that role differences were very common in ancient societies. The original readers would have understood Paul, then, to defend such role differences, and he does so on the basis of the created order. In other words, Paul thinks such differences are good and proper and not the result of sin or the fall. Scholer's observation that Genesis is cited in a selective manner is irrelevant. Douglas Moo rightly observes that the Old Testament is *always* cited selectively.[147] The question is how the citation fits into the flow of the argument in which it is used.

Some scholars contend that Paul's interpretation here is forced and illogical.[148] This position at least has the virtue of understanding the

---

139. For further discussion on this point, see Schreiner, "Head Coverings," 128–30.

140. Evans, *Woman in the Bible*, 104.

141. Fee, *Gospel and Spirit*, 58.

142. Harris, "Eve's Deception," 343.

143. Keener, *Women's Ministry*, 116.

144. Scholer, "1 Timothy 2:9–15," 208–13.

145. Motyer, "Expounding 1 Timothy," 97–98. He finally resolves the issue (p. 100) by accepting the Kroegers' understanding of v. 13.

146. Hurley, *Man and Woman*, 207–8.

147. Moo, "What Does It Mean?" 498, n. 32.

148. Hanson, *Pastoral Epistles*, 72; Jewett, *Male and Female*, 116, 126; Krijn A. van der Jagt, "Women Are Saved Through Bearing Children (1 Timothy 2.11–15)," *The Bible Translator* 39 (1988): 205.

Pauline intention and meaning, even though his argument is rejected as inferior. My purpose is not to engage in an apologetic for the Pauline position here; it should simply be noted that most evangelicals have a higher view of biblical authority than these scholars. We should not miss, however, that these scholars agree exegetically with the historic position, although they see a contradiction with Pauline teaching elsewhere because of their own philosophical commitments.

Many scholars suggest that the reason women could not teach men is because they were promulgating the heresy or were uneducated.[149] This theory cannot be exegetically validated because it reads something into the text that is not present. Paul could have easily said that the women were prohibited from teaching because they were spreading the heresy or were uneducated.[150] Yet he does not breathe a word about these matters. Instead, he appeals to the created order. Those scholars who posit that false teaching or lack of education was the reason for the prohibition upon women ignore the reason the text actually gives (the created order) and insert what is not said in the text (false teaching and lack of education) to explain the proscription. I do not deny that women were influenced by the false teaching (1 Tim. 5:11–15; 2 Tim. 3:6–9), and it is even possible (though not certain) that some of the women were teaching the heresy.[151] But this alone does not explain the Pauline wording here. If both men and women were involved in the heresy, why does Paul forbid only the women from teaching men?[152] If the reason for the limitation were participation in the heresy or lack of education, then we would expect Paul, as a good egalitarian, to prohibit all men and women, who were spreading the heresy or who were uneducated, from teaching. This point is particularly important because we know without a doubt from the Pastoral Epistles that men were spreading the heresy (1 Tim. 1:20; 2 Tim. 2:17–18; 3:5–9). Yet he forbids only women from teaching. As Don Carson says about another text, the Pauline limitation on women would only be sensible if *"all* the women and *only* women . . . were duped—which perhaps I may be excused for finding hard to believe."[153]

Philip Towner says the real point of the passage is that one must adapt to societal norms and institutions, but this can take place as time

---

149. Barron, "Women in Their Place," 455; Bilezikian, *Beyond Sex Roles*, 180–81; Gritz, *Mother Goddess*, 137–38; Kroegers, *I Suffer Not a Woman*, 113, 117, 120–25; Mickelsen, "Egalitarian View," 204; Payne, "Libertarian Women," 176, 185–91; idem, "Surrejoinder," 96; Scholer, "1 Timothy 2:9–15," 218.

150. Rightly Moo, "Rejoinder," 203; idem, "What Does It Mean?" 193.

151. Towner (*Goal of Our Instruction*, 39, 216) cautions that the evidence is insufficient to prove that women were teaching the heresy.

152. Rightly Moo, "Rejoinder," 203.

153. Carson, "Silent in the Churches," 147.

progresses.[154] Once again, though, he leaps over the argument given to provide one not stated in the text. Towner's view is attractive, but the appeal to creation shows that the Pauline proscription here is not just part of societal norms but is rooted in the created order. Richard Longenecker avers that redemption transcends creation, and thus creational norms are not necessarily binding.[155] Again, this would neatly solve the problem, but it stumbles on the stubborn fact that Paul himself apparently did not believe redemption in Christ overturned the created order. We must bypass Paul, then, to say that redemption transcends creation in the relationship between men and women. Those who erase the distinction in roles between men and women in the present age are probably guilty of falling prey to a form of overrealized eschatology, for the creational order established with reference to men and women will be terminated in the coming age (cf. Matt. 22:30).

Others protest that we are selective in what we accept as universally valid.[156] We do not, for instance, command all younger widows to marry (1 Tim. 5:14), and little is said today about the applicability of 1 Timothy 5:3–16. We all have blind spots and thus we need to beware of bracketing out texts that are distasteful to us. Perhaps we have not been serious enough about applying 1 Timothy 5:3–16 to our culture. But if we have been avoiding the message of this passage, it does not logically follow from this that we can also jettison the prescriptions in 1 Timothy 2:9–15. Our responsibility in such a situation is to obey both texts. A full exegesis of 1 Timothy 5:3–16 cannot be engaged in here, but it seems that one principle in the text is that godly widows in financial need, who can no longer support themselves, need to be supported by the church. If widows in our churches need financial help, then the church should provide it. Bruce Waltke rightly observes that Paul's authorial intent must be gleaned in his advice to the younger widows (1 Tim. 5:11–15).[157] He recommends marriage for the younger widows to restrict sexual sin (cf. 1 Cor. 7:9). One principle here is that believers should not pledge themselves to a life of celibacy without taking into account the strength of their sexual desires. Paul commends the single state (1 Cor. 7), but even then (vv. 2, 9) he recognizes that sexual desires may be one indication that one should marry. In any case, the prohibition in 1 Timothy 2:12 is grounded by an appeal to creation, indicating that the command has universal validity.

154. Towner, *Goal of Our Instruction*, 219, 221. For an argument that is similar in some respects, see Wiebe, "1 Tim. 2:11–15," 71–79.

155. Richard N. Longenecker, *New Testament Social Ethics for Today* (Grand Rapids: Eerdmans, 1984), 70–93.

156. Fee, *1 Timothy*, 77; idem, *Gospel and Spirit*, 59–61; Scholer, "1 Timothy 2:9–15," 214.

157. Bruce K. Waltke, "1 Timothy 2:8–15: Unique or Normative?" *Crux* 28 (1992): 26.

Ronald Pierce, in dependence on Sherwood Lingenfelter, asserts that women are often banned from ministry on the basis of verse 13 because we assume that Paul is using Western logic when he is actually using "practical logic."[158] Lingenfelter says that Paul taps into the "generative core of beliefs" to justify his prohibition. But how does labeling this "practical logic" show that the prohibition is no longer applicable? If this represents Paul's "generative core of beliefs," on what basis do we discard it today? Interestingly, Pierce slides from this observation to the thesis that Paul wanted women to practice humility and patience as they slowly moved from their lowly status to their new liberty in Christ.[159] But Pierce reads this latter idea into the text, for it is hardly apparent from verses 13–14 that Paul envisions a time when the restriction in verse 12 will be lifted.[160]

One might object, however, that not all commands rooted in creation are normative. Paul commends food and marriage as good since they are grounded in creation (1 Tim. 4:1–5), yet we know from 1 Corinthians 7 and Romans 14–15/1 Corinthians 8–10 that in some situations he counsels believers to abstain from marriage or certain foods. Is this not an indication that an appeal to creation is not necessarily normative? Actually a subtle equivocation has occurred in such an objection. What Paul argues in 1 Timothy 4:1–5 is that all foods and marriage are good, *not that one must eat all foods and must get married*. Thus, the fact that some believers are called to celibacy or should abstain from certain foods in particular situations hardly constitutes an exception to the argument from creation in 1 Timothy 4:1–5. In 1 Corinthians 7 Paul continues to maintain that marriage is good and counters the idea that marriage and sexual relations must be eschewed. Moreover, in Romans 14–15/1 Corinthians 8–10 those who abstain from certain foods are even considered weak in faith, and the strong must abstain occasionally so as not to offend the weak. What would violate the principle of 1 Timothy 4:1–5 is if one were to argue that marriage and certain foods were always to be avoided because they were inherently defiling, and this is precisely what the false teachers in the Pastoral Epistles were saying.

Even if we were to accept the analogous argument from 1 Timothy 4:1–5, so that the argument from creation in 1 Timothy 2:11–13 admits

158. Pierce, "Gender Roles," 350.

159. Ibid., 350–51.

160. Indeed, Pierce is actually the one who falls prey to Western logic, for his whole thesis depends on the view that Gal. 3:28 sits awkwardly with the restrictions in 1 Tim. 2:11–15. He finds this difficult because he has imbibed deeply the Western view of equality, which perceives any differences in function as a threat to equality. This is remarkably different from the biblical worldview, in which equality of personhood did not rule out differences in role and function. Once we grasp how dissimilar the Western view of equality is from the conception of equality in the Scriptures, then we can understand why this issue is so pressing in our time and was not as troubling for people in previous centuries.

exceptions, the conclusion progressives want to draw from the parallel does not follow logically. For at least in the case of 1 Timothy 4:1–5 the principle of the goodness of the created world stands, whereas in the case of 1 Timothy 2:13 progressives would have to argue that the exception exists when women are prohibited from teaching men, but the norm permits them to do so. In the case of 1 Timothy 2, then, the appeal to the created order would justify *the exception*, not the rule. The parallel from 1 Timothy 4:1–5 falters on this analysis because in that text the created order is invoked to support the *rule*, not the exception. In other words, Paul supports the idea that women cannot teach men by invoking the created order, and yet progressives who would use this argument do not say that women may in some exceptional circumstances teach men (in analogy with the argument from 1 Tim. 4:1–5). Instead, they insist that prohibiting women from teaching men is the exception. The analogy from 1 Timothy 4:1–5, therefore, is turned around. And if women can usually teach men, we are left wondering why an argument from creation is given at all. In principle, one could similarly argue that the prohibitions against polygamy and homosexuality are exceptional, even though an argument from creation is used to support the commands (Matt. 19:4–6 par.; Rom. 1:26–27). The fundamental problem with this suggestion, then, is that it provides no explanation as to why an argument from creation is given. It appeals to alleged exceptions and renders no account as to why Paul appeals to a creational norm. This seems to be a clear case of evading the positive reason given for the prohibition.

Perhaps we can preserve the principle of the command in verse 12 without denying women the right to teach men. After all, it was argued that the principle underlying verses 9–10 permits women to wear jewelry and clothing that is not seductive or ostentatious. However, the principle in verse 12 cannot be separated from the practice of teaching or exercising authority over men.[161] There are some instances in which the principle and practice (e.g., polygamy and homosexuality) coalesce. This is one of those cases. Public teaching of men by women and the concomitant authority it gives them violate the principle of male leadership.

The Argument from the Woman Being Deceived

If verse 13 is a strong argument for the historic view, progressives declaim that verse 14 is quite problematic for the historic position.[162] For

---

161. So Moo, "What Does It Mean?" 191; Köstenberger, "Gender Passages," 270.
162. Note, for example, how Fee (*1 Timothy*, 74; *Gospel and Spirit*, 58) says that Paul's real purpose in citing the Genesis narrative emerges here (cf. Witherington, *Women*, 123; Evans, *Woman in the Bible*, 104). One wonders, then, why he bothered appealing to the

instance, Towner notes that the former position would seem to lead to the conclusion that women are more easily deceived and gullible than men.[163] Bruce Barron says that the historic position cannot explain how Adam was not deceived, for he was as guilty as Eve.[164] And if Adam sinned rebelliously with his eyes wide open, and Eve sinned because she was deceived, then why would this qualify men to teach women? It would seem the more serious sin would be the blatant rebellion practiced by Adam, and thus men would be disqualified from teaching. Progressives believe they have a much more credible solution to the meaning of this verse. They argue that the reference to Eve's deception points either to women being responsible for the heresy or to the influence of false teachers on women and/or their lack of education.[165] It is suggested, for instance, that Adam knew of God's prohibition in the garden firsthand, while Eve only knew the command secondhand. Thus, Eve sinned because she was ignorant of God's command, and so too the women in Ephesus were being deceived by the false teachers and, in turn, were propagating the heresy. They could not teach until they were adequately educated.

Doubtless the verse is difficult, but I would like to suggest that defenders of the progressive view actually have a weaker interpretation of the text than defenders of the historic interpretation. It cannot be stressed emphatically enough that verse 14 scarcely justifies the thesis that women were *teaching* the heresy, although it is likely that the prohibition is given because some women were teaching men.[166] Neither Genesis nor Paul suggests that Eve taught Adam. Instead, both texts affirm that she was deceived (cf. Gen. 3:13).[167] The emphasis is on what transpired in Eve's heart—deception—not on the fact that she wrongly taught Adam. Verse 14, therefore, does not provide any clue that

---

order of creation at all. Fung ("Ministry," 338, n. 204) observes that if v. 13 is merely an introduction to the substantial argument, it could have easily been jettisoned.

163. Towner, *Goal of Our Instruction*, 217; Barron, "Women in Their Place," 455.

164. Barron, "Women in Their Place," 455.

165. Bilezikian, *Beyond Sex Roles*, 180, 259; Perriman, "What Eve Did," 139; Evans, *Woman in the Bible*, 105; Gritz, *Mother Goddess*, 140; Harris, "Eve's Deception," 345, 347–50; Keener, *Women's Ministry*, 117; Kroegers, *I Suffer Not a Woman*, 237–42; Payne, "Libertarian Women," 177, 182; 112; Scholer, "1 Timothy 2:9–15," 195–200, 210–11; Spencer, "Eve at Ephesus," 219–20. Of course, not every scholar here describes the situation in precisely the same way, but the common elements in their reconstruction are striking.

166. Rightly Hugenberger, "Women in Church Office," 349–50; Moo, "Rejoinder," 217; idem, "What Does It Mean?" 189–90.

167. The prepositional prefix could indicate that Eve was completely deceived (ἐξαπατάω), whereas the verb used in reference to Adam is simply ἀπατάω. More likely, though, the shift to ἐξαπατάω is stylistic and no significance should be ascribed to the change (cf. Knight, *Pastoral Epistles*, 144; Moo, "1 Timothy 2:11–15," 69). In support of this latter conclusion, Gen. 3:13 uses the verb ἀπατάω.

women were forbidden from teaching because they were spreading the heresy. Verse 14 can only be used by progressives to say that the women of Ephesus—like Eve—were *influenced* by false teaching, and thus fell into sin. Progressives can only reasonably argue, therefore, that the women in Ephesus were prohibited from teaching because they were temporarily deceived by the false teachers, and they could function as teachers later on by acquiring sound doctrine. But again it must be emphasized that verse 14 does not provide any evidence that women were promulgating false teaching.

Neither does the appeal to the Genesis narrative in verse 14 support the idea that women were disallowed from teaching merely because they were duped by false teaching or uneducated. If Eve was at a disadvantage in the temptation, as some progressives declare, because she received the commandment from God secondhand through Adam, then the implication is that Adam somehow muddled God's command in giving it to Eve. If he gave it to her accurately and clearly, then we are back to the view that Eve (before the fall!) could not grasp what Adam clearly said, which would imply that she was intellectually inferior. But if Adam bungled what God said, so that Eve was deceived by the serpent, the argument of 1 Timothy 2:11–15 makes little sense in its historical context. For then Eve was deceived because Adam muddled God's instructions. And if Eve sinned because a man communicated God's command inaccurately, then why would Paul recommend here that men should teach women until the latter get their doctrine right? If a man teaching a woman is what got the human race into this predicament in the first place, Paul's appeal to Eve's being deceived would be incoherent and would not fit the argument he is attempting to make in 1 Timothy 2.

What I am suggesting is that progressives, who often complain that the proponents of the historic view cannot handle verse 14, are actually in an even more indefensible position. The verse cannot be used to say that women were teaching the heresy. Nor does it make sense to say that women were deceived because they lacked knowledge. Such a view would pin the blame on Adam as a teacher, not Eve. If such were Paul's understanding of the events associated with the fall, his admonition that men should teach women (even temporarily) on the basis of the Genesis narrative would be incoherent.

Moreover, the author of Genesis is not suggesting that Eve was at a disadvantage because she was ignorant of or poorly instructed in God's command (Gen. 3:2–3).[168] What Genesis 3 indicates (and Paul is a careful

---

168. I do not think that the addition of the words "or touch it" in Gen. 3:3 represents a distortion of God's command. Even if it does, this would hardly help progressives. We are faced again with the scenario I just traced. Either Eve distorted God's command on her own or Adam bungled what God said.

interpreter of the account here in 1 Tim. 2:14) is that the serpent deceived Eve, not Adam. We should not read into the narrative that Eve was at any disadvantage in terms of knowledge during the temptation. Deceit may occur because of lack of knowledge or education, but Genesis does not attribute Eve's deception to her being uneducated. Indeed, the idea that sin originated because of ignorance is a Platonic view, not a biblical one. The serpent deceived Eve by promising her that she could function as a god, independent of the one true God (Gen. 3:4–6). Eve was deceived not because she had an intellectual deficiency, but because of a moral failing.

In conclusion, progressives cannot provide an interpretation of verse 14 that makes sense of the contexts of both Genesis 2–3 and 1 Timothy 2:9–15. What we need to probe is the significance of this verse in the context of 1 Timothy 2. Some scholars, depending on parallels in Jewish tradition, suggest that Eve was sexually seduced by the serpent.[169] But this is unwarranted. The appeals to Jewish parallels are unpersuasive since the latter postdate the New Testament.[170] And the word ἐξαπατάω (I deceive) elsewhere in Paul does not refer to sexual seduction (cf. Rom. 7:11; 16:18; 1 Cor. 3:18; 2 Cor. 11:3; 2 Thess. 2:3). The parallel from 2 Corinthians 11:3 is particularly illuminating, for Paul fears that the entire church will fall prey to the same deception Eve did. His concern is scarcely that the whole church will fall into sexual sin!

Others argue that the point is that Adam sinned with full knowledge and rebelliously, for the text says that "Adam was not deceived," whereas Eve was deceived and committed transgression.[171] The verse thereby signals that Adam was responsible as the leader and the religious teacher. This interpretation is surely a possibility, and it has the virtue of taking the words "Adam was not deceived" straightforwardly. Nevertheless, it is hard to see how this argument would function as a reason for men teaching women. An appeal to Adam sinning willfully and Eve sinning mistakenly (because deceived) would seem to argue against men teaching women, for at least the woman wanted to obey God, while Adam deliberately sinned.[172] This view would be strengthened if the corollary were also drawn: Paul implies that women are more prone to deceit than men. Yet most of the modern adherents of this view are reluctant to draw this latter conclusion.[173]

---

169. Dibelius and Conzelmann, *Pastoral Epistles*, 48; Houlden, *Pastoral Epistles*, 71–72; Holtz, *Pastoralbriefe*, 70; Hanson, *Pastoral Epistles*, 73; Roloff, *Timotheus*, 139; cf. Falconer, "Interpretive Notes," 376.

170. Towner, *Goal of Our Instruction*, 313–14, n. 78; cf. Gritz, *Mother Goddess*, 139; Witherington, *Women*, 123.

171. Gritz, *Mother Goddess*, 139; Guthrie, *Pastoral Epistles*, 77; Knight, *Pastoral Epistles*, 143–44; Moo, "Rejoinder," 204.

172. Cf. Fung, "Ministry," 201–2.

173. An exception here is Clark, *Man and Woman*, 202–4.

Historically, a very common interpretation is that Paul is forbidding women from teaching because they are more liable to deception, more gullible, and more easily led astray than men.[174] This interpretation is usually dismissed out of hand today because it is so shocking to modern sensibilities. Our task, though, is to interpret texts according to the intention of the author, and thus we must be careful that an interpretation is not rejected merely because it offends our sense of justice. For those who hold a high view of biblical authority the text must reign over and correct what we think is "just." This interpretation, then, is quite possible and is much less speculative than those advanced by progressives. Some features of this interpretation should be rejected since they imply that women are ontologically and intellectually inferior. Serious objections have also been raised against this view.[175] Women teaching other women and children is saluted elsewhere in the Pastorals (2 Tim. 1:5; 3:15; Titus 2:3–4). It is unlikely, critics of this view say, that Paul would commend this if women are prone to deceit by nature, for then their error would be passed on to children and other women. I will return to this issue shortly when I propose my own interpretation of the verse.

Paul Barnett intriguingly suggests that the point of the text is that Adam was not deceived first, but Eve was deceived first.[176] The word "first" (πρῶτος) would be implicitly understood from verse 13. Timothy Harris rightly objects that the text does not say that Eve was deceived first, and this weakens Barnett's suggestion.[177] But Barnett's suggestion is a possibility when we recall that Paul was writing to Timothy, who was quite familiar with his theology. Paul would be reminding Timothy that Eve transgressed first, and yet Adam was held responsible for the sin that was imputed to the whole human race (Rom. 5:12–19). The reference to Eve sinning first along with the recognition that Adam bore primary responsibility for sin entering the world (note in Gen. 3 that God approached Adam first after the sin) reveals the reality of male headship. In this scenario, then, verse 14 would function as a second argument for male leadership in teaching.

The problem with the above view is that so many assumptions need to be added to the text. Gordon Fee makes a suggestion that is more

174. Jewett, *Male and Female*, 61; Clark, *Man and Woman*, 203–4; Culver, "Traditional View," 36–37; Hanson, *Pastoral Epistles*, 73 (but he says that this proves the letter is not Pauline); Holtz, *Pastoralbriefe*, 71–72; Kelly, *Pastoral Epistles*, 68; Moo, "1 Timothy 2:11–15," 70 (but he changed his mind on this point; see "Rejoinder," 204). Daniel Doriani in the appendix of this volume argues a variant of this view.

175. For arguments against the idea that women are more gullible, see Barnett, "1 Timothy 2:11–15," 234; Evans, *Woman in the Bible*, 104–5; Foh, *Women and the Word of God*, 127; Fung, "Ministry," 201–2; Harris, "Eve's Deception," 346; Hurley, *Man and Woman*, 215; Moo, "What Does It Mean?" 190; Payne, "Libertarian Women," 175–77.

176. Barnett, "1 Timothy 2:11–15," 234.

177. Harris, "Eve's Deception," 346.

fruitful in terms of a solution.[178] What Paul emphasizes is that it was Eve (not Adam) who was deceived *by the serpent*. Thus, we need not conclude that Adam was undeceived in every respect, or that he was without sin. The latter would contradict Romans 5:12–19, and the former is hard to understand in any case, for it seems that all sin involves deceit. Do people sin with their eyes wide open, understanding the nature and consequences of their sin? Paul's purpose is more restricted here. He wants to focus on the fact that the serpent approached and deceived Eve, not Adam. The significance of the serpent targeting Eve is magnified, for apparently Adam was with Eve (Gen. 3:6) during the temptation.[179] In approaching Eve, then, the serpent subverted the pattern of male leadership and interacted only with Eve during the temptation.[180] Adam was present throughout and did not intervene. The Genesis temptation, therefore, is a parable of what happens when male leadership is abrogated.[181] Eve took the initiative in responding to the serpent, and Adam let her do so. Thus, the appeal to Genesis 3 serves as a reminder of what happens when God's ordained pattern is undermined.[182]

But the explanation cannot stop here as Daniel Doriani rightly explains in more detail in appendix 1.[183] God's order of creation is mirrored in the nature of men and women. Satan approached the woman first not only because of the order of creation but also because of the different inclinations present in Adam and Eve. Generally speaking, women are more relational and nurturing and men are more given to rational analysis and objectivity. Women are less prone than men to see the importance of doctrinal formulations, especially when it comes to the issue of identifying heresy and making a stand for the truth. Appointing women to the teaching office is prohibited because they are less likely to draw a line on doctrinal non-negotiables, and thus deception and false teaching will more easily enter the church. This is not to say women are intellectually deficient or inferior to men. If women were intellectually inferior, Paul would not allow them to teach women and children. What concerns him are the consequences of allowing women in the authoritative teaching office, for their gentler and kinder nature inhibits them from excluding people for doctrinal error. There

178. Fee, *1 Timothy*, 74; idem, *Gospel and Spirit*, 59; cf. Moo, "1 Timothy 2:11–15," 69. I realize Fee would not agree with the conclusions I draw from his observation.

179. Rightly Scholer, "1 Timothy 2:9–15," 210.

180. Oden remarks (*First Timothy*, 100) that the rabbis believed that the fall also included a reversal of the creation order, in that Eve took the leadership over Adam.

181. For a similar suggestion in some respects, see Fung, "Ministry," 202; Hurley, *Man and Woman*, 214–16; Moo, "Rejoinder," 204.

182. Cf. Moo, "What Does It Mean?" 190.

183. My own understanding of this verse was changed upon reading Daniel Doriani's exegesis in appendix 1. I refer readers to his discussion for a more extended explanation.

is the danger of stereotyping here, for obviously some women are more inclined to objectivity and are "tougher" and less nurturing than other women. But as a general rule women are more relational and caring than men. This explains why most women have many more close friends than men. The different inclinations of women (and men!) do not imply that they are inferior or superior to men. It simply demonstrates that men and women are profoundly different. Women have some strengths that men do not have, and men have some strengths that are generally lacking in women. Some people become enraged at any suggestion that men and women have different strengths and weaknesses, but interestingly enough, as Doriani observes, many feminists are now arguing that men and women have different inclinations. To sum up: The traditional view of verse 14, when shorn of any misogynistic implications, is not far from the mark. Women are prohibited from the teaching office not only because of the order of creation but also because they are less likely to preserve the apostolic tradition in inhabiting the teaching office.

Women Being Saved through Childbirth

Verse 15 literally reads, "But she shall be saved through childbirth, if they remain in faith and love and sanctification along with discretion." Susan Foh's opinion that the verse is "a puzzle and a sort of non sequitur" is unsatisfying, for the verse functions as the conclusion to the paragraph and must be integrated with the rest of the argument.[184] On the other hand, some scholars think that this verse is climactic, the key to the whole text.[185] This latter opinion goes to the other extreme. It is better to take the verse as providing a qualification to what is said in verse 14 and as rounding out the argument.[186]

Many questions emerge from this verse.[187] What is the subject of the verbs σωθήσεται (she shall be saved) and μείνωσιν (they remain)? Does the verb σωθήσεται refer to spiritual salvation or preservation through childbirth? What does the noun τεκνογονία (childbirth) refer to: the birth of Christ, rearing children, or bearing children? What is the precise meaning in this context of the preposition διά? Does this text teach salvation by works? How does it fit with the rest of the paragraph?

184. Foh, *Women and the Word of God*, 128.
185. Keener, *Women's Ministry*, 118; Scholer, "1 Timothy 2:9–15," 196.
186. Cf. Clark, *Man and Woman*, 207; Gritz, *Mother Goddess*, 141; Stanley E. Porter, "What Does It Mean to Be 'Saved by Childbirth' (1 Timothy 2.15)?" *Journal for the Study of the New Testament* 49 (1993): 93.
187. Of course, the verse is difficult and debated. One should not conclude that the interpretation of v. 15 proposed below is necessary for the understanding of vv. 11–14 that has been argued for in this chapter.

We will begin by examining the meaning of the verb σωθήσεται. Some understand it to mean "preserve," so that the verse says that women shall be preserved safely through childbirth.[188] Craig Keener defends this interpretation by appealing to parallels in Greco-Roman literature, where women often prayed for safety in childbirth; the verb σώζω (save) most commonly bears the idea of physical preservation.[189] This interpretation should be rejected for at least two reasons. The fact that Christian women have often died in childbirth raises serious questions about this interpretation.[190] More important, σώζω always has the meaning of spiritual salvation in the Pastoral Epistles (cf. 1 Tim. 1:5; 2:4; 4:16; 2 Tim. 1:9; 4:18; Titus 3:5) and the other Pauline writings.[191] Keener commits the error of making the meaning of the term in other writings more important than in the Pauline writings. In addition, since σώζω always refers to eschatological salvation in Paul, it is also not compelling to say that women "are saved" from the error of usurping authority over men by keeping to their proper function.[192] Once again a definition is supplied for σώζω that does not accord with the Pauline usage. In addition, verse 12 is too far from verse 15 for this latter interpretation to be plausible.[193] The difficulty of this verse, therefore, cannot be swept aside by finding a different meaning for σώζω; the verse does say that a woman will be spiritually saved through bearing children.

Perhaps the biting edge of this verse can be explained by investigat-

188. NASB; Barrett, *Pastoral Epistles*, Barron, "Women in Their Place," 457; Jewett, *Male and Female*, 60; Keener, *Women's Ministry*, 118–19.

189. Keener, *Women's Ministry*, 118–19.

190. Cf. Evans, *Woman in the Bible*, 106; Gritz, *Mother Goddess*, 141; Hilde Huizenga, "Women, Salvation, and the Birth of Christ: A Reexamination of 1 Timothy 2:15," *Studia Biblica et Theologica* 12 (1982): 21; Oden, *First Timothy*, 100.

191. So Gritz, *Mother Goddess*, 141; Fung, "Ministry," 203; Houlden, *Pastoral Epistles*, 72; David R. Kimberly, "1 Timothy 2:15: A Possible Understanding of a Difficult Text," *Journal of the Evangelical Society* 35 (1992) 481–82; Krijn van der Jagt, "Women Are Saved through Bearing Children: A Sociological Approach to the Interpretation of 1 Timothy 2.15," in *Issues in Bible Translation*, ed. Philip C. Stine; UBSMS 3 (New York: United Bible Societies, 1988), 293; Lock, *Pastoral Epistles*, 31; Moo, "1 Timothy 2:11–15," 71; idem, "What Does It Mean?" 192; Payne, "Libertarian Women," 178; Porter, "Saved by Childbirth," 93–94.

192. So S. Jebb, "A Suggested Interpretation of 1 Ti 2.15," *Expository Times* 81 (1970): 221–22; Hurley, *Man and Woman*, 222. Against this interpretation, see Fee, *1 Timothy*, 75; Hanson, *Pastoral Epistles*, 74; Kimberly, "1 Tim 2:15," 482; Porter, "Saved by Childbirth," 95; Roloff, *Timotheus*, 141.

193. The same error is committed by Roberts ("1 Timothy 2:15," 6–7) who adopts a nonsoteriological definition for σώζω. Roberts' interpretation is even more arbitrary. He says by giving birth to the Messiah (and continuing in the faith) women will be saved from their subordinate role, and thus can be restored to teaching men. There is no evidence, however, that Paul contemplated that the "saving" in v. 15 involved liberation from the injunctions in vv. 11–12!

ing the meaning of the word τεκνογονίας. A common view in the history of the church is to detect a reference to the birth of Christ.[194] The near context is invoked by supporters of this reading, for the reference to the deceit and transgression of Eve (v. 14) is qualified by the promise that she will be saved by the childbirth, that is, the birth of Christ. Since Paul had just cited Genesis 3 in verse 14, it is argued that he would have naturally turned to the promise of salvation through the seed promised in Genesis 3:15. The singular "she" could be ascribed to Eve as the representative of all women, or to Mary who gave birth to the Messiah. The definite article τῆς (the) preceding τεκνογονίας is also cited to defend the idea that Paul was thinking of the birth of Christ.[195]

The unpalatable flavor of this verse would certainly be removed if it says that salvation comes through the birth of Christ. This view, unfortunately, is quite improbable. Anthony Hanson says that it "is more romantic than convincing."[196] Donald Guthrie trenchantly observes that Paul "could hardly have chosen a more obscure or ambiguous way of saying it."[197]One must also slide from seeing Eve as the subject of σωθήσεται to Mary, but to read the latter into the verse is highly arbitrary.[198] Moreover, even if we accept Mary as the subject, the meaning is still problematic. Mary was not saved by virtue of giving birth to Jesus, nor does Paul elsewhere say that salvation is through the incarnation. The noun τεκνογονία emphasizes the actual giving birth to a child, not the result or effect of childbirth.[199] Those who posit a reference to Jesus' birth have subtly introduced the notion that salvation is secured as a *result* of giving birth to him, whereas the text speaks not of the result of birth but the actual birthing process. A defense of the christological interpretation cannot be sustained by the presence of the article. The article is notoriously perplexing in Greek since it has a wide range of uses and is thereby difficult to categorize definitively. Thus, we should be wary of concluding that the presence of the article

194. For references in the early fathers, see Porter, "Saved by Childbirth," 90, n. 8. Recent advocates of this view include Knight, *Pastoral Epistles*, 146–47; Lock, *Pastoral Epistles*, 33; Padgett, "Wealthy Women," 29; Payne, "Libertarian Women," 177–78, 180–81; Roberts, "1 Timothy 2:15," 6–7; Spencer, "Eve at Ephesus," 220; Oden, *First Timothy*, 101–2; Huizenga, "Birth of Christ," 17–26.

195. Huizenga, "Birth of Christ," 22; Oden, *First Timothy*, 102; Payne, "Libertarian Women," 180–81.

196. Hanson, *Pastoral Epistles*, 74.

197. Guthrie, *Pastoral Epistles*, 78; cf. Evans, *Woman in the Bible*, 107; Fee, *1 Timothy*, 75; Foh, *Women and the Word of God*, 128; Gritz, *Mother Goddess*, 141; Hurley, *Man and Woman*, 222; Kelly, *Pastoral Epistles*, 69; Moo, "1 Timothy 2:11–15," 71; Porter, "Saved by Childbirth," 92.

198. Keener, *Women's Ministry*, 118; Porter, "Saved by Childbirth," 92; Dibelius and Conzelmann, *Pastoral Epistles*, 48; Brox, *Pastoralbriefe*, 136.

199. Cf. Fee, *1 Timothy*, 75.

indicates particular reference to Christ's birth.[200] The article is probably generic in any case.[201] A reference to the birth of Christ, although
immensely attractive, must be rejected. Neither is it persuasive to see
in the word τεκνογονία the idea of rearing children.[202] The word
τεκνοτροφέω (I bring up children) was available and used in 1 Timothy
5:10 to communicate this idea, while the verbal form τεκνογονέω (I
bear children) by contrast is used in 1 Timothy 5:14 for the bearing of
children.[203]

The significance of διά is also a matter of debate. E. F. Scott tried to
soften the scandal of the verse by saying that a woman shall be saved
"in spite of" or "even though" having children.[204] Any notion of women
being saved "through" having children is excluded. Unfortunately, the
semantic range of διά is violated by this interpretation, and thus Scott's
proposal has been consistently rejected.[205] Neither is it persuasive to
see διά referring to attendant circumstances, so that women will be
saved "in the experience" of childbirth.[206] This interpretation is dictated
by theology rather than syntax.[207] Probably the common instrumental
sense of διά is intended here (cf. Titus 3:5).[208] I shall take up how this
fits with Paul's theology of salvation shortly.

Who is the subject of the verbs σωθήσεται and μείνωσιν, and why
does the tense switch from the singular to the plural? It has already
been argued above that we can eliminate the options that Eve or Mary
is the subject of σωθήσεται. The context clarifies that nonbelievers are
not included, for they will not be spiritually saved. Thus, the reference
is to the Christian women of Ephesus and by extension to all Christian
women everywhere.[209] The switch from the third singular to the third
plural is awkward.[210] It has been suggested that the third plural refers

200. For a lucid discussion of the article with warnings about misuse, see D. A Carson, *Exegetical Fallacies* (Grand Rapids: Baker, 1984), 182–88.

201. See Porter, "Saved by Childbirth," 92; Moo, "Rejoinder," 206.

202. Cf. Falconer, "Interpretive Notes," 377; Moo, "1 Timothy 2:11–15," 71–72; Brox,
Pastoralbriefe, 136; Barrett, *Pastoral Epistles*, 56–57; Jeremias, *Timotheus*, 19; Hanson,
Pastoral Epistles, 74; Spîcq, *Epîtres pastorales*, 383–84.

203. So Holtz, *Pastoralbriefe*, 70–71; Huizenga, "Birth of Christ," 18; Kimberly, "1 Tim.
2:15," 482; Payne, "Libertarian Women," 178–79; Porter, "Saved by Childbirth," 95–96.

204. E. F. Scott, *The Pastoral Epistles* (New York: Harper & Bros., n.d.), 28.

205. Cf. Evans, *Woman in the Bible*, 107; Guthrie, *Pastoral Epistles*, 78; Moo, "1 Timothy 2:11–15," 71; Porter, "Saved by Childbirth," 96–97.

206. Cf. Falconer, "Interpretive Notes," 376; Roloff, *Timotheus*, 141–42.

207. So Porter, "Saved by Childbirth," 97.

208. So Porter, "Saved by Childbirth," 97–98; Dibelius and Conzelmann, *Pastoral
Epistles*, 48; van der Jagt, "Bearing Children," 292; Moo, "1 Timothy 2:11–15," 72.

209. See Porter, "Saved by Childbirth," 101; Dibelius and Conzelmann, *Pastoral Epistles*, 48; Brox, *Pastoralbriefe*, 137; Moo, "1 Timothy 2:11–15," 71.

210. But the idea that v. 15b stems from another source is unpersuasive contra Falconer, "Interpretive Notes," 378; Hanson, *Pastoral Epistles*, 74; rightly Porter, "Saved by
Childbirth," 98.

to the children of the women, or husbands and wives.[211] It is too jarring, though, to detect a sudden reference to children or husbands here. The third singular at the beginning of the sentence refers to women generically, and thus Paul shifts to "women" plural in the latter half of the verse.[212] This fits with the structure of the passage as a whole, where Paul begins by speaking of women in the plural (vv. 9–10), shifts to the singular (11–15a), and then reverts back to the plural.[213] The singular in 15a may also be accounted for from the reference to Eve in verses 13–14, for the latter is understood as representative of all Christian women.

The discussion so far has simply established that the verse says what it appears to say on first glance, and thus the theological and contextual questions posed earlier remain.[214] If women are saved by bearing children, then is this not salvation by works and a contradiction of Pauline theology?[215] Understanding the historical situation will aid us in answering this question. The false teachers, in trumpeting an overrealized eschatology, prohibited marriage and certain foods (1 Tim. 4:1–5). If marriage was banned, then bearing children was probably also criticized.[216] Childbearing was selected by Paul, then, as a specific response to the shafts from the false teachers. Referring to childbearing is also appropriate because it represents the fulfillment of the woman's do-

211. For a reference to children, see Houlden, *Pastoral Epistles*, 72–73; Jeremias, *Timotheus*, 19; while Brox (*Pastoralbriefe*, 137) sees a reference to husbands and wives.

212. So Barrett, *Pastoral Epistles*, 57; Fung, "Ministry," 204; Gritz, *Mother Goddess*, 144; Holtz, *Pastoralbriefe*, 72; Porter, "Saved by Childbirth," 98–99; Scholer, "1 Timothy 2:9–15," 196; Towner, *Goal of Our Instruction*, 221.

213. The same shift occurs with "men." Paul begins with ἄνδρας in v. 8 and shifts to ἀνδρός in v. 12. The latter is obviously generic.

214. Pierce ("Gender Roles," 351, 353) suggests that v. 15 promises "partial healing" for women in childbirth and gives "them hope that deliverance from the curse of male dominance is also possible." This is an unconvincing interpretation. It has already been argued that the verb σωθήσεται in the Pauline literature does not refer to healing but to eschatological salvation. Thus, it does not refer to mitigating the pain of childbearing in this age. To say that the verse offers hope of deliverance from male dominance is puzzling, since nothing is said about that subject in the verse. It is certainly understandable that some would see the admonitions in these verses as having temporary validity, but one looks in vain anywhere in 1 Tim. 2:9–15 for any hint that the text is actually promising eventual deliverance from male dominance. Nowhere is male leadership *criticized!*

215. So Barron, "Women in Their Place," 457; Hanson, *Pastoral Epistles*, 74; Huizenga, "Birth of Christ," 197–98; Hurley, *Man and Woman*, 221; Knight, *Pastoral Epistles*, 145; Payne, "Libertarian Women," 179; idem, "Surrejoinder," 115; Oden, *First Timothy*, 100.

216. Many scholars have rightly seen that the reference to childbirth was precipitated by the impact of the false teachers. See Barron, "Women in Their Place," 457; Fee, *1 Timothy*, 74–75; idem, *Gospel and Spirit*, 59; Gritz, *Mother Goddess*, 143; Harris, "Eve's Deception," 350; Jeremias, *Timotheus*, 19; Kelly, *Pastoral Epistles*, 70; Kimberly, "1 Tim 2:15," 484–86; van der Jagt, "Bearing Children," 293–94; Kroegers, *I Suffer Not a Woman*, 171–77; Moo, "What Does It Mean?" 192; Padgett, "Wealthy Women," 28; Scholer, "1 Timothy 2:9–15," 197–98. It should be noted that Barron, the Kroegers, and Kimberly unfortunately read into the text gnosticism from the second century A.D.

mestic role as a mother in distinction from the man.[217] Childbearing, then, is probably selected by synecdoche as representing the appropriate role for women. This rounds out the passage because a woman should not violate her role by teaching or exercising authority over a man; instead, she should take her proper role as a mother of children. It could be argued that the reference to women bearing children is culturally limited to the domestic and maternal roles of Paul's day.[218] More likely, Paul saw in the woman's function of giving birth a divinely intended and ongoing difference of function between men and women.

This does not mean that all women must have children in order to be saved.[219] Paul is hardly attempting to be comprehensive here. He has elsewhere commended the single state (1 Cor. 7). He selects childbearing because it is the most notable example of the divinely intended difference in role between men and women, and most women throughout history have had children. Thus, Paul generalizes from the experience of most women in using a representative example of women maintaining their proper role. To select childbearing is another indication that the argument is transcultural, for childbearing is not limited to a particular culture, but is a permanent and ongoing difference between men and women. The fact that God has ordained that women and only women bear children indicates that the differences in role between men and women are rooted in the created order.

When Paul says that a woman will be saved by childbearing, he means, therefore, that they will be saved by adhering to their ordained role.[220] Such a statement is apt to be misunderstood (and often has been), and thus a further comment is added for explanation. Women will be saved "if they remain in faith and love and sanctification along with discretion." Thereby Paul shows that it is not sufficient for salvation for Christian women merely to bear children; they must also persevere in faith, love, holiness, and presumably other virtues.[221] The reference to "discretion" (σωφροσύνης) hearkens back to the same word in verse 9 and also functions to tie the entire text together.[222] Paul does not imply that all women must bear children to be saved. His purpose is to say that women will not be saved if they do not practice good works. One indica-

---

217. So Barnett, "1 Timothy 2:9–15," 235; Clark, *Man and Woman,* 207; Evans, *Woman in the Bible,* 107; Falconer, "Interpretive Notes," 377; Perriman, "What Eve Did," 140–41; Hurley, *Man and Woman,* 222–23; Kelly, *Pastoral Epistles,* 69; Padgett, "Wealthy Women," 28; Roloff, *Timotheus,* 141; Scholer, "1 Timothy 2:9–15," 197.

218. E.g., Scholer, "1 Timothy 2:9–15," 197.

219. Contra Huizenga, "Birth of Christ," 18.

220. Fung, "Ministry," 204.

221. For a careful analysis of the conditional clause used here, see Porter, "Saved by Childbirth," 99–101.

222. Cf. Barnett, "1 Timothy 2:11–15," 235 (although the chiasm he detects is not clear to me).

tion that women are in their proper role is if they do not reject bearing children as evil, but bear children in accord with their proper role.

Many will complain that this is salvation by works and contradicts Pauline theology. A contradiction with Pauline theology would only exist if the text were claiming that one must do these good works in order to *earn or merit* salvation. Elsewhere Paul insists that good works are necessary as *evidence* of a salvation already given (e.g., Rom. 2:6–10, 26–29; 1 Cor. 6:9–11; Gal. 5:21).[223] Paul is not asserting in 1 Timothy 2:15 that women *merit* salvation by bearing children and doing other good works. He has already clarified that salvation is by God's mercy and grace (cf. 1 Tim. 1:12–17). The term σωθήσεται is used rather loosely here, so that Paul does not specify in what sense women are saved by childbearing and doing other good works. I think it is fair, though, since Paul often argues elsewhere that salvation is not gained on the basis of our works (e.g., Rom. 3:19–4:25; Gal. 2:16–3:14; 2 Tim. 1:9–11; Titus 2:11–14; 3:4–7) to understand the virtues described here as *evidence* that salvation is genuine.[224]

The same problem arises in 1 Timothy 4:11–16.[225] There Paul exhorts Timothy to live a godly life ("be an example for believers in speech, in conduct, in love, in faith, in purity," v. 12) and keep instructing believers in the truth of the gospel. Paul sums up these instructions in verse 16. He says to Timothy, "Pay heed to yourself and to your teaching; remain in them." In other words, Timothy is to keep practicing the virtues specified in verse 12 and to continue instructing the church. In verse 16b a reason is supplied as to why Timothy should be virtuous and keep teaching: "For by doing this, you will save both yourself and your hearers." Once again the verb σώζω is used with reference to spiritual salvation. Paul certainly does not mean that Timothy and his hearers will be "physically preserved" if they live godly lives and continue in godly instruction. One could protest that Paul is teaching salvation by meritorious works here, since he says that Timothy and his hearers will be saved *if* they live godly lives and continue in right instruction. But this would be a mistake. What Paul means is that abiding in godly virtues and apostolic instruction constitute necessary *evidence* that one has been saved. Those who fall away have no assurance that they belong to the redeemed community (cf. 1 Cor. 9:24–10:22). Indeed, the necessity of doing good works or persevering to end in order to realize salvation is

223. For an investigation of this issue in more detail with a defense of the notion that works are necessary as an evidence of salvation, see my "Did Paul Believe in Justification by Works? Another Look at Romans 2," *Bulletin for Biblical Research* 3 (1993): 131–58.

224. So Witherington, *Women*, 124.

225. Witherington (ibid.) also notices the parallel and comments that those spoken of were already Christians.

often taught in the New Testament (cf., e.g., Heb. 2:1–4; 3:7–19; 5:11–6:12; 10:26–31; 12:25–29; James 2:14–26; 1 John 2:3–6; 2 Pet. 1:5–11).[226]

The parallel text in 1 Timothy 4:11–16 indicates that it is too simplistic to wave aside the reference to salvation by bearing children as salvation by meritorious works. Upon examining the context and historical situation carefully, we see that Paul selected childbearing because of the emphasis of the false teachers who denigrated marriage and the maternal role of women. Other virtues are added in the conditional clause to prevent misunderstanding. Salvation is not evidenced by childbirth alone. But the genuineness of salvation is indicated by a woman living a godly life and conforming to her God-ordained role. These good works are one indication that one belongs to the redeemed community.

Conclusion

I can scarcely claim that I have given the definitive and final interpretation of this passage. I would argue, however, that verses 9–15 yield a coherent and comprehensible meaning. Paul has argued that women should adorn themselves appropriately with good works, not with ostentatious or seductive clothing. Moreover, women should not arrogate a teaching role for themselves when men and women are gathered in public meetings. They should learn submissively and silently, and not engage in teaching or the exercise of authority. Women are prohibited from teaching or exercising authority because of the creation order. The creation of Adam before Eve signaled that men are to teach and exercise authority in the church. Moreover, the events in Genesis 3 confirm the necessity of male leadership. Eve, beguiled by the serpent, took leadership in responding to the serpent. Adam, although he was with Eve, did not intervene and properly exercise leadership. Instead, he allowed Eve to respond improperly to the serpent. Verse 14, then, signals a second reason women should not teach or exercise authority over men. They are more prone to introduce deception into the church since they are more nurturing and relational than men. It is not that they do not have the capacity to teach doctrine or the ability to understand it. Women are less likely to perceive the need to take a stand on doctrinal non-negotiable since they prize harmonious relationships more than men do.[227]

---

226. For how this fits with Christian assurance, see D. A. Carson, "Reflections on Christian Assurance," *Westminster Theological Journal* 54 (1992): 1–29.

227. It must be said again that this does not mean that women are inferior to men. Men and women have *different* weaknesses, and that is why there are different roles. Men who value acuracy and objectivity can easily fall into the error of creating divisions where none should exist and become hypercritical. They should learn from the women in the church in this regard!

Women, Paul reminds his readers, will experience eschatological salvation by adhering to their proper role, which is exemplified in giving birth to children. Of course, adhering to one's proper role is not sufficient for salvation; women must also practice other Christian virtues in order to be saved.

Our problem with the text is not in the main exegetical but practical. What Paul says here is contrary to the thinking of the modern world. We are confronted here with an alien and shocking word from the Scriptures. This alien word should modify and correct both our thinking and our behavior. In the next chapter we will explore the basis for application of Paul's teaching to our modern world. These are not idle topics, for the happiness and strength of the church today will be in direct proportion to our obedience to the biblical text.

6

The Hermeneutics of 1 Timothy 2:9–15

Robert W. Yarbrough

Exegesis and 1 Timothy 2:9–15

How should we interpret the Bible? That apparently simple question has called forth untold reams of discussion since the time of Christ—and even before Christ, who found himself engaged in controversies, already long-standing when he appeared, over how to interpret the Old Testament.[1]

Some say the answer is easy: Just read what it says. While ultimately too naive, those words can be valuable initial counsel. In a sense "reading what it says" has been the focus of this book thus far. The technical name for such "reading," for determining textual meaning in the light of a text's historical setting broadly conceived, is exegesis. Preceding chapters have reexamined the exegetical ABCs of 1 Timothy 2:9–15. Scholars have sought to shed fresh and, to the extent possible, definitive light on basic questions of cultural background (chap. 1), genre (chap. 2), word meaning (chap. 3), syntax (chap. 4), and "signification" (meaning of the passage in its original setting) of the passage as a whole (chap. 5).[2]

"What the Bible says" (to keep the matter simple for a moment), the signification of 1 Timothy 2:9–15, is tolerably clear, as the preceding chapter showed. In Paul's understanding men and women, while equal

---

1. See, e.g., D. I. Brewer, *Techniques and Assumptions in Jewish Exegesis before 70 CE* (Tübingen: J. C. B. Mohr/Paul Siebeck, 1992).

2. M. J. Erickson, *Evangelical Interpretation: Perspectives on Hermeneutical Issues* (Grand Rapids: Baker, 1993), 59, uses "signification" to refer to the meaning of a statement in its original setting. "Significance" would be the meaning it has, or should have, for some other setting (e.g., the modern situation). Erickson seeks here to refine E. D. Hirsch's terms "meaning" and "significance." Hirsch's outlook has been the subject of voluminous comment; for a recent brief defense, see J. F. Harris, *Against Relativism: A Philosophical Defense of Method* (LaSalle, Ill.: Open Court, 1992), 120–22.

in value and importance before the Lord, were not accorded identical places in church and home. Precisely the same offices in the church were not open indiscriminately to either sex. In the overall scope of biblical teaching this was not, apparently, felt to be a penalty or restriction. Women's gifts, callings, and ministries are delineated and even exalted in numerous passages both in Paul's letters and across the whole of Scripture. They are hallowed in the innumerable situations arising in home, church, and public life that call for those expressions of Christian graces that lie uniquely within the purview of regenerate[3] female nature and competencies. But a corollary to this is that at certain points women's gifts, callings, and ministries were differentiated from the gifts, callings, and ministries of men.[4] The historic position of the church on the sanctity of motherhood (for married females only), fatherhood (for married males only), and certain church offices (for males only) recognizes this.

First Timothy 2, it has been argued above, lends support to this historic position, in spite of recent proposals to the contrary.

E. Earle Ellis has pointed out that this understanding of 1 Timothy 2 is no anomaly in early Christian teaching; in fact it is quite in keeping with parallel passages in earlier Pauline and Petrine texts:[5]

1 Cor. 14:34f.
The women should keep *silent* in the churches. For they are not *permitted* to speak, but they are to *subject themselves*, as the law says. If they wish to *learn*, let them ask *their own husbands* at home. For it is disgraceful for *a woman* to speak in church.

1 Tim. 2:9–13
Likewise also [I want] *women* [everywhere] to *adorn* themselves in *respectable* deportment with modesty and decency, not in *braids* and *gold*

---

3. E. E. Ellis, *Pauline Theology, Ministry and Society* (Grand Rapids: Eerdmans, 1989), stresses that Paul's pronouncements on men, women, and their interaction assume the presence of Christ in hearts, of covenant commitment on the parts of the recipients of his counsel. Much misuse of Paul by Christians, and maligning of Paul by non-Christians, might be avoided if the primary horizon of Paul's admonitions were recognized. His epistles are addressed to persons "in Christ," not "in Adam" (12–14). Women's offices and roles in church and (Christian) family as Paul (and other biblical writers) outlines them ought not be treated by the church as automatically and necessarily binding on society at large, though they may well be commended as worthy of respect because grounded in the creation order.

4. At most points they were not, as any number of theological pronouncements, moral commands, ethical expectations, and promises attest.

5. This chart is an adaptation of Ellis, *Pauline Theology, Ministry and Society*, 73. I have not always followed Ellis's translation but have preferred my own at some points and the rsv at others. Italicized words are common expressions that suggest early tradition to Ellis.

or pearls or *high-cost clothing, but rather* [in] that which befits women professing godliness, with good works. Let *a woman learn* in *silence* in *full submission*. Teaching is something I do not *permit a woman* [to do], nor to exercise authority over *a man*; she is to be *quiet* [not teach]. For Adam was formed first . . .

1 Pet. 3:3–6
Likewise you *wives* . . . let not your *adornment* be the outward *braiding of hair*, wearing *gold jewelry*, or *putting on dresses, but rather* . . . *quietness* of spirit, which is *costly* in the sight of God. For thus also the holy *women* who trusted in God formerly *adorned* themselves, *subjecting themselves to their own husbands*, as Sarah obeyed Abraham . . .

Because this kind of biblical teaching is *not* restricted to 1 Timothy 2,[6] interpreters with a high view of Scripture—a view that seeks to let "signification" determine "significance" as much as possible—will be slow to reject it as merely the products of culpably patriarchal writers[7] or to relativize it as culturally outmoded.[8]

The findings of previous chapters, however, will not bring an end to the debate over the responsibilities and offices most appropriate to women in the body of Christ generally or even to the significance of 1 Timothy 2:9–15 in particular. This is because the discussion is not guided by exegesis alone (nor can it be); it is influenced by hermeneutics as well.

The Need for Hermeneutical Wisdom

Exegesis (determining the "signification") of a text must be informed by sound hermeneutics to determine "significance," or the present implications, with any degree of validity.[9] Hermeneutics refers to the principles (and other factors, whether acknowledged by the interpreter or not) that tend to govern interpretation. "Hermeneutics" is a broader term than "exegesis," and the relationship of the two calls for clarification. It is easy to see why.

The matter of moving from the original message of the text in its historic setting to today, from "signification" to "significance," is complicated. Exegesis, determining "what the Bible says," is always informed by the hermeneutics, a constellation of assumptions, principles, and

6. In addition to the parallels above, see especially Eph. 5:22–33.
7. See, e.g., *The Women's Bible Commentary*, ed. C. Newsom and S. Ringe (London: SPCK/Westminster/John Knox, 1992), 353ff.
8. As previous chapters have shown, and as this chapter confirms, many interpreters who profess a high view of Scripture have done precisely this. It is one of the goals of this chapter to question the wisdom of appeal to 1 Tim. 2:9–15 for support of this move.
9. On "signification" and "significance," see n. 2.

modi operandi, of the exegete. And this hermeneutical orientation is, in turn, likely informed by previous exegesis, which has been influenced by an earlier level of hermeneutical understanding, and so on. The spiral extends back endlessly into the imponderables of each individual interpreter, the interpretive community he or she inhabits, and the full range of experiences and native tendencies that lie behind the exegesis he or she does.

But while the spiral is endless with respect to the circumstances of each interpreter, it is not endless with respect to the object to be interpreted, in this case the text of 1 Timothy 2. These words stand before all interpreters in their literary, historical, and theological givenness. Both better and worse interpretations of them are conceivable. They can be appropriated faithfully or wrested wrongly. Some interpretations do more justice to the whole range of relevant factors that bear on Paul's meaning, and others do less.[10] As R. Douglas Geivett states, "The much-paraded contention that objectivity is impossible at all levels of inquiry is exaggerated and self-referentially defeating."[11]

With respect to any given question aimed at any given text—for example, does a passage like 1 Timothy 2:9–15 accord to women in Christ precisely the same position in the family and offices in the church as

---

10. While interpretation struggles with the problem of the interpreter's limited horizon and preunderstanding, we do not agree that "radical relativity" must necessarily describe the interpretive process. Those who insist on absolutizing their experience of reality as a normative interpretive grid are obviously free to do so; in this case the verdict of "radical relativity" is apt as a description of their interpretive philosophy and work. But the declaration of "radical relativity" for all interpretations of anything is, finally self-refuting—by what standard can any interpreter call all others relative? This pronouncement itself presumes a standard by which to measure. Thus, either there is a standard after all, in which case "radical relativity" does not necessarily describe interpretation; or there truly is not a standard, and solipsism (the view that the self knows only its own knowing; perception and meaning are fundamentally different for every single person) is the human predicament. In the latter case there is no need for anyone to heed anyone else's charge of "radical relativity." Such a charge would be a meaningless truism—if there could be a truism in a solipsistic world. For a philosophical refutation of "radical relativity," see Harris, *Against Relativism*. For a briefer and more accessible defense of the notion of objectivity despite the social construction of knowledge, see S. Dex, "Objective Facts in Social Science," in *Objective Knowledge*, ed. P. Helm (Leicester, U.K.: Inter-Varsity, 1987), 167–90. On theological grounds it may be noted that the Bible holds humans accountable for responsiveness to events and words addressed to them, ultimately, from outside their own experience. This invalidates the solipsistic thesis, unless God were unjust, which Scripture insists he is not. Further, the Bible portrays the human condition since the fall, not as radically relative to shifting immanent considerations, but as profoundly absolute in view of universal condemnation under God's law. The standards of a sovereign God, who is absolute, confer a substantial degree of nonrelativity on humans. This shatters the "radical relativity" thesis for those who acknowledge this God's dominion over their lives—and, if they are correct, over everyone else's life, too.

11. "Is Jesus the Only Way?" in *Jesus Under Fire*, ed. Michael J. Wilkins and J. P. Moreland (Grand Rapids: Zondervan, 1995), 202 n. 37.

men?—there is in theory one truly best answer. That answer will be the one that best accords with the author's meaning in the text under scrutiny, given certain *hermeneutical considerations that permit exegesis,* "reading what the Bible says," *to liberate the biblical message* for contemporary application rather than confine it due to the interpreter's improper assumptions, principles, or procedures. By "liberate" I mean permit the message to convey to the reader the signification that inheres in the original document and that the author intended to pass on. Below we will see that much modern interpretation, by employing a *sachkritische* ("content-critical") approach, effectively imprisons the text's claims or imperatives in an unsatisfactory fashion.

This is not the place for a complete hermeneutical guidebook; this need is amply provided for in other studies.[12] Even if we could canvass such works, we might be disappointed with the results, for, as Howard Marshall comments, "discussions on biblical hermeneutics have given us a fair amount of guidance on how to elucidate what the text said" but "have not done a lot to help us make the passage from what the text said to what the text says."[13] Nor will an attempt be made to arrive at a full-orbed application of 1 Timothy 2:9–15. Finally, this is not the place to handle several other significant issues of an integrative-theological kind, such as relating 1 Timothy 2:9–15 to Galatians 3:28, 1 Corinthians 11:11, 14, or other pertinent passages in the Pauline epistles or the Gospels.

We will rather survey a selection of hermeneutical issues bearing on the move from our text's signification in Paul's day to its significance for the present day. Perusal of current literature indicates that for many readers the major impediment to applying what 1 Timothy 2 says, as interpreted in earlier chapters of this volume, lies in three arguments. These are based on Western culture's liberalized views of women, the putative meaning of Galatians 3:28, and an alleged tie between women's subordination and slavery. Below I attempt to clear the ground of current popular but possibly mistaken views in each of these three areas that prevent the scriptural testimony from being accepted as it ought to be.

12. The recent literature alone is extensive. For seminal readings, see K. Mueller-Vollmer, ed., *The Hermeneutics Reader* (New York: Continuum, 1985). On hermeneutical theory, see A. C. Thiselton, *New Horizons in Hermeneutics* (Grand Rapids: Zondervan, 1992). For wide-ranging coverage of the history and theological dimensions of biblical hermeneutics, see G. Maier, *Biblical Hermeneutics*, trans. R. Yarbrough (Wheaton: Crossway, 1994). More generally, see R. Morgan with J. Barton, *Biblical Interpretation* (Oxford: Oxford University Press, 1988); G. Osborne, *The Hermeneutical Spiral* (Downers Grove: InterVarsity, 1991); W. Klein, C. Blomberg, and R. Hubbard, Jr., *Introduction to Biblical Interpretation* (Dallas: Word, 1993); D. Black and D. Dockery, eds., *New Testament Criticism and Interpretation* (Grand Rapids: Zondervan, 1991).

13. Marshall, "The Use of the New Testament in Christian Ethics," *Expository Times* 105, no. 5 (February 1994): 136.

More broadly, the survey below will serve to make understandable major features of the hermeneutical rationale informing previous and following chapters. It will provide a hermeneutical framework[14] for cautious but firm affirmation of the reading of 1 Timothy 2:9–15 that has the weight of historic Christian interpretation, as well as the most plausible understanding of related biblical passages, to commend it. And it will constitute a challenge to those who take exception with those chapters to examine their own hermeneutical outlook lest it prevent them from coming to grips with the divine Word addressed to us all.

Copernican Revolution and Aftermath

No single hermeneutical question is of greater consequence than this one: Was it, is it, and will it continue to be well advised for Christians to follow the recent lead of Western society in liberalizing attitudes toward women's and men's identities and roles?

By "liberalizing" I have in mind not theological liberalism (though that is an important concern, too) but rather the individualistic "liberal faith," the "particular social doctrine," which stresses individual rights rather than social or institutionally mandated responsibilities in both civil and moral matters.[15] I have in mind the view of persons that dominates the West at the twentieth century's end, a view that stresses self-realization and personal fulfillment rather than fellowship and self-sacrifice for others by involvement in an inherited or adopted family and perhaps also religious tradition. Liberalism in this sense is the grand "cause of the liberty of the human spirit, the cause of opportunity of human beings for full development of their powers."[16] While it is tempered today by impulses calling for selective subordination of personal good to social good (national health care, gun control), the move in the United States, at least, is still toward an "expressive individualism"[17]

---

14. In other words, this discussion will not seek to arrive at a set of discrete "principles" or interpretive rules which, applied to 1 Timothy 2, will yield the proper understanding. Thiselton, *New Horizons*, has already performed the service of showing the ways that much feminist-leaning interpretation runs afoul of weighty theoretical philosophical and theological considerations. We cannot duplicate, or even apply in any extensive and systematic way, his insights here due to space constraints. We have chosen instead to deal with more practical (rather than theoretical) issues that seem to be exerting the most influence on the interpretation and application of 1 Timothy 2 in many circles at the present time.

15. See John Dewey, *Liberalism and Social Action* (New York: Capricorn, 1935, rpt. 1963), 2–3.

16. Ibid., 93.

17. Robert N. Bellah et al., *Habits of the Heart* (San Francisco: Harper & Row, 1986), *passim*.

that tends to "obliterate all prior culture"[18] in its own narrow liberal self-interest.

The harrowing fascist and communist experiments of the twentieth century have not provided promising models or motivation for an alternate socialist[19] vision that would check America's seemingly endless self-obsession. Instead, successive philosophical movements stretching as far back as John Stuart Mill (1806–73) have fueled feverish demands for "the rights and liberty of individuals" along lines "supportive of today's feminist principles."[20] These movements (and representative seminal thinkers) are utilitarian (Mill), existential (Simone De Beauvoir [1908–]), Marxist (Friedrich Engels [1820–95], Lenin [Vladimir Ilyich Ulyanov] [1870–1924], Herbert Marcuse [1898–79]), and analytic (Bertrand Russell [1872–1970]).

In its views of women's roles, the church in the West has followed the world's lead. On this point there can hardly be debate. "The women's movement of the 1960s and 1970s and the increasing number of women attending seminaries renewed interest in what it might mean to read the Bible self-consciously as a woman."[21] As feminism entered its "second wave" in the 1960s and 1970s (the "first wave" arose in the late 1700s, a spin-off from the rise of liberalism itself[22]), it began to read the Bible in light of its own distinct, emancipated, and increasingly authoritative view of reality. Today it is a commonplace that biblical authority for feminist biblical interpretation is secondary to feminist experience.[23] For instance, in sharp contrast to the uniquely normative character of Scripture, white feminist theologians "view scripture as only secondarily normative, subjecting scripture, with other sources, to an-

---

18. Ibid., 283.

19. Dewey's *Liberalism and Social Action* (see n. 14) was an attempt to reassert liberal values in the dark years of German fascist and Soviet Stalinist expansion. On the socialist nature of Nazi fascism, see G. Huntemann, *The Other Bonhoeffer*, trans. T. Huizinga (Grand Rapids: Baker, 1993); he rightly calls Hitler's reign a "socialist dictatorship" (52). A 1935 German *Reichsmark* (5 DM coin) has embossed on its edge the words "Gemeinnutz geht vor Eigennutz (Community use takes precedence over personal use)"—the antithesis of the liberal creed.

20. M. B. Mahowald, ed., *Philosophy of Woman: An Anthology of Classic and Current Concepts*, 2nd ed. (Indianapolis: Hackett, 1983), 45.

21. *The Women's Bible Commentary*, ed. Newsom and Ringe, xiv.

22. M. A. Kassian, *The Feminist Gospel* (Wheaton: Crossway, 1992), 1. On "third wave" feminism, see "Feminism's Daughters," *U.S. News & World Report* (September 27, 1993), 68–71. For valuable primary source readings and bibliography, see Mahowald, ed., *Philosophy of Woman*; "Religion and Feminism," in *Border Regions of Faith*, ed. K. Aman (Maryknoll, N.Y.: Orbis, 1987), 7–93; Susannah Heschel, "Jewish and Christian Feminist Theologies," in *Critical Issues in Modern Religion*, ed. R. A. Johnson et al., 2nd ed. (Englewood Cliffs, N.J.: Prentice Hall, 1990), 309–45.

23. Cf. R. Groothuis, *Women Caught in the Conflict* (Grand Rapids: Baker, 1994), 103–8.

other norm: the liberation of women from oppressive, patriarchal structures, of which scripture and its interpretation is one."[24] While evangelical feminist interpreters seek to maintain full biblical authority, it has been the larger sanction of liberalizing feminist social forces that has given both impetus and credence to new interpretations (or dismissals) of key texts like 1 Timothy 2 in evangelical circles.[25] K. Stendahl speaks for a great many in arguing that the two questions of societal liberation for women and full ecclesiastical powers for women (i.e., their ordination) ultimately cannot be separated; a positive answer to the former inexorably requires a "progressive" view regarding the latter.[26] "The only alternative . . . is to recognize the legal, economic, political, and professional emancipation of women . . . as a great achievement. . . . If emancipation is right, then there is no valid 'biblical' reason not to ordain women."[27]

Relatively ignored in the wrangling over Christian women's demands to be as free from so-called traditional constraints in church and marriage as their non-Christian sisters has been the plight of women and children in the years since the Copernican social revolution of the 1960s. But it can be ignored no longer.

Disaster has overtaken women and children as divorce rates more than doubled from 1970 to 1980, eventually leveling off at a distressingly high rate.[28] "The war against women: Violence, poverty and abuse" trumpets a *U.S. News & World Report* cover story. Its theme: "Women are falling further behind in country after country—and their men like it that way."[29] *U.S. News* puffs the international scene, but the domestic picture is frightening enough. As M. N. Ozawa notes: "Something extraordinary is happening to American women. Although their

24. E. K. Wondra, "By Whose Authority? The [sic] Status of Scripture in Contemporary Feminist Theologies," *Anglican Theological Review* 74, no. 1 (1993): 84. Feminist interpreters of color are no more likely to be subservient to the biblical text, though there are sure to be exceptions.

25. Kassian, *Feminist Gospel*, 205: "But conservative evangelical Christians are not unaffected by feminism. Many of them view the philosophy of feminism as a valid adjunct to their faith. They believe that the basic tenets of feminism are supported by the Bible and that feminism can naturally, easily, and homogeneously be combined with Christianity. . . . They believe in the Bible, but also believe in feminism."

26. In n. 3 we argued that care must be taken in transferring principles of church order into the larger social sphere. There may be important correlates and analogies, but these must be worked out with caution. In Stendahl's zeal for modernity's social order, he and evangelicals who too facilely endorse such thinking commit this error in the opposite direction.

27. *The Bible and the Role of Women*, trans. E. Sander (Philadelphia: Fortress, 1966), 40f.

28. My thanks to Margaret Boyd for bibliographic aid in the next few paragraphs.

29. 116, no. 12 (March 28, 1994), 42–56. Quotes from table of contents and cover, respectively.

individual economic capability has never been as great as it is today, their economic well-being in relation to that of men has been slipping. . . . [W]omen's economic lot is deteriorating in comparison to that of men."[30] Women have gained great freedom—but at a great price. They are arguably more the victims of male tyranny or indifference than ever before. "The determining factor [of women's increasing social plight] is social, not economic: *the weakening tie between men and women* as a result of the increasing incidence of childbearing out of wedlock (whether by teenagers or by adults), divorce, and the growing likelihood that women will become widows."[31]

Children's plight is, however, perhaps even more depressing to contemplate.[32] The ills besetting women "have profound ramifications" for "the future of American children—the future of American human capital."[33] "[F]or the first time in American history, the educational skills of the current generation of children will not surpass, will not equal, and will not even approach those of their parents."[34] "Never before has one generation of American children been less healthy, less cared for, or less prepared for life than their parents were at the same age," according to the National Commission on the Role of School and the Community in Improving Adolescent Health Care.[35]

On a closely related front, adolescents who are not yet legally adults wield lethal weapons and murder not only adults but each other by the hundreds on America's streets. Youth deaths by homicide have doubled since 1985, with a child dying by gunshot at the rate of one every two hours.[36] The world was recently shocked by details of a trial in Britain of two boys who lured a mere toddler away from his mother, then tortured him much as boys in other times might have toyed with a toad.

The short- and long-term emotional and psychological effects of divorce on the high percentage of American children affected by it are far more damaging than once thought.[37] Judith S. Wallerstein's research

30. Martha N. Ozawa, ed., *Women's Life Cycle and Economic Insecurity* (New York: Praeger, 1989), 1. See also Terry Arendell, *Mothers and Divorce* (Berkeley: University of California Press, 1986).

31. Ozawa, *Women's Life Cycle and Economic Insecurity*, 2 (my emphasis).

32. See, e.g., Irwin Garfinkel and Sara McLanahan, *Single Mothers and Their Children* (Washington, D.C.: The Urban Institute Press, 1986); J. B. Elshtain, "Family Matters: The Plight of America's Children," *Christian Century*, July 14–21, 1993, 710–12.

33. Ozawa, *Women's Life Cycle and Economic Insecurity*, 3.

34. Ibid.

35. Quoted in Susan S. Phillips, "Caring for Our Children: Confronting the Crisis," *Radix* 22, no. 1 (1993): 4.

36. Angela E. Coloumbis, "New Report Finds Youth Deaths by Homocide [*sic*] Doubled since 1985," *Christian Science Monitor*, April 25, 1994, 18, reporting on the Annie E. Casey Foundation's 1994 Kids Count Report.

37. Barbara Defoe Whitehead, "Dan Quayle Was Right," *Atlantic Monthly* (April 1993), 47–84.

has documented "the sleeper effect."[38] Children may not show the trauma of divorce for a decade or more after it occurs. Even if Waller-stein's ground-breaking work proves flawed at points,[39] the fact re-mains that "each divorce is the death of a small civilization."[40] And the problem is worsening, it seems, with the passage of time.[41] Yet there "remains extraordinary reluctance to acknowledge its seriousness and its enormous impact on all our lives."[42]

Society has changed markedly in recent decades. A revolution has occurred. There is no turning back; but there must be adjustments. And for Christians the question remains: Is it responsible for the church to assume the intrinsic desirability for the church of ideals—like the liber-alization of views of women's (and inevitably of men's) roles as defined above—which appear to be organically linked with bringing such woe to the world?[43] From a Christian perspective both sexes have sinned grievously against each other as evidenced in rampant divorce, the sex-ual infidelity that often attends it, and the ripple effects of drastic life-style changes. Corporate adult offense against children, and increas-ingly by children against each other, is incalculable. Adult women themselves have been adversely affected in areas other than economics: Between 1980 and the end of 1992 the number of women in state and federal prisons increased 275 percent.[44]

Yet remarkably the implicit assumption has been and continues to be that changes in society require parallel changes in the church. Nowhere has this been truer than in the area of biblical teaching on sex and gen-der roles.[45] As Spencer Perkins remarks with an eye to the African

38. "Children after Divorce: Wounds That Don't Heal," *New York Times Magazine*, Jan-uary 22, 1989, 19ff.

39. See, e.g., Andrew J. Cherlin, *Marriage, Divorce, Remarriage*, rev. ed. (Cambridge, Mass., 1992), 76ff.

40. Pat Conroy, quoted in Judith Wallerstein and Sandra Blakeslee, *Second Chances* (New York: Ticknor & Fields, 1989), xxi.

41. Ibid., xx.

42. Ibid., xix.

43. It is not being argued here that all the woes are the direct result of liberalization of women's and men's roles. But it would be unconscionable special pleading to deny that the emancipation of women and men from the moral and familial expectations common until the 1960s (reflected, e.g., in strict divorce laws) has nothing to do with the break-down of marriages and increasing plight of children since the 1960s. We are arguing only that there is enough of a connection between the woes and the liberalization that the church would have been well advised to be wary of the latter if it wished to avoid being implicated in the former. Too often the church has been uncritical on this score.

44. "Mandatory Sentences Lead to Surge of Women in Prison," *Christian Science Monitor* (November 29, 1993). The number of male inmates increased 160 percent in the same period. Four out of five women inmates are mothers; their incarceration is at the same time apt to be punitive for their children.

45. C. Keener insists that the "progressive" (to use Schreiner's term from the previous chapter) reading of New Testament texts on women's and men's roles "is not, as some

American inner-city scene: "After three decades of civil rights laws, wars on poverty and drugs, and billions of dollars in urban programs we have not fewer but more dead young Black men, more babies born out of wedlock, and an overall decrease in the quality of life in our inner cities. And still we have been unwilling to look at the obvious connection between family breakdown and the growing instability of our cities."[46]

All this points to a hermeneutical watershed. Those who feel justified in endorsing our *Zeitgeist*'s convictions that women ought to hold church office and be on radically equal footing with husbands in marriage will continue to hold 1 Timothy 2:9–15 as interpreted elsewhere in this volume at arm's length. But for others, omnipresent heartbreaking social carnage, the scope of which we have only sketchily documented, could encourage a new look at much-vilified "traditional" Christian teaching.

Some will claim that the challenge is to appropriate society's positive new direction without succumbing to its evils.[47] This is to overlook that numerous passages in the Bible may be understood as forbidding the people of God facilely to adopt the liberal (in the political sense sketched earlier) attitudes toward personhood, sexuality, morality, marriage, children, and (if this book's thesis proves correct) church leadership that have arisen in recent decades. As we will see below, these attitudes have spawned much debate and many creative new renderings of passages like 1 Timothy 2, which are taken to legitimate the essential implications of society's new direction. But viewing society's drift in its application for Christian gender roles as essentially "positive" could only have taken place when key biblical texts were set to the side long enough for the drift to be endorsed. This in turn enabled creative renderings of the problem texts so as either to reinterpret them, declare them culturally relative, or both. The soundness of this interpretive strategy deserves careful questioning.

It might also be argued that endorsement of the liberalizing agenda that has taken shape since the 1960s was required because of the evils

---

would argue, an agenda borrowed from the secular world" (*Paul, Women and Wives* [Peabody, Mass.: Hendrickson, 1992], 10). Keener attempts valiantly to be true to the biblical text rather than a secular mind-set. But his own work is studded with references to current progressive objections to "historic" (to use Schreiner's terms again) Christian interpretation and practice. These references do not necessarily furnish him his agenda, but they certainly affect it. F. F. Bruce's statement may be closer to the truth: "We too are culturally conditioned; only we do not notice it. The women's liberation movement has conditioned not only our practices but our very vocabulary" ("Women in the Church: A Biblical Survey," in *A Mind for What Matters* [Grand Rapids: Eerdmans, 1990], 266).

46. "Saving Our Children in a World without Fathers," *Urban Family* (Winter 1994): 12.

47. See, e.g., Stendahl, *Bible and Role of Women*, 41, who endorses the direction but speaks of not "being blind to" the problems.

of bourgeois society and attendant victimization of women stemming from the 1950s or before. Here the reply must be that Christians should not have been letting some earlier sordid status quo determine treatment of women, either. When they were doing so—and they often did—they should have repented. But repenting of the 1950s should have taken some other form than acquiescence to the social debacle chronicled above. It should have involved a renewed draught of grace and compassion from Christ and submission to Scripture by all parties, not attenuation of the Bible's counsel.

To summarize, a fundamental hermeneutical question is whether the prevailing secular mind-set should continue in the future to exercise the strong influence on exegesis of biblical texts that it has had in the recent past. An affirmative answer here is conceivable from those who choose to ignore the mounting social devastation, for others who think that the gains for some women are worth the pain for other women and millions of children, and for all who believe that continued liberalization will at some point begin to reverse the current vast and burgeoning misery.[48] R. Groothuis offers rallying words: "We must weather the storm of change—keeping our wits about us and our spirits submitted to the truth that sets us free."[49]

Others, however, may find veteran social critic John Perkins' counsel worth pondering: "We are fools if we depend on the same people that got us into the mess to get us out of it."[50] Or, as W. Ramsay more temperately states, bringing us back to Paul and 1 Timothy 2: "How far Paul's opinions about women should be regarded as springing from his insight into the divine force that moves the world, we do not venture to judge; they are out of harmony with ours; but the fault may well lie with

---

48. Groothuis, *Women Caught in the Conflict*, 135, is willing (for somebody) to pay the price. She attempts to distinguish between social breakdown and social liberalization understood as "women's liberation," as she terms it. She denies any causal link between the two. I agree that "women's liberation" is not the sole cause of breakdown. In fact I think that men are more to blame than women. But the reasoning on which Groothuis bases her view does not begin to deal with the widely recognized fact that recent innovations in views of gender roles are of a piece with recent demolition of the social fabric. Nor is her appeal to nineteenth-century feminism convincing: by comparison with recent feminism, the nineteenth-century version was hardly feminism in the fundamental philosophical sense at all. In particular, the earlier version tended to affirm a Christian ethos rather than militantly oppose it. (Groothuis [46] admits that "The anti-Christian element was a minority one in the nineteenth century, whereas today it characterizes the secular feminist movement.") Finally, Groothuis's belief that the disintegration "would not happen if the beliefs of today's evangelical feminists were implemented in church and society" is a moot point and a naive confession of utopian hope. The horse is already out of the barn, in fact out of sight. How long before we can retrieve it if we must wait for church and society to embrace evangelical feminist views?

49. Ibid., 216.

50. As quoted by his son Spencer in *Urban Family* (Winter 1994): 14.

us, and we may be judging under the prepossession of modern custom, which will perhaps prove evanescent and discordant with the plan of the universe and the purpose of God."[51]

Are "Progressive" Readings of 1 Timothy 2:9–15 Concessions to the Spirit of the Age?

Some will be loath to concede what the previous section argued: that the "progressive" interpretation of Paul is indebted significantly, and at times probably culpably, to the prevailing social climate rather than to the biblical text. Such reticence is conceivable from two groups. One would be those who fail to realize how novel some of the arguments currently being advanced for "progressive" readings of 1 Timothy 2 are.[52] A second group would be those who are probably aware that the arguments are novel but who feel they are justified by an equally novel assessment of another Pauline text: Galatians 3:28. We will take up the question of Galatians 3:28 in the next section when we deal with the views of K. Stendahl and F. F. Bruce.

By way of reply to the first group, a survey of scholarly articles on 1 Timothy 2:9–15 listed in the standard bibliographical reference tool *New Testament Abstracts* may prove informative.[53] Following is a survey of most (not all[54]) "progressive" and "historic" offerings that have appeared.

New Testament Abstracts goes back to 1956. Perusal of its volumes turns up a relevant article first in 1969. N. J. Hommes argues along "progressive" lines that 1 Timothy 2:11–12 excludes domestic bossiness and does not address the issue of women holding church office at all.[55] The "progressive" theme continues and extends in various directions in subsequent years. In 1974 A. D. B. Spencer warns against generalizing from the women at Ephesus addressed in 1 Timothy 2 to women in

51. W. Ramsay, *The Teaching of Paul in Terms of the Present Day*, 2nd ed. (London: Hodder & Stoughton, 1914), 212.

52. Groothuis, *Women Caught in the Conflict*, 240f. ("For Further Reading") is an example. She cites only post-1980 evangelical feminist literature and clearly relies on it for her own exegetical conclusions. There is little to no precedent for much of this exegesis in serious exegetical discussion prior to the 1960s and 1970s. See also Daniel Doriani's work in appendix 1.

53. For a discussion of the history of interpretation of 1 Tim. 2:11–14 leading up to the present day, see appendix 1.

54. A few do not fall readily into either "progressive" or "historic" categories. More than a half-dozen others deal with 1 Tim. 2:15 and the question of women being "saved by childbirth." These articles are included in the total number of articles published but are not counted as either "progressive" or "historic" contributions.

55. Hommes, "Let Women Be Silent in the Church," *Calvin Theological Journal* 4, no. 1 (1969): 5–22.

other times and places.[56] In 1975 J. A. Díaz suggests that 1 Timothy 2:11–15 is a later addition reflecting the Montanist controversy.[57] Also in 1975 C. Butler laments that the Pastorals were wrongly viewed as Pauline, causing their assertions on women's roles to be imputed mistakenly to dominical and apostolic teaching.[58]

In 1980 D. Scholer upholds the burgeoning new understanding in arguing that the concerns of 1 Timothy 2 and 1 Peter 3 for women's outward appearance, seemly submission, and silence are not fitting in the same way in the contemporary setting.[59] G. D. Fee in 1985 argues on genre grounds that 1 Timothy's strictures are ad hoc and therefore not applicable in other situations in the same way.[60] A. Padgett in 1987 comes to the same conclusion as Scholer and Fee but on different grounds related to social context.[61]

Only a couple articles advancing a "progressive" understanding of 1 Timothy 2 are indexed in 1988 and 1989, followed by a complete hiatus in 1990. In 1991 alone, however, *New Testament Abstracts* records some nine articles. These include pieces by G. Redekop, D. Scholer, C. Kroeger, G. Fee, T. Harris, B. Barron, A.-L. Danet, and M. Grey.[62] The steady flow of "progressive" advocacy becomes a torrent. Since that

56. Spencer, "Eve at Ephesus (Should Women Be Ordained as Pastors According to the First Letter of Timothy 2:1–15?)," *Journal of the Evangelical Theological Society* 17, no. 4 (1974): 215–22.

57. Díaz, "Restricción en algunos textos paulinos de las reivindicaciones de la mujer en la Iglesia," *Estudios Eclesiásticos* 50 (1975): 77–93.

58. Butler, "Was Paul a Male Chauvinist?" *New Blackfriars* 56 (1975): 174–79.

59. Scholer, "Women's Adornment: Some Historical and Hermeneutical Observations on the New Testament Passages," *Daughters of Sarah* [Chicago] 6, no. 1 (1980): 3–6.

60. Fee, "Reflections on Church Order in the Pastoral Epistles, with Further Reflections on the Hermeneutics of ad hoc Documents," *Journal of the Evangelical Theological Society* 28, no. 2 (1985): 141–51.

61. Padgett, "Wealthy Women at Ephesus: 1 Timothy 2:8–15 in Social Context," *Interpretation* 41, no. 1 (1987): 19–31.

62. Redekop, "Let the Women Learn: 1 Timothy 2:8–15 Reconsidered," *Studies in Religion/Sciences Religieuses* 19, no. 2 (1990): 235–45; Scholer, "Women in the Church's Ministry. Does 1 Timothy 2:9–15 Help or Hinder?" *Daughters of Sarah* [Chicago] 16, no. 4 (1990): 7–12; Kroeger, "Women in the Church: A Classicist's View of 1 Tim 2:11–15," *Journal of Biblical Equality* 1 (1989): 3–31; Fee, "Women in Ministry: The Meaning of 1 Timothy 2:8–15 in Light of the Purpose of 1 Timothy," *Journal of the Christian Brethren Research Fellowship* 122 (1990): 11–18; idem, "Issues in Evangelical Hermeneutics, Part III: The Great Watershed—Intentionality and Particularity/Eternality: 1 Timothy 2:8–15 as a Test Case," *Crux* 26, no. 4 (1990): 31–37; Harris, "Why did Paul Mention Eve's Deception? A Critique of P. W. Barnett's Interpretation of 1 Timothy 2," *Evangelical Quarterly* 62, no. 4 (1990): 335–52; Barron, "Putting Women in Their Place: 1 Timothy 2 and Evangelical Views of Women in Church Leadership," *Journal of the Evangelical Theological Society* 33, no. 4 (1990): 451–59; Danet, "I Timothée 2,8–15 et le ministère pastoral féminin," *Hokhma* 44 (1990): 23–44; Grey, "'Yet Women Will Be Saved through Bearing Children' (1 Tim 2.15): Motherhood and the Possibility of a Contemporary Discourse for Women," *Bijdragen* 52, no. 1 (1991): 58–69.

banner year four additional articles tending in the "progressive" direction have appeared.[63]

On the "historic" side one finds considerably fewer studies. *New Testament Abstracts* lists one each in the years 1977, 1981, and 1984.[64] Two are indexed in 1989,[65] one in 1990,[66] none in 1991, two in 1992,[67] and one each in 1993 and (so far) in 1994.[68]

All told, taking *New Testament Abstracts* since 1956 as a rough barometer of contemporary discussion on the topic of 1 Timothy 2:9–15 and its relation to the question of women's role in the church, some ten articles seem to support a "historic" view, while more than twice that many (twenty-three) argue for a "progressive" interpretation. The year 1969 marks the beginning of the "progressive" voice. Prior to that time, apparently, while there is no lack of rejection of Paul's teaching in 1 Timothy 2:9–15 on other grounds,[69] the distinctive features of "progressive" understanding as these have taken shape in contemporary discussion had not emerged.

63. D. F. Kuske, "An Exegetical Brief on 1 Timothy 2:12 (οὐδὲ αὐθεντεῖν ἀνδρός)," *Wisconsin Lutheran Quarterly* 88, no. 1 (1991): 64–67; J. Murphy-O'Conner, "St. Paul: Promoter of the Ministry of Women," *Priests and People* 6 (1992): 307–11; G. Hugenberger, "Women in Church Office: Hermeneutics or Exegesis? A Survey of Approaches to 1 Tim 2:8–15," *Journal of the Evangelical Theological Society* 35, no. 3 (1992): 341–60; A. C. Periman, "What Eve Did, What Women Shouldn't Do: The Meaning of αὐθεντέω in 1 Timothy 2:12," *Tyndale Bulletin* 44, no. 1 (1993): 129–42.

64. In their order of appearance these are N. Lightfoot, "The Role of Women in Religious Services," *Restoration Quarterly* 19, no. 3 (1976): 129–36; D. Moo, "1 Timothy 2:11–15: Meaning and Significance," *Trinity Journal* 1, no. 1 (1980): 62–83; G. W. Knight, "*Authenteo* in Reference to Women in 1 Timothy 2.12," *New Testament Studies* 30, no. 1 (1984): 143–57.

65. H. W. House, "A Biblical View of Women in the Ministry," *Bibliotheca Sacra* 145 (1988): 301–18; K. Sandnes, "'et liv som vinner respekt.' Et sentralt perspektiv på 1 Tim 2:11–15," *Tidsskrift for Teologi og Kirke* 59, no. 2 (1988): 97–108.

66. P. W. Barnett, "Wives and Women's Ministry (1 Timothy 2:11–15)," *Evangelical Quarterly* 61, no. 3 (1989): 225–37.

67. B. K. Waltke, "1 Timothy 2:8–15: Unique or Normative?" *Crux* 28, no. 1 (1992): 22–23, 26–27; A. L. Bowman, "Women in Ministry: An Exegetical Study of 1 Timothy 2:11–15," *Bibliotheca Sacra* 149 (1992): 193–213.

68. R. Yarbrough, "I Suffer Not a Woman: A Review Essay," *Presbyterion* 18, no. 1 (1992): 25–33; E. Lassman, "1 Timothy 3:1–7 and Titus 1:5–9 and the Ordination of Women," *Concordia Theological Quarterly* 56, no. 4 (1992): 291–95.

69. See, e.g., R. F. Horton, ed., *The Pastoral Epistles: Timothy and Titus* (Edinburgh: T. C. & E. C. Jack, 1901), 102f. Commenting on 1 Tim. 2:12, Horton posits a misogynist "personal element" in Paul and declares, "The question after all must be, not, Does Paul prohibit women from teaching? but Does the Spirit of God use them as teachers?" A more recent critical strategy is to relegate the Pastorals to non-Pauline status and therefore not indicative of his theology; see, e.g., M. Dibelius and H. Conzelmann, *The Pastoral Epistles*, trans. Philip Buttolph and Adela Yarbro (Philadelphia: Fortress, 1972), 49; S. Terrien, *Till the Heart Sings: A Biblical Theology of Manhood and Womanhood* (Philadelphia: Fortress, 1985), 190f.

One can, therefore, hardly argue that social pressure has not exerted considerable influence on how 1 Timothy 2 is being understood today. It strains credulity to the breaking point to maintain that it is mere coincidence that "progressive" readings of 1 Timothy 2, which were virtually unheard of in church history prior to the women's movement of the 1960s, are not indebted to that movement in fundamental respects for their plausibility. "Contemporary interest in vindicating the pastoral ministry of women"[70] is at work from about 1970 onward.

A brief look at *Religious Index One* (RIO), which casts a slightly broader bibliographic net than *New Testament Abstracts*, will shed additional helpful light on the matter. A footnote below contains a tally of its contents from the first volume in which a "progressive" reading of 1 Timothy 2:9–15 appears.[71] This tally indicates that prior to 1970–74 *Religious Index One* cites no "progressive" articles arguing that 1 Timothy 2 gives no impediment to women holding pastoral office at full parity with men. Since that time articles on the subject, whether "progressive" or "historic" in orientation, have swollen to account for about 40 percent of all catalogued published discussion on Timothy or 1 Timothy generally. While lulls do occur, in some years the percentage is much higher. Not all of the 40 percent are arguing the "progressive" view, it is true. But

70. *New Testament Abstracts* 20, no. 1 (1976): 45, commenting on Díaz, *Estudios Eclesiásticos* 50 (1975): 77–93.

71.

RIO volume	Year	Total articles on (1) Timothy overall	Articles on women in 1 Tim. 2
10–11	1970–74	9	2
12	1975–76	7	–
13	1977–78	4	1
14	1979–80	8	–
15	1981–82	4	4
16	1983–84	14	5
17	1985	4	2
18	1986	2	–
19	1987	2	1
20	1988	4	1
21	1989	1	–
22	1990	10	6
23	1991	6	–
24	1992	10	8
25/1	1993	4	4
		Total: 89	Total: 34

Note: In the above chart, the "Total Articles" column tallies the number of all articles in *Religious Index One* dealing with any aspect of "Timothy" or "Timothy I." Articles listed under the heading "Timothy II" are not included. The "Articles on Women in 1 Tim 2" column tallies the number of all articles cited in *Religious Index One* dealing only with studies touching directly on the meaning of 1 Timothy 2 for the women's issue. Articles related to women in other chapters of 1 Timothy are not included.

many do.[72] And virtually all of the 40 percent are best accounted for as symptomatic of the rise and onward march of the "progressive" outlook.

We conclude that the "progressive" claim simply to be interpreting the text with no fundamental indebtedness to the larger social milieu cannot be taken seriously.

But has the effect of the cultural milieu been deleterious? It can be argued that "progressive" exegetes are merely exercising cultural sensitivity, letting the Bible speak to cultural questions as new developments pose them. Whether one ought to accept this argument depends on whether the "progressive" hermeneutic constitutes a critical attenuation of the New Testament's content.

The Content-Critical Challenge

So far we have suggested the following: (1) based on chapters 1–5 of this book, the "historic" understanding of 1 Timothy 2:9–15 has firm exegetical support; (2) hermeneutics is central to one's understanding of how to apply the fruits of exegesis; (3) the spirit of social revolution of the last quarter century has brought woe to women and children, yet has generally received widespread endorsement in North American and European society and therefore churches; and (4) this same social pressure has exerted marked influence on the exegesis of 1 Timothy 2:9–15. The influence of this pressure is minimized by some who claim that they are merely interpreting what the text (when seen in the light of ancient social conditions, new lexical findings, or other considerations) had been saying all along. We believe this claim to be questionable.

In the present section we will make the argument that "progressive" exegesis of 1 Timothy 2:9–15 is hermeneutically risky because it is, if not formally, then at least materially Cartesian in nature, resulting in a content-critical hermeneutic that threatens the integrity of gospel belief and proclamation in the modern world.

"Cartesian" is a term used by H. Thielicke to describe the hermeneutical tendency of mainline biblical and theological studies since the Enlightenment.[73] This approach accepts the limits on its perception that

---

72. Not every article cataloged in *Religious Index One* was accessible to me for making precise determinations.

73. *The Evangelical Faith*, vol. 1, *Prolegomena: The Relationship of Theology to Modern Thought Forms*, trans. G. Bromiley (Grand Rapids: Eerdmans, 1974). By "Cartesian" Thielicke seems *not* to have in mind the (ontologically significant) "'real distinction' between mind and body" but rather Descartes' (epistemologically significant) "egocentric approach which is one of the most characteristic features of his philosophy and which, with its related insistence on epistemology as the starting point of philosophy, serves to distinguish it and much that followed it from most philosophy that preceded it" (B. Wil-

were established by Kant, essentially endorsing a Kantian epistemology[74] or some version of it. It is Cartesian in that it makes "the relevance of the knowing self the center of thought."[75] It is distinctly modern[76] in that it wants "to bring theological statements into harmony with the sense of truth as this has been transformed by historical and scientific study."[77] The Cartesian approach does not, at least not intentionally, set out "to give the modern self-consciousness a dominant position and then to accommodate Christian truth to it as a function."[78] Its concern is rather "to work out the possibilities of understanding Christian truth."[79] It is thus chiefly concerned with "the possible appropriation of the kerygma rather than its content."[80] In other words, it applies the text in the modern situation within the cognitive framework of modern thought instead of seeking from the text the means to construct a cognitive framework that might well clash with presumed modern certainties.

Yet Thielicke also mentions the danger of this approach: it might "do what was not intended and invest the subject of understanding with a normative rank for what is understood."[81] Instead of being a careful receptor, the reader might become an impatient editor, too hastily conforming the message of biblical utterances to his or her own prior understanding.

We will argue below that recent "progressive" handling of key biblical texts reflects a Cartesian, content-critical approach that calls for serious rethinking if current corrosive social pressures are to be offset and transcended by the gospel of Jesus Christ.[82]

---

liams, "Descartes, René," in *The Encyclopedia of Philosophy*, ed. P. Edwards, vol. 2 [New York: Macmillan & The Free Press/Collier Macmillan, 1967], 348, 346). Cf. Thielicke himself, 34f.; also more recently R. Bernstein, *Beyond Objectivism and Relativism*, 16ff., 115ff

74. What is meant by "Kantian epistemology" with reference to theological-historical understanding is partially outlined by D. McKenzie, "Kant and Protestant Theology," *Encounter* 43 (1982): 157–67; J. Luick, "The Ambiguity of Kantian Faith," *Scottish Journal of Theology* 36 (1983): 339–46. For more extended exposition, see R. Kroner, *The Primacy of Faith* (New York: Macmillan, 1943). In broad terms Kant "divorced reason from reality and reduced it to a subjective (though universal) grid our mind imposes upon an unknown and unknowable reality ('things-in-themselves'). In this post-Kantian climate, reason, no longer anchored in reality, floats on a subjective sea, blown by every wind: sociological, psychological, 'politically correct,' or even hormonal" (P. Kreeft, *Christianity for Modern Pagans* [San Franciso: Ignatius, 1993], 235).

75. Thielicke, *Evangelical Faith*, 1:34.

76. Thielicke (ibid., 33) points out that such modernity existed at least as far back as Semler (1725–91).

77. Ibid., 32.

78. Ibid., 33.

79. Ibid.

80. Ibid., 41.

81. Ibid., 33.

82. Owing to the fairly technical nature of the following section, the reader may want to scan or skip it and resume reading with the section below.

The Cartesian Character
of Post-Enlightenment Biblical Studies

As we have shown, interpretation of 1 Timothy 2 is currently dominated by voices calling for a new understanding of it. To grasp where
these voices come from, and where they may be leading, it will be useful
to track the history of modern scholarly biblical study since its inception in the late 1700s.[83] The late Martin Albertz (1882–1956) furnishes
a historical overview of the five major dominant syntheses in New Testament theology in the past two hundred years. To these we will add a
sixth.

To anticipate the point to be made from Albertz's survey: since the
inception of Enlightenment "critical" study of the Bible, the Bible's own
voice has been muffled by the intellectual constructs used to interpret
it. In other words, the presumed certainties of modern systems of
thought have suppressed the Bible's own message. If current new readings of 1 Timothy 2 and related passages follow this pattern—and it
seems that they do—then Albertz's typology is a useful tool for understanding the nature of those readings.

Albertz's starting point is the observation that New Testament theology from Gabler forward can be shown to have subordinated its subject
matter—the content of the Bible—"to the thought forms of the opinions
of schools of theology, which in the nineteenth and twentieth centuries
change like clothing fashions."[84] In all its various forms it is "content-
critical" *(sachkritisch)*.[85] That is, to borrow here from Rudolf Bultmann, it reads the Bible so as to distinguish "between what is stated and
what is meant, and assesses what is said in the light of what is meant."[86]
By this Bultmann was saying that the modern reader must constantly

---

83. Its inception might be traced back earlier—to Galileo, Richard Simon, Descartes,
Spinoza, or other key figures. See, e.g., K. Scholder, *The Birth of Modern Critical Theology*,
trans. J. Bowden (London/Philadelphia: SCM/Trinity Press International, 1990); W.
Baird, *History of New Testament Research*, vol. 1 (Minneapolis: Fortress, 1992). These
ideological giants all have their place. But my own studies lead me to find today's currents
most readily explicable in terms of trajectories arising at the time of J. Gabler's inaugu-
ration of the discipline of biblical theology in the modern sense (1787). This is also the
era that Schleiermacher's epoch-making synthesis was taking shape. Few if any dominant modern theological impulses are not rooted more or less directly either in the dynamics set in motion by post-Enlightenment "biblical theology" in all its critical, "historical," and synthetic rigor, or in the theological currents that Schleiermacher (with the
help of others of his day and since) set in motion.

84. Albertz, "Die Krisis der sogenannten neutestamentlichen Theologie," *Zeichen der
Zeit* 8 (1954): 371.

85. Unless otherwise indicated, translations of German language works are my own.

86. Bultmann, "Das Problem einer theologischen Exegese des Neuen Testaments," in
Das Problem der Theologie des Neuen Testaments, ed. G. Strecker (Darmstadt: Wissenschaftliche Buchgesellschaft, 1975), 256.

assess the text's surface assertions—"what is stated," or the signification—in the light of its significance, or what the enlightened modern
scholar believes that the text ought to be taken to mean. In this view the
arbiter of the text's meaning is ultimately not what the itself text says
but what the interpreter's own prior certainties decide that the text
must mean. This is the essence of the Cartesian approach.[87]

Albertz sees this as the logical outcome of technical New Testament
scholarship's roots in rationalism.[88] An integrated understanding of the
New Testament might well imply, from the New Testament's own point
of view, that in New Testament theology, "one ought to have started
from the premise of the living Christ, whose attestation the Bible is."[89]
But because of Gabler's (and others') rationalistic response to both orthodoxy and pietism of his day, scholars "fell prey, in the foundational
stages of our discipline, out of deference to an autonomous philosophy,
to an autonomous theology."[90] In other words, Gabler's program did not
just rightly invite evaluation of the historical remains of the Christian
tradition from a modern standpoint, a task whose legitimacy few would
question today. Additionally and sadly, it implicitly facilitated an a priori sacrifice of the content of that tradition in favor of the successive
ideological and hermeneutical certainties of the critics who assessed it.

Albertz identifies five different trends to which New Testament theology has submitted.

First is the Hegel–F. C. Baur line of thought.[91] This was the genius of
the well-known Tübingen school. Second is the "doctrinal concepts"
(lehrbegriffliche) method.[92] It was epitomized in B. Weiss's New Testament theology, which countered Tübingen's grand philosophical sweep
with painstaking detailed exegesis—but in the process reduced the New
Testament message to a passel of variegated messages conveying primarily didactic content. This was not always an adequate response to
the Tübingen challenge.

Third is the approach of "psychology of religion" *(Religionspsycholo-
gie)*, which Albertz sees much in evidence in his former teacher A. Harnack.[93] Albertz faults this approach for its uncritical endorsement of
Ritschlian liberalism, resulting in systematic misrepresentation of the
New Testament's message. Fourth is the history of religions direction

87. On the question of whether there can be "objectivity" in interpretation, see n. 10.
88. Apparently unwittingly, Albertz's argument is strikingly similar to the line taken
by A. Schlatter in the foreword to volume 2 of his New Testament theology (*Theologie der
Apostel* [Stuttgart: Calwer, 1922], 3).
89. Albertz, "Die Krisis," 371.
90. Ibid.
91. Ibid., 371f.; cf. Albertz, *Die Botschaft des Neuen Testaments*, vol. II/1 (Zollikon-
Zürich: Evangelischer Verlag, 1954), 15f.
92. Albertz, *Botschaft* II/1, 16f.; "Die Krisis," 372.
93. Albertz, *Botschaft* II/1, 17; "Die Krisis," 372.

of research, typified by W. Bousset and H. Weinel.[94] The whole of biblical history is reduced here to "a phenomenon of human culture." Albertz protests that "the Lord whom the gospel proclaims is not to be understood as merely one of the founders of the world's great religions."

Fifth, Albertz turns to the work of R. Bultmann (1884–1976), probably the single most influential New Testament scholar of the twentieth century. Bultmann, says Albertz, takes up and follows to their logical conclusions the vital characteristics of all four preceding research trajectories.[95] Following F. C. Baur he reduces New Testament theology to an evaluation of Paul and John, deducing the system of both on the basis of a predetermined theological position which, when necessary, reads Paul even against himself when his thought does not hew to the lines of the dictates of Bultmann's overarching method (we will come back to Baur's "content-critical" method below). Following the "doctrinal concepts methods" *(Lehrbegriffsmethode),* Bultmann's chief concern is the thought and "theologies" of the various writers, while the message of the New Testament itself furnishes for Bultmann "merely the presuppositions of this theology."[96] Following Schleiermacher and ultimately Harnack in their psychology of man and religion, Bultmann's New Testament theology comprises the "dismantling of theology in favor of anthropology."[97] Following the history of religions school, Bultmann understands early Christianity as "syncretistic religion."[98] Following social pressure (if unconsciously) as well as E. Stauffer's precedent in his *New Testament Theology,*[99] Bultmann's New Testament theology is "conditioned by a worldview."[100]

Albertz concludes with the penetrating observation: "Like all his great liberal predecessors [Bultmann] does homage to the absolute demands of the philosophical system he employs. He does the same thing that the theological students following Hegel once did: he does violence to the message using the categories of a modern philosophy."[101]

Bultmann's New Testament theology thus epitomizes the "erroneous development which characterizes all New Testament theological research."[102] From Gabler to Bultmann one travels full circle: still today, just as when Gabler felt constrained to set forth fresh guidelines for New

94. Ibid.
95. Albertz, "Die Krisis," 374; *Botschaft* II/1, 18ff.
96. Ibid.
97. Ibid.
98. Ibid.
99. Trans. J. Marsh (London: SCM, 1955). Stauffer's work was first published in Germany during Nazi dominance. Albertz detected in it a thinly veiled polemic against the Nazi position based on the worldview that Stauffer believed the New Testament implies.
100. Albertz, "Die Krisis," 374; *Botschaft* II/1, 18ff.
101. Albertz, "Die Krisis," 374; *Botschaft* II/1, 20.
102. Ibid.

Testament scholarship, New Testament theology does not faithfully explicate the message of its sources but rather systematically subjects them to reigning—and fleeting—modes of philosophical thought. New Testament theology has consistently let "the standards of its criticism" be dictated to it "by the surrounding culture."[103] Recently S. Hauerwas has voiced similar criticism of academic handling of the Bible in the current American setting, speaking of the need to "free theology from its academic captivity" in which theologians have generally "abandoned Scripture."[104] The result is that "New Testament theology" can from one point of view be seen largely as a learned revisionist enterprise that in the end loses sight of its subject matter's living reality and message.

Concern arises immediately that Albertz has in mind "foolishly . . . a repudiation of the historical-critical work of the last century and a half."[105] Yet his remarks, coming from a product of vintage German liberal theological education (his teachers included Gunkel, Harnack, and Zahn) and a seasoned veteran of lectern, pulpit, and prison[106] are hardly the one-sided charges of a novice or outsider. Albertz's concern and position are, in fact, echoed in more recent remarks by P. Stuhlmacher, among others, as he has attempted "critically to ponder the historical method as such."[107] G. Maier's recent work in hermeneutics belongs in the same category.

To Albertz's five schools of thought we may add a post-Bultmannian sixth: liberation theology. It repudiates classic "modernist" liberalism as too bourgeois, too set on scientific certainty, and too white, male, and Euro-American in orientation. And if it scorns "modernist" liberals, it ridicules "precritical" Christians when it mentions them at all.[108] Liberation theology is but one expression of a wider movement of thought called postmodernism. Its confessed fundamental characteristic is epistemological relativism.[109] It is possible, however, to see it as just a more recent version of one of the many "modernist" constructs that have come and gone since the Enlightenment.[110] It makes no essential

---

103. Albertz, "Die Krisis," 375.

104. *Unleashing the Scripture* (Nashville: Abingdon, 1993), 8f.

105. O. Merk's charge in *Biblische Theologie des Neuen Testaments in ihrer Anfangszeit* (Marburg: N. G. Elwert, 1972), 2.

106. Albertz was jailed for his opposition to Nazi policies.

107. Stuhlmacher, ". . . in verrosteten Angeln," *Zeitschrift für Theologie und Kirche* 77 (1980): 223.

108. Well-known liberation advocate W. Brueggemann, *Texts under Negotiation* (Minneapolis: Fortress, 1993), viii, seems to have traditional confessional Christians in mind when he speaks of "some important enclaves of eighteenth-century faith that deserve eighteenth-century criticism."

109. F. B. Burnham, ed., *Postmodern Theology* (San Franciso: Harper & Row, 1989), x.

110. Diogenes Allen, "Christianity and the Creed of Postmodernism," *Christian Scholars Review* 23, no. 2 (1993): 117–26. I am indebted to Matthew Floding for calling my attention to this article.

break with the five schools of thought outlined above in terms of their Cartesian character. Like its predecessors, it reifies a given worldview that is foreign to that of the biblical writers, then interprets (some of) the biblical writers' words in the light of that worldview.

For our purposes liberation theology is especially significant because it is the rubric under which we find Christian variations on feminism. Liberation theology, with its broad international influence, formidable establishment backing by university and mainline church, and professed antipathy toward classic Christian orthodoxy is the ideological shield behind which feminist theologies of any description find their legitimacy and make their advance. Evangelical feminists seek to appropriate some of liberation theology's key insights without endorsing its liabilities,[111] but they are faced with a delicate balancing act in which they at best preserve their own souls and, in their view, better women's lot in the small world of evangelical hegemony; they are certainly not altering the face of liberation theology in its much larger and virulent worldwide influence and appeal.

How do the six movements in theology described above relate to the hermeneutics of 1 Timothy 2? Simply this: they remind us of "modern" thought's systemic inability over the past two hundred years to let the biblical texts stock its conceptual larder with the gospel's own content of truth as it is in Jesus. Instead, successive intellectual constructs have dictated to biblical interpreters what they must find when they look at the biblical texts. They have employed a Cartesian method along the lines defined by Thielicke. This is not surprising, since Enlightenment biblical interpretation and its offshoots share the premise that with the help of critical reason they can (and must) liberate the Bible from the dogmatic chains of pre-Enlightenment Christian theology.[112] In other

---

111. See recently Groothuis, *Women Caught in the Conflict*, who wants to embrace feminism's freedoms without committing its sins. Her admission (111) that evangelical feminism continues "along the lines of a tradition [i.e., early American feminism] begun nearly two hundred years ago" is highly damaging, since "early American feminism maintained that the Bible had been mistranslated and misinterpreted so as to appear to teach the subordination of women as a universal norm. This twisting of the true message of Scripture, they believed, occurred at the hands of men who approached Scripture from the premise that men are primary and women secondary" (ibid.). There is little to separate this watershed hermeneutical premise from that held by secular, liberal, and liberationist understanding of Scripture today, and few would argue that most modern evangelical feminists first came to their views by reading early American feminists. They were influenced rather by modern nonevangelical ideologues and exegetes (who also knew nothing of the obscure figures and exegetical lightweights like Sarah Grimké that Groothuis cites) and the prevalent spirit of emancipated selfhood.

112. Gabler's method ultimately presupposes a rationalist foundation for understanding Scripture, thereby according dogmatic status to rationalism in place of the Christian dogmas that rationalism repudiated; cf. G. Strecker, "Das Problem der Theologie des Neuen Testaments," in *Das Problem der Theologie des Neuen Testaments*, 9.

words, the only scholarly reading of the Bible could be one that was at its core anti-Christian, taking Christian in its classic creedal sense.[113] But what is surprising is the extent to which the intrinsically quasi- if not anti-Christian bent of biblical scholarship has been glossed over by those who practice it. Scholars perform formidable feats of erudition requiring lifelong devotion and sacrifice with the ostensible aim of interpreting the Bible, but their underlying aims appear inimical to the gospel cause. A good example may be observed in the preface and introduction to a celebrated study that assumes the high moral ground of fidelity to Jesus, yet casts doubt on some 82 percent of Jesus' words contained in the four Gospels and heaps scorn on anyone who questions its premises and results, especially Bible-believing Christians.[114]

Something similar may be developing at the moment in the way that 1 Timothy 2 is being handled. If it can be shown that "progressive" interpretation of it is seriously indebted to the Cartesian, content-critical tendency outlined by Albertz and typified in postmodern-liberation-feminist interpretation, then "progressive" hermeneutics may risk compromising the text's message by subjecting it to contemporary certainties that are at least foreign and possibly hostile to it.

Content Criticism of 1 Timothy 2:9–15: Stendahl and Bruce

We have alluded to a group of exegetes, theologians, and others who are probably aware that the arguments for "progressive" readings of 1 Timothy 2:9–15 are novel but who feel they are justified by an equally novel assessment of another Pauline text: Galatians 3:28.[115] This group

113. Many scholars have tried, with varying degrees of success, to integrate the goal of post-Enlightenment biblical research with premises and methods not hostile to the gospel. But in historical perspective these scholars' contributions, while laudable, have not won the day on the international scene: The secularization of Western cultural and of mainline Western Christendom has continued apace. A plausible application of this observation: It is important that evangelicals today not overestimate the extent to which they are changing the world by their renewed scholarly production since the 1950s. Until these gains translate into markedly transformed community life, both in the church and beyond, any proclamation of a new Reformation would be premature. In the postmodern setting all kinds of ideas proliferate in print, and all kinds of religious movements make their mark. But there is negligible indication at the moment that the emergent truth of the world of tomorrow is the Christian gospel (though it would be pleasant to discover otherwise). And this means it is dangerous to be naive about the fundamentally anti-Christian character of much scholarly biblical study. See Craig M. Gay, "The Uneasy Intellect of Modern Evangelicalism" *Crux* 26, no. 3 (1990): 8–11.

114. See R. Funk, R. Hoover, and the Jesus Seminar, *The Five Gospels* (New York: Macmillan, 1993), ix–xviii, 1–38.

115. The present book's focus on 1 Timothy 2 does not permit the detailed exegetical and hermeneutical demonstration of how Gal. 3:28 fits neatly with the "historic" interpretation of 1 Timothy 2. Suffice it to say that it is equally wrong to allow "content criticism" to give priority to 1 Timothy 2 over Gal. 3:28 as vice versa. For some pertinent remarks regarding fallacious hermeneutical approaches to Gal. 3:28, including discussions

is perhaps best typified by two well-known New Testament scholars, K. Stendahl and the late F. F. Bruce.[116] Stendahl's voice was seminal in raising the issue of hermeneutics and the interpretation of New Testament passages dealing with women's roles. Bruce will go down as perhaps the most influential evangelical New Testament scholar in English-speaking Christendom in the latter half of the twentieth century. We will argue that in handling New Testament passages on gender roles, both employ a Cartesian and content-critical method reminiscent of the six major schools of New Testament theology just described.

Stendahl's essay was written to further the cause of women's ordination in the Church of Sweden in the late 1950s. He criticizes liberal theology for its "conscious or unconscious tendency to judge and evaluate texts and ideas from the first century by the anachronistic standards of modern Western values and sentiments."[117] He praises what he calls "realistic interpretation," by which he appears to refer to what others called the "biblical theology movement" with roots in the 1920s and whose flower lasted from about the end of World War II to sometime in the 1960s. "Realistic interpretation" is invaluable because unlike both liberal and fundamentalist interpretation, it recognizes the enormous gap "between the first and the twentieth centuries."[118] The realistic interpreter "is a good enough historian to recognize that everything is conditioned by the actual situation of the time," so that "Jesus and Paul shared the exegetical and cultural presuppositions of their time" even when speaking of matters that "they considered . . . 'timeless truths' of fundamental significance."[119] The realistic interpreter "may even question whether the idea of 'timeless truth' is congenial to the biblical material in which the revelation in the Scriptures is always open to interpretation."[120] Such statements indicate already that Stendahl is prepared to

---

of an integrative nature, see Andreas J. Köstenberger, "Gender Passages in the NT: Hermeneutical Fallacies Critiqued," *Westminster Theological Journal* 56 (1994): 269–94.

116. Similar hermeneutical approaches, and a use of Gal. 3:28 virtually unheard of in technical exegesis prior to the latter half of the twentieth century, are available in P. K. Jewett, *Man as Male and Female* (Grand Rapids: Eerdmans, 1975); R. Longenecker, *New Testament Social Ethics for Today* (Grand Rapids: Eerdmans, 1984); C. Boomsma, *Male and Female, One in Christ* (Grand Rapids: Baker, 1993). For trenchant criticism of Longenecker, see T. Tiessen, "Toward a Hermeneutic for Discerning Universal Moral Absolutes," *Journal of the Evangelical Theological Society* 36, no. 2 (1993): 189–207, esp. 203ff. For nineteenth-century adumbrations of current views, see D. Dayton, *Discovering an Evangelical Heritage* (Peabody, Mass.: Hendrickson, 1976), 90–93. These earlier interpretations grew up more in connection with the application of Gal. 3:28 to the slavery issue than to the theories of personhood that make Gal. 3:28 so central at present.

117. Stendahl, *The Bible and the Role of Women*, trans. E. Sander (Philadelphia: Fortress, 1966), 10.

118. Ibid., 11.

119. Ibid., 13.

120. Ibid.

sweep aside the Bible's certainties—even those stated by Christ himself—when these conflict with modern cultural presuppositions.

Stendahl's key insight is that rightly interpreting the New Testament requires a sense for what is absolute and enduring in its pages, on the one hand, and what is ephemeral and nonbinding for later times, on the other. This is the heart of his call for attention to "hermeneutics." For Stendahl "the center of revelation" in the Bible is "God and his mighty acts." In contrast, biblical statements about persons are peripheral and nonrevelatory: "The understanding of man in the biblical view is valuable for our reading of the content and consequences of revelation, but it can hardly be the revelation itself."[121] He concludes: "Against this background it seems natural to see the understanding of man in the New Testament—an integral part of the 'biblical view'—as distinct from the revelation itself, as anchored in the event, in the Christ event. Then this must also refer to the question concerning the relationship between male and female both in home and congregation."[122]

For Stendahl, then, when the Bible speaks of humans, its outlook is not authoritative for later times. This enables him to preserve the theory of biblical authority in purely theological matters, while at the same time admitting that there is hardly any "element in the gospels which transcends the essentially Palestinian Jewish frame of ideas. Jesus' sayings touching on the relationship between men and women all fall within this fundamental view,"[123] a patriarchal[124] outlook quite out of line with modern convictions about persons and roles. The claim to hallow the Bible by frankly critiquing and finally correcting it is a hallmark of content-critical approaches since Gabler.

But, Stendahl continues, even in the New Testament, if not in Jesus' example or teaching then at least in the course of early church developments, there is hope. This hope rests in Galatians 3:28 ("There is neither Jew nor Greek, slave nor free, male nor female, for you are all one in Christ Jesus"), which represents a "breakthrough."[125] It is the wave of the future for those "in Christ" and in fact for the world as a whole.

Stendahl's "progressive" hermeneutic thus involves pitting Galatians 3:28 (and a few other Pauline phrases he thinks hint in the same egalitarian direction) against other passages that speak of women's subordination. This includes 1 Timothy 2:9–15. No clearer example of the "content-critical" procedure alluded to above could be imagined. What the Bible repeatedly states (classic passages include Col. 3:18–19; Eph. 5:22–33; Titus 2:5–8; 1 Pet. 2:18–25) and everywhere as-

121. Ibid., 23.
122. Ibid., 24.
123. Ibid., 26.
124. Ibid., 27.
125. Ibid., 32.

sumes[126] is set aside by the hermeneutical move of declaring the Bible culturally bound when it speaks about people. Prophetic, dominical, and apostolic insight take a back seat to the presumed superior vantage point of the modern or postmodern West.

Stendahl's "breakthrough" verse, Galatians 3:28, carries virtually the whole weight of his argument because of its reference to "slave and free." If this verse is properly understood to mandate the abolition of slavery in society, or even declare it to be sinful, then why cling to distinctions that fail to realize that "male and female" are likewise distinctions requiring abolition in ecclesiastical and home settings?[127] This is an important issue and one to which we will return in the next section when we discuss a recent and impressive study of the slavery issue and its relation to the hermeneutics of 1 Timothy 2.

For now, we note that Stendahl calls for doing away with the "serious hermeneutical naïveté" that failed to realize that "the New Testament contain[s] elements, glimpses which point beyond and even 'against' the prevailing view and practice of the New Testament church."[128] Christians dare not play "First-Century Semites," accepting some "static 'biblical view'" of the past that is no longer appropriate today, nor pursue a "nostalgic attempt to play 'First-Century'" or "'First-Century Bible Land.'"[129]

Stendahl's confident, even flippant *ad absurdum* argumentation in these passages is a clue to his confidence in the plank upon which he builds: contemporary affirmation of women's liberation or "emancipation." "If emancipation is right, then there can be no valid 'biblical' reason not to ordain women."[130] He candidly admits that "the ideology or dogma which underlies both the movements of emancipation and the demand for the ordination of women is a secularized philosophy of

---

126. Cf. V. Hasler, *Die Briefe an Timotheus und Titus* (Zurich: Theologischer Verlag, 1978), 25: "In ancient thought people did not think of themselves as individuals but only as members of a community. This community was in turn a constituent element in a comprehensive order that encompassed heaven and earth. As a result, believers in their churches, synagogues, and other religious affiliations ordered their social and religious lives according to set ranks and classes. Thus Paul speaks of the baptized Christian's embeddedness in the body of Christ (1 Cor 12:27, Rom 12:5), of a God who does not promote disorder but peace (1 Cor 14:33), and even of the coiffure and proper place of the woman in the worship setting (1 Cor 11:2–16)." Hasler's statement is too sweeping and unqualified, but it does point out how out of sympathy with biblical anthropology Stendahl seems to be—not on exegetical grounds, but because of his cultural commitment to his own (unredeemed) social order.

127. G. Bilezikian, *Beyond Sex Roles*, 2nd ed. (Grand Rapids: Baker, 1989), 128, argues on this basis that "Sex distinctions are irrelevant in the church. Therefore, the practice of sex discrimination in the church is sinful."

128. Stendahl, *Bible and Role of Women*, 35, 34.

129. Ibid., 17, 35, 36.

130. Ibid., 41.

equality with roots in the Enlightenment or in Hellas or in the cult of Baal—in any case alien to the Bible."[131] But he thinks the "fruits" of recent social developments confirm their rightness. The basis, then, for his hermeneutical move is pragmatic. On that basis secular Western society's "belief in unlimited human freedom"[132] must be true, at least for the present world, while the Bible's counsel about persons and social order even in the church is wrong. Stendahl would perhaps say "wrong for today," though adequate for their own time.[133] This outlook seems reasonable in the current hermeneutical climate in which there are no universal transcendent verities. But is it compatible with a Christian view of revelation that takes the Bible as its authority? Or is it ultimately Cartesian and content-critical to a fault?

Ironically, Stendahl is as guilty of letting modern certainties determine his exegesis as the liberal and fundamentalist elements he opposes. For as Madeleine Boucher states in a study rejecting Stendahl's exegesis (though agreeing with his hermeneutics), "the ideas of equality before God and inferiority in the social order are in harmony in the New Testament. To be precise, the tension did not exist in first-century thought, and it is not present in the texts themselves. The tension arises from *modern man's* inability to hold these two ideas together."[134]

We conclude that in elevating certain underlying premises of "realistic biblical interpretation" and Bultmann's demythologizing program, both of which Stendahl admires, he is rightly placed in the mainstream of the Cartesian and content-critical flow of post-Enlightenment biblical criticism with its tendency to uphold modernity at the expense of biblical authority in its full-orbed, rightful sense.

F. F. Bruce, despite his unquestioned evangelical credentials, takes up where Stendahl leaves off. If the latter argues for the need to appreciate the phenomenon of cultural relativity and incorporate it into one's hermeneutic, Bruce baptizes it at the outset; the first words of his treatment read, "The phenomenon of cultural relativity, with the adaptations it imposes, is repeatedly illustrated within the Bible itself."[135]

---

131. Ibid. One could wish that subsequent "progressive" thinkers were more honest in their historical judgments and less prone to revisionism.

132. Allen, *Christian Scholars Review* 23, no. 2 (1993): 121, calls this a "pillar of the modern mentality" and one of the key points at which postmodernism has not in any way separated from modernism.

133. This is also the underlying conviction of Keener, *Paul, Women and Wives*.

134. Boucher, "Some Unexplored Parallels to 1 Cor 11,11–12 and Gal 3,28: The NT on the Role of Women," *Catholic Biblical Quarterly* 31 (1969): 57. Boucher's insightful remark not only uncovers an irony; it creates a new one. In using "inferiority" to describe women's subordination in the biblical social order she seems to be using the same modern criteria of judgment that she cautions others not to employ.

135. Bruce, "Women in the Church: A Biblical Survey," in *A Mind for What Matters* (Grand Rapids: Eerdmans, 1990), 259.

The problem which Stendahl, writing in Swedish in the mid–1950s, could not have anticipated, and of which Bruce, writing in the late 1970s, seems unaware, is the meaning of "cultural relativity" in postmodern parlance. It is fundamental to what Diogenes Allen calls the "postmodern creed."[136] It is not simply a matter of cultures differing (the fact to which Bruce probably means to point). It is the claim that all science, literature, philosophy, and religion generally are "wholly imbedded in culture" (which Stendahl seems prepared to accept).[137] This is the entrée into what Diogenes Allen has called

> a particular kind of relativism. We not only construct the world, so that all knowledge, value, and meaning are relative to human beings, as Idealists since Kant have argued, but now the radical conclusion is drawn that there is no reality that is universally constructed because people in different periods of history and in different societies construct it differently. There is no definitive procedure or universal basis to settle disputes in the natural sciences, in ethics, and in the interpretation of literature. Every domain of inquiry and every value is relative to a culture and even to subcultures.[138]

Bruce would doubtless not have agreed with such an approach to knowledge. But his hermeneutical moves in the question at hand do little to discourage it. He calls for separating the temporal husk from the enduring kernel[139]—a hermeneutical tool so reminiscent of rationalists like Lessing that the student of the Enlightenment may be shocked to witness an evangelical scholar wielding it with such aplomb.[140] How do we know what is permanent? Whereas we might expect an appeal to Scripture, Bruce's sole stated criterion is that "whatever in Paul's teaching promotes true freedom is of universal and permanent validity; whatever seems to impose restrictions on true freedom has regard to local and temporary conditions."[141] Such language can only be under-

136. *Christian Scholars Review* 23, no. 2 (1993): 119.
137. Ibid.
138. Ibid. Challenging this view in a comprehensive way is Harris, *Against Relativism*.
139. Bruce, "Women in the Church," 260: "The local and temporary situation in which the message was first delivered must be appreciated if we are to discern what its permanent essence really is and learn to re-apply it in the local and temporary circumstances of our own culture."
140. Maier, *Biblical Hermeneutics*, 299ff., notes the use of this figure in Lessing, Strauss, Harnack, Dibelius, Dobschütz, and others. He points out that such separation of revelation's form from its content destroys "the Reformation foundation of *sola scriptura*" and ultimately attacks "the very foundation of being Christian itself" (301). Cf. Groothuis, *Women Caught in the Conflict*, 102, who attributes the masculine imagery for God in the Bible not to any truth about God's person or being but to God's need to "reveal himself to people in a patriarchal culture." Here the kernel of a more feminine God is removed from the husk of a paternal God required by the cultural order.
141. Bruce, "Women in the Church," 263.

stood as positing an extrabiblical standard—true freedom—which we may use to recognize the Bible's true utterances and to cancel out teachings of less lofty quality.

Given Bruce's restrained but consistent suspicion of the written Word (the Bible[142]) as inferior to the insight given by the living Spirit, there seems little to distinguish his approach in the question at hand from Stendahl's, in which the "fruit" and social acceptability of liberalized understanding of women's roles is decisive for determining what Christians today should make of the Bible's counsel. Bruce, like Stendahl, ultimately calls for pragmatics to determine hermeneutics: "experience shows that [the Holy Spirit] bestows . . . gifts, with 'undistinguishing regard,' on men and women alike. . . . That being so, it is unsatisfactory to rest with a halfway house in this issue of women's ministry, where they are allowed to pray and prophesy, but not to teach or lead."[143] This constitutes, of course, a distinctly Cartesian approach.

And for Bruce as for Stendahl, Paul's "revolutionary sentiment" of Galatians 3:28[144] serves to qualify 1 Timothy 2:9–15 in such a way as to set it to the side.[145] Bruce does affirm the Pastoral Epistles' canonicity and acknowledges that in 1 Timothy 2:11–12, "women are quite explicitly not given permission to teach or rule."[146] But he claims to be puzzled by verses 13–14 and unable to see how they support verses 11–12. Galatians 3:28 plays a key role in his puzzlement, since for Bruce it mandates what Paul in 1 Timothy 2 seems to forbid. Bruce cuts the Gordian knot by declaring "Nothing that Paul says elsewhere on women's contribution to church services [he refers to 1 Corinthians 14 and 1 Timothy 2] can be understood in a sense which conflicts with these statements of principle"[147] related to Galatians 3:28. "Content criti-

---

142. Ibid.: "In applying the New Testament text to our own situation, we need not treat it as the scribes of our Lord's day treated the Old Testament. We should not turn what were meant as guiding lines for worshipers in one situation into laws binding for all time. . . . The freedom of the Spirit, which can be safeguarded by one set of guiding lines in a particular situation, may call for a different procedure in a new situation." Bruce's dim view of written Scripture in comparison to the living Spirit who transcends written definition comes to the fore repeatedly in his *Paul: Apostle of the Heart Set Free* (Grand Rapids: Eerdmans, 1977), e.g., 80, 124, 182, 186f., 188ff., 463. In explicating Paul's alleged view of the Torah Bruce continually separates the (written) form of Scripture and its (spiritual) content. With due respect for the fact that Paul was not a legalist or even a nomist as such, Bruce's separation is more reminiscent of Semler or Gabler than of Paul.

143. Bruce, "Women in the Church," 264.

144. Ibid., 262.

145. For a more recent example of this move, see R. Pierce, "Evangelicals and Gender Roles in the 1990s: 1 Tim 2:8–15: A Test Case," *Journal of the Evangelical Theological Society*," 36, no. 3 (1993): 343–55.

146. Bruce, "Women in the Church," 263.

147. Ibid., 262.

cism" of 1 Timothy based on Galatians 3, grounded in the foundation of a pragmatic hermeneutics of cultural relativity, is Bruce's way to settle the impasse.

The problem with Bruce's and Stendahl's method is not that it recognizes tensions in the Bible. The Reformation principle that Scripture interprets Scripture (*sacra scriptura sui interpres*) implies the presence of obscure or ostensibly conflicting passages. The problem lies in their recourse to a distinctly modern consciousness to adjudicate Scripture's meaning. This is to step outside the horizon of Scripture to determine Scripture's significance. It is to imperil the *sola Scriptura* doctrine of the Reformation and even before.[148]

The Hermeneutical Problem of Slavery

The case for Cartesian and content-critical handling of New Testament passages like 1 Timothy 2:9–15 has received recent strong support from K. Giles.[149] His article is ultimately not so much about slavery as about what he calls "the subordination of women," by which he appears to mean applications of exegesis following a "historic" rather than "progressive" line. His thesis nicely summarizes what both Stendahl and Bruce argued with less comprehensiveness and verve:

> If it can be shown that the Bible does in fact unambiguously endorse both the institution and the practice of slavery, although we cannot now accept slavery in any form, then we will have discovered something about the nature of biblical revelation which will help resolve the present debate about the status and role of women. We will have learnt that Scripture can endorse social structures no longer acceptable, just as we have learnt that the Bible can endorse scientific ideas no longer tenable. The Bible is authoritative in matters of faith and conduct but not necessarily in science, or on how to order social relations.[150]

At a number of points one can only agree with Giles' analysis, which centers on American slavery in the Old South and its purportedly biblical defense by Reformed theologians like Dabney, Thornwall, and Charles Hodge. Southern slavery was a great evil. Much of the defense

---

148. Augustine, e.g., states on the one hand: "Thus whatever evidence we have of past times in that which is called history helps us a great deal in the understanding of the sacred books [i.e., the Bible], even if we learn it outside of the Church as a part of our childhood education." Yet on the other hand: "[T]he truth of propositions is a matter to be discovered in the sacred books of the Church [i.e., the Bible]." See Augustine's *On Christian Doctrine*, trans. D. W. Robertson Jr. (Indianapolis: Bobbs-Merrill, 1983), 63, 68. Augustine does not disparage extrabiblical learning in principle, yet refuses to grant it parity with biblical revelation.

149. "The Biblical Case for Slavery: Can the Bible Mislead? A Case Study in Hermeneutics," *Evangelical Quarterly* 66, no. 1 (1994): 3–17.

150. Ibid., 4.

mounted in its favor deserves criticism and not a little of it rejection. Racism is roundly condemned by both Testaments. Devout Christians with sophisticated hermeneutical understanding and formidable learning can be wrong in interpreting and applying the Bible. Giles rightly drives these important points home.

Nevertheless, Giles' point is not well taken that the slavery analogy as he presents it proves that those who hold the "historic" view of women's roles in church and home are guilty of the same heinous sins as Old South slaveholders and those who defended them, while "progressive" interpreters are the modern equivalent of righteous abolitionists. A number of considerations serve to vitiate Giles' claims.

First, by Giles' logic his own "progressive" hermeneutic is responsible for the social evils of post-Enlightenment, post-slavery liberal governments and nations. If Southern Reformed "historic" hermeneutics should be blamed for endorsing the social order of its day with all its attendant ills, then Giles' theology, which defends and enshrines the modern liberal social order of emancipation, must share the guilt of the wars, injustices, and inequities that the liberal social order since, say, the American or French Revolution, has produced. Christians who argue a just war theory in the modern world must be blamed for Hiroshima and Nagasaki. American Christians whose fear of federal control moves them to oppose the abolition of the right to bear arms are guilty for the thousands of homicides committed with handguns. Such charges are, of curse, ludicrous. But if they are, then so is the basic logic on which Giles depends.

Second, Giles' case (and all like it) makes the fundamental mistake of seeing in modern enlightened Western social orders the opposite of ancient repressive social orders, like those that dominate the whole of biblical history in which slavery was a universal fact of life. To the contrary, the opposite of the social order that prevailed in biblical times, cursed as it was with many sins and inherent inequities, is the kingdom of God in its endtime fullness. Other alternatives are likely to be some version or mix of the following: a world of intensified Western materialistic decadence; stifling collectivist oppression;[151] or mass anarchy, from whose horrors none is likely to escape. In any case, to imagine that the Western world order of the twentieth century is so superior to that of biblical times that we can declare slavery a thing of the past is tastelessly self-congratulatory. It fails to take seriously the social wreckage of just this century alone, much of it the fruit of our supposedly enlightened modern age. While it is true that the biblical world (if we may

---

151. "Totalitarianism always brings slavery with it. The totalitarianism of the Kingdom of God alone is an affirmation of freedom" (Nicolai Berdyaev, *Slavery and Freedeom*, trans. R. M. French [New York: Charles Scribner's Sons, 1944], 206).

speak of it monolithically) was far from utopian, it is not as easy as Giles imagines to demonstrate the inherently higher moral ground of modernity in the area of social relations.

Giles overlooks the all-important sense in which the modern equivalent to slaves has not disappeared. It is present in the form of those who work for a living—which, in all social orders yet devised, including liberal Western ones, means virtually everyone.[152]

True, we are not "slaves" in the most restricted sense imaginable, following Giles' definition: (1) the property of another human being, (2) completely subject to an owner's authority, and (3) granting our labor under coercion.[153] But the sentiment voiced in an old Tennessee Ernie Ford pop song, "I owe my soul to the company store,"[154] is the heart cry of all laborers, white- or blue-collar, sometimes, and of many at all times. The same curse that decreed sweat from the brow and thorns from the earth and that lay behind the social expression that was slavery in the ancient Near East takes the form of a much different social order today—and yet very similar in its essence. A few still reign, and most still serve them with the best efforts of their productive years. The alternative is to suffer the consequences—at best welfare or the dole, otherwise life on the streets.

Tolstoy saw this clearly. Surveying the situation in both Europe and America in 1900 he noted, "People of our day consider the position of labourers to be a natural, inevitable, economic condition, and they do not call it slavery. . . . [T]he majority as yet are convinced that among us no slavery exists."[155] He explains: "A thing that helps people today to misunderstand their position in this matter is the fact that we have, in Russia and in America, only recently abolished slavery. But in reality the abolition of serfdom and of slavery was only the abolition of an obsolete form of slavery that had become unnecessary, and the substitu-

---

152. Some of the most tortured souls I ever met were Romanians soon after the 1989 revolution who had been "employed" in factories which, due to the collapsing economy, had done no work for years. The most bitter epithet they could hurl at the Communists: "They would not let us work." Work, even in the coercive world of Nicolae Ceausescu, may be a more redeemable fate than many jaded, relatively affluent, and chronically employed Westerners seem to realize. "Slavery" in its sometimes relatively benign ancient forms was not always as hellish as might be imagined (as Giles rightly recognizes: *Evangelical Quarterly* 66, no. 1 [1994]: 15f.).

153. Ibid., 3.

154. I am told by a historian that miners using company stores truly were in slavery. Employers calculated how much miners needed to earn in order to purchase sufficient supplies at the store—and then deliberately paid them slightly less than this amount, extending them credit to make up the difference. The longer they worked, the "deeper in debt" (to quote Ford's song again) they were mired. At worst this is only nominally different in kind from plantation slavery.

155. Leo Tolstoy, "The Slavery of Our Time," in *Government Is Violence: Essays on Anarcihsm* [sic] *and Pacifism* (London: Phoenix Press, 1990), 130.

tion for it of a firmer form of slavery, and one that holds a greater number of people in bondage."[156] In socioeconomic terms, to say nothing of the underlying spiritual level of slavery to the hankering for things and pleasures for which the consumerist Western worker toils,[157] Tolstoy rightly sees that enslaving social orders have by no means disappeared in the modern West.[158]

It is certainly true that in many respects the modern order is more urbane. But is it necessarily more humane? Historians of other times paint surprisingly civilized portraits of daily life in classical antiquity or medieval feudal times long before the European Enlightenment and the Declaration of Independence. Personally I would rather read about those times, I think, than trust the historians enough to volunteer to relive them. I am spoiled by today's creature comforts and ostensible liberties. But we must reject the view that modern societies free of slavery (granting for now that they exist) so nearly embody the social order of the eschaton that we can let those societies' social relations provide the content-critical key for critiquing revealed Scripture when it touches on social relations. This would be unwise. Furthermore, it is a most implausible reading of Galatians 3:28, since Paul here envisioned an order that resulted from being "in Christ." That describes only a small percentage of North Americans and probably fewer Europeans if missiological reports are correct. Berdyaev sternly warns that slavery, "the spell and slavery of collectivism," is the inevitable result of attempting to project the depersonalized virtues of truly spiritual Christian camaraderie onto the social institutions of a society in general apart from the personal transformation of the members of that society.[159]

It is possible that Giles is inadvertently echoing liberation theological reasoning that "redemption" means political, economic, and ultimately personal self-determination; this is the "emancipation" for which Jesus of Nazareth died and to which all, including slaves and women are entitled.[160] But Romans 6:12–14 is typical of an overarching

---

156. Ibid.

157. See Berdyaev, "The Lure of the Bourgeios Spirit: Slavery to Property and Money," in *Slavery and Freedom*, 181–89.

158. Cf. W. Ramsay, *A Historical Commentary on St. Paul's Epistle to the Galatians* (Grand Rapids: Baker, 1965 [1900]), 385: "nominally we have abolished slavery, but really slavery is far from abolished in any country."

159. *Slavery and Freedom*, 201.

160. See, e.g., J. Cavanaugh, *Following Christ in a Consumer Society* (Maryknoll, N.Y.: Orbis, 1989). In such a paradigm salvation becomes primarily political: "To become a Christian means, in my perspective, to be enabled to participate in the liberation struggle" (Dorthy Sölle, response to H. D. Betz, in Betz, "Paul's Concept of Freedom in the Context of Hellenistic Discussions about the Possibilities of Human Freedom," in *Protocol of the Colloquy of the Center for Hermeneutical Studies in Hellenistic and Modern Culture* [Berkeley, Calif.: Center for Hermeneutical Studies, 1977], 29).

biblical conviction that all persons in all times are either free with regard to God's righteousness, being slaves to sin, or redeemed from sin's tyranny and thereby handed over to enslavement to God. The transformation of the social order as such, then, while not unimportant, is far less a key to kingdom actualization for (say) Paul than it seems to be to many moderns. Whether we choose to embrace Paul's or moderns' insight into the human condition vis-à-vis Christ's redemption will make a considerable difference in the hermeneutic we employ.

A third and final hermeneutically significant objection to Giles' case is the gravity of his claim, "The Bible is authoritative in matters of faith and conduct but not necessarily in science, or on how to order social relations."[161] It is not clear how this can be taken seriously as an adequately biblical understanding of scriptural authority. How much of life can be safely regarded as bereft of implications related to "social relations"? The great commandment to love others is surely inseparable from "social relations." Yet in Giles' view we are now suddenly without necessarily trustworthy biblical counsel for our lives in this crucial area of spiritual response. The leap from the correct observation that God contextualizes his message for the peoples and times he addresses through Scripture to the programmatic assertion that we do not regard Scripture as authoritative when it touches on "social relations" is a fateful hermeneutical move that many will rightly hesitate to endorse.[162]

We conclude that Giles fails to sustain the parallel he posits in a satisfactory way. The tragic Reformed defense of Southern slavery is insufficient ground to accuse the Bible of deception or culpable cultural embeddedness.[163] The self-congratulatory appeal of modern Westerners overlooks that modern liberal economic and labor structures[164] are

---

161. *Evangelical Quarterly* 66, no. 1 (1994): 4.

162. See, e.g., A. Schlatter, *Die Kirche der Griechen im Urteil des Paulus*, 2nd ed. (Stuttgart: Calwer, 1958), 91n. for detailed examples of the close ties in Paul's writings between sanctification and relations between the sexes.

163. I. H. Marshall attempts something of a mediating position, absolving Paul of guilt in the slavery issue without denying that he failed to see the heinousness of the institution per se with the clarity made possible by the modern social order: "We find ourselves concluding that the fuller implication of Paul's teaching [in Philemon] is that the Christian faith is incompatible with the ownership of slaves. Paul himself may not have come to this realisation, but he had charted a route which leads to this destination" ("The Theology of Philemon," in K. P. Donfried and I. H. Marshall, eds., *The Theology of the Shorter Pauline Epistles* [Cambridge: University Press, 1993], 190). This appears to be a more workable, because nuanced, postion than Giles', though the notion that "the fuller implication" of apostolic teaching in one place might support "the Christian faith" in calling into question apostolic teaching in another place may be a hermeneutical principle easier to formulate than control.

164. "Liberalism in economic and social life has been the ideology of capitalism. . . . The wage system is a system of slavery" (Berdyaev, *Slavery and Freedom*, 211).

in essential respects too reminiscent of the ancient institution of slavery to condemn the Bible's world order, praise our own, and then use it as a standard to give biblical counsel on social relations our thumbs-up or -down.

We have dwelt at length on Giles' contentions because his stance epitomizes a by now stock justification for "progressive" reinterpretations of biblical pronouncements about men, women, and their respective places in God's economy.[165] If Giles be followed and the implications of his views traced out fully in years ahead, then we may have seen only the beginning of revised understandings of social, and inevitably sexual, relations in ostensibly Bible-believing circles. We may be at the threshold of any number of behavioral and philosophical adjustments rendered plausible even in evangelical churches by unfolding social mores now that the Bible is silent for us, if not flatly wrong, on these topics. (In many nonevangelical circles, of course, society's mores replaced the Bible in the area of social relations long ago.)

But if Giles' arguments lack the sweeping powers to validate "progressive" hermeneutics that he claims, then that hermeneutic loses the powerful rhetorical and comparative validation of the slavery analogy in interpreting 1 Timothy 2:9–15. It must be content to bear full responsibility for its content-critical procedure in which some parts of Scripture (in this case Gal. 3:28) serve to cancel out others. And it must face squarely the exegetical liabilities set forth elsewhere in this volume.

Toward a Progressive "Historic" Hermeneutic

To the extent that the preceding arguments are sound, the hermeneutics informing the "progressive" interpretation of 1 Timothy 2:9–15 deserve to be called into question. The "historic" exegesis of the passage should be allowed to stand, as the first five chapters of this book maintain. Some offices and responsibilities in church and home[166] are biblically mandated as the peculiar province of men and husbands. No necessary or even sufficient hermeneutical grounds (exegetical grounds

165. See, e.g., Groothuis, *Women Caught in the Conflict*, 31–39, and elsewhere.

166. "Progressive" interpreters in favor of women's ordination who do not wish to set aside the apostolic teaching of Christian wives' deference to their husbands sometimes try to separate New Testament teaching on the home from teaching on order in the church. This view overlooks that the early church was probably of a house church nature throughout the New Testament period. See V. Poythress, *The Church as Family* (Wheaton, Ill.: Council of Biblical Manhood and Womanhood, 1990), rpt. in *Recovering Biblical Manhood and Womanhood* (Wheaton, Ill.: Crossway, 1991), 233–47. There is no compelling biblical ground for declaring church order a thing hermetically sealed off from home order in subsequent times (despite the fact that this is often come about in the course of church tradition).

have been matters for earlier chapters) for overturning the "historic" interpretive framework for understanding of biblical counsel on this subject have been found. We have tried to show that hermeneutical moves to circumvent "historic" exegesis fall short of being persuasive.

In conclusion, we wish briefly to summarize the liabilities of the "progressive" hermeneutic. We will also call for refinement of the hermeneutic underlying the "historic" exegesis of 1 Timothy 2:9–12 for which this book argues.

Summary Reflections on a "Progressive" Hermeneutic

It should be underscored that the Stendahl–Bruce approach, now widespread even in evangelical circles,[167] is fraught with considerable danger. This comes especially clearly to light in the historical perspective we established in the previous section. It may be easy for pragmatic Americans and anti-intellectual evangelicals to ignore the sweep of history, but, like it or not, Stendahl and Bruce are very much indebted to it, as is the "progressive" approach in general. It is novel and depends on modernity for its persuasive power. It is Cartesian and content-critical. It is easy to see these qualities looking as far back as the Enlightenment, the Tübingen school, Harnack, and Bultmann. All these movements were, in the end, inimical to the gospel, though they all protested innocence at the time, typically saying that they were not contradicting the gospel, just reinterpreting it in keeping with an altered intellectual climate. It takes little imagination, though perhaps considerable will and nerve, to see the same dynamics at work in the "progressive" movement now as it follows the postmodern and liberation theological lead.

It is helpful to recall the social track record of modernity in its present treatment of women and children. Their fate in "emancipated" America hardly argues for the biblical sanction of social developments that have brought their woes into being, and promise to extend them for at least the next generation, if not longer. For the cycle will not be easy to break.

---

167. Gal. 3:28 as Stendahl and Bruce understand it is the foundation of Groothuis, *Women Caught in the Conflict*; this verse or its context accounts for nine of only fifty-four Scripture references in a book of over two hundred pages. On the opening page (1) Groothuis defines "the gospel of Jesus Christ" with reference to Gal. 3:28, expanded on later with the assertion that "the biblical truth of the equality of all persons under God is entailed by the biblical message of salvation" (155). In this understanding Gal. 3:28 essentially replaces the function of, e.g., Rom. 1:16–17 or John 3:16 in earlier understandings of the heart of the gospel. Similarly J. W. Cooper, *A Cause for Division? Women in Office and the Unity of the Church* (Grand Rapids: Calvin Theological Seminary, 1991), 42f. establishes "the analogy of Scripture" along a continuum stretching from "The First Word" of Gen. 1:26–28 to "The Last Word" of Rev. 22:5 with "Paul's Middle Word" being Gal. 3:28. It is no wonder that he dismisses 1 Corinthians 14 and 1 Timothy 2 because "the right exegesis cannot be established with certainty" (53). Preset hermeneutical parameters have ruled out certain exegetical conclusions—the danger of a Cartesian approach.

But it is unlikely that the so-called feminization of poverty will be effectively addressed by further feminization of what male leadership in Christian homes there may still be and of the ministry of Christian churches. Something far more profound and less cosmetic is called for.

To phrase the matter positively, there is freedom, emancipation, liberty, whatever it be called, only in Christ. This is true for all, Jew and Greek, slave and free, male and female.[168] Embracing the modern social (dis)order as somehow preevangelistic for a newly discovered gospel of equal rights in church and home is a dubious strategy for at least two weighty reasons.

First, it would appear to be disobedient to those Scriptures that call for reflection of the creation order in marriage (Eph. 5:31–33) and ministry (1 Tim. 2:12–13). We may perhaps scoff at what harm could come from disobeying Scriptures' commands when current social conditions make it seem not only expedient but necessary to do so. But unless weighty hermeneutical considerations constrain us to transpose the form (never the substance) of what Scripture commands (an example might be the biblical kiss of greeting, for which some modern cultures possess different equivalents[169]), we do well to keep transgressions as defined by Scripture to a minimum. To love God and one another involves more than obeying his commands, but it does not involve less.

---

168. Martin Luther took Gal. 3:28 to be underscoring that only in Christ lies justification: Even if the Jew does his best under the law, even if the Gentile arrives at his highest wisdom, even if the slave fulfills the highest standards set for him, even if the master performs in the most upright fashion, even if husband and wife comply fully with their duties by the best of works—"yet are all these nothing in comparison of that righteousness which is before God" (*A Commentary on St. Paul's Epistle to the Galatians* [London: James Clarke, 1953], 342). Despite fashionable polemic against Paul's understanding, not only of social roles but even of the doctrine of salvation by grace through faith itself (see T. Schreiner, *The Law and Its Fulfillment* [Grand Rapids: Baker, 1993]) as Reformers like Luther propounded it, this exegesis of Gal. 3:28 is probably a firmer basis for Christian ethics than that pioneered by Stendahl and now common currency in "progressive" circles. This view will be less attractive to those who follow Stendahl in feeling increasingly less bound to understand the Pauline gospel in reformational terms; see Stendahl, "The Apostle Paul and the Introspective Conscience of the West," *Harvard Theological Review* 56 (1963): 199–215.

169. Another might be the ancient Near Eastern head covering or veil, a convention much discussed with respect to 1 Corinthians 11. See, e.g., C. Keener, *Paul, Women and Wives*, 46f., who points out that while Paul was not "making a transcultural argument in favor of women wearing head coverings in church, we can notice some transcultural points in his argument." It is definitely not the case that if women go without head coverings now, they are also free to set aside 1 Tim. 2:11–12. See T. Schreiner, "Head Coverings, Prophecies and the Trinity: 1 Corinthians 11:2–16," in *Recovering Biblical Manhood and Womanhood* (Wheaton, Ill.: Crossway, 1991), 124–39, 485–87. In many (not all) settings it is quite possible to be in full compliance with the apostolic directives of 1 Corinthians 11 without wearing headgear, just as missionaries can be in full compliance with the so-called Great Commission (Matt. 28:19–20) without applying Jesus' commands about belt, bag, tunic, and staff (Matt. 10:9–14) with pendantic precision.

Second, "progressive" hermeneutics removes the social scandal of the cross of subordination—for husbands the call to place their wives' welfare above that of their own, for wives the call to respond to their husbands' leadership; for men the solemn charge that some of their number will give account of the souls under their ordained oversight (Heb. 13:17), for women the mandate to minister aggressively in the expansive spheres delegated to them. True, there is here a reciprocity that forbids a simplistic "chain of command" schema (1 Cor. 11:11). Spouses are partners, not master and slave. Pastors are shepherds, not commandants. But the Bible does envisage a divine ordering within redeemed human relationships, domestic and ecclesial, redolent of God's own diversity in unity, which humans together bear and mirror in their divinely bestowed social potential and destiny. The Bible does this, among other reasons, because of its high view of persons and the intrinsic connections it affirms between sexuality and identity. Groothuis writes, "Sexual identity is not conflated with personal identity" in the evangelical feminism she urges as middle ground in the current debate.[170] This is hardly middle ground at all, since it is a direct challenge to the scriptural claims that each of us is, essentially, human *qua* male or human *qua* female. Our corporate wholeness as divine image-bearers emerges through our respective acquiescence to God's will in creating us as he did, with all that implies for our respective stations in his household.

To obliterate our God-given gender distinctions (or to follow Marxist or other social theories in declaring all such distinctions to be no more than social conditioning) on the flimsy grounds offered by postmodern humanism is an affront and basic alteration to the message of the cross. To the contrary, our call is to the renunciation of treasured societal values, where necessary, in order to follow Christ.[171] In the current climate it is becoming increasingly necessary. *"The cross transforms present criteria of relevance; present criteria of relevance do not transform the cross. Salvation is pro-active, not re-active, in relation to the present."*[172]

It is not enough, however, to point to deficiencies in "progressive" thought or practice. There must also be renewal among those who affirm "historic" exegesis.

Refining a "Historic" Hermeneutic

In kingdom hermeneutics the interpreter's own life and soul are integral to the blessedness of the message he or she propounds.[173] This

---

170. *Women Caught in the Conflict*, 126.

171. See, e.g., A. McGrath, *The Mystery of the Cross* (Grand Rapids: Zondervan, 1988).

172. Thiselton, *New Horizons*, 610.

173. See, e.g., "The Interpreter," in Maier, *Biblical Hermeneutics*, 45–63; Augustine, *On Christian Doctrine, passim*; Thiselton, *New Horizons*, 609.

means that rightly applying 1 Timothy 2:9–15 is not only, and in a sense not primarily, about exegetical rigor and conceptual sophistication. It has everything to do with how the Lord regards the state of our hearts and the intent behind the arguments we marshall.

There is need for détente in the "historic-progressive" debate. This will be no easier in days ahead than it has been in times past. Both sides sling stinging salvoes. Strong differences of opinion are unavoidable. There is need for the inevitable conflicts over different points of view to be waged "with honorable and clean weapons."[174] It is helpful to note that there is a wide range of mediating positions between hard-core male dominance views and full-blown biblical feminist positions—even among those who claim the highest possible understanding of scriptural authority.[175] In the end we may be convinced that the other side's understanding of what the Bible says is wrong and that this vitiates their claim to be honoring Scripture's authority. But we should strive to keep lines of peaceable exchange open.

We should, however, not be oblivious to those voices that see evangelicalism in trouble. *Christianity Today*'s 1994 Book Awards were dominated by jeremiads: "Many of the titles communicate anxiety—we are concerned that we may be ignoring the institutional church, that we no longer value truth or theology, that we have been unduly influenced (and harmed) by psychology and marketing techniques, that heresy is creeping into our churches."[176] "Progressive" hermeneutics may be part of the problem (as may "historic" understanding when pressed too far, as Giles shows[177]). A Neville Chamberlain response to gathering doctrinal storm clouds, whether we detect them in the opposing camp or in our own, will not do. At a time when the basic parameters of evangelical theology are being questioned and repositioned,[178] we must be as wary of untoward innovation as we are hopeful of positive alteration. For the time may come, if it is not already here, when the issue at hand will not merely comprise a secondary matter (like mode of baptism or form of church government) but an essential one. It will become a confessional issue, a question on which hinges one's understanding of the essence of the gospel itself.

Communities who affirm "historic" exegesis should be aware that

174. Cf. A. Schlatter, "The Theology of the New Testament and Dogmatics," in R. Morgan, ed., *The Nature of New Testament Theology* (Naperville, Ill.: Allenson, 1973), 202, commenting on academic biblical studies generally.

175. J. G. Stackhouse, Jr., "Women in Public Ministry in 20th-century Canadian and American Evangelicalism: Five Models," *Studies in Religion/Sciences Religieuses* 17, no. 4 (1988): 471–85.

176. M. Maudlin, "1994 Book Awards," *Christianity Today* (April 4, 1994), 39.

177. *Evangelical Quarterly* 66, no. 1 (1994): 3–17.

178. See, e.g., S. J. Grenz, *Revisioning Evangelical Theology: A Fresh Agenda for the 21st Century* (Downers Grove: InterVarsity, 1993).

their own hierarchical excesses are probably the most effective apologetic for the "progressive" view at the popular level. When wives are less loved than utilized, when their myriad legitimate ministries are repressed or trivialized rather than respected and furthered, when women continue to be the objects of thin humor and innuendo, when husbands fob off on long-suffering spouses all the drudgery of housework and child care and make no attempt to share the burden, no amount of biblical evidence can legitimate a "historic" community hermeneutic.[179] There arises a relative justification for "progressive" understanding of biblical texts that are being used to subjugate women rather than accord them the dignity that even the "subordination" passages presuppose.[180]

By the same token male pastoral incompetence or chauvinism or laziness gives point to the argument that some women could do the job a whole lot better. In the end, this pragmatic argument should not overrule Scripture's insistence that men bear a few strategic burdens that women normally[181] do not. The Lord reigns; we gain nothing by mistrusting his counsel and taking matters into our own hands. But men must be careful not to hide their own sinfulness behind the presumed privilege that pet verses seem to afford. Too many confuse the *necessary* condition of maleness for certain biblically mandated responsibilities with a *sufficient* condition. Being male alone is not a sufficient qualification for proper execution of leadership responsibilities in the household of God, in either church or home.

Finally, the call for renewed affirmation of a "historic" hermeneutic is a call for repentance. Where that hermeneutic has not been abandoned today, it tends to be in such ill repair as to be, so far, largely undiscovered in its fullness. Just as the church through its neglect of social need was in some ways responsible for the rise of anti-Christian socialist forces in Europe last century,[182] the church in the twentieth century has brought sex role confusion on itself by a variety of quintessentially

179. This is not to minimize the existence of analogous miscues on the part of women. It is doubtful that they are significantly less guilty than men of failing to love God and others as they ought, though in the current climate an air of feminine moral supremacy may occasionally be detected. But our focus here lies elsewhere.

180. It is hard to imagine, e.g., that F. F. Bruce's views were not affected by chauvinist excesses in his own conservative denomination.

181. The qualifier is important. Scripture itself portrays God's willingness to use women to serve as judges or prophets (though there are no indisputable examples of pastors) to fill a void in men's devotion or in other special circumstances. The "historic" position needs to be as open to unusual situations today as the Lord was in times past according to Scripture. But the scriptural exception cannot be used to establish an extrascriptural rule.

182. K. Bockmühl, *The Challenge of Marxism* (Colorado Springs: Helmers & Howard, 1986).

male sins often tolerated in its own midst. In some churches these are even legitimated by male-exalting mores or teachings: failure to love wives and children even in intact families as Scripture calls for; bogus division of labor in the home so that child care and housework were unjustly heaped exclusively on the wife (and daughters when available); throwaway attitudes toward marriage and family leading to divorce and followed by negligence in child support; use of the family as chattel rather than cultivating it as a dynamic center for spiritual renewal and ministry through the church;[183] idolization of crass materialism leading to occupational or leisure fixations (sports, hunting, fishing) at the expense of loving God and others wholeheartedly; indulgence of moral double standards that exploited wives by cheating on them and other women by defiling them. Even this casual representative sampling of historic male malfeasance ought to make "historic" proponents wince, since churches in the past that championed their hermeneutic often failed to address, much less rectify, such evils.

Behind every confirmed "progressive" exegete there is probably personal experience of self-serving "historic" use of the Bible. My source of information for many of the male sins just listed was the (nominally Protestant) home I grew up in; the (Irish Catholic) childhood home life of my wife of over twenty years was no better. As a result we began married life as self-centered egalitarians (or "equalitarians" in Groothuis's parlance[184]). But we repented, in part due to the stubborn testimony of passages like 1 Timothy 2, and are still discovering how glad we are that we did. Perhaps other modern women and men alike will find the grace to abide in the "subordinate" roles Scripture sets for us all under Christ as a "historic" hermeneutic results in revolutionary acts of male love instead of reactionary exhibits of male power. Here, too, godless cultural patterns require the wondrous transformation that Jesus Christ's own strength of leadership and deference can provide.

183. Cf. R. Clapp, *Families at the Crossroads* (Downers Grove: InterVarsity, 1993).
184. *Women Caught in the Conflict*, 126.

7

The New Testament Against Itself:
1 Timothy 2:9–15 and
the "Breakthrough" of Galatians 3:28

Harold O. J. Brown

As Jesus himself said, and Abraham Lincoln quoted, "A house divided against itself cannot stand" (Matt. 12:25). The late Francis Schaeffer trained his students to look not merely at specific doctrines or exegetical assertions, but to examine the presuppositions behind them and to observe the conclusions to which they would lead. Is it possible that at times the presuppositions lead directly to the conclusions, without actual recourse to the texts, exegesis, or doctrines on which the conclusions are supposedly based?

The "Divided" Apostle and the Power of Presuppositions

For about eighteen centuries, 1 Timothy 2:12, as well as 1 Corinthians 14:34 and related texts, was assumed to have a clear and self-evident meaning. Then, rather abruptly, some, hardly a quarter century ago, began to "discover" a different meaning in the apostle's words.[1] Did God suddenly permit "more light to break forth from his holy Word," as the old Congregationalist put it? Or is there reason to suspect that the many modern interpretations of 1 Timothy 2 are primarily the result of certain conscious or unconscious presuppositions?

To what extent is the Bible, in the present case the New Testament, still functioning as the church's "perfect rule of faith and practice"? No

---

1. Cf., e.g., Letha Scanzoni and Nancy Hardesty, *All We're Meant to Be: A Biblical Approach to Women's Liberation* (Waco, Tex.: Word, 1974). Cf. more recently John Temple Bristow, *What Paul Really Said about Women* (San Francisco: Harper, 1988).

longer a "rule," an authoritative prescription for acts of belief and of conduct, Scripture, in the hands of some, has become so flexible that it is no longer able to serve as a firm standard in the life of the church.

As Robert Yarbrough has shown in the preceding chapter, the contemporary interpretation of 1 Timothy 2:9–15 as permitting rather than prohibiting women from the church's teaching and ruling offices has frequently come about as a consequence of extratextual presuppositions that in effect foreordained the actual interpretation of the text. The work of Krister Stendahl, one of the trendsetters of recent decades, offers a prime example.

According to Stendahl, it is naive not to recognize the fact that the New Testament points "beyond and even 'against' the prevailing view and practice of the New Testament church."[2] Stendahl turns the "glimpses" of sexual egalitarianism he discovers in the New Testament into a polemic against what he perceives as the simplistic literalism and play-acting of conservative Christians in our day who make "a nostalgic attempt to play 'First Century.'"[3]

Some Christians in academia make little effort to conceal their disdain for unsophisticated Christians and their simple, perhaps naive, pieties. Indeed, more sophisticated Christians may be tempted to abandon such simple pieties and the simpler Christians who hold them, in order to avoid similar ridicule and disdain. But there is more at stake here than ridicule and reputation: we are facing a question of truth.

It is not the purpose of this essay to disparage honestly struggling women, even less to justify the male abuse of authority, intentional or unintentional. The Christian church has, as in many other areas, a poor history of putting into practice the highest ideals and best intentions of its founding figures. Doubtless God is grieved by the experiences of women who have been demeaned and made to feel worthless and inferior by men.

Ultimately, beside being an issue of truth, the present question is also a deeply personal one. For those struggling with the proper roles of women and men in the church today, it may be helpful to consider that, in the final analysis, the issue is larger than the analysis of ancient culture, word studies, Greek syntax, exegesis, and hermeneutics. The egalitarian position represents a symptom of a culture, even an entire civilization, which has increasingly strayed from God's order of creation, indeed, of the very notion that such an order can exist or even would be

---

2. Krister Stendahl, *The Bible and the Role of Women*, trans. Emilie T. Sander (Philadelphia: Fortress, 1966), 34. This work has had an effect totally out of proportion to its size. It may also be seen as a precursor of many egalitarian arguments in recent years. It seems therefore justified to give Stendahl's contribution a significant place in the following discussion.

3. Cf. ibid., 36.

desirable. Predictably, therefore, even after all the evidence set forth in the present work, many can be expected to retain their opposing views, since embracing the position advocated here would be too radical in a world where postmodern relativistic pluralism and pressures of political correctness maintain an uneasy coexistence.

The point under dispute does not seem to be a crucial issue by which the church stands or falls. The proper role of women and men in the church is not generally considered to be one of the cardinal doctrines of the faith. However, when opinions and convictions suddenly undergo dramatic alteration, although nothing new has been discovered and the only thing that has dramatically changed is the spirit of the age, it is difficult to avoid the conclusion that that spirit has had an important role to play in the shift.

In fact, some of the most strident voices calling for an egalitarian interpretation of 1 Timothy 2 appear to have made the prior decision that the New Testament need not be interpreted according to its actual explicit message, and that one should not accord the Scriptures authoritative status. Why, then, do these interpreters use scriptural passages to support a conviction they appear to have formed already on another basis? Evidently, Scripture does possess some residue of authority in their eyes, or at least they expect their use of the Bible to add persuasiveness to their arguments in the eyes of their audience. Scripture can thus lend impact to a position.

There is also another dynamic at work. The traditional Christian community has taken a conservative stance on the issue of sexual equivalence, and where its influence remains strong, it is hard for those desiring radical egalitarianism to obtain acceptance for such a view. If these proponents were able to show, however, that Scripture permits, even demands, what more traditionally minded Christians think it forbids, these egalitarians would secure readier acceptance for their program.

An effect that is probably unintended is the way in which such an approach tends to undermine the confidence of many people in both the authority and the clarity of Scripture itself. If Scripture does not mean what people have taken it to mean for centuries, then the Bible is obscure, and, due to its lack of clarity, it cannot possess the authority it once had.[4]

---

4. It is evident that this is an approach that eventually will cease to be effective. As long as what the Scripture teaches is held to be authoritative and binding by large numbers of people, it will be helpful to use (or abuse) Scripture to induce the attitudes and actions that one desires. However, if one can make Scripture teach such things only by effectively denying those attributes of Scripture that commanded the respect and obedience of believers in the first place, especially its authority and clarity, then before long the recourse to scriptural authority will become totally ineffectual. Indeed, this has already happened across broad segments of Christendom, with the result that once sober and godly institutions now go, not to the Bible, but to dreams of witchcraft and recrudescent gnostic aeons and visions to justify their programs.

There are, of course, some who are generally committed to the authority of Scripture but who nevertheless take an egalitarian position.[5] One may ask why these interpreters are willing to depart from their usual high interpretive standards in this particular case. What good is achieved? It appears that the desire to establish total sexual equivalence in the church as well as in larger society is felt so strongly that this concern tends to override, consciously or unconsciously, the fidelity that such evangelical writers otherwise maintain toward the text and the generally accepted sense of Scripture.

Creation: Adam and Eve, or Adam, Then Eve?

Behind the traditional interpretation of 1 Timothy 2 stands the literal, or, as some would call it, "fundamentalist" interpretation of Genesis 1 and 2. In giving what appear to be gender-specific instructions, both Jesus and Paul refer to God's special creation (Matt. 19:4–5; 1 Cor. 11:2–16; 1 Tim. 2:13–14). If God has acted in a specific and special way to create first Adam, the man, then Eve, the woman, to be Adam's wife, it need not surprise us if in special revelation he should turn out to have given us diverse instructions for the conduct of men and women. Inasmuch as these were created separately, with an apparent time lapse between them, it is not the least unreasonable to suppose that God had different roles for each in mind.

Now one interpreter argues, "[T]his order [i.e., the distinction between men and women] rests upon the Scriptures, and can only be incidentally corroborated by 'nature,' as is clear in 1 Corinthians 11:14."[6] Of course this is precisely the point at issue. Biologically speaking, it is self-evident that certain differences between man and woman are there already at creation and cannot be eradicated—at least not by anything short of dramatic surgical intervention and the use of (as of yet not available) devices such as artificial wombs for gestation.

In 1 Corinthians 11 Paul refers not to an unalterable biological function such as the ability to bear children, but to an alterable sexual characteristic, even less sex-specific than facial hair, namely, to the style in which the hair on a person's head is worn. Some may find fault with Paul's observation that it is nature itself that teaches us that long hair is

5. Cf., e.g., Gordon D. Fee, "Issues in Evangelical Hermeneutics, Part III: The Great Watershed—Intentionality and Particularity/Eternality: 1 Timothy 2:8–15 as a Test Case," *Crux* 26 (1990): 31–37; David M. Scholer, "1 Timothy 2:9–15 and the Place of Women in the Church's Ministry," in *Women, Authority and the Bible*, ed. Alvera Mickelsen (Downers Grove: InterVarsity, 1986), 193–219; and scholars such as F. F. Bruce, W. Ward Gasque, and Richard N. Longenecker.

6. Cf. Stendahl, *Bible and the Role of Women*, 34.

a disgrace to a male. It might be argued that, although the general be-havior of human societies throughout history does show a preference for longer hair for women and shorter hair for men, there are numerous variations in style and custom.

Indeed, for some, the implication seems to be that, if differences in the length of one's hair are primarily a matter of taste rather than of the natural order, then all of the other, greater, differences claimed to result from the natural order are likewise matters of taste or style rather than being fundamental. Nevertheless, the fact that nature does not teach us all that clearly how we ought to cut our hair, does not mean that nature teaches us nothing about the differences between the sexes. This fact may merely indicate that nature by itself is not always sufficient to es-tablish gender-specific norms.

Those interpreters denying nature any validity thus, in effect, polem-icize not merely against doctrines traditionally found in Scripture, such as the teaching that the ministry of the Word and of the sacraments is reserved for men, but against the objective, ordered structure of reality that faith holds to have been set up by the Creator. What is at issue is not merely a revolt against the traditional stereotyping of sexual roles. The revolt is a symptom of a very deep and strong resistance to the con-cepts of both authority and reality. Not only does Scripture not mean what sixty-odd generations of Christians thought it meant, but the world is not what human common-sense observation has taken it to be.

It is this type of approach that Ernst Voegelin stigmatized as gnostic and described as the fundamental human temptation. Nothing is as it seems; all must be understood by virtue of a special key.[7] If we do not like the world as it is and want it to be different, we can change it only by first challenging the Order of Being. Therefore, we deny that there actually are orders and commands given by the One who has estab-lished that Order. In the case at hand, the central conviction is that dif-ferences between the sexes arise merely from culture rather than being rooted in creation.[8]

There are two levels at which the question of presuppositions should be examined: at the level of what may be called "anthropogenesis" (i.e., the origin of the race of man) and at the level of, to coin a term, "gyno-genesis" (i.e., the origin of the woman). Much depends on the way in

7. See Ernst Voegelin, *Science, Politics, and Gnosticism* (Chicago: Regnery, 1968), esp. 53–73.

8. This is one of the bedrock principles undergirding the egalitarian position. Any structure of authority and subordination between men and women is viewed as stem-ming from after the fall and as subsequently eradicated by Christ. Cf., e.g., Mary Hayter, *The New Eve in Christ: The Use and Abuse of the Bible in the Debate about Women in the Church* (Grand Rapids: Eerdmans, 1987). But see Mary A. Kassian, *Women, Creation and the Fall* (Westchester, Ill.: Crossway, 1990).

which Genesis 2:18–25 is interpreted. Does the passage relate an actual event? Does it communicate a specific truth to be believed on the basis of the authority of the divine Author? Or does the account merely reflect a human etiological myth?

Genesis 2 tells us that Adam was created first, then Eve. As is well known, the apostle Paul makes use of this account.[9] If God indeed fashioned Eve later than Adam, for a purpose for which another male human being was not suited, then it is not difficult to argue that, in principle, there are things for which the woman may be suited for which the man is not, and vice versa. This observation appears to provide some substantiation for the kinds of functional distinctions between men and women in the Creator's purpose that have traditionally been held.

The account of the creation of Eve, "the mother of all the living," in Genesis 2:18–25, has proved to be perplexing for many, including Luther who wrote, "We have talked enough about the creation of Eve. Although it sounds like a fairy tale to reason [even in the sixteenth century!], it is the most certain truth."[10] If the account indeed represents the "most certain truth," then certain less fundamental texts, such as 1 Timothy 2:12, appear far less arbitrary and shocking.

Calvin, in commenting on verse 13, observes: "The Apostle justly reminds us of that order of creation in which the eternal and inviolable appointment of God is strikingly displayed."[11] It is evident that Calvin assumes Genesis 2:22 to refer to a real event. He does not use the fact that Adam was created first as a justification for his position. Indeed, Calvin does not see 1 Timothy 2:12 as a categorical prohibition, "for a necessity may occur of such a nature as to require that a woman should speak in public; but Paul has merely in view what is becoming in a duly regulated assembly."[12]

The quarrel between Calvin and some later egalitarian interpreters, therefore, does not hinge on Calvin's insistence that 1 Timothy 2:12

9. See the essay on the exegesis of 1 Tim. 2:9–15 by Thomas Schreiner in the present work. See also Andreas J. Köstenberger, "Gender Passages in the NT: Hermeneutical Fallacies Critiqued," *Westminster Theological Journal* 56 (1994): 267–71.

10. Martin Luther, *Works*, vol. 1, *Lectures on Genesis, Chapter 1–5*, ed. Jaroslav Pelikan (St. Louis: Concordia, 1958), 135.

11. John Calvin, *Commentaries on the First Epistle to Timothy*, trans. William Pringle (Edinburgh: Calvin Translation Society, 1861), 68.

12. John Calvin, *Commentary on the Epistles of Paul the Apostle to the Corinthians*, trans. John Pringle (Edinburgh: Calvin Translation Society, 1848), 468. Calvin also discourses briefly on the relationship of men and women in society, maintaining that "It is the dictate of common sense, that female government is improper and unseemly." Recognizing the role of Deborah (cf. Judg. 4:4) and others, he comments, "Extraordinary acts done by God do not overturn the ordinary rules of government, by which he intended that we should be bound." Cf. *Commentaries on the First Epistle to Timothy*, 67.

constitutes a categorical requirement but rather on his assumption that the Genesis account recounts a real event from which one may infer that there is a general order to creation, an order that is to be respected.

Although separated by almost four centuries from Luther and Calvin, Barth, too, sees the specific patterns chosen by God in his creation as establishing basic principles for human conduct in society and, as in the present case, in the church. While these norms are not mandatory without exception, they are nevertheless generally valid. This is apparent in Barth's discussion of God's covenant as the inner reason (*der innere Grund*) of creation where Barth briefly mentions the reference to the woman's silence (ἡσυχία) in 1 Timothy 2:12. Barth notes that in this injunction "the New Testament did not see a deficiency, but precisely the special distinction of the woman."[13]

Those who disagree with Luther, Calvin, Barth, and the universally accepted interpretation of 1 Timothy 2 until recently will not be satisfied with the kind of exception Calvin was prepared to make, that is, when "a necessity may occur." These interpreters want to see the traditional understanding discarded and their own view put in its place. It is precisely this idea of order—the concept that there are some binding principles, and that not every function and role is open to the choice of every rational human being—that is apparently so obnoxious to many contemporary interpreters.

Indeed, it seems plausible to suggest that it was often this order that was rejected first, while many modern reinterpretations of 1 Timothy 2 are the result, rather than the cause, of such a rejection. Of course, in specific cases, 1 Timothy 2:12 may be set aside if certain circumstances warrant such an exception, provided the general principle is observed. If, however, one claims that the prohibition of 1 Timothy 2:12 can be disregarded as a general principle altogether, one may also, implicitly or explicitly, reject the idea that such things as divinely ordained relationships exist at all.

Unlike Barth, later Lutherans, and indeed most contemporary scholars, have difficulty echoing Luther's conviction about the "most certain truth" reflected in the Genesis 2 account and may in fact prefer not to think about the unique creation of Eve. It is therefore hardly surprising that many of these interpreters stumble over the resulting implication that there are divinely ordained and abiding differences in role between women and men.

Theoretically, it may be possible for someone to accept the idea that God has established certain social patterns he wants to be observed, and even to accept the account of Eve's creation from Adam's rib in

---

13. Karl Barth, *Die kirchliche Dogmatik*, 4th ed. (Zurich: Evy-Verlag, 1970), vol. 3/1, 374.

Genesis 2 while rejecting the traditional interpretation of 1 Timothy 2. In fact, however, the rejection of that interpretation by radical feminists often takes place in the context of a prior rejection of the doctrines of special creation and of the idea that there are explicit *mandata Dei* that hold good for all time and in every place.

The rejection of the special and separate creation of man and of woman is so common in our day that many may not even notice the psychological pressure placed on them to deny every principle of order derived from it.[14] It is in this climate that rejects (or ignores) the fundamental doctrine of creation in which egalitarian (re)interpretations of 1 Timothy 2:12 have flourished. It seems hardly promising to dispute the details, for it is often the fundamental principles that effectively control the outcome of one's interpretation.

Nevertheless, it is to the details that many interpreters arriving at an egalitarian position draw our attention. Could the reason for this possibly be that Christians can often be persuaded more easily to reject something that is presented as a cultural accretion than a truth as fundamental as the doctrine of special creation? Experience shows that, once the "cultural accretion" has been rejected, other doctrines are frequently discarded with unexpected rapidity.

Of course, scholars who take an egalitarian position argue that it is the facts, not their presuppositions, that determine their interpretive conclusions. But it seems difficult to deny that certain generally accepted, but seldom explicitly stated, assumptions tend to influence, if not determine, the egalitarian interpretation of 1 Timothy 2:12, regardless whether such conclusions are supported by proper exegetical procedure or not.[15]

In fact, for many radical liberal feminists (although not for evangelical feminists), the evolutionary hypothesis may well be the most powerful hidden presupposition in this entire debate. The theory of evolution is so widely accepted today that many assume it as fact without further questioning it.[16] The conviction that evolution is the fundamental principle of all reality undergirds much of contemporary public discourse. Thus, a certain kind of process in the intellectual development of humanity is presupposed.

14. For a curious recent example of the transposition of the evolutionary model into the social sciences, see the cover article of *Time* (August 15, 1994): 28–36, "Infidelity: It May Be in Our Genes," by Robert Wright. Indeed, the doctrine of creation is generally rejected in our society, even by many Christians who pray the Apostles' Creed. This is done not so much by explicit denial that God did create as by taking as fact an evolutionary doctrine and a general evolutionary worldview that makes divine creation implausible and God in effect superfluous.

15. Cf. Köstenberger, "Gender Passages," 261–63.

16. In fact, the evolutionary hypothesis is far from assured. See esp. Philip E. Johnson, *Darwin on Trial* (Downers Grove: InterVarsity, 1991).

One important implication of such a process is the belief that words spoken in a previous century do not necessarily need to be heeded in a later century. What is more, earlier insights generally ought to be discarded and be superseded by practices and values that are different, better, and more in synchrony with the spinning wheels of progress.

Thus, there seems to be a connection in practice, if not in theory, between egalitarianism and evolutionism. If belief in the literal special creation of Adam out of the "dust of the earth" and of Eve from Adam's rib is retained, the idea of a discrete and distinctive divine purpose for the human race and its members is often rejected. Thus it is no longer Scripture but the wisdom of the present age that undergirds one's views, in the biological (evolution) as well as the religious realm (egalitarianism).

Indeed, the present age all but imposes materialistic evolution with all of the pressure it can bring to bear on individuals, short of actual violence and persecution. To submit to such pressure, however, be it wittingly or unwittingly, amounts to sacrificing truth for acceptability in the world's eyes.[17] For the consistent and committed Christian, this is not an acceptable option.[18]

Yet this is precisely what some interpreters, consciously or unconsciously, are doing. Indeed, some radical feminists (though not necessarily so-called biblical feminists) go so far as not only to imply that nature and the roles of male and female are not planned by God, but even to reject, in effect, the concept that there *is* an order of creation to which the Christian must submit.

Even Stendahl does not shrink back from the heavy theological implications of his interpretation: "If one counters that this [understanding Gal. 3:28 to prescribe the full equivalency of men and women] would lead to a conflict with the order of creation, and hence must be wrong, we must say that it does indeed lead to such a conflict, and that

---

17. From the perspective of the present argument, the acceptance of evolutionary doctrine as true has the advantage that it militates against the traditional view that our attitudes and behavior may properly be prescribed by the One who has created us. In the long run, however, it could have the contrary effect of permitting discrimination of an invidious kind. One could argue that certain races, having progressed further and shown more promise than the rest, deserve to be favored and helped to increase, while others should be granted something resembling "death with dignity," and helped to withdraw gracefully from the world's stage. Although a similar argument seems less plausible with respect to the two different sexes, it is not altogether impossible, for there are feminists who, in a perhaps unconscious parallel to Gen. 2:21, see Eve, or rather the woman, as later, and therefore better and more advanced than the man, and thus as the sex that should carry the human mission into the future, with males reduced to the small numbers necessary to provide—at least as things are at present—sperm for reproduction.

18. Cf. J. Renié, *Les origines de l'humanité d'après la Bible* (Lyon: Emmanuel Vitte, 1950), 90: "Materialistic evolution is to be rejected; spiritualistic evolution that does not admit a special divine intervention in the production of Adam's body seems to me difficult to accept."

this is precisely what it should do and intends to do."[19] This writer thus appears to view the apostle as taking a position not merely set against the creation order but against what Voegelin calls the Order of Being.[20] The ultimate implication of this approach is that there is no Order of Being at all, but rather, as Milton's Satan says,

> The mind is its own place, and of itself
> Can make a Heav'n of Hell, a Hell of Heav'n.[21]

Indeed, some view Paul as in conflict with himself, for the great insight, the "'breakthrough' of Galatians 3:28," as Stendahl terms it, becomes clouded in 1 Corinthians 11, not to say totally buried in 1 Timothy 2 (which, of course, most modern interpreters no longer attribute to Paul, but merely to the creative imagination of the early church).[22]

We do well to echo Robert Yarbrough's question of the preceding chapter: "Was it, is it, and will it continue to be well advised for Christians to follow the recent lead of Western society in liberalizing attitudes toward women's and men's identities and roles?" Only if we are willing to accept the contention that Scripture as traditionally understood is in conflict with what the apostle actually intended and that the apostle implicitly rejects the Genesis story, indeed, the order of being itself, can we answer this question in the affirmative.

Kings, Priests, and Cultures

Much has been written regarding the alleged cultural conditioning of 1 Timothy 2.[23] Some have charged Paul, or the author of 1 Timothy, with assuming the social order of patriarchy and of attempting to impose this pattern on the church. The "breakthrough" of Galatians 3:28 has often been viewed as not merely requiring the abolition of slavery, but also of all vestiges of patriarchy or of any form of sexism, as well as of nationalism and perhaps of ethnicity altogether.[24]

19. Stendahl, *Bible and the Role of Women*, 34.

20. Was Paul hostile to the Order of Being in Voegelin's sense? This hardly appears to be the case. It is, however, apparently what Stendahl contends.

21. John Milton, *Paradise Lost*, Book 1, 254–55.

22. Cf. Hans Dieter Betz, *Galatians: A Commentary on Paul's Letter to the Churches in Galatia* (Hermeneia; Philadelphia: Fortress, 1979), 200.

23. See on this the contributions by S. Baugh, D. Gordon, and R. Yarbrough in the present work.

24. Cf. Willard M. Swartley, *Slavery, Sabbath, War and Women* (Scottdale, Pa.: Herald, 1983); and the discussion by Robert Yarbrough above. The degree to which the current interpretation of Gal. 3:28 serves the perceived need of the hour, and only that specific need, is illustrated by the fact that no one on the American church scene has ventured to

Now it is, of course, impossible for a sociocultural system to step outside itself and view its own time, or other times, from some Archimedean point of total objectivity.[25] Interpreters on both sides of the issue are, to some degree, susceptible to the influence of the spirit of this age. Yet the Zeitgeist is a tyrant to be resisted, not embraced, and certainly not one to which one ought to sacrifice all the values of the past, to say nothing of the truths of saving faith.

Of course, if one, on the one hand, is unwilling to conceive that God in his infinite wisdom created the first humans for a purpose and with a plan, then it is hardly reasonable to seek purpose and plan in the time and place of the sending of Christ. If, on the other hand, one supposes that God actually does things, and that there is purpose and providence in God's actions, then the time, the language, and the culture into which Christ came should not easily be dismissed as insignificant.

Reference is often made to the pacification of much of the world by Roman power at the time of Christ, to the cultural unity of the Hellenistic world, to the wide usage of Greek, indeed to the otherwise somewhat jarring fact that the New Testament, and even the utterances of Jesus and his Semitic band of apostles, are all transmitted in Greek. Is it not conceivable that the fullness of time mentioned in Galatians 4:4 relates not only to the stage reached in the history of redemption, but also to the stage of world history when God sent his Son?

If so, one may argue, contra Adolf von Harnack, that the second century was not a century of the "acute Hellenization of Christianity," but rather the century during which the faith began to grow and mature in the nurturing environment of Hellenistic thought into which God had deliberately placed it. One may even agree with Georges Florovsky that God was entirely aware of the Hellenists and of their learning, and that he actually intended for the faith to be formulated and expressed in such un-Semitic terms as οὐσία and ὑπόστασις.

No century is in itself normative. Yet in this same vein, we must ask, is it adequate to conclude that the setting of the first century for the writing of the New Testament is purely an "accident of history"? Surely it is no less reasonable to suppose that the intellectual culture of the first century has ongoing validity than it is to allow the political correctness of the late twentieth century to determine our interpretations of Scripture.

---

argue that it should make us blind to minority interests, which would have to be the case if we accepted "neither Jew nor Greek" as a mandate, just as we are told to accept "neither male nor female." On such a reading, for example, Gal. 3:28 should make Christians regard affirmative action as unbiblical.

25. For an extensive examination of the roles of men and women in light of Scripture and the social sciences, see Stephen B. Clark, *Man and Woman in Christ* (Ann Arbor, Mich.: Servant, 1980).

Many scholars express reservations regarding the development of Christian theology that took place as a result of the dissemination of the gospel message in Greek and the influence of Hellenistic thought and culture on the expression of Christian doctrine. The thoughtful reader should consider, however, whether it is not more appropriate to accept the idea that the application of Hellenistic language and concepts to the New Testament message was no accidental intrusion unforeseen and undesired by God but rather fully intended by him.

What, then, of the other aspects of culture? Specifically, what of the roles of men and women in society and religion as they existed when Paul and his fellow apostles wrote? Were they patterns from which to learn, perhaps to be taken over in more or less modified form? Were they imprisoning bars to be broken? Is the present age so much closer to the divine plan that its patterns have the authority to supersede those of earlier centuries?[26]

We live at the end of the twentieth century in an extremely individualistic, highly intellectualizing culture. Little or nothing is supposed to depend on the Order of Being described by Voegelin. Everything is a matter of choice, or, as we recall, "The mind is its own place." One may *choose* one's sexual "preference." One may *choose* whether to "terminate" a child before birth.

These fundamental aspects of human biological-physiological reality can be disregarded by modern men and women if they choose to do so. With such choices, the covenant aspect of creation, stressed by Barth, becomes irrelevant as the original creation complementarity between man and woman is rejected, both as a fact and as an interpretation.

How can we possibly expect, in a society and an intellectual milieu that trivializes, disregards, or even denies such fundamental aspects of created reality, that obedient attention will be paid to such secondary aspects of human relationships as the distribution of the roles in the pulpit or at the Lord's Table? Are we not in some danger of becoming like the poet Dryden's vision of the ancient Hebrews,

> God's pampered people, whom, debauch'd with ease,
> No king could govern, and no God could please?

God has indeed called all of us to be kings and priests (1 Pet. 2:9). Most of us, however, will recognize that, even in our individualistic culture, not everyone can function in society as king. Must everyone nevertheless function in the church as priest?

---

26. It may be unnecessary to remind the reader that the suggestion that the values and tastes of our own era should be determinative in effect means that there are no such things as values and tastes that have the specific approval of God. But ironically, this would mean that therefore there is nothing to be gained—at least not in God's sight—by following the egalitarian approach to gender roles.

Epilogue

The controversy over the role of women in the church has gripped virtually every denomination in Christendom. The Roman Catholic Church resists the ordination of women, at least in part if not primarily, because of church tradition. Notwithstanding the recent watershed decision to ordain women in the Anglican Church, there, too, a significant number oppose such a practice, be it on scriptural grounds (evangelicals) or for traditional reasons (High Church Anglicans).[1] This book could easily be assessed by some as a defense of the church's traditional position on the issue and an effort to resist the new winds of freedom that are blowing in the churches. The contributors to this volume, as evangelicals, do not grant ultimate authority to tradition, for practices and beliefs contrary to the Scriptures can infiltrate the church. We are not committed to defending the historic view on women in the church merely because it is the venerable tradition of the church.

Of course, long-held traditions in the church should not be jettisoned casually or without careful reflection, for we are all liable to the chronological snobbery of the modern age and apt to dismiss the contribution of thoughtful Christians who have preceded us. Indeed, the virtually universal agreement on the role of women in the church by Christian believers from a variety of communions in the nineteen centuries of the Christian era constitutes presumptive evidence against the progressive view. Nonetheless, Scripture functions as our sole authority only if we are willing to reexamine every cherished doctrine and practice. New circumstances may provoke us to see that we have defended a certain view of women in the church because of our prejudices and cultural encumbrances. Thus, we have attempted to probe in this book whether the central biblical text that forbids women from teaching or ruling men, 1 Timothy 2:11–15, actually justifies role distinctions between men and women in the church.

We explored the social world that must inform any rigorous exegesis of 1 Timothy—the world of first-century Ephesus. We have shown that the "feminist Ephesus" is a figment of the modern imagination. The role of women in Ephesian society was not vastly different from that in the other Greek cities of the period. That role has both significant

---

1. For a recent treatment from an Anglican perspective, see Michael Harper, *Equal and Different: Male and Female in Church and Family* (London: Hodder & Stoughton, 1994).

points of continuity and some discontinuities with the role of women in modern societies. Nor does the particular purpose or genre of 1 Timothy restrict Paul's admonition in 1 Timothy 2:12 so that it is limited only to first-century Ephesus. Paul applies universal norms to the particular situation encountered in the church at Ephesus.

We have also demonstrated through an exhaustive analysis of the term αὐθεντέω that the word has the meaning "to have or exercise authority" in 1 Timothy 2:12. That αὐθεντεῖν means authority in 1 Timothy 2:12 has been accepted by nearly all interpreters of the passage until modern times. The syntactical structure of 1 Timothy 2:12 is reflected elsewhere in biblical and extrabiblical writings. An analysis of the structure reveals that teaching and authority are a conceptual pair. Moreover, Paul sees both teaching and authority as positive concepts; it is the *right* teaching and *right* exercise of authority of women over men that Paul forbids.

We proceeded, then, to interpret 1 Timothy 2:9–15 in detail, examining the foundation on which the prohibition in 1 Timothy 2:12 is based. Paul's restriction was not based on some ephemeral or culturally conditioned situation. Rather, the prohibition of women teaching and exercising authority over men is rooted in the created order. The final two chapters reflect on the reception of Paul's perspective in modern culture, and we contended that insofar as modernity has strayed from the apostle's word it has failed to understand that 1 Timothy 2:12 is an apostolic norm. It is a norm, as appendix 1 demonstrates, which has been the standard for the church throughout its history. In the light of our research, we have concluded that the historic view of the church is substantially correct and that it did not impose an alien meaning on 1 Timothy 2:9–15.

We have not investigated in detail how the meaning of 1 Timothy 2:9–15 should be applied in today's world. At a minimum, our understanding of the text would prohibit women from functioning as teaching pastors or teaching elders/overseers of churches. In our context this means that women should not proclaim the Word of God from the pulpit to the congregation of the saints. Many other questions, however, could be asked. May women teach Sunday school classes made up of both men and women? May they teach in a seminary? If women function as missionaries, why are they prohibited from functioning as pastors? If women cannot teach men in the church, is it permissible for them to teach children? If so, at what age do boys become men: high school, college, age twenty-five? It is not our intention to provide answers to these difficult questions in a brief epilogue. To answer these questions adequately more discussion would be needed than is possible here. There are inevitably some gray issues involved in applying any teaching of Scripture. We may concur on what the text means and yet disagree in some respects on how to apply it to the variety of circumstances that

Epilogue   211

arise. The church has generally agreed that 1 Timothy 2:11–15 at least prohibits women from functioning as teaching and ruling pastors or elders, but even among those who espouse the historic view there have been differences regarding the application of this text to other circumstances. Such differences should propel us to prayer and discussion (and humility!) so that greater clarity emerges on how the Word of God should be related to contemporary situations. What we hope to have provided with the present work is a firm framework for such discussion.

Lance Morrow, in a recent "Convert's Confession," says the reason he does not go to Mass much anymore is his church's opposition to the ordination of women.[2] He urges a "full, welcoming embrace of women as ordained equals in the priesthood," charging that anything less clings to "an unimportant or incidental distinction—one that is rooted in custom of distant time and [one that] becomes essentially inhuman." "I hate the doctrinaire reductionism that coarsens all relationships between men and women into trench warfare," he writes. This is strong language. Increasingly, this appears to be the cultural climate in which evangelicals operate. Those who maintain that the Scriptures affirm functional gender distinctions in church and home are often considered to be male chauvinists, or, if they are women (such as Mary Kassian and Susan Foh and many women in churches throughout the world) betrayers of the feminist cause. They appear to some as "doctrinaire reductionists" who resist the swift progress of a gender-blind, discrimination-free society.

But is the church to take its cue from the world and succumb to its pressure? In a climate of religious freedom, all Christians should resist the effort on the part of the larger society to squeeze the church into its mold. To contend that the Scriptures prohibit women from functioning in roles of ultimate responsibility and authority over Christ's church does not amount to devaluing women's contributions in the church, or to relegate them to roles of insignificance, as is often alleged. While there is room for disagreement and constructive dialogue—hence this book—each person ultimately stands before God himself, with the responsibility to search the Scriptures with an open mind and a heart ready for obedience. If such obedience involves a certain amount of suffering and being misunderstood, this, after all, has always been part of the calling of followers of Christ, and we live in a time where being conservative may be the most radical thing of all.

Andreas J. Köstenberger,
Thomas R. Schreiner,
and H. Scott Baldwin

2. *Time*, October 3, 1994, p. 71.

Appendix 1

A History of the Interpretation of 1 Timothy 2

Daniel Doriani

A Personal Word

Feminism has suffused the cultural air I have breathed since I was about fourteen. My father, an ordained minister, participated in the ordination of my mother, whom I love and admire, in 1973. I have three daughters, no sons. Twelve, nine, and five years old as I write, they already display flashes of spiritual zeal and maturity exceeding that of some male elders I know. So I lack no personal motive to align myself with the evangelical feminist movement.[1] Yet I am chastened by one of Francis Schaeffer's final remarks: "Tell me what the world is saying today, and I'll tell you what the church will be saying in seven years." I decline, furthermore, to believe in the inevitability of progress (theological or otherwise) and the superiority of all things new. So I gladly surveyed the thought of the church's most profound and influential theologians to see how they viewed gender issues, particularly the interpretation of 1 Timothy 2:11–14, hoping their unhurried reflections can illumine the urgent agonies of current debate.

The Conceptual Matrix of Interpretation

The uninitiated tend to enter the battle over 1 Timothy with presuppositions blazing: "Paul can't *possibly* mean . . . *Everybody* knows . . . Paul

---

1. The terms "feminist" and "traditionalist" are epithets for some, a badge of honor for others. This essay uses the terms without positive or pejorative connotations. "Feminist" will be used interchangeably with "egalitarian"; "complementarian," with "traditionalist."

obviously means. . . ." So feminists and traditionalists often talk past each other in casual discussions. Scholars and exegetes also forget that interpreters come to texts with more than a set of linguistic competencies. We, too, have an array of convictions and presuppositions—some the product of critical inquiry, some not—which influence or even determine our reading of the text. Awareness of presuppositions runs high when they differ, but if opposing debaters share presuppositions, they may be overlooked.

Christians have differed, first, over the nature and value of creation, its order, and its crowning inhabitants, man and woman. Is the material world intrinsically good or evil? Are marriage and sexuality good or evil? How did the fall alter them? Second, on what basis has God ordered human relations: by a system of merit or divine fiat? Are service and subordination intrinsically demeaning or not? Are women spiritually superior, inferior, or intrinsically equal to men? Are they made in the image of God, or in the image of man? Are they irrational and easily deceived, or perhaps more spiritually sensitive than men? Are women more, less, or equally open to God and his righteousness? Are men capable of leading without dominating? Can they be servant-leaders? Why do men lead? Because they are stronger or smarter than women, more aggressive and educated? Because patriarchal social structures favor them? Because God ordained it so?

Cultural conditions also shape our presuppositions. If contemporary hedonism begets Christian versions of "the joy of sex," ancient asceticisms may have prompted Christian versions of "the joy of abstinence." At the beginning of the Christian era cynics, stoics, Neo-Pythagoreans, Neo-Platonists, and gnostics all had ascetic tendencies, so that Christians may have praised virginity and belittled marriage and women, in part to outdo them.[2] Whatever the causes, most early theologians who wrote about women never married. Some knew few women who could provide them with the vital insiders' critique of their theories. The church's subculture of virginity surely influenced its views of women as well.

Second, the argument over women and the meaning of 1 Timothy 2 is complicated by differing presuppositions regarding mission and calling. Theologians explicitly contest one question today: Is the cause of the gospel advanced or harmed if women teach and lead in the church? Egalitarians ordinarily say female leaders would have been an obstacle in Ephesus, the destination of 1 Timothy, and perhaps throughout the apostle Paul's world. On the other hand, the exclusion of women from leadership in the church hinders the missionary cause today, driving off

2. M. Rosamond Nugent, *Portrait of the Consecrated Woman in Greek Christian Literature of the First Four Centuries* (Washington, D.C.: Catholic University Press, 1941), 1–5.

women with egalitarian sympathies and depriving the church of valuable leaders.[3] They also propose that Paul only temporarily opposed female leadership in the church. Some, therefore, call attention to the present tense of the verb ἐπιτρέπω in 1 Timothy 2:12. Paul, they allege, used the present tense to indicate that while he did not presently permit women to teach or exercise authority in the church, he might permit it in the future.[4]

Presuppositions also play a role in the major arguments regarding the gifts and calling of women. A leading egalitarian rationale for women's ministry, which I will label the "All Gifts Argument," can be stated as a syllogism. Major premise: All who have gifts should be free to exercise them. Minor premise: Women have received the Spirit and his gifts. Conclusion: Therefore, women should be free to exercise their gifts in every setting, as leaders as well as followers.[5] For the egalitarian, "Women have spiritual gifts" means "Women receive every kind of spiritual gift." Complementarians question the universality of the major premise, and read the minor premise differently. They often skirt the question of women's spiritual gifts, and speak vaguely of women having "all kinds of spiritual gifts."[6]

Egalitarians also use the "Subjective Calling Argument." Stated simply, it says, "Women sense a call from God to Christian ministry. How can anyone question this call?" Women have put it to me more personally: "I believe God is calling me to preach and lead. Who am I, and who are you, to question a call from God?" The woman may add that she did not seek the call, that it frightens her, but that she cannot resist or deny it. The implicit premise is that subjective communication from God is (ordinarily) unquestionable.[7]

Another egalitarian presupposition produces what might be called

3. Clarence Boomsma, *Male and Female, One in Christ* (Grand Rapids: Baker, 1993), 80.

4. Gloria Redekop, "Let the Woman Learn: 1 Timothy 2:8–15 Reconsidered," *Studies in Religion* 19, no. 2 (1990): 235–45. I have not encountered this argument in antiquity.

5. Mary Stewart Van Leeuwen, *Gender and Grace* (Downers Grove: InterVarsity, 1989), 34–37, 231–50; Faith Martin, *Call Me Blessed* (Grand Rapids: Eerdmans, 1988), 3–5, 10; Gretchen Hull, *Equal to Serve* (Old Tappan, N.J.: Revell, 1987), *passim;* Boomsma, *Male and Female*, 23–29, 103–5.

6. The "All Gifts Argument" appeared in the nineteenth century. See, for example, both the text (below) and introductory letters to Frances E. Willard's *Women in the Pulpit* (Boston: D. Lothrop, 1888). Joseph Cook's letter says "women have eminent natural endowments for the ministry," plus necessary "spiritual and intellectual and social qualities." He asks, "What Scriptural authority can be quoted of greater weight than the divine command not to keep a light under a bushel, or talents in a napkin?"

7. See E. Margaret Howe, *Women and Church Leadership* (Grand Rapids: Zondervan, 1982), 162–68. Howe assumes the validity of the calling rather than arguing it. Her segment on the call to ministry (162–68) often uses the terminology of gift, calling, and freedom to serve, and assumes the "All Gifts" argument and the high value of freedom (see below).

the "Gamaliel Argument." In Acts 5 Gamaliel urged his fellow members of the Sanhedrin to wait a season before punishing the apostles for preaching the gospel. If their movement is human, Gamaliel reasoned, it will fail. But if it is of God, they might find themselves opposing the Lord himself. So they should watch and wait. Egalitarians propose, similarly, that an experiment with female leaders seems judicious, given the current condition of the church. Men have created such a mess; why not give women a chance?

As I read feminist literature, many authors believe their position is obviously correct. Therefore, feminists sometimes argue that traditionalists operate in bad faith, not strictly believing their own arguments, but using them to obtain or retain control of the church. Or perhaps the church's fathers feared their own sensual nature and avoided it by demonizing women. Or perhaps they simply hate women. (Is that not what the accusation of misogyny means?) This essay, on the contrary, will maintain that the traditionalist position principally rises from theologians' belief that crucial texts such as 1 Timothy 2 and 1 Corinthians 11 must be taken at face value.

The egalitarians have confidence because their position rests on three putatively impregnable principles: (1) women are spiritually equal to men—equally created in God's image, equally recreated by Christ; (2) women receive all spiritual gifts; and (3) women must be free to exercise them. Christian thinkers have questioned all three principles, as we shall see. But the third, though rarely questioned today, is particularly suspect in historical terms.

Freedom and Order

Imagine that a group of contemporary Christians could assemble thinkers from the fourth to seventeenth centuries to discuss Paul's statement, "I do not permit a woman to teach or to exercise authority over a man." Even if we should overcome linguistic barriers, contemporary Christians would have to bridge other gaps, including their predecessors' presuppositions. Past generations assumed that women were uneducated, perhaps uneducable, and largely without experience in the ways of the wide world. Some considered celibacy superior to marriage, and virginity superior to fecundity. They considered the body to be evil, and sexuality to be corrupting under almost every circumstance, even within marriage. Denigrations of marriage sometimes correlate with a misogynistic devaluation of female abilities.

At many points we might hope to introduce our predecessors to more mature Christian notions. For example, today we believe that women are receptive to formal education and that they are rapidly gaining experience. But in time they would want to educate us as well—on the fundamental importance of order for the good of any society. In the past, the positions one took about the structure of life in family, government, or church had to be able to answer the question, Will it promote or at least preserve order? Today, Americans assume that freedom is foundational to every good society, and "order" gets short shrift. Whether the topic is women's issues, sexual orientation and behavior, or the rise of hate groups, contemporary American debaters have to answer the question: Will your view enhance (or at least preserve) or restrict human freedom?

In secular settings, it is almost axiomatic to every popular debate that, as long as they inflict no direct harm on another, people should be free to do whatever they want. Populist philosophy, from public schools to public advertisements, agrees that people should be free to dream any dream, to aspire to any legal goal. In this atmosphere, secular and secularized thinkers find it half-quaint, half-revolting that some Christians actually debate whether women should be *allowed* ("free") to preach, teach, and lead the church.

We can only suggest the causes of this shift. Perhaps a call for more consideration of "order" is to twentieth-century America what a call for more consideration of "guilt" was to fifteenth-century Germany. Interest is small because the sense of deficit is lacking. Perhaps, therefore, arguments based on the need for order would garner better audiences among people suffering through the internecine tribal warfares of Africa or the Balkans. Perhaps we have blindly carried the principles of individual rights, personal choice, and egalitarian relationships from the political to the social arena, and allowed them to define social as well as political relationships. Perhaps we have found ways to make freedom an ordering principle—just as past societies found pathways to freedom through the principle of order.

Whatever the cause of the shift, the consequence remains: just as past Christians accommodated their deliberations about women's roles to the concern for order, so contemporary Christians—both feminists and traditionalists—have accommodated theirs to the concern for freedom. Freedom is central to the "All Gifts Argument." The major premise, again, is that anyone who has a gift should be free to exercise it, and it concludes that women should be free to exercise their gifts. Freedom looms large, implicitly, in other feminist arguments. The "Subjective Call Argument" assumes that women should be free to follow any call they may sense. The "Gamaliel Argument" assumes the church should be free to experiment with the benefits of female leadership. Complementarians sometimes presuppose the importance of freedom too—although they surely define the term differently. They argue that traditional concepts of male leadership, contrary to appearances, actually liberate women and grant them true freedom.[8]

The current preoccupation with freedom is unusual, historically speaking. Past generations would have said maintaining order and discharging duties were higher goods than freedom, and that freedom could be sacrificed for them. Classically, then, scholars readily took 1 Timothy 2 at face value, because, even though it limited woman's freedom to minister, it provided order. It also seemed consistent with the principle that the man is the head of the home, where order outranked freedom again. This does not prove that the twentieth century has erred. But it does question whether the proposition, "Women should be free to minister," deserves to be a first-order principle.

Past traditionalists did not simply call for order. To speak in archetypes, there are Thomist and Scotist views of order.[9] The Thomist says God's order must and does have a reason, and readily propounds natural and theological reasons why women may not teach and exercise authority in the church. The Scotist says we know God's will, but cannot explain it, for God orders the world as he wills, whether with, against, or beyond reason. The Thomist expects and examines a coherence between natural law and divine law; the Scotist does not.

On the Right and Profitable Use of Church History

Traditionalists and feminists agree that the church has historically interpreted 1 Timothy 2:11–14 in a straightforward manner. For over nineteen centuries most theologians shared several beliefs. Women ought to learn, but quietly and submissively (1 Tim. 2:11). They could teach informally, but not formally, not with authority (2:12). Paul forbids them to teach, said the theologians, due to both God's sovereign decree and the nature of man and woman (2:13–14). The phrase, "Adam was formed or created first," means God chose and decreed to make males the spiritual heads of churches and homes (2:13). Eve's deception compounds or explains woman's subordination. Her subordination, said the teachers, became subjugation as a punishment for her departure from her place. God possibly subordinated woman to man in the church because women are prone to deception, whether

8. John Piper, "A Vision of Biblical Complementarity," in *Recovering Biblical Manhood and Womanhood*, ed. J. Piper and W. Grudem (Wheaton, Ill.: Crossway, 1991), 46–47, 57. The index contains twenty-two references to freedom, although some mean freedom in another sense. On the other side, *Gender and Grace* by Van Leeuwen has ten entries, referring to twenty pages, in its index.

9. That is, this paragraph does not necessarily do justice to the precise views of Aquinas and Scotus, but makes use of their stereotypes.

due to diminished intellectual capacity or lack of interest in theological analysis.

Today, however, egalitarians reject the old consensus on 1 Timothy. They interpret it through the lens of Acts 2, Galatians 3, and the stories of female prophets, judges, and kingdom laborers, whose lives, they say, prove that women may indeed teach and lead in the church. Women have the gifts, the calling, and the fruit that demonstrate their freedom to minister in any capacity. Therefore, egalitarians say, 1 Timothy 2:11–14 cannot be understood as literal, permanently binding instructions for the church. Either the text has been misunderstood, or it applies only to temporary, local conditions in Ephesus.

Complementarians accomplish little by stressing the novelty of this view. Feminists are not impressed by the counting of hands or the polling of heroes of theology past. Sophisticated feminists already know the church insisted on male leadership throughout most of its history. Honest complementarians should agree with egalitarians that most leaders accepted the teaching of the church without giving sustained attention to women's issues.

Traditionalists should also admit that past discussions were often framed in terms that could demean women. For example, the Greek question, "Do women have souls?" loitered in the theological discussions of the spiritual capacities of women into the Middle Ages, the Reformation, and beyond. The wise egalitarian might ask, "If the all-male theologians' guild is still debating whether women even have souls, is it a wonder if they do not consider whether they can lead?" Furthermore, in the past women lagged so far behind men in education and experience outside the home that few could attain the qualifications needed for leadership. Consequently, egalitarians concede that Christian orthodoxy has barred women from exercising formal positions of authority. But, a cheeky egalitarian might ask, since when do polls of dead theologians determine truth? All Protestants, mindful of Luther contra mundum and committed to the principle of *sola Scriptura,* must admit that mere polling is futile.

Egalitarians can abuse the past, too. By selective quotation and interpretation, some make proponents of male headship sound misogynistic or incoherent. It is at best misleading to cull the worst excesses of the past, and cite them again and again, as if they were typical of traditional thought. A more subtle error is hero-hunting, the quest for forerunners, whose existence validates modern feminist positions. All theological innovators search for forerunners in an effort to validate themselves, because orthodoxy is communal, whereas heresy is solitary. Therefore, to prove they lie in the mainstream of Christian thought, they comb through church history, searching for protofeminists, and proto-feminist remarks. These protofeminists become "precursors" of the full flower of the egalitarian interpretation of Scripture. Given the vast scope and diversity of Christian thought, feminist historians inevitably find both egalitarians and egalitarian sentiments. But the mere discovery of precursors proves almost nothing, for so much has been written that one can find a precursor for almost any idea. After all, every imaginable aberration that has plagued the church also claimed precursors.

The history of interpretation serves current interpretation of 1 Timothy 2 by recovering the best thought of the best minds of the church. This means more than a mere collation of "who believed what about female teachers," an exercise that mixes the quaint and the cogent. We hope to discover the reasoning of the church's best theologians, especially where most trenchant and compelling. We weigh witnesses, listening more carefully to writings that have stood the test of time, to writers actively engaged in the life of the church, to theologians who apparently interacted with opposing viewpoints. Among the reasons given, which seem culturally accommodating or idiosyncratic? Which have substance and universality?

We wish it were superfluous to add that those who invoke the names of theologians past should take the trouble to read them. Aquinas, for example, is routinely vilified as a prejudiced and misogynistic thinker. Yet most of his critics admit, by citing nothing but secondary sources in their footnotes, that they never read the man they easily accuse.[10] Genuine inquiry into the past entails reading and comprehending the sources, then reporting what they said, without massaging data to fit preferred theses. The first goal of honest researchers must be to write reports on Chrysostom and Calvin that Chrysostom and Calvin would judge accurate.

The Ancient Church

By modern standards, ancient discussions of 1 Timothy 2 and women's issues were rare and unsophisticated. Yet there was debate, even if it rose from general convictions about God, men, and women, rather than exegesis. Further, neolithic misogyny did not suffuse all; no major Christian theologian has ever advocated a total ban on fe-

10. See, for example, Ronald W. Pierce, "Evangelicals and Gender Roles in the 1990s: 1 Tim 2:8–15: A Test Case," *Journal of the Evangelical Theological Society* 36, no. 3 (1993): 345. Pierce criticizes Aquinas for saying women are "defective and misbegotten." He cites not Aquinas but Patricia Gundry, "Why We're Here," in *Women, Authority and the Bible*, ed. Alvera Mickelsen (Downers Grove: InterVarsity, 1986), 21. Gundry's source is not Aquinas either, but Susan G. Bell, *Women from the Greeks to the French Revolution* (Belmont, Calif.: Wadsworth, 1973), 122. Examples abound; see also n. 60.

male teachers. All recognized the teaching activity of Abigail and Huldah, Philip's daughters, and Priscilla. All agreed that women teach in the church by instructing their children, by leading other women, by living and dying nobly. On the other hand, many centuries passed before any orthodox theologian granted women the right to hold formal teaching offices.

Isolated remarks about women lie scattered thinly over the most ancient sources. For example, Ignatius's (d. 115) letter to Polycarp urges him to convene a council and to appoint a man as courier for his message.[11] Among the dozens of "precepts" of the Lord that Cyprian gathered, his forty-sixth says, "A woman ought to be silent in the church." To demonstrate his view, Cyprian quotes 1 Corinthians 14:34–35 and 1 Timothy 2:11–14, without further explanation.[12] The famous letter from Pliny, the governor of Bythinia, to Emperor Trajan, from A.D. 111–113 reports that Pliny, using torture, extracted the real truth about the Christians "from two female slaves, who were styled deaconesses" ("ex duabus ancillis, quae ministrae dicebantur").[13] These women, slaves or lower-class servants, possibly held a minor office in the church.[14]

It is possible that women played a larger role in heretical sects, though the evidence is fragmentary and disputed. For example, gnostic literature is said to exalt women as recipients of revelation.[15] But the gnostic gospel of Thomas, speaking of Mary and women in general, says, "every woman who will make herself male will enter the kingdom of heaven."[16] So even egalitarian historians admit to tensions in the gnostic view of women.[17]

11. The term ἀνήρ does not appear, but the pronouns in the passage (ὅν, ὅς, τοῦτον) are all masculine rather than neuter. Ignatius, "Letter to Polycarp," in *The Apostolic Fathers: Greek Texts and English Translations of Their Writings*, ed. Michael Holmes, trans. J. B. Lightfoot and J. R. Farmer (Grand Rapids, Baker, 1992), 199.

12. Cyprian, "The Treatises of Cyprian," trans. Ernest Wallis, in *Ante-Nicene Fathers*, ed. Alexander Roberts and James Donaldson, 9 vols. (Grand Rapids: Eerdmans, 1979–85), 5:546. The absence of argumentation is common. He "proves" most precepts simply by quoting prooftexts. (Subsequent references will cite the *Ante-Nicene Fathers* as *ANF*.)

13. Pliny the Younger, "Letter to Trajan, Epistle 96," in *Pliny, Letters*, trans. William Melmouth, in Loeb Classical Library (Harvard: Harvard University Press, 1963), 2:404–5.

14. Jean Danielou, *The Ministry of Women in the Early Church*, trans. Glen Symon (New York: The Faith Press, 1961), 15.

15. Catherine Kroeger, "1 Timothy 2:12—a Classicist's View," in *Women, Authority and the Bible*, ed. Alvera Mickelsen (Downers Grove: InterVarsity 1986), 235, 238; Bruce Barron, "Putting Women in Their Place," *Journal of the Evangelical Theological Society* 33 (December 1990): 454–56.

16. Gospel of Thomas, in *The Nag Hammadi Library*, ed. James M. Robinson (San Francisco: HarperCollins, 1978), 138.

17. Ruth Tucker and Walter Liefeld, *Daughters of the Church* (Grand Rapids: Zondervan, 1987), 97–99; Elaine Pagels, *The Gnostic Gospels* (New York: Random, 1979), 62–63.

Tertullian, Origen, and the Apostolic Constitutions

Tertullian (d. 225) had reason to grant full ministerial rights to women, for two female prophetesses, Priscilla and Maximilla, played foundational roles in the Montanist movement he joined later in life. Nonetheless, Tertullian's discussion of the gifts of the Spirit insists on the silence of women in the church, for "women should be under obedience." He parenthetically grants them "the right of prophesying" when covered with a veil.[18] But he also says women should not be too bold in their learning and must not be permitted to teach.

In a treatise that grants laymen the right to administer baptism in emergencies, Tertullian also made a few comments about women's rights and restrictions in the church. Citing both 1 Corinthians 11 and 1 Timothy 2, he asks, "For how credible would it seem that he who has not permitted a woman even to *learn* with over boldness, should give a female the power of teaching and of baptizing!" Rather women should "be silent . . . and at home consult with their own husbands."[19] Women may only hold the office of widow, in which they may "counsel and comfort" other women, and that office only opens to them at age sixty, if they have been the wife of one husband, and if they have traveled down the whole course of probation "whereby a female can be tested."

All women should be veiled, according to Tertullian, because of "the necessity for humility," because they are subject, because, "the man is the head of the women," because men have authority and deserve honor.[20] Although mitigating passages exist, the following excerpt, loaded with both rhetoric and misogyny, seems to mean Tertullian also believed women were spiritually inferior to men: "And do you not know that each of you is an Eve? . . . You are the devil's gateway: you are the first deserter of divine law: you are she who persuaded him whom the devil was not valiant enough to attack. You destroyed so easily God's image. On account of your desert—that is, death—even the Son of God had to die."[21]

Origen (ca. 185–250) rejected Montanism and the public prophetic role of the women Priscilla and Maximilla within it. Origen believes Paul's dictum, "The women should keep silence in the churches," discredits female teachers, yet he took up "the arguments which they judge convincing." Of the Bible's female prophets, Origen says,

> If the daughters of Philip prophesied, at least they did not speak in the assemblies; for we do not find this fact in evidence in the Acts of the Apos-

18. Tertullian, "Against Marcion," trans. Peter Holmes, *ANF,* 3:446.
19. Tertullian, "On Baptism," trans. S. Thelwall, *ANF,* 3:677.
20. Tertullian, "On the Apparel of Women," trans. S. Thelwall, *ANF,* 4:33.
21. Ibid., 14.

tles. Much less in the Old Testament. It is said that Deborah was a prophetess. . . . There is no evidence that Deborah delivered speeches to the people, as did Jeremias and Isaias. Huldah, who was a prophetess, did not
speak to the people, but only to a man, who consulted her at home. The
gospel itself mentions a prophetess Anna . . . but she did not speak publicly. Even if it is granted to a woman to show the sign of prophecy, she is
nevertheless not permitted to speak in an assembly. When Mary the
prophetess spoke, she was leading a choir of women. . . . For "I am not
giving permission for a woman to teach," and even less "to tell a man what
to do."[22]

Origen finds that Titus 2:3–4 confirms his position. There Paul commands older women to be an example and to teach "what is good in
order to form young women is wisdom." Paul does not simply command "let them teach," Origen explains, because "men should not sit
and listen to a woman . . . even if she says admirable things, or even
saintly things, that is of little consequence, since they come from the
mouth of a woman."[23] In a passage on the washing of feet, Origen explains that the washing is figurative and occurs through good teaching.
In that sense, women may not wash men, for "'I permit no woman to
teach or to have authority over men.'"[24]

Origen never explains why women should not teach men. He does
permit women to be deacons, for "even women are instituted deacons
in the church."[25] Origen's teacher, Clement of Alexandria, notes that if
women teach women it prevents scandal, and perhaps Origen also fears
that sexual temptation may arise if women teach men.[26] But Origen
rests his position on a literal understanding of 1 Timothy 2:12.

The Apostolic Constitutions (late fourth century) limit both private
and public teaching by women. If someone should ask a widow about
her faith, she should send them to the church's governors. She may refute polytheism and assert monotheism, "but of the remaining doctrines let her not answer anything rashly, lest by saying anything un-
learnedly she should make the word to be blasphemed." Defective
explanations produce scorn for God, so women ought to teach as little
as possible.[27] The Constitutions restrict public teaching even more. "We

22. Origen, "Fragments on 1 Corinthians," in Roger Gryson, *The Ministry of Women
in the Early Church*, trans. Jean Laporte and Mary Louise Hall (Collegeville, Minn.: Liturgical Press, 1976), 28.
23. Ibid., 28–29.
24. Origen, "Homilies on Isaiah, 6,3," in Gryson, *Ministry of Women*, 27.
25. Ibid., 31, from Rom. 16:1–2.
26. Clement of Alexandria, *Commentary on 1 Corinthians*, in Gryson, *Ministry of
Women*, 30.
27. "The Constitutions of the Holy Apostles," trans. J. Whiston and Irah Chase, *ANF*,
7:427. The anonymous Constitutions claim to be written by the twelve apostles.

do not permit our 'women to teach in the church,' but only to pray and hear those that teach." Why? "For our Master and Lord, Jesus himself, when he sent us the twelve to make disciples of the nations, did nowhere send out women to preach, although he did not want [lack] such. For there were with us the mother of our Lord and his sisters; also Mary Magdalene and Mary the mother of James, and Martha and Mary the sisters of Lazarus; Salome, and certain others." If Jesus had wanted women to teach, he would have appointed one of them. Further, the Constitutions explain, the ban on the ordination and teaching office of women is logical. "'If the head of the woman be the man,' it is not reasonable that the rest of the body should govern the head." So, if women were ordained and did teach, it would abrogate the order of creation, in which the man was created first.[28]

The Constitutions did permit widows and female deacons to minister to women. As unordained servants of priests and bishops, they ranked far below presbyters and bishops.[29] They could not baptize in an emergency. That would be "dangerous, or rather wicked and impious." For the man is the head of the woman, and "it is not just to abrogate the order of creation." For women to teach, to baptize or to be ordained is forbidden, for the ordination of women is "one of the ignorant practices of Gentile atheism."[30] So the Constitutions deny women the teaching office because they are less capable of defending the faith, because it disrupts the order of creation, and because it follows the practices of atheists.

Tertullian, Origen, and the Apostolic Constitutions all sharply restrict women in the church, and agree that men must teach with authority and lead officially in the church. Yet they do allow women freedom to prophesy, to minister to women, and to answer polytheists. Thus, even the strictest traditionalists respected the impulses women have for ministry.

Jerome

Though he was initially reluctant to teach women, Jerome (331–420) demonstrated his faith in the intellectual abilities of some women by sharing the fruits of his study, and praising them when they passed those fruits on to others. Paula, a widowed Roman aristocrat, was so devoted to Jerome's teaching that she and her daughter Eustochium followed him to Palestine when he left Rome. "She was slow to speak and swift to learn. . . . The holy Scriptures she knew by heart," Jerome says. Paula pressed hard for the truth. "Whenever I stuck fast and hon-

28. Ibid., 427–28, 394.
29. Ibid., 430–31, 492.
30. Ibid., 429.

estly confessed myself at fault [i.e., ignorant] she would by no means rest content but would force me by fresh questions to point out to her which of the many different solutions seemed to me most probable." Jerome almost implies that Paula and her daughter acquired Hebrew more readily than he, the ancient church's preeminent Hebrew scholar and translator: "While I myself beginning as a young man have with much toil and effort partially acquired the Hebrew tongue and study it now unceasingly, [lest when I] leave it, it may also leave me; Paula, on making up her mind that she too would learn it, succeeded so well that she could chant the Psalms in Hebrew and speak the language without a trace of the pronunciation peculiar to Latin. The same accomplishment can be seen to this day in her daughter Eustochium."[31]

Paula effectively taught and led women, most notably in a women's monastery she founded alongside Jerome's monastery for men in Bethlehem. Yet at least once she also taught men. In Jerome's absence a man began to teach heresy concerning the character of eternal life, and Paula resisted both the heresy and its proponents. In time, "she publicly proclaimed them as enemies of the Lord."[32]

Marcella, another noble Roman widow within Jerome's circle, taught even more. Widowed just seven months after her wedding, Marcella dedicated herself to chastity and asceticism. An older woman when Jerome arrived in Rome, she never met him without asking some question about Scriptures. Hearing his reply, she "would bring forward points on the other side; this, however, was not for the sake of argument but that by questioning she might learn as answer to such objections as she saw might be raised."[33] In this way Marcella became something of a teacher herself, Jerome said.

> After my departure from Rome, in case of a dispute on any subject, recourse was had to her to settle it. And so wise was she and so well did she understand what philosophers call τό πρέπον, that is, the becoming, in what she did, that when she answered questions, she gave her opinion not as her own but as from me or someone else, thus admitting that what she taught she had learned from others. For she knew that the apostle had said: 'I suffer not a woman to teach' and she would not seem to inflict a wrong upon the male sex many of whom (including sometimes priests) questioned her concerning obscure and doubtful points.[34]

31. Jerome, "To Eustochium" (Letter 108), trans. W. H. Freemantle, in *Nicene and Post-Nicene Fathers*, 28 vols. in two series, ed. Philip Schaff (Grand Rapids: Eerdmans, 1952–56), second series, 6:209–10. (Subsequent references will cite the *Nicene and Post-Nicene Fathers* as *NPNF*).

32. Ibid., 207–9.

33. Jerome, "To Principia" (Letter 127), in *Select Letters of St. Jerome*, trans. F. A. Wright (Cambridge, Mass.: Harvard University Press, 1954), 453.

34. Ibid., 455. Jerome, writing in Latin, slips into Greek for just the two words cited in the Greek.

When a potent heresy "fouled the clear waters of the faith of Rome," Marcella took a more public role. After holding back for a time she became convinced that the faith of Rome was endangered, and "threw herself into the breach." She "publicly withstood its teachers, choosing to please God rather than men." By letter she challenged the heretics to appear to defend themselves, and when they refused to come, they were discredited.[35]

Jerome's understanding of 1 Timothy 2, as expressed in this panegyric to Marcella, is problematic. Marcella taught what she had learned from Jerome (2:11) to other believers, including males and even some priests. Yet Jerome believes she did so without violating 1 Timothy 2:12. How? First, when she gave her opinion she admitted that it came from Jerome or another man. But how precisely does this save her from violating the apostolic teaching? In *Daughters of the Church*, Tucker and Liefeld, perhaps seizing on the idea of what is becoming and citing the term "seem," interpret the passage to mean that Jerome approved a bit of duplicity on Marcella's part. They editiorialize, "In other words, Marcella, with Jerome's concurrence, *ascribed her theological opinions to him* so she would not *seem* to be taking over the position of a teacher."[36] This interpretation is possible. But if we remember Jerome's passion for probity, and, it must be admitted, his vanity, it is more likely that we should emphasize that she "confessed" or "admitted" (Lat.: *fateratur*) that her ideas originated with a man, not herself. Marcella was, as Jerome sees it, his delegate in Rome. As he put it, "All that I had gathered together by long study, and by constant meditation made part of my nature, she first sipped, then learned, and finally took for her own."[37] Just as people had come to him when he was in Rome, so now people came to her, because she had acquired the fruits of his study.

Jerome therefore approves the teaching activity of Marcella, a mature widow. She filled the breach when heresy roiled the church. On the other hand, it does not even occur to Jerome that Marcella should be ordained or hold a teaching office. It was fitting that she teach privately and discreetly when others sought her, especially since she operated under the distant authority of a man, Jerome. Thus, as a traditionalist Jerome limits women's ministry. But as a teacher, he trained women for ministry.

Chrysostom

A preacher renowned for rhetorical prowess, for blunt critique of social sins, and for sensible, allegory-free exposition of Scripture, Chrysostom

35. Ibid., 457–61.
36. Tucker, *Daughters*, 118. Emphasis mine.
37. Jerome, *Select Letters*, 455.

(345–407) preached through 1 Timothy and many other texts that treat women. The critical reader easily detects some tension in his works. Compared to other ancients, his homilies on Ephesians 5 manifest a singular sensitivity toward marriage and women.[38] This very tenderness makes us puzzle longer over some of his harsh remarks about women.

Like other ancients, Chrysostom despised the indulgence and venality of Greco-Roman culture, and preached more passionately on the vain and immodest apparel of women than on the riddles of 1 Timothy 2:11–12.[39] So Chrysostom read 2:11–12 in light of 2:8–10. Women, Chrysostom asserts, are "naturally somewhat talkative," and disrupt the church with their clamor as they converse "upon unprofitable topics."[40] Thus, women should be silent for the same reason that they should dress modestly, so the church can fulfill its task of teaching, and so they can learn something.

Nonetheless, the command to be silent is not merely utilitarian. Women should be silent, Chrysostom says, because Adam was created first, and Eve was deceived. He anticipates the objection, "What does the creation and subsequent sin of Adam and Eve have to do with women of the present?" First, the law that made women subject to men rests on creation. By forming man first, God "shows their superiority." God created Adam first to show that "the male sex enjoyed the higher honor" and "had preeminence in every way."[41] Second, the fall sealed woman's subordinate status. "For the woman taught the man once, and made him guilty of disobedience, and wrought our ruin. Therefore, because she made bad use of her power over the man, or rather her equality with him, God made her subject to her husband." She was a poor teacher because she was "captivated by appetite, and deceived by "an inferior and subordinate animal."[42] Third, Eve's sin was typical for "the sex is weak and fickle . . . collectively." The whole female sex transgressed when Eve was deceived and deceived her husband in turn. Yet Paul does not wish woman to be cast down. God has granted her "another opportunity of salvation"; in bringing up children she can be saved, not only by herself, but by others.[43]

Such comments understandably draw feminists' ire. Yet Chrysostom's homily on Romans 16 gathers positive attention, for he generously lauds woman's ministry there. Warning his auditors not to skip

38. See Chrysostom, "Homilies on Ephesians" (Homily 20), trans. Gross Alexander, *NPNF,* First Series, 13:143–52.

39. For the concern regarding apparel, see Nugent, *Portrait of the Consecrated Woman*, 48–63.

40. Chrysostom, "Homilies on Timothy" (Homilies 8–9), trans. Philip Schaff, *NPNF,* First Series, 13:432–35.

41. Ibid., 435.

42. Ibid.

43. Ibid., 436.

over the "gold" found in the praise the apostle distributes to his co-
laborers, Chrysostom enthusiastically praises all the men and women
whom Paul greets.[44] As he expounds these encomia, Chrysostom ac-
claims several women—Mary, Tryphena, and Nereus's sister. Above all,
he takes the Junia/Junias of 16:7 to be a woman. Junia was Paul's relative, fellow prisoner, and an "apostle" (16:7). But Chrysostom's exegetical decision concerning Junia's gender is not as important as it might
seem, for he does not take "apostle" to mean one equal to the twelve
who laid the foundation for the church in doctrine and evangelism.
Rather he takes it in a secondary sense, such as one commissioned by
the church for a certain task (Acts 13:2–3; 14:14).

This conclusion rests on Chrysostom's comments about Mary, the
first woman whom Paul praised in the previous verse (one paragraph
earlier in the homily). Like other women, Mary puts men "to shame,"
by leaving them "so far behind" as she carries on "the race apostles and
evangelists ran."[45] Immediately, Chrysostom asks, "In what sense then
does he [Paul] say, 'I suffer not a woman to teach?' He means to hinder
her from publicly coming forward (1 Cor. 14:35), and from the seat on
the bema [a raised seat for clergy], not from the word of teaching." So,
he adds, women may admonish children (1 Tim. 2:15) and teach unbe-
lieving (1 Cor. 7:16) and even believing husbands. "Private conversing
for advantage" Chrysostom approves, public instruction by women "before all . . . in the public assembly," he does not. Now if public instruction by women has been prohibited in the first paragraph, on Mary
(Rom. 16:6), he cannot permit it in the next, on Junia (Rom. 16:7).
Hence, Chrysostom praises women who perform "all other ministries,"
indicating all but public teaching.[46]

This is Chrysostom's consistent position. His commentaries on Acts
18 and Romans 16 never imagine that Priscilla's instruction of Apollos
indicates that women can regularly teach doctrine to men. He stresses
instead her willingness to minister, to show hospitality, and to teach
women privately.[47] Further, his treatise "On the Priesthood" discusses
the proper pastoral care of virgins, not pastoral work by virgins.[48] Else-

---

44. "It is worth learning from this how he distributes to each his different praise,"
Chrysostom says, and nearly every one is singularly great, excellent, noble, or honorable
in his generous eyes. The greeting to Epenetus (16:5) is "very great." Andronicus and
Junia (16:7) enjoy "very great praise." For Apelles (16:10), "There is no praise like this."
The greeting to Philologus, Julius, Nereus, and his sister Olympias is "the greatest dignity
and unspeakable height of honor." Chrysostom, "Homilies on Romans, Homily 31,"
trans. George B. Simcox, *NPNF,* First Series, 11:553–56.

45. Ibid., 554–55.

46. Ibid., 554.

47. Chrysostom, "Homilies on Romans, Homily 30," *NPNF,* First Series, 11:550–52.

48. Chrysostom, "On the Priesthood," trans. T. W. Chambers, *NPNF,* First Series,
9:33–83. See esp. 56–59.

where, he interprets 1 Corinthians 14:34–35 quite literally. Paul re-presses the "babbling" of women; he "sews up their mouths"; he "not only enjoins on them silence, but silence with fear." They are "not even to ask any question in the church." Why is Paul so strict? Because "the woman is in some sort a weaker being and easily carried away and light minded." So they are subject to their husbands "for the benefit of both."[49] Chrysostom's interpretation of Timothy evinces a certain harshness and an absence of precision.[50] Nonetheless, Chrysostom enunciated several enduring arguments for male leadership and female silence in the church: (1) Man was created first, and thereby was des-tined to preeminence by God. (2) The woman abused her initial equality with man by leading him into sin, and was punished for it. (3) Women are less rational than men, somehow weaker and less honorable.

The Middle Ages

Medieval commentary on 1 Timothy 2 is also rare and incidental. Me-dieval concepts of 1 Timothy and other texts about women must be in-ferred from behavior of the church, from theological discussions of church law regarding ordination, gifts, and the administration of bap-tism, and from the monastic movement.

Hildegard (1099–1179), Benedictine abbess in Disebodenberg, vi-sionary, healer, and contemporary and female counterpart of Bernard of Clairveaux, dispensed counsel, sought and unsought, to four popes, two emperors, and the patriarch of Jerusalem (who heard that a "divine force operated in and through her"). She reached monks, abbots, dukes, sundry ecclesiastical officials, and humbler folk. She denounced the sins of the church, and called it to look to Christ rather than to priests for salvation.[51] Her authority devolved from her visions. "From my infancy my soul has always beheld this light," she asserted. Without trances or dreams, her soul soared. "I perceive these matters in my soul. . . . I do not hear them with my outer ears, nor do I perceive them by the cogitations of my heart, or by any collaboration of my five senses; but only in my soul, my eyes wide open . . . wide awake . . . I see these things."[52]

---

49. Chrysostom, "Homilies on 1 Corinthians, Homily 37," trans. T. W. Chambers, *NPNF*, First Series, 12:222.

50. For example, he unconsciously vacillates on the critical exegetical issue of the ref-erent of woman (γυνή) in 1 Timothy 2.

51. David S. Schaff, *The Middle Ages: From Gregory 7, 1049, to Boniface 8, 1294*, vol. 5 of *History of the Christian Church*, ed. and principal author Philip Schaff, 9 vols. (Grand Rapids: Eerdmans, 1953–57), 5:371–73; Henry Osborn Taylor, *The Medieval Mind* (Cam-bridge, Mass.: Harvard University Press, 1949), 462–75.

52. Taylor, *Medieval Mind*, 465–66.

In her forty-third year, she reported a vision and a voice commanding her to speak and write what she saw and heard. In that vision, "A
flashing fire of light . . . transfused my brain, my heart. . . . And suddenly
I had intelligence of the full meaning of the Psalter, the Gospel, and the
other books of the Old and New Testaments, although I did not have the
exact interpretation of the words of their text, nor the division of sylla-
bles nor knowledge of cases and moods."[53] After years of silence, Hildegard began to write, with an authority suggested by her eponymous
opening, "Lux vivens dicit." Framed as visions, her writings are artless
but orthodox.[54] By her books and her letters Hildegard taught the
church. Yet she soothed male sensibilities by calling herself an unlearned woman who received visions and wrote them down as ordered.[55] Hildegard, therefore, claimed that her ideas were not her own,
that she was merely the vessel for divine truth. Thus, she taught without
ordination, and without offending the orthodox consensus against
women in office.

The theological discussion of ordination begins roughly when
Hildegard began to publish her visions, with Peter Lombard's Sentences of 1148. Yet no one discussed women's ordination until Thomas
Aquinas and Bonaventure, who addressed it almost simultaneously.
Perhaps with Hildegard in mind, Thomas asks whether "the charism
of wisdom in speech and knowledge pertains to women" as well as
men. It appears so, says Aquinas, because "Prophecy is granted to
women," and the grace of prophecy is greater than that of speech." Further, all have received gifts, and women cannot administer the grace of
wisdom and knowledge unless they speak. On the other hand, Aquinas
counters, "St. Paul says . . . 'I permit no woman to teach or to have authority over men.'"

Aquinas (1225–74) finally decides women may not teach publicly in
the church.[56] He distinguishes private speech, which "becomes a
woman," and public speech, before "the whole church," which does not.
Public speech "is not conceded to women" because they "must be subject to man, according to Genesis. But to teach and persuade publicly
in the Church is not the task of subjects but of prelates." The subjection
of women has two aspects. Woman's penalty for her role in the fall requires that she "be subject to the man's domination," that she "bear

---

53. Ibid., 466–67.

54. Ibid., 466, 470–75. But Gies says Hildegard's work betrays familiarity with Augustine, Boethius, and contemporary science; Frances and Joseph Gies, *Women in the Middle
Ages* (New York: Harper & Row, 1978), 76–85.

55. Taylor, *Medieval Mind*, 466–68.

56. Thomas Aquinas, *Prophecy and Other Charisms*, trans. Roland Potter, in *Summa
Theologica*, ed. Thomas Gilby and T. C. Gilby, 60 vols. (New York: McGraw Hill, 1963–74),
45:133.

with her husband's will against her own." This, the first subjection, is accidental, pertaining to woman's history, but not her nature. But the second subordination is permanent and essential to woman, "since even before the Fall the man was the head of the woman."[57]

Why would woman be subject even without the fall? Women "generally speaking are not perfected in wisdom," and so should not minister publicly, Aquinas contends.[58] They "seldom keep a firm grip on things," they lack "in firm rational judgment. . . . Despite instances to the contrary . . . their conduct is not based on solid reason, but easily swayed by feeling." They do "not pursue what reason has counseled."[59] It is not necessary to read these remarks as chauvinistic insults, for Thomas knows subtlety. He says women seldom keep a firm grip, that they are easily swayed, that they do not pursue the counsels of reason. So Aquinas evaluates feminine inclinations as much as feminine capacities.

Thomas bans women from office for several reasons. Female priests might incite men to lust.[60] Tonsure, which is required for ordination, is impossible due to 1 Corinthians 11. But above all, women cannot receive ordination and the teaching office in the church because of their subjection to men. Subjection, though not a state of radical inferiority, is woman's natural state.[61] Her state of subjection promotes order, for the human family should be governed by the wise, and "the power of rational discernment is by nature stronger (Lat. *abundat*) in man."[62] But Thomas does not believe in a global moral and intellectual inferiority of women. Some women are virtuous, and husband and wife can delight in each other's virtue and in their marital relationship.[63] Similarly, Aquinas never denies that some women are governed by reason, although he does consider it less common in women than in men.

Parenthetically, those who accuse Aquinas of misogyny do so on the basis of dubious scholarship. In a section titled "The production of woman," Aquinas observes that some say woman should not have been part of the original creation. In describing their position, he cites Aristotle's view that "the female is a misbegotten male" and that "woman is

---

57. Thomas Aquinas, *Well Tempered Passion*, trans. Thomas Gilby, in *Summa Theologica*, 44:177.

58. Ibid., 45:133.

59. Ibid., 44:21.

60. Ibid., 45:133.

61. Ibid., *Man Made to God's Image*, trans. Edmund Hill, *Summa Theologica*, 13:35–39.

62. Ibid., 13:36–39.

63. Aquinas believes a "delightful" friendship can develop between a husband and a wife, through pleasure in the "generative act," by providing for "mutual needs" for the common good, and by the "virtue proper to . . . husband and wife." Thomas Aquinas, *Commentary on the Nicomachean Ethics*, trans. C. I. Litzinger, 2 vols. (Chicago, 1964), 2:766–68.

naturally of less strength and dignity than man." These two statements argue for a position on women that Aquinas rejects. Though he grants them plausibility in that he replies to them, he believes they fail to establish the question. Reasoning from erroneous biological notions, Aquinas does agree that "as regards the individual nature, woman is defective and misbegotten." Yet, he immediately adds, God rightly created her at the beginning, for "as regards human nature in general, woman is not misbegotten, for her creation is part of God's plan for the race and its procreation." Therefore, the accusation of misogyny on the basis of the "female is a misbegotten male" line is unjustified.[64]

Bonaventure (1221–74) agreed that only males may receive ordination. He first cited the consensus that women should not be ordained. Even though Deborah judged Israel and women have shown virtue in martyrdom and in religious life, woman has a "natural incapacity" for ordination. It is necessary, Bonaventure held, for an ordinand to bear the image of God, "because in this sacrament the person *[homo]* in some way becomes God or divine, since he participates in the divine power." But the male is in the image of God by reason of his sex. Further, a male must administer the sacrament because he signifies Christ, and only a male can represent the male Christ. Further, spiritual power is conferred in ordination, but women cannot receive or exercise such power.[65]

Duns Scotus (ca. 1266–1308) agrees that women should not be ordained, but argues that women cannot receive ecclesiastical orders simply because that is the will of Christ. "The church would not have presumed to deprive the entire sex of women, without any fault of their own, of an act which would licitly have been theirs, and which might have been ordained for the salvation of women and others in the church through her." Scotus implies that pastoral benefits might accrue from the ordination of women. So the ban rests on the pure will of Christ, not the good of the church, not on the inability of woman to bear the image of Christ (per Bonaventure), nor on a nature suited to subjection (per Aquinas). Yet once Scotus has established that this is Christ's will, he adds that it is also just (so Scotus is not a "Scotist"). For example, Jesus

64. For the charge, see Tucker, *Daughters*, 164–65. It must be noted here that Tucker quotes Will Durant's summary of Aquinas's view of women as if Durant's words were Aquinas's (see Will Durant, *The Age of Faith* [New York: Simon & Schuster, 1950], 973). The words chosen from Durant preserve and accentuate all of Aquinas's most negative remarks about women, but none of the positive. Durant, as cited by Tucker at least, sometimes takes Aquinas's words out of context. Furthermore, it is not clear from his footnotes that Durant ever read Aquinas. Once, Durant quotes Aquinas's description of an error as if it were his own belief! So Aquinas's views may be offensive and erroneous, but he is unjustly called a woman-hater.

65. Francis Cardman, "The Medieval Question of Women and Orders," *The Thomist* 42 (1978): 588–90.

did not ordain his mother; therefore, no woman should be ordained. Furthermore, reason teaches that after the fall women cannot enjoy eminence. Scotus might allow women to be deaconesses and "official" widows, but their offices would entail neither ordination nor authority.[66]

Women's Ministry in the Middle Ages

A tiny number of women, many of them somewhat like Hildegard, taught men privately, by letter or by audiences with church leaders. More often women taught other women. Female monasteries arose occasionally throughout the Middle Ages. Abbesses wielded considerable power over their sisters in some cases. Double monasteries, with male and female monastics in close proximity, occasionally flourished, especially among the Benedictines in the eighth and twelfth centuries. In exceptional cases, female abbesses ruled double monasteries, but they might have essentially been nunneries, with men present to perform male functions, such as manual labor, saying Mass, and hearing confession.[67] A few abbesses may have rivaled the authority of local bishops, but such situations depended on local conditions, social rank, and assertiveness.[68]

If medieval women became teachers and leaders, they did so by circumventing the ordinary channels to power. None taught or exercised authority through the ordinary paths to church office.[69] They did not attend universities, let alone teach at them; they did not receive ordination or celebrate the Mass. Female mystics claimed divine illumination and often denigrated their own skills and status. Though she seems to have been a learned woman and a Latinist, Julian of Norwich (late fourteenth century) called herself a "simple, unlettered creature . . . lewd, feeble and frail." A modest woman, she still felt she had to record her visions. "Because I am a woman, should I therefore believe that I ought not to tell you about the goodness of God, since I saw at the same time that it is his will that it be known?"[70] At the end of the account she, or her scribe, warned her readers, "beware thou take not one thing after thy affection and liking, and leave another. . . . But take everything with

---

66. Ibid., 590–92.
67. Gies, *Women in the Middle Ages*, 66.
68. Schaff, *History*, 5:638–39, Tucker, *Daughters*, 140–45.
69. For the view that the church has deliberately suppressed the truth that women held ordained office in the Middle Ages, see Joan Morris, *The Lady Was a Bishop: The Hidden History of Women with Clerical Ordination and the Jurisdiction of Bishops* (New York: Macmillan, 1973).
70. Edmund College and James Walsh, "Editing Julian of Norwich's Revelations: A Progress Report," *Medieval Studies* 38 (1976): 410–16, 420–23.

other, and truly understand that all is according to Scripture."[71] Even if Julian is a self-effacing woman,[72] we must ask, "If one has received a vision, who needs formal authority?"

In some contrast, the German nun and playwright Hroswitha (or Hrotsvith) admitted she is "capable of learning . . . divinely gifted with abilities" with "moderate knowledge" of philosophy. Yet she also declared herself "unlearned and lacking in thoroughness . . . a lowly woman" producing "rude" works, limited by "my woman's understanding."[73] Hroswitha's vacillations make us wonder whether she believed in female weakness or merely struck a pose for the sake of accommodation to a male world.

Gertrude of Helfta (thirteenth century) was even less prone to question her "female capacity" and confidently accepted authority.[74] Orthodox, supportive of the monastic community, and generally positive toward the sacramental system, she, like Julian, claimed she received visions that instructed her and granted her powers like those of a priest. "Behold, I give my words into your mouth," Christ said to her, qualifying her and commanding her to teach, advise, counsel, and preach. Her visions opened roles the thirteenth century formally denied to women.[75]

Whatever they thought of their abilities, the medieval female teachers shared the advantage of singleness and freedom from the authority of a husband or a father. Hildegarde, Hroswitha, Gertrude, and Julian were all single nuns. Catherine of Siena, famed for mystical visions and for a crusade for reform during the "Babylonian Captivity" of the papacy, never married. Brigitta, another fourteenth-century reformer, began her career after her husband died. Margery Kempe is the apparent exception that proves the rule. A wife and mother of fourteen children, she began her public work as a visionary and traveling evangelist only after she convinced her husband to join her in a pact of chastity and separation, sworn before a bishop.[76] In short, if a woman wanted to teach in the Middle Ages, the unwritten rule was, "Have a vision, but not a husband."

71. Julian of Norwich, *Revelations of Divine Love*, in *Women and Religion: A Feminine Sourcebook of Christian Thought*, ed. Elizabeth Clark and Herbert Richardson (New York: Harper & Row, 1977), 104; Julian of Norwich, *Revelations of Divine Love*, trans. Clifton Walters (New York: Penguin, 1966), 213. Clark and Richardson ascribe the line to Julian; Walters attributes it to a scribe.

72. College and Walsh, "Editing Julian," 406, 410, 421–32; See Julian, *Revelations of Divine Love*, 75, 139, passim.

73. Lina Eckenstein, *Women under Monasticism* (New York: Russell & Russell, 1896), 180–82. The quotation is from a letter to patrons of her plays.

74. Caroline Bynum, *Jesus as Mother: Studies in the Spirituality of the High Middle Ages* (Berkeley: University of California Press, 1982), 207–8.

75. Ibid., 184–87, 196–202.

76. Clark and Richardson, *Women and Religion*, 105–7.

Among the explanations of female mystics' visions, some find their roots in woman's propensity toward emotionalism. But if so, why has the church not had a steady stream of mystics in all ages? More plausibly, mysticism granted women "direct authorization to act as mediators to others."[77] By their visions they circumvented the strictures that the official church used to deny them ordination. No one had to argue against the accepted interpretation of 1 Timothy 2; the Lord himself transcended it with a vision.

The history of medieval sects corroborates this "Theory of Circumvention." Frequently persecuted by the church for nothing more heretical than their critique of its excessive authority, medieval sects often allowed women to minister publicly. The Waldensians of the twelfth and thirteenth centuries promoted the popular use of Scripture, the importance of preaching, and the right of laymen to preach. They even claimed that women could preach as well as men. When Paul's words concerning the silence of women were quoted to them, they replied that the women taught rather than formally preaching, and counterquoted Titus 2:3. They probably allowed women to administer the sacraments as well.[78] The Hussites also admitted the laity, including women, to the office of preaching.[79] The Cathari, a truly heretical movement, allowed both men and women to administer the Consolamentum, their central rite, which guaranteed the absolution of sin.[80]

To summarize, even though the ancient and medieval churches lack a full-orbed exegesis of 1 Timothy 2, the ancient and medieval churches consistently opposed the ordination of women to formal offices of teaching and authority in the church. When women did teach men, they justified it by claiming that God had commissioned them directly. On the other hand, the church allowed women to teach privately, to teach other women, and to publish their visions. Tertullian and Aquinas explicitly permitted women to prophesy, if inspired by God. Yet they denied that this should be likened to church office, since they spoke as God moved them directly.

The church's position rested primarily on a straightforward interpretation of 1 Timothy 2 and related passages in 1 Corinthians. The explanations of the ban on women in office varied, but the root was not merely a desire to control women or misogyny.[81] Some theologians be-

---

77. Bynum, *Sprituality*, 184.

78. Schaff, *History of the Christian Church*, 5:503–4.

79. Philip Schaff, *The Middle Ages: From Boniface 8, 1294, to the Protestant Reformation, 1517, History of the Christian Church*, 6:393.

80. Schaff, *History of the Christian Church*, 5:477.

81. Rosemary Ruether, "Misogynism and Virginal Feminism in the Fathers," in *Religion and Sexism: Images of Women in Jewish and Christian Tradition* (New York: Simon & Schuster, 1974), 150, 157–64, 179.

lieved women were intellectually inferior to men, and prone to deception, others held that they were simply less interested in reason. Some
believed the sensual nature dominated women.[82] One way or another,
most theologians doubted that women had the moral and intellectual
capacity to meet the doctrinal and apologetic needs of the church's public life. But without significant debate, no one compelled a thorough development of their rationale. That task began in the Reformation and
stretches to the present.

The Reformation

If the Reformation was a theological earthquake, with justification by
faith alone, salvation by grace alone, and the authority of Scripture
alone at the epicenter, its shock waves reached women and the family.
With the Reformation, the praise of marriage supplanted the praise of
virginity and the support of marriage replaced its vilification. As the status of marriage rose, so did that of women, and theologians began to
rethink their views of women, their role in the church, and the meaning
of texts such as 1 Corinthians 11, Ephesians 5 and 1 Timothy 2:9–15.

Luther

Luther (1483–1546) revered women as wives, mothers, and household
managers. He embraced marriage as God's good will for the vast majority of humankind, clergy included. He perceived the bustling household
as God's school of character and defended women from the contempt
of misogynists. Luther said woman is "much weaker" than man, "not
the equal of the male in glory and prestige," like the moon to man's sun.
Yet Eve was and woman is "similar to Adam so far as the image of God
is concerned, that is, in justice, wisdom, and happiness." She "may not
be excluded from any glory of the human creature," although women
are "inferior to the male sex," weak, often foolish, and prone to chaotic
talk.[83] Yet commenting on Genesis 2, Luther explains that God created
women "according to a definite plan," and that if she had not sinned,
"she would have been the equal of man in all respects." Before her sin,

---

82. Gies, *Women in the Middle Ages*, 41–52. Dominican Humbert de Romans was one
of the rare men who argued that women are superior to men, possessing more grace and
more glory; ibid., 37–41.

83. Martin Luther, *Lectures on Genesis: Chapters 1–5*, trans. George V. Schick, vol. 1
of *Luther's Works*, ed. Jaroslav Pelikan and Walther T. Lehman (St. Louis: Concordia,
1955–72), 1:68–69, for the quotation. For the rest, *Table Talk*, trans. and ed. Theodore G.
Tappert, *Luther's Works*, 54:221, 183, 428.

Eve "was in no respect inferior to Adam, in body or mind." After the fall, even apart from procreation and facing their defects, man cannot get along without woman.[84]

To be sure, Luther's occasional recklessness lets critics charge him with misogyny. One widely quoted, and heedlessly decontextualized, comment on childbearing says, "If women get tired and die of bearing, there is no harm in that; let them die as long as they bear; they were made for that."[85] But a little context makes a big difference. "God has created both man and woman to produce seed and to multiply," the full text begins. The rejection of marriage produces both immorality and poor health. "We see how weak and sickly barren women are. Those who are fruitful, however, are healthier, cleanlier, and happier. And even if they bear themselves weary—or ultimately bear themselves out—that does not hurt. Let them bear themselves out. This is the purpose for which they exist. It is better to have a brief life with good health than a long life in ill health."[86] Thus, Luther's intent is nearly the opposite of what his accusers say. Childbearing may result in death, he admits. But ordinarily, childbearing begets health for both women and men.

Luther wrote the first significant commentary on 1 Timothy 2:8–15 since Chrysostom. Like Chrysostom, Luther labored more over immodest dress than women's ecclesiastical rights. He wanted women to be modest and sensible in their dress, and believed a plain wardrobe helps in "controlling women." Women may dress up for weddings, Luther allows, but not in church, "when they gather for prayer, and when the Word is about to be taught."[87] Luther believed 2:11 treated public ministry, in the public assembly of the church. There, Luther declares, "a woman must be completely quiet, because she should remain a hearer and not become a teacher. She is not to be the spokesman among the people. She should refrain from teaching, from praying in public. She has the command to speak at home. This passage makes a woman subject. It takes from her all public office and authority."[88]

Luther concedes that sacred literature has many examples of women who "have been very good at management," such as Huldah, Deborah, Jael, and Queen Candace (Acts 8:27). Why then, Luther asks, does Paul

---

84. Luther, *Works*, *Genesis*, 1:115; *Table Talk*, 54:160–61; see also 54:171, 223.

85. The first American source of the quotation may be Will Durant, *The Reformation: A History of European Civilization from Wyclif to Calvin, 1300–1564* (New York: Simon & Schuster, 1957), 416.

86. Martin Luther, "The Estate of Marriage," in *The Christian in Society*, trans. Walther I. Brandt, *Works*, 45:46. For the German, see Weimar Ausgabe, vol. 10, pt. 2, 301.

87. Martin Luther, *Lectures on 1 Timothy*, trans. Richard Dinda, *Luther's Works*, 28:270–76.

88. Ibid., 276.

deprive women of the administration of the word in 1 Timothy? "Where men and women have been joined together, there the men, not the women, ought to have authority. An exceptional example is where they are without husband, like Huldah and Deborah. . . . He forbids teaching contrary to a man or to the authority of a man. Where there is no man, Paul has allowed that they can do this, because it happens by a man's command."[89]

Luther justifies Paul's ban on women in authority in several ways. First, Paul wants "to save the order preserved by the world—that a man be the head of the woman, as 1 Corinthians 11:3 tells us. . . . There would be a disturbance if some woman wished to argue against the doctrine that is being taught by a man. . . . Where a man teaches there is a well-rounded argument. . . . If she [a woman or wife] wants to be wise, let her argue with her husband at home."[90] So men ought to teach to maintain the natural order in the church. But, he implies, men are better able to teach, more rounded, and perhaps more logical or less argumentative.

When Paul forbids women to have authority over a man, Luther adds that he does not advocate a "real physical domination" by men. He means the woman should not "have the last word" or appear wiser or more learned in church or in home. Rather, "the principal role belongs to the man . . . not only because of what God intended but also from the history of Adam and Eve." Man deserves authority because "God himself has ordained that man be created first—first in time and first in authority." Adam has the right of primogeniture. But man also rules because of merit. "Not only has God's wisdom ordained this, but there was more wisdom and courage in Adam. . . . Experience has been witness of this. . . . It was not Adam who went astray. Therefore there was greater wisdom in Adam than in the woman."[91] Luther ponders Satan's strategy in the fall, stressing that "Satan did not attack Adam." He avoided "the fearless person [Adam] and attacked the weaker one." She "became a transgressor" and sin entered the world "by her fault." Thus, woman's position is also a punishment, "a memorial of that transgression which by her fault entered into the world."[92] So men lead because God ordained it, because they are stronger, wiser, and more courageous, and because woman deserves to be punished for Eve's role in the fall.

89. Ibid., 276–77. In this section Luther says he takes "woman" to mean wife and "man" to mean husband. But this exegetical decision concerning γυνή and ἀνήρ had no discernible influence on his broader interpretation.

90. Ibid., 277.

91. Ibid., 277–78.

92. Ibid., 278–79.

Calvin

Calvin (1509–64) reads 1 Timothy 2:11–12 as a description of church life rather than family life; the man and woman in the text are not husband and wife, but members of the church. Calvin says verses 10 and 11 describe "with what modesty women ought to conduct themselves in the holy assembly." When Paul bids the women to learn quietly, he means they cannot "speak in public" or teach publicly.[93] By nature, women are subject; "by the ordinary law of God" they are "formed to obey." Government by women "has always been regarded by all wise persons as a monstrous thing." So they must be quiet, for "to teach implies the rank of power and authority."[94]

Of course, women may instruct their families, but Paul "excludes them from the office of teaching, which God has committed to men only." If anyone adduces Deborah, Philip's daughters, Abigail, and other female prophets and teachers, Calvin answers that these women never held "the office to speak in the assembly."[95] Further, their cases are "extraordinary and do not overturn the ordinary rules of government, by which he intended that we should be bound." The God "who is above all law" can do such things without affecting his ordinary system.[96] So, if a woman should teach or govern for a season, we should conclude not that women may hold authority, but that evil behavior brings "great confusion," that "God will shame us [males] . . . and show us that we are not worthy" by causing "women and little children to reign."[97] But such free acts of God set no precedent for human government.[98]

Commenting on 2:13, Calvin observes that Paul "assigns two reasons why women ought to be subject to men; because not only did God enact this law at the beginning, but he also inflicted it as a punishment on the woman" for her sin. Women have never been received into public office, because "nature" imprints the knowledge that it is "unseemly . . . to have

93. John Calvin, *Commentaries on the Epistles to Timothy, Titus and Philemon*, trans. William Pringle (Edinburgh: The Calvin Translation Society, 1856), 67.

94. Ibid., 68.

95. Calvin, *Commentaries*, 67; John Calvin, *Sermons on Timothy and Titus* (Oxford: Banner of Truth Trust, 1983), 226. The latter is a facsimile of a 1579 London edition, printed by G. Bishop, and translated by L.T. [sic]. The pagination is egregiously erratic; where erroneous, the number given in the text will appear first, followed by the correct number, in parentheses.

96. Ibid.

97. Calvin, *Sermons*, 227.

98. Calvin, *Sermons*, 225. We hear the Scotist in Calvin saying, "we must make a difference between the common order which God will have to be observed among men for a rule" and his unusual work. "For we may not make God subject to a law, because all laws proceed from his will."

women govern men."[99] So when Paul says Adam was created first, he reflects on all the circumstances of creation, not just "the order of time." Specifically, "woman was created" as "a kind of appendage to the man." She was joined to him to "be at hand to render obedience to him," as "an inferior aid."[100] Woman's subjection is also a punishment for her sin. Adam was entangled in deceit along with Eve, but she was the "cause or source" of their sin, and more at fault than he. Therefore, "because she had given fatal advice, it was right that she should learn that she was under the power and will of another." Calvin explains that "the condition of obeying" was "natural from the beginning," but after Eve's disobedience, "the subjection was now less voluntary and agreeable." Because she exalted herself against her Creator as well as her husband, her subjection now admits a "note of ignominy and shame."[101]

Calvin imagines someone wondering why women should be subject to men. Calvin's explanation for a male-dominated order borrows from both Thomas and Scotus. God "appointed a certain kind of policy and order . . . to provide for the weaker sort," says the Thomist in Calvin.[102] In a passage from the commentary on John 20 that condemns Jewish unbelief and the disciples' sluggishness, Calvin wonders why the Lord chose women to be the first witnesses to Jesus' resurrection. Quoting 1 Corinthians 1:27, Calvin explains that "God chooseth what is weak in the world and foolish" that he may confound the wise and powerful. It was "a mild and gentle chastisement . . . [an] inconceivable kindness" that God would instruct the twelve through women. If someone objects that the women "are not less carnal and stupid" than the apostles, Calvin replies, "It does not belong to us to estimate the difference between the Apostles and the women."[103] Moments later, commenting on Deborah's rule over Israel, the Scotist in Calvin explains, "when God maketh a law . . . it derogateth nothing from his liberty, so that he may not upon occasion work otherwise. . . . For we may not make God subject to a law, because all laws proceed from his will."[104] So the Scotist sounds the dominant chord. Why did God establish a male-governed order? Because "it pleased God [that] it should be so." Moreover, "we can allege no desert why God preferred us before women." Yet even if men have no worthiness, women have no right to murmur against the

99. Ibid., 212.

100. Calvin, *Commentary*, 68–69. The term "inferior" ordinarily referred to social rank at the time of the Reformation, and does not necessarily imply incapacity.

101. Ibid., 69–70; *Sermons*, 209 (213).

102. Calvin, *Sermons*, 223.

103. Calvin's references to the weakness of women are very rare, and seem to allude to either 1 Cor. 1:27 or 1 Pet. 3:7. Nonetheless they earn him feminist ire (see Tucker, *Daughters*, 176–77). John Calvin, *Commentary on the Gospel According to John*, trans. John Pringle (Grand Rapids: Baker, 1981), 247–48, 260–61.

104. Ibid., 225.

divine order. If they chafe, let them remember that they bear God's image and rule the lower creation.[105] So, while Calvin is slightly agnostic ("it does not belong to us to estimate," above), he leans toward the idea that men and women are intrinsically equal.

Calvin's voluminous writings let scholars shift from collecting scraps of a theology of women, to selecting from the most telling remarks from an ever fuller theology of woman and gender roles. Scholars can even play texts against each other in Calvin, although most conclude that Calvin is simply a nuanced traditionalist.[106] Jane Douglass, however, claims that the *Institutes* have hermeneutical priority over the commentaries, and proposes that, for Calvin, woman's silence in the church is "adiaphora," that is, an indifferent matter. Although she concedes that Calvin knew his society would never accept women as pastors, she believes Calvin was theoretically open to female church leaders.[107] Her evidence is that, according to the *Institutes*, woman's silence in the church is merely a matter of order and decorum, hence changeable, rather than immutable divine law.[108] Douglass's key text is a paragraph describing order and decorum in worship. Decorum, Calvin asserts, requires "that profane drinking bouts should not be mingled with the Sacred Supper of the Lord [1 Cor. 11:21–22], and that women should not go out in public with uncovered heads [1 Cor. 11:5]." Order means "hours set for public prayers, sermons and sacraments." It requires silence for sermons, "fixed days for the celebration of the Lord's Supper,

105. Ibid., 214–12 (215). Calvin's commentaries on Genesis, John, and Corinthians sound similar. The latter especially insists on the spiritual equality of men and women, that the differences flow from "civil order and honorary distinctions, which cannot be dispensed with in ordinary life." In John Calvin, *Commentary on the Epistles of Paul the Apostle to the Corinthians*, trans. John Pringle (Grand Rapids: Baker, 1981), 353–55.

106. Georgia Harkness, *John Calvin: The Man and His Ethics* (New York: Abingdon, 1958) 155; John Bratt, "The Role and Status of Women in the Writings of John Calvin," in *Renaissance, Reformation, Resurgence: Colloquium on Calvin and Calvin Studies*, ed. Peter DeKlerk (Grand Rapids: Calvin Theological Seminary, 1976), 1–17. According to Bratt, Calvin believed women receive spiritual gifts from God, deserve dignity, may rule nations, and have conjugal rights equal to those of a man, but they cannot hold public office in the church because they are permanently subordinated to men. See also Willis P. DeBoer, "Calvin on the Role of Women," in *Exploring the Heritage of John Calvin: Essays in Honor of John H. Bratt*, ed. D. E. Holwerda (Grand Rapids: Baker, 1976), 236–72; Rita Mancha, "The Woman's Authority: Calvin to Edwards," *Journal of Christian Reconstruction* 6 (1979–80): 86–98.

107. Ibid., 106–7. "Calvin . . . specifically includes Paul's advice for women to be silent in the church among the adiaphora where the church should be open to change." Of course, if "silent" means totally mute, Douglas is correct. But if (as appears to be the case) the end of the silence means teaching and exercising authority, then we must demur.

108. Douglass, *Women and Calvin*, 7. Her preface declares that she "continued to puzzle over Calvin's unexpected inclusion of women's silence in church among matters of order and decorum that are "indifferent," matters of human law that are adaptable to changing circumstances.

the fact that Paul forbids women to teach in the church [1 Cor. 14:34], and the like. Especially are there those things which maintain discipline, such as catechizing, church censures, excommunication, fasting, and whatever can be referred to the same list."[109]

Against Douglass, the close observer will have noticed that "adiaphora," the key term for Douglass, appears neither in the quotation nor in the broader section. Further, Calvin's list of ecclesiastical ordinances contains some true adiaphora—matters touching decorum alone, such as head coverings and hours for worship—but also some points that are far from indifferent, such as drunkenness at the Lord's table and the maintenance of church discipline. The custom of kneeling for prayer, says Calvin "is human," but "it is also divine." So "decorum" is part of "the sum of true righteousness." But God left the particulars of decorum unspecified because he "did not will in outward discipline and ceremonies to prescribe in detail what we ought to do." So believers suit the details of decorum to local cultures, even while they guard "the general rules" God has given.[110] Therefore, matters of decorum may be adiaphora, but that does not mean they are absolutely indifferent morally. Rather it means the *form* of obedience is indifferent as long as the the underlying principle remains.

Calvin does use the term "adiaphora" in his commentary on 1 Timothy 2:10. He urges women to dress according to the rule of moderation, but refrains from making specific regulations. He explains that "dress is an indifferent matter [adiaphora]" so that "it is difficult to assign a fixed limit." The "adiaphora" comment notwithstanding, Calvin says women must dress with modesty and sobriety; he censures the prominent display of gold and jewels. "The dress of a . . . godly woman must differ from that of a strumpet . . . in chaste and becoming dress."[111] So Calvin insists on the principle of modesty, while saying the particular application of the principle is "adiaphora."[112]

Applying this understanding of adiaphora to the case of male/female relations, we see that Calvin believed the form of woman's deference to male leadership could vary, as long as the substance, male leadership, remained. So Douglass has not proved that the substance of the

109. John Calvin, *Institutes of the Christian Religion*, trans. Ford Lewis Battles, 2 vols. (Philadelphia: Westminster, 1960), 2:1207.

110. Ibid., 2:1208.

111. Calvin, *Commentary*, 66–67.

112. On this reasoning, the difficulty attending the quotation most troublesome to our argument, Calvin's comment on "let the women be silent in the churches" (1 Cor. 14:34), becomes innocuous. The line is "The discerning reader should come to the conclusion that the things which Paul is dealing with here are indifferent, that is, neither good nor bad; and none of them is forbidden unless it works against order and decorum." But as we read it, Calvin is only affirming that the form is indifferent; the need for decorum and the male leadership that allows it remains.

women's issue is adiaphora for Calvin. Calvin believed men should always lead: "God hath set an order which may in no wise be broken, and must continue even to the world's end."[113] His numerous, widespread, and forceful affirmations of male leadership in home and church stand. Since even feminist historians admit that the rest of the Reformers were traditionalists, we conclude that all the leading theologians of the Reformation adopted the traditional interpretation of 1 Timothy 2.

The Puritans

The English Puritans (1560–1645) developed a theology of marriage and gender roles that provides a complete context for the interpretation of 1 Timothy 2.[114] The Puritans believed God structured human society by ordaining "degrees of superiority and inferiority, of authority and subjection."[115] He governs the world through a series of relations between inferiors and superiors: magistrates and subjects, ministers and churches, husbands and wives, parents and children, masters and servants. In each relationship, superiors obtain and hold authority through their position, not their virtue, even though they must discharge and uphold their position through virtue.

In marriages this order means that, "by virtue of the matrimonial bond the husband is made the head of his wife, though the husband were, before the marriage, a very beggar, and of mean parentage, and the wife very wealthy and of a noble flock."[116] If someone should argue that servitude is against the law of nature, "it is indeed against the law of nature as it was before the fall, but against the law of corrupted nature it is not." A servant may, in "the inner man be equal to his master . . . yet in regard of the outward man and the civil order amongst men, the master is above the servant and the servant is and must be subject to the master."[117]

But what if a woman's husband is "lewd and beastly . . . a drunkard, an impious swearer" and his wife is a "sober, religious matron"? Must she "account him her superior, and worthy of an husband's honor"? Certainly, for his evil disposition does not deprive him of the "civil

113. Calvin, *Sermons*, 227.

114. William Gouge wrote a 700-page tome on the family, devoting over 300 pages to the mutual duties of husbands and wives (21–132, 213–427). Daniel Rogers wrote a 400-page tome, *Matrimoniall Honour*; John Dod, Robert Cleaver, Thomas Gataker, William Whately, Paul Baynes, and Nicholas Byfield all wrote at less, yet comparable, length on marriage and family.

115. William Gouge, *Of Domesticall Duties* (London, 1622), 591. The Puritans' original spelling, punctuation, and capitalization have been modernized in this section, except in titles.

116. Gouge, *Duties*, 272–73.

117. William Perkins, *Works*, 3:698.

honor" that God bestows on "his place and office."[118] The best wife, therefore, always retains her inward reverence. If she wants to rule, she should do it through his heart. The wife may disobey only if a husband's commands contradict the word of God.[119]

While these remarks bind women in some ways, they loose them in others.[120] First, the Puritans addressed women directly, something unknown in Chrysostom, Aquinas, Luther, and Calvin. Second, they assume that women have the competency to judge the legality of their husbands' directives, and that they have the courage to resist their husbands' orders when necessary. Third, the Puritans respected woman's conscience. They commanded husbands to rule legally and only "to procure their wives' good." Before executing major decisions husbands must persuade their wives of their wisdom, granting them time to deliberate, exercising their authority gently.[121] Moreover, if she cannot bring her mind to his, though the husband patiently instruct her, he must not enforce his will, lest he damage her conscience.[122]

William Gouge's commentary on 1 Timothy 2:12 draws some practical conclusions from the Protestant position. Gouge said a wife's words should be "few, reverend and meek" in her husband's presence, "for the apostle enjoineth silence to wives in their husbands' presence . . . in these words, 'I permit not the woman to usurp authority over the man, but to be in silence." Gouge contended that in 1 Timothy 2:11 Paul "speaketh not only of a woman's silence in the church, but also of a wife's silence before her husband."[123] A wife may speak a little, as long as she "somewhat restrain her tongue," Gouge explains, for complete silence suggests "stubbornness of heart" as much as loquacity implies disrespect. But a wife who speaks on "just occasion" is willing to listen to the husband. Therefore, "silence" means that a wife speaks sparingly and reverently. Gouge explains that for the term ἡσυχία, "the original signifieth also quietness." Women manifest subjection by quietly learning from their husbands.[124]

Nonetheless, women may teach, according to Gouge. As joint governor of the family with her husband, she rightly teaches the women and

118. Gouge, *Duties*, 272–73.

119. Ibid., 654.

120. Gouge, at least, offended some prominent women of London, and heard about it. See ibid., 272–73, and esp. the preface to the second edition.

121. William Whately, *A Bride Bush* (London, 1617), 21, 29f. Whately urged husbands to conceal their use of authority (rather than loudly insisting on it), much as speakers conceal their use of logic and rhetoric.

122. Rogers, *Honour*, 264–65; Gouge, *Duties*, 378; Whately, *Bride*, 33–34.

123. Gouge, *Duties*, 281–82. Regarding the translation of αὐθεντεῖν as "usurp authority," Gouge does not argue for his translation; he is merely quoting the King James translation. I have discovered no debate about the meaning of αὐθεντεῖν until the modern era.

124. Ibid., 282.

children, and even the male servants, in her husband's absence. Such teaching does not conflict with 1 Timothy 2:12, Gouge explains, for that teaching "hath respect to public assemblies, and Churches, in which she may not teach: but not to private families, in which she may, and ought to teach: for Bathsheba taught Salomon. When Apollos was brought to the house of Aquila, Priscilla the wife of Aquila did help to expound to Apollos the way of God more perfectly." Further, although husbands have primary responsibility for leading household worship, wives may even lead "in praying, reading, teaching, and performing like exercises herself, so far as she is able, when her husband is absent, or negligent, or careless, and will not himself do them."[125]

What, then, is the extent of a wife's subjection to her husband? The husband's authority is very large, Gouge says, because "it hath no restraint but God's contrary command," and if a wife is not "assured" that her husband's command is contrary to God's will, "she must yield to her husband's will." The wife must not only yield in practice, she also "must labor to bring her judgment . . . to her husband's." This is what it means to "learn in silence with all subjection (1 Timothy 2:11)." Gouge admits that the text "principally meant . . . learning in the church, yet it excluded not her learning at home of her husband: for in the next words he addeth, 'I suffer not a woman to usurp authority over a man, but to be in silence.'"[126] Stringent as these requirements are, we must recall that when Gouge addressed husbands, he ordered them not to force their wives to act against their conscience.

The Puritans also explored why men ought to lead and women ought to follow. The Thomists among them asserted that men lead because they are superior to women in mind and body and so deserve to rule. Robert Bolton said the husband, as the head is "the glory of the body. . . . The head is the seat of understanding and wisdom. . . . The husband, by the benefit of a more manly [!] body tempered with a natural fitness of the soul to work more nobly in; doth or ought to exceed the wife in understanding, and dexterity to manage business." The wife's soul, on the other hand, is "something damped by the frailty of that weaker body, with which God's wise providence hath clothed it."[127] William Whately agreed that "nature hath framed the lineaments" of the male's body "to his superiority, and set the print of government in his very face, which is sterner and less delicate than the woman's; and he must not suffer this order of nature to be inverted."[128] Similarly, John Winthrop,

125. Ibid., 256–60; quotations from 258, 260.
126. Ibid., 337–38.
127. Robert Bolton, *Some General Directions for a Comfortable Walking with God* (London, 1625), 245.
128. William Whately, *Directions for Married Persons*, ed. John Wesley, *A Christian Library in Thirty Volumes* (London: T. Cordeux, 1821), 12:299.

governor of the Massachusetts Bay Colony, reported that the wife of the governor of Connecticut went insane because she had meddled "in such things as are proper for men, whose minds are stronger."[129]

Most Puritans argued that men lead primarily because of the need for order. As William Perkins put it, "there must be orders of men" for family, church and commonwealth to stand.[130] Gouge said God commands all men to submit to one another, "because everyone is set in his place by God, (not so much for the good of himself, as for the good of others.)"[131] Thomas Gataker argued for male leadership three ways: order, nature, and history. Order requires husbands to lead because, "the man was first created . . . and therefore the man hath the birthright (1 Tim 2:13)." But the nature of the genders proves the same thing, for Genesis 2:22 says "the woman was made for the man, and not the man for the woman." Further, the woman is the "image and glory of the man, as the man is the image and the glory of God (1 Cor 11:7)." And historically the woman sinned first and drew the man into sin with her, so woman's position was sealed.[132]

The Puritans refined the complementarian position in important ways. Perhaps because they emphasized order more than capacity, the Puritans granted women substantial freedom. In New England, Samuel Sewall and Samuel Whiting both turned all of their finances over to their wives.[133] Gouge permitted wives to lead family worship if husbands were absent or indisposed.[134] Applying the Protestant principle of the priesthood of believers, they largely abandoned notions of the intellectual inferiority of women. They respected women's conscience and expected them to exercise spiritual judgment. Although the Puritans did not entirely abandon the idea that men might be more fit to lead, the principal rationale for male leadership is the need for order in society.

The Reformation recognized the mental and spiritual capacities of women. But affirmations of woman's ability invite a challenge. If women are as capable and spiritual as men, why are they barred from office? If they feel a subjective call, exercise it, and see fruit, should they not be free to lead in church and home? The challenge came soon enough. In England, women became active in the religious sects that emerged during the Civil War. In America Anne Hutchinson troubled the Massachusetts Bay Colony with her semipublic critiques of ser-

129. John Winthrop, *History of New England, 1630–1649*, ed. James Kendall Hosmer, 2 vols. (New York: Barnes & Noble, 1908, 1966), 2:225.

130. Perkins, *Works*, 3:511.

131. Gouge, Duties, 5–7. He comments on Eph. 5:21.

132. Thomas Gataker, *Certaine Sermons* (London, 1635), 2:188–89.

133. Morgan, *Puritan Family*, 43.

134. Gouge, *Duties*, 256–60.

mons and the pastors who preached them.[135] In 1666 Margaret Fell, the second wife and co-laborer of George Fox, published perhaps the earliest protofeminist tract, "Women's Speaking Justified, Proved, and Allowed by the Scriptures." More a protest or diatribe than a theological treatise, it asserts that "the Church of Christ is a woman, and those that speak against the Woman's speaking, speak against the Church of Christ . . . such speak against Christ and his Church and are of the Seed of the Serpent." Since Jesus spoke to women, loved women, and poured out his Spirit on women, and used women in ministry, 1 Timothy 2 cannot forbid all women to speak or preach in the church. Rather 1 Timothy addresses women who dress immodestly, and *they* should not teach or usurp authority.[136] Fell's tract seems to have had little influence, but it suggests that reappraisals of female spiritual capacity invite egalitarian developments.

The Eighteenth Century: Wesley and Edwards

John Wesley and Jonathan Edwards shared a "relaxed" traditionalism. For Wesley, 1 Timothy 2:11–12 and 1 Corinthians 14:34 meant women should not teach in public "unless they are under an extraordinary impulse of the Spirit." Normally, women must refrain from public teaching because woman was originally the "inferior" or subordinate of man (1 Tim. 2:13), and because woman "is more easily deceived, and more easily deceives." So Wesley permitted women to say a few words, or "exhort" audiences of both men and women at public gatherings on occasion while remaining in the traditionalist camp.[137]

Edwards discussed the women's issue in the context of spiritual pride in the New England revival. Citing 1 Timothy 2:9–12, Edwards says all persons owe each other a civil reverence, including a "modesty and shamefacedness," which social "inferiors," owe their "superiors," in both civil and spiritual realms. "Not that . . . women's mouths should be shut up from Christian conversation," Edwards quickly adds. But there is room for women to be reverent toward men, says Edwards:

> 'Tis beautiful for persons when they are at prayer . . . to make God only their fear . . . and to be wholly forgetful that men are present. . . . And 'tis beautiful for a minister, when he speaks in the name of the Lord of hosts

135. Winthrop, *History*, 1:243–55, 260–63.

136. Margaret Fell, *Womens Speaking Justified, Proved, and Allowed by the Scriptures* [sic] (London, 1666), 3–12; reprinted by Mosher Book and Tract Committee of the New England Yearly Meeting of Friends, Amherst, Mass., 1980.

137. John Wesley, *The Letters of Rev. John Wesley*, 8 vols., ed. John Telford (London: Epworth, 1931), 5:257; John Wesley, *Explanatory Notes upon the New Testament*, 11th ed. (New York: Carlton & Porter, 1754), 440, 540.

. . . to put off all fear of men. And 'tis beautiful for private Christians, though they are women and children to be bold in professing the faith of Christ . . . and in owning God's hand in the work of his power and grace, without any fear of men, though they be reproached as fools and madmen. . . . But for private Christians, women and others, to instruct, rebuke, and exhort, with a like sort of boldness as becomes a minister when preaching, is not beautiful.[138]

Nineteenth-Century Thinkers and Doers

Intensive debate about the role of women arose in the nineteenth century. Though the church was officially traditionalist in doctrine and practice, women taught Sunday school classes, wrote hymns, and battled social sins. At revivals, women began to say a few words, then to give more formal addresses, typically with an expressed allegiance to the notion of male leadership of the church. But as more women participated in revivals, some, such as Jerena Lee, Salome Lincoln, and Antoinette Brown, began to hear or feel a call from God to preach the gospel. Most reported that they had resisted God's pursuits before succumbing to its irresistible attraction (the "Subjective Call Argument").[139] As the missions movement expanded, both married and single women took active roles abroad, teaching, training, and even preaching. Most female missionaries worked primarily with women. But the harvest was plentiful and the workers were few, so they inevitably spoke to men from time to time. For example, Charlotte (Lottie) Moon worked first with women and children, but she believed that she had to reach men if she wanted tangible results for her work. She could not resist working with inquiring men on occasion. Likewise, Hudson Taylor said no offense is given if men in China sometimes listen to the Bible lessons of a missionary sister.[140] New practices inevitably prompted a reconsideration of the issues, and publications followed events.

Three Early Feminist Writers

In *Female Ministry; or Woman's Right to Preach the Gospel*, Catherine Booth (1829–90), already an active speaker in the Salvation Army, at-

---

138. Jonathan Edwards, *The Great Awakening*, ed. C. C. Goen, vol. 4 of *Works of Jonathan Edwards*, gen. ed. John E. Smith (New Haven: Yale University Press, 1972), 4:426–28.

139. Tucker, *Daughters*, 259–63, *passim*.

140. Irwin Hyatt, *Our Ordered Lives Confess: Three Nineteenth Century American Missionaries in East Shantung* (Cambridge, Mass.: Harvard University Press, 1976), 104, 109–11; *Missionary Review of the World* 11 (November 1898): 874; see Tucker, *Daughters*, 303–18.

tacked the chief facets of the traditionalist position: the intrinsic incapacity of women to minister and God's will to bar them from it. Concerning woman's nature Booth asseverates that she is fit for both
platform and pulpit because "God has given to woman a graceful form
and attitude, winning manners, persuasive speech, and, above all, a
finely-toned emotional nature, all . . . eminent natural qualifications for
public speaking." Amiable and unobtrusive, women are no more prone
to vanity than men.[141]

Scripture also permits women to preach, Booth avers. "The public
ministry of women [is] absolutely enjoined by both precept and example in the Word of God." She cites Joel 2:28, Acts 2:17, and 1 Corinthians 11:4–5, which assume that women pray and prophesy in
churches. Her work with historical figures includes both stimulating
and fanciful readings. Besides Deborah and Huldah, Booth emphasizes
the women who labored alongside men, as she sees it, in virtually equal
capacities: Miriam alongside Moses, Anna beside Simeon welcoming
the Christ in the temple.[142]

Contrary to complementarians, Booth believes that if women prophesied, they also preached. Further, the right of women to prophesy is
beyond debate. First Corinthians only discusses whether women
"might do so without their veils," says Booth.[143] When women prophesy
in the New Testament, it is "not the foretelling of events, but the preaching to the world at large the glad tidings of salvation by Jesus Christ."
So if women prophesied, they also preached and taught. Quoting from
a contemporary, Booth declares that "whoever prophesied spoke unto
others to edification, exhortation, and comfort, and, that no preacher
can do more, every person must acknowledge. Because, to edify, exhort,
and comfort, are the prime ends of the Gospel ministry. If women thus
prophesied, then women preached."[144] Thus, Phoebe the deacon (Rom.
16:1) was also a minister, a preacher. Indeed, "she traveled much and
propagated the gospel in foreign countries."

The injunctions for women to keep silent cannot, therefore, refer to
the religious exercises of the church. First Corinthians only disallows
inconvenient questions, disputing, finding fault. What Paul forbids in
1 Corinthians 14:34 is inappropriate speech; λαλεῖν can mean im-

141. Catherine Booth, *Female Ministry or Woman's Right to Preach the Gospel* (New
York: The Salvation Army, 1859, reprinted 1975), 5–6.

142. Ibid., 6–7, 14–17.

143. Ibid., 7. This section summarizes a long quotation from "Dr. Barnes." Lengthy
quotations from Barnes and others loom large in an otherwise energetic and well-modu-
lated work.

144. Ibid., 10–11, 17. The source is Barnes again. The paragraph argues that Tryphena and Tryphosa were prophetesses and preachers alongside Paul (Rom. 16:12). See
also p. 8.

proper speech, according to Booth, and she believes the context requires just that meaning. Paul is banning questionings, disputations, or
any other speech that violates Christian obedience. Booth admits that
men ought to avoid such speech, too, but she never wonders why Paul
would particularly command women to avoid wicked speech if men
should shun evil too.[145]

Booth believed 1 Timothy 2:11–12 was meant to bar women from
domineering in the home, not the church. The "usurpation of authority
over the man . . . is the only teaching forbidden by St. Paul in the passage." Men have altered or mistranslated Scriptures that advance
women and flesh out the freedom Paul grants women in Galatians 3:28,
Booth alleges. Therefore, women may teach publicly on various subjects, "provided it be not dictatorial, domineering, nor vociferous. . . .
An ignorant or unruly woman is not to force her opinions on the
man."[146] But many women, such as Phoebe, Junia, and Philip's daughters "actually did preach and teach in the early churches. Since then
many women have felt the Spirit's constraining call, and have led excellent and fruitful lives. Woman, therefore, has a right to teach."[147]

Poor in argumentation, rich in pathos, *Women in the Pulpit*, by
Frances Willard (1839–98), protests and testifies more than it does theology or exegesis.[148] Willard maintains that the notion of women's silence in the church and subjection to men, "grows out of the one-sided
interpretation of the Bible by men." Male theologians are guilty of a selective and self-serving literalism in biblical interpretation. They explain away the uncomfortable commands such as Romans 13:7 on subjection to government, or 1 Corinthians 7 on celibacy, but take passages
on the subjection and silence of women literally. They lay "the most solemn emphasis" on 1 Timothy 2:11–12 "as an unchangeable rule of faith
and practice for all womankind in all ages" while they "pass over the
specific command relative to . . . expensive attire" in 1 Timothy 2:9.[149]

"Personal predilection" and a desire to control women lie behind literal interpretation of one text and "fast and loose" explanations of the
next, Willard asserts.[150] Men seem "comparatively willing" to let
women in any profession but their own; doctors permit women to be

145. Ibid., 8–10.

146. Ibid., 12–13; but see p. 17 for the charge of prejudiced mishandling of Scripture.

147. Ibid., 15–19.

148. Frances Willard, *Women in the Pulpit* (Boston: D. Lothrop, 1888). Pages 17–62
are Willard's own work; but her chief ideas all appear in pages 17–50. Pages 63–112 consist primarily of testimonies by dozens of men and women to the efficacy of the women
in the ministry. The last sixty pages contain a critique and countercritique of Willard's
views by two male theologians.

149. Ibid., 37, 17–20.

150. Ibid., 21–22, 39–40, 45. In the first pages Willard compares women's rights and
liberation with slaves' rights and liberation.

lawyers, but bar them from medicine, while the reverse holds for lawyers. "This is true of ministers with added emphasis, for here we have the pride of sex plus the pride of sacerdotalism. 'Does a woman think to rank with *me?* . . . Does a woman think she has a right to stand with *me* in the most sacred of all callings?'"

Women, Willard declares, are actually more suited to ministry than men because of their moral superiority. "If the purest should be called to purest ministries, then women, by men's own showing, outrank them in actual fitness for the pulpit . . . and woman's holiness and . . . pure heart, specially authorize her to be a minister of God." She continues with a diatribe against men.

> It is *men* who have . . . lighted inquisitorial fires, and made the Prince of peace a mighty man of war. It is men who have taken the simple, loving, tender Gospel of the New Testament, so suited to the proclamation of women's lips, and translated it into terms of sacerdotalism, dogma, and martyrdom. It is men who have given us the dead letter rather than the living Gospel. The mother-heart of God will never be known to the world until translated into terms of speech by mother-hearted women. . . . Men preach a creed, women will declare a life. Men deal in formulas, women in facts. Men have always tithed mint and rue and cumin . . . while the world's heart has cried out for compassion, forgiveness, and sympathy. Men's preaching has left heads committed to a catechism, and left hearts hard as a . . . millstone.[151]

Willard reasoned that the literal interpretation of 1 Timothy 2 contradicted other Scriptures such as Judges 4, Luke 2, Galatians 3:28, 1 Corinthians 11:5; Romans 16:1–4, and Philippians 4:3, as well as Jesus' decision to make women his witnesses, which all show that women may speak and teach.[152] Willard also believed the female temperament must complement the male if the world is to hear the whole message of Christianity. "Love and law will never balance in the realm of grace until a woman's hand shall hold the scales." When women begin to minister, the power of the gospel will be doubled, for "religion is an affair of the heart" and woman has heart.[153]

God's Word to Women, an exegetical monograph by Katherine Bushnell (1856–ca. 1925), explores 1 Timothy 2 at length. The importance of 1 Timothy has been greatly exaggerated, she says. Merely a "personal epistle," 1 Timothy has many universal truths, but "strong masculine prejudice" leads men to use it "as a pretext for subordinating women,

151. Ibid., 46–47. These remarks, she briefly notes at the end, apply only to the "intolerant sacerdotal element" of the church, not to all. But the disclaimer follows pages of general remarks about men.
152. Ibid., 28–33, 40–43.
153. Ibid., 47–50.

ecclesiastically." Paul's comments about women teaching merely state "his own practice," a mere wish and example, "advice of temporal use only," which Christians may disregard "with impunity," just as one may disregard Paul's desire that all men be single in 1 Corinthians 7:7.[154]

Bushnell claims that 1 Timothy 2 addresses a time of "supreme peril to Christian women," during Nero's persecution, a peril, "not only to life . . . but to virtue also."[155] In this time the "common decency" of Christians was under attack. Paul responded to it "by separating the women from the men and having them keep quiet." Ten years earlier, when the church faced no persecution, Paul allowed women to pray and prophesy, and made "no distinctions as regards sex in the Christian body."[156] Bushnell says the historical situation required "very unobtrusive costume (2:9)." Through this, and good deeds, women "proclaim godliness (2:10)." Citing a linguist's claim that the verb ἐπαγγέλομαι (used as a participle in 2:10) may refer to public speeches and promises in Ephesians 6:21, Bushnell asks why the verb cannot refer to a public, verbal proclamation here too, "where it relates to women?"[157]

Bushnell sees 2:11 as an affirmation of woman's right to learn. The quietness Paul requires is "the serious purpose of harmonizing her life to the religion she is taught." Such quietness entails subjection to God, "or perhaps to a teacher (man or woman)" but not to men in general. Obedience to man's law "contravenes the Lord's own warning" against serving two masters. According to Bushnell, men may teach the Scriptures to women; but women may also teach men, as the cases of Priscilla and Timothy's mother and grandmother show. Paul's prohibition in 2:12 "merely states . . . his own practice in times of fierce persecution and a fierce attack upon the moral reputation of Christians—under those conditions he did not allow women to teach men."[158] In that hour "man should go first," leading the church and bearing the brunt of persecution. Since the world cultivates in women "a habit of immaturity of mind and character," woman has a "social condition of inexperience and immaturity . . . leaving her vulnerable to deception." Therefore, "at a time of great peril to the church . . . an inexperienced and immature person should not be put at the rudder of the ship."[159]

154. Katherine C. Bushnell, *God's Word to Women: One Hundred Bible Studies on the Place of Women in the Divine Economy* (North Collins, N.Y.: Ray B. Munson, 1976, reprint, 1919 ed.), paragraphs 306–9. (No pagination; paragraphs average about three-fifths of a page.)

155. Bushnell is alluding to rape.

156. Ibid., 310–26, esp. 325–26.

157. Ibid., 330–33, 340.

158. Ibid., 334–37.

159. Ibid., 338, 341–42.

Portions of the thought of Booth, Willard, and Bushnell have fallen by the way, but several of their arguments have entered the evangelical egalitarian arsenal: (1) temporary social conditions led Paul to ban women from teaching; (2) the ban contradicts other Scriptures; (3) men have used 1 Timothy 2 to keep women in a subordinate position; (4) the distinction between public and private teaching is denied, so that the private teaching by women relativizes Paul's ban on public teaching; (5) many egalitarians equate prophesying with preaching and other kinds of public teaching.

Three Traditionalists

Patrick Fairbairn, Abraham Kuyper, and Charles Hodge represent traditionalist exegesis of 1 Timothy 2 in roughly the same era as the women we just discussed. The first two, leaning toward the Thomist camp, notice the natural differences between men and women, while the third stresses the essential equality of man and woman and God's interest in order. According to Fairbairn (1838–1912), 1 Timothy 2:8–12 refers to the "public assemblies of the church." Men have a more prominent place in worship than women, who are given duties "of a more retired and quiet kind."[160] Fairbairn stresses the importance of modest apparel, yet encourages women to "learn in all subjection." Learning is important because women have the "rational power of thought" and the "right to prove all things—only in a manner suited to her position—in order that she may hold fast what is good and reject what is otherwise." The Pauline dictum, "But to teach I do not permit a woman," applies to the church's public life. Women may teach informally, Fairbairn says, but may not "act the part of a teacher in the meetings of the faithful."[161] In the next phrase, "nor to lord it over the man," Fairbairn asserts that αὐθεντεῖν "scarcely means to *usurp* authority . . . but only to exercise it in an imperious manner. . . . She is not to assume the part of ruling and domineering over man" for that would not be "compatible with her natural constitution or her distinctive vocation."[162]

Whatever women actually do in church and society, Fairbairn says both the constitution and vocation of women require men to lead. The phrase, "Adam was first formed (1 Tim 2:13)," means that "precedence in time" implies "superiority in place and power." Man has headship, Fairbairn explains, and it is "his right, and . . . obligation, to hold di-

---

160. Patrick Fairbairn, *Commentary on the Pastoral Epistles* (Grand Rapids: Zondervan, 1974; reprint of 1874 edition), 121.
   161. Ibid., 122–27.
   162. Ibid., 127–28.

rectly of God, and stand under law only to him; while woman, being
formed for his helpmate and partner, stands under law to her husband." The inversion of this order overthrew paradise.[163] Fairbairn con-
fesses that the invocation of Eve's deception as a ground of male leadership (1 Tim. 2:14) "has often been deemed strange." Still, the fall is

> a grand though mournful example . . . of the evil sure to arise if . . . woman
> should quit her proper position as the handmaid of man, and man should
> concede to her the ascendancy. She wants, by the very constitution of
> nature, the qualities necessary for such a task—in particular the equabil-
> ity of temper, the practical shrewdness and discernment, the firm, inde-
> pendent, regulative judgment which are required to carry . . . leaders . . .
> above first impressions and outside appearances, to resist solicitations,
> and amid subtle entanglements and fierce conflicts to cleave unswerv-
> ingly to the right. Her very excellencies in other respects—excellencies
> connected with the finer sensibilities and stronger impulses of her emo-
> tional and loving nature—tend in a measure to disqualify her here. With
> man, on the other hand . . . the balance . . . between the intellectual and
> the emotional inclines as a rule in the opposite direction.[164]

The woman's weakness becomes evident when the serpent's "subtler
intellect" deceives her and she heeds "impressions" gained from him.
Fairbairn says Paul cites Eve's sin "as a beacon to future generations . . .
lest amid the liberty of gospel times [women] might be tempted to assume functions which they were not qualified or called in providence to
fill."[165] While Fairbairn criticizes women here, elsewhere he stresses
that they have rational powers and the "right to prove all things." Like
Aquinas, he believes woman's emotional nature "tends in a measure" to
disqualify her; man "as a rule" inclines in the opposite direction. So
Fairbairn generalizes regarding the propensities of men and women
without stereotyping.

Compared to Fairbairn, Abraham Kuyper's devotional *Women of the
Old Testament* sounds condescending. Beginning with 1 Timothy 2:9–
15, Kuyper (1837–1920) asserts that Eve "is the woman who embodied
potentially all that is female," including her "grace and independence,
her susceptibility to Satan, but her susceptibility to faith as well." Adam
"represented more" because he "embodies not only all that is male, but
also all that is human." Adam "existed first," and was both "her head
and the root from which she sprang." Yet she is also "the product of divine creation" and "Adam could not get along without her."[166] Accord-

163. Ibid., 128.
164. Ibid., 129.
165. Ibid., 130.
166. Abraham Kuyper, *Women of the Old Testament*, trans. Henry Zylstra (Grand Rapids: Zondervan, 1933), 5–6.

ing to Kuyper woman is no less holy than man, and may even be less sinful, yet Satan knew she was more susceptible to temptation than Adam. "Her sensibilities are more alert to impression of the concrete and the attractive." Constitutionally, she is "less well adapted to offering resistance" to temptation. Seduced by the beauty of the tree of knowledge, she "dragged Adam with her into sin."[167] Kuyper's descriptions of faithful women often diminish them. He stresses the jealousy of Miriam, rather than her role as a prophetess. He says God achieved victory through Deborah "so that because of her weakness His Omnipotence might more gloriously be made manifest." Huldah's career allegedly shows that women rise to prominence "when masculine vigor is wanting."[168] So Kuyper often praises individual women, while belittling womankind.

Charles Hodge (1797–1878), by contrast, dignifies women. Woman's subordination to man, he explains, rests on the principle that "order and subordination pervade the whole universe, and is essential to its being." A woman must "recognize her subordination to her husband" and use symbols of it, such as a veil.[169] But Hodge refuses to step from subordination to inferiority. There are different kinds of subordination, but it is possible that even where two beings have "the same nature," one can be subordinate to the other. Since the Son is subordinate to the Father, even though he is equal with him in nature, "the subordination of the woman to the man" can also be "perfectly consistent with their identity as to nature."[170]

Nonetheless, Hodge says, for a woman to be a "public teacher" would be "contrary to the relation of subordination" of woman to man, and contrary to the facts of biblical history. Adam was created first, and "Eve was formed out of Adam." She was made for him, "derived her origin from him," and "always assumes his station."[171] Yet, as the example of the Son and the Father shows, her subordination is "perfectly consistent with the essential equality and mutual dependence of the sexes." Since woman has the same spiritual capacity as man, she "may receive and exercise the gift of prophecy." Further, "the desire for knowledge in women is not to be repressed, and the facilities for its acquisition are not to be denied to them." Yet "the refinement and deli-

---

167. Ibid., 6–8.

168. Ibid., 60–63, 71–74, 163–64.

169. Charles Hodge, *An Exposition of the First Epistle of the Corinthians* (Grand Rapids: Eerdmans, 1956), 206, 211.

170. Ibid., 205–7. Incidentally, Hodge's view that equality and subordination are perfectly consistent is no novelty, but the consensus view of the church until this century, which suddenly "views distinctions of class and rank as evil per se." E. E. Ellis, *Pauline Theology: Ministry and Society* (Grand Rapids: Eerdmans, 1989), 57.

171. Ibid., 205, 210, 305.

cacy" of woman, and the need for order, require that women neither speak nor prophesy in public in the church.[172]

In our typology, Kuyper and Fairbairn are Thomists, Hodge a Scotist. Within the Thomist camp, Kuyper leans toward the negative Thomist "women are inferior" school, one that gradually disappears in the twentieth century. Fairbairn leans toward the positive Thomist "women have different inclinations" school. Hodge's Scotism closely approximates current complementarians. They say men and women are equal in value and nature, but the need for order throughout creation requires that one lead and one be subordinate in marriage. In this view, male leadership says more about the plan of God than about the nature of men and women. Though other chapters also analyze current thought, we hope to chart the trajectories of recent thought in the light of the past.

Trajectories of the Twentieth Century

The shape of current debate would astonish most major theologians from the church's first eighteen centuries, both in the dominance of egalitarian thought and in the Scotist proclivities of current traditionalists. Conservatives emphasize God's decisions and God's order, but largely ignore or deny the echoes of those decisions in human nature. On the egalitarian side, theologians have ignored arguments based on the need for social order. Some have also minimized the differences between male and female, suggesting that women can do anything men can do. This is changing, however, as increasing numbers of social science researchers—perhaps most of them women—explore the differences between the language, social behavior and cognitive styles of men and women.[173] I expect Christian feminists to acknowledge and explore the differences between men and women, then to argue that women should be present at all leadership levels in the church in order to balance certain negative tendencies within the masculine style.

Current critical theologies are almost monolithically feminist. Critics typically dismisses the literal reading of 1 Timothy in one of three ways: (1) 1 Timothy is pseudepigrapha, a pious forgery, and no part of authentic apostolic tradition. The apostolic truth resides in Galatians

172. Ibid., 304–5.
173. In the field of psycho-linguistics, for example, see the work of Dennis Baron, *Grammar and Gender* (New Haven: Yale University Press, 1986); Carol Gilligan, *In Different Voice: Psychological Theory and Women's Development* (Cambridge, Mass.: Harvard University Press, 1982); and Deborah Tannen, *You Just Don't Understand: Men and Women in Conversation* (New York: Ballantine Books, 1990). There is also a stream of research on the subtle differences between the male and the female brain.

3:28 and 1 Corinthians 11:5, 11–12 and 12:7–11, where Paul declares male and female one in Christ in salvation and giftedness. (2) Paul erred in 1 Timothy, accidentally contradicting his earlier, nobler sentiments. (3) First Timothy 2:12 applies only to local circumstances in Ephesus around the end of the first century A.D.

In evangelical feminism, a few join the critics and disregard 1 Timothy 2 as subapostolic, but the great majority are loyal to the biblical text. Yet a bundle of axioms constrains them to deny that the text indeed means what a straightforward reading of it seems to mean. They presuppose that patriarchy is oppressive. They assume that women must have opportunity to use the many gifts they possess, that they should be free to serve according to God's sovereign call.

For evangelical egalitarians, the example of Miriam, Deborah, Huldah, Anna, Priscilla, Philip's daughters, Phoebe, and others show that women are free to serve as leaders and teachers in the church. Pivotal texts such as Acts 2:17–18, Galatians 3:28, and 1 Corinthians 11:5 remove the last reasonable doubts. The real task of feminist exegesis—I say this without malice or irony—is to decide what 1 Timothy 2:11–14 does mean once it has been established that the apparent meaning is impossible. So egalitarians gather evidence that Paul combated a gnosticism that advocated the supremacy of women, or that a heresy had swept through the female membership of the church at Ephesus, or that female leadership would have hampered the cause of the gospel in that culture, or that women's lack of education and experience made them unfit to lead.

Conservative studies of 1 Timothy 2, almost by definition, advance few novel readings of the text. Rather, they attempt to confirm and defend the straightforward grammatical-historical reading. So, for example, complementarians chide egalitarians for failing to draw vital distinctions between offices and function, between preaching and prophecy. They stress the difference between private teaching, which they grant to women, and public teaching, which they do not. They argue that evangelical egalitarianism rests on an overrealized eschatology that leaps directly from Acts 2 to the perfect equality and freedom the saints will enjoy in heaven.[174] They question the egalitarians' ability to resist cultural trends, such as America's zeal for freedom and self-actualization.

Nonetheless, the complementarian position has developed. Assertions of the ontological inferiority of women have become rare, so natural law or Thomistic arguments based on the size, bearing, and ratio-

---

174. Of course, not all traditionalists draw the distinctions the same way. Generally, however, traditionalists assert that preaching, public teaching, and office entail something more permanent, authoritative, doctrinal, and foundational to the church.

nality of men have virtually disappeared from serious discourse. Most declare that women are different in function, but equal to men in spiritual, mental, and emotional being. Woman "may be given gifts of ruling or teaching, but she may not use them as an elder in the church." She bears the image of God in all but authority.[175]

The recent traditionalist anthology, *Recovering Biblical Manhood and Womanhood,* represents this type of argument.[176] The editors state that their fundamental argument for "the loving headship of husbands or the godly eldership of men" is "the created order of nature."[177] Men lead in ministry not because of women's "doctrinal or moral incompetence" but because of "God's created order for manhood and womanhood."[178] They observe that in 1 Timothy 2:12, "Paul does not give lack of education as a reason for saying that women cannot 'teach or have authority over a man,' but rather points back to creation."[179] Other contributors use similar reasoning, even when they also rely on other arguments.[180] Commenting on 1 Timothy 2:12, Douglas Moo emphasizes that Paul grounds his prohibition of female leadership not in cultural factors, nor even in the sin of Eve, but in "the created role relationship of man and woman," which "always remains in effect."

Vital to the shift toward creation order and away from ontological arguments is a reinterpretation of 1 Timothy 2:14. Traditionalist interpreters increasingly join feminists in denying that the phrase, "Adam was not deceived but the woman was deceived," means that women are liable to deception. They deny that Eve's deception, described in Genesis and 1 Timothy, typifies womankind. The idea, they admit, that women are prone to deception proves too much. If women lack discern-

175. Susan Foh, *Women and the Word of God* (Philipsburg, N.J.: Presbyterian & Reformed, 1979), 171, 177–78; James Hurley, *Man and Woman in Biblical Perspective* (Grand Rapids: Zondervan, 1981), 173–74. Hurley repeatedly asserts that male is differentiated from female by dominion, not dignity or worth (ontological value); the quotation is from Foh.

176. *Recovering Biblical Manhood and Womanhood,* ed. John Piper and Wayne Grudem (Wheaton, Ill.: Crossway Books, 1991), *passim.* The concept of creation order also appears on some pages lacking the terminology.

177. Piper and Grudem, "An Overview of Central Concerns," in ibid., 65.

178. Ibid., 73–74.

179. Ibid., 81–82.

180. Nineteen of its twenty-two authors argue for their position on the basis of creation or the order of creation, and they do so in twenty-one of the book's twenty-six chapters, on at least eighty-one pages. For example, D. A. Carson argues that men rather than women must weigh the prophecies at Corinth because of the "creation order" ("Silent in the Churches," 152–53). While George Knight stresses that Christ's redemptive love dictates the manner of headship, the institution of "male headship is of divine appointment" and is "rooted in creation and in God's eternal purposes, not just the passing trends of culture" ("Husband and Wives as Analogues of Christ and the Church: Ephesians 5:21–33 and Colossians 3:18–19," 170, 176).

ment, they should not be permitted to teach other women or children either. Yet the whole Bible, even the Pastorals themselves, permit women to teach women and children (2 Tim. 1:5, 3:15; Titus 2:3–4, cf. Acts 16:1).[181] Besides, if women are prone to deception after the model of Eve, is not man prone to wanton rebellion after the model of Adam? And if so, how would that qualify Adam to lead? This would give us a church in which rebels instruct fools.[182] Recent conservatives therefore maintain that the text describes or illustrates what happens when men abdicate and women usurp leadership. The race fell into sin because Adam stood by while Eve took the lead in responding to the serpent's challenge, and Ephesian women who make Eve's mistake and seek the roles of men will, as Douglas Moo puts it, "bring similar disaster on themselves and the church."[183]

But this line of traditionalist thought is open to critique. Why do traditionalists expect "similar disasters" to occur if Eve in no way typifies women? If women have no more propensity toward doctrinal error than men, why should the church expect disaster if roles reverse? Regardless of this difficulty, recent conservative theologians have shied from ontological arguments for male headship.[184] James Hurley has explained that Adam, as the first-formed, was trained by God to be the spiritual leader of the family. Eve was not deceived due to a fragile or gullible mind, but because God had not appointed and prepared her to encounter Satan at the temptation. She fell, therefore, because she was tricked into taking Adam's role as leader and defender of the faith.[185] This view, while attractive, has two crucial flaws. First, as a comparison of Genesis 2:16–17, 3:2–3, and 3:11 shows, Eve did have the essential knowledge about the tree of knowledge at the time of her interchange with the serpent. Second, by using questions rather than assertions at critical junctures (asking, "Can verse 14 . . . be understood from such a perspective?" and "Could it be that his point in verse 14 is . . . ?") Hurley virtually admits that his view depends on speculative deductions based on the concept of primogeniture.[186] Why must men lead and teach in the church, egalitarians,

181. Douglas Moo, "What Does It Mean Not to Teach or Have Authority over Men? 1 Timothy 2:11–15," in *Recovering Biblical Manhood and Womanhood*, 190; Foh, *Women and the Word*, 127; Hurley, *Man and Woman*, 214–16.

182. Martin, *Call Me Blessed*, 153.

183. Moo, "What Does It Mean?" 190.

184. Significantly, two of the strongest advocates of ontological differences between men and women in *Recovering Biblical Manhood and Womanhood*, are David Ayers, a sociologist, and Gregg Johnson, a biologist. See "The Inevitability of Failure: The Assumptions and Implementations of Modern Feminism," and "The Biological Basis for Gender-Specific Behavior" (312–31, 280–93, respectively.)

185. Hurley, *Man and Woman in Biblical Perspective*, 206–16.

186. Ibid., 215–16.

children, and recent converts ask? Because of God's will and decree, because of God's knowledge of the need for order, traditionalists reply. At its best, what I call the "Family Order / Church Order Argument" runs this way:[187]

1. God has ordained in Scripture, notably Ephesians 5, that the male, the husband and father, lead the home and marriage. Even if the husband is not intrinsically superior to the wife, someone must bear final responsibility for making decisions, for charting the course, in a society of two. For when two are equally responsible, no one is finally responsible. Marriage needs a leader, and God has ordered that the male ought to be that leader.
2. If the husband/father leads the home, he must in turn lead the church, for two reasons. First, success or failure at leadership of the nuclear family effectively tests whether someone can manage the church (1 Tim. 3:4–5). Second, if the husband spiritually leads his family, it is fitting that he also lead in the church, the family of God. Besides, if the men lead their wives at home while wives lead their husbands in the church, conflicts could easily develop. For example, a gifted woman could test her husband's teaching in public, thereby offending both propriety and her role as a wife.[188]

This basic argument seems valid, and it often persuades those who still believe husbands ought to head their homes. But it is too slender a reed to support and advance the entire traditionalist position. Of course, many Christians will accept the traditional view on the mere authority of the Bible. But without supplementary arguments, I doubt its ability to hold waverers, let alone convince the skeptical, as our society becomes more monolithically, confidently, aggressively egalitarian. For confirmed egalitarians the claim that men must lead seems counterintuitive at best, suspicious at worst. But to argue that men must lead women because God has ordered it so, and to say little more, sounds like special pleading, like a deus ex machina. Perhaps many complementarians believe there are no ontological differences between man and woman; perhaps they are reluctant to state unpopular ideas. Either way, few traditionalists explain God's reasons or ex-

---

187. For a far more sophisticated version, see Vern Poythress, "The Church as Family," 233–47, esp. 238–42. See also D. A. Carson's article, "Silent in the Churches: On the Role of Women in 1 Corinthians 14:33b–36," in *Recovering Biblical Manhood and Womanhood*. Carson argues that while women may prophesy, men must weigh prophecies because the weighing is the act of authority and headship. If a woman weighed her husband's prophecy, she would be exercising authority over him, which violates the creation order.

188. See Ellis, *Pauline Theology*, 68–70.

plore how he may have etched his decree in nature.[189] Meanwhile egalitarianism, volunteerism, and the self-esteem movement whisper that anyone—any woman—should be free to aspire to whatever she chooses.

In this atmosphere, how persuasive is the Scotism that says men lead simply because God willed it? Yes, it can reinforce the "choir" of confirmed traditionalists. But will it convince evangelical feminists? They already have their evidence that women can minister (Deborah, Anna, Philip's daughters, and more). In this situation we must ask if Scotism has the ability to enlist them for the unpopular side of the gender wars. Of course, it is fantasy to imagine that an appeal to God's pure decree would convince secular feminists.

The Family Order / Church Order Argument has another weakness: it implicitly exempts single women from the principle of male leadership in the church, and permits them to serve as spiritual leaders of the church.[190] Scarcely anyone *argues* that the church should give single women special ministerial prerogatives, but the church has long had an instinct for the idea.[191] Portions of the early church recognized an order of widows, above sixty years in age, who performed limited diaconal functions. The medieval abbesses, writers, and visionaries were all single women. Later, the mission field became the great outlet for single women who longed to minister. Lottie Moon, for one, turned down a marriage proposal after she was on the field, in part to preserve her freedom for ministry.[192] In each epoch, most female leaders had never married; some were widows. Most telling are the exceptions that prove the rule—the married women who left their husbands when they started to lead within the church: the Montanists Maximilla and Prisca, the visionary Margery Kempe, this century's evangelists Aimee Semple McPherson and Kathryn Kuhlman.[193] The Family Order / Church

---

189. In *Recovering Biblical Manhood and Womanhood*, co-editor John Piper argues on the basis of innate differences between men and women. Poythress also says that a woman simply is "not constituted" to be a father in the family or "in God's household." See John Piper, "A Vision of Biblical Complementarity," and Vern Poythress, "The Church as Family: Why Leadership in the Family Requires Male Leadership in the Church," in *Recovering Biblical Manhood and Womanhood*, 35–52 and 239, respectively.

190. Certain popular teachers assert that single women remain under their fathers' governance until they marry, but their thought rarely reaches print and does not seem to be influential.

191. Ellis, *Pauline Theology*, 75, is rare in his brief note that single women might form a special case.

192. Irwin T. Hyatt, *Our Ordered Lives Confess* (Cambridge, Mass.: Harvard University Press, 1976), 98–99.

193. It is long alleged, but not quite certain that Maximilla and Prisca left their husbands. McPherson's husband briefly rejoined her and their children four years after she separated from him to start her ministry. See Tucker, *Daughters*, 100, 364–65, 392. For Kempe, at n. 72.

Order Argument bypasses this issue—no trivial matter in a society where nearly 40 percent of adult women are single.

Conclusions

Throughout the ages the church has traditionally interpreted 1 Timothy 2:11–14 in a straightforward manner. This book has presented extensive data to demonstrate that the traditional reading is correct. Women ought to learn, but in a quiet and submissive manner (2:11). They may teach informally, but may not hold teaching offices or formally authoritative positions in the church (2:12). Paul forbids that women teach both because of God's sovereign decree and because of the history and nature of man and woman (2:13–14). For complementarians, the phrase, "Adam was formed or created first," refers beyond chronology to God's sovereign decree that made males the spiritual heads of God's kingdom, churches, and homes (2:13). Eve's deception either compounds or explains woman's subordination. Some traditionalists say woman's subordination became onerous as a punishment for her role in the fall. Others say God subordinated women to men in the church because women are more prone to deception, whether due to lower intellectual capacity or less interest in disciplined intellectual pursuits.

Egalitarians interpret 1 Timothy through the lens of Acts 2, Galatians 3, and the stories of female prophets, judges, and kingdom laborers whose lives prove that women may indeed teach and lead in the church. Women have the gifts, the calling, and the fruit that demonstrate their freedom to minister in any capacity. Therefore, 1 Timothy 2:11–14 cannot be a literal, permanently binding instruction for the church. Egalitarians argue either that the text has been misunderstood, or that it applies only to temporary local conditions.

The preceding discussion shows that traditionalists have used varied rationales to defend male leadership. So egalitarians might accuse traditionalists of knowing what they want and using theology to justify the taking. But there are finally only three types of traditionalist reasoning.[194]

1. The archetypal Scotist emphasizes 1 Timothy 2:13 ("Adam was formed first") and argues that men lead simply because God so willed it, that men are in no way more fitted to lead than women. No "masculine" traits—physical size and strength, stern disposi-

---

194. We must observe that many, perhaps most, traditionalists never explain their position; when all agree, as they did throughout much of church history, explanation is superfluous! So this discussion applies only to those who do explain why men should lead, whether in a study of 1 Tim. 2:13–15 or otherwise.

tion, grave voice, assertiveness, rationalist mental style—have any connection with God's decision that men should lead. They do not even present tokens of it to the world. Men lead because of the divine will, period.

2. The archetypal (negative) Thomist, by contrast, emphasizes 1 Timothy 2:14 ("The woman was deceived") and searches for confirmations of divine law in natural law. Negative Thomists discern physical, mental, and spiritual differences between male and female that ultimately make them say women are weaker or less rational than men.

3. Most complementarians, including Duns Scotus and Thomas Aquinas themselves, take a mediating position that attempts to give 1 Timothy 2:13 and 14 equal weight. Hereby labeled the Congruent Creation View, it asserts that men lead in home and church because God desired an ordered creation. He sovereignly chose to order it through male headship, a headship given to them without a view to any merit on their part. Yet God established a coherence or congruence between his decree and his creation. Congruence thinkers affirm that God shaped the minds, proclivities and perhaps even the bodies of humans to reflect his decree. A few mark the size, bearing, voice, or aggressiveness of the male. Others resonate with Aquinas's comment that women ordinarily do not pursue the counsels of reason, but are more easily swayed by other factors. These factors include the "stronger impulses of her emotional and loving nature."[195] Calvin, Gataker, Hodge, Fairbairn and perhaps Jerome and Gouge agree that women are as capable as men, but have other interests, and have developed their capacities in different directions.[196]

Some recent egalitarian thought takes a similar direction. For example, Van Leeuwen believes that female theologians recognize the emotional and relational aspects of God and the social nature of the faith more readily than men.[197] Her views would cohere with those of egalitarians who believe that female leaders enrich the church by developing its communal aspects, its feminine virtues, such as tenderness and compassion, and its character as the family of God.[198] Van Leeuwen

195. Fairbairn, from n. 166.

196. I cite Jerome because negative remarks about women notwithstanding, he honored his female students' abilities. I cite Gouge because, despite his affirmations of women's ability, he assumes their interests are domestic, and assumes they tend to become irrational. See *Duties*, 287–308, 315–23, 337–40.

197. Van Leeuwen, *Gender and Grace*, 39–41.

198. See Willard, n. 153. I have heard this point in several private conversations with egalitarians; I have not yet seen it in print from a recent evangelical feminist.

admits that woman's sociability becomes a liability when it descends toward social enmeshment. The abuse of sociability uses "the preservation of relationships as an excuse not to exercise accountable dominion . . . to avoid taking risks that might upset relationships."[199] Secular social scientists have increasingly explored gender differences in the last two decades. They perform sophisticated analyses of the male tendency toward competition, conflict and disputation, and the female tendency toward relatively more cooperation and affiliation.[200]

Here traditionalist and feminist analyses partially converge. Both sides note that women tend toward enmeshment, which entails an unwillingness to see and condemn harsh truths about loved ones. Mindful of many individual exceptions to the rule, they sometimes say that women generally have more interest in persons and less interest in detached rational analysis of ideas. But the capacity for detached, critical assessment is absolutely essential for discerning and rooting out heresy, for carrying out discipline in the church. Of course, the defense of the faith and the challenge of heresy was a problem in the church at Ephesus and has remained one ever since.[201] This reasoning does not propose that men are more capable of discerning doctrinal error. But if, as analysts past and present maintain, men can more easily "forget" that the heretic before them is their neighbor, then we can see one reason why Paul said men should promulgate and guard doctrine. Their greater willingness to disagree openly, while no intrinsic virtue, does suit them for the task of guarding doctrine and condemning error.

It is not popular, today, to propose that men and women have equal gifts but different interests. Yet past traditionalists said such things as they attempted to explain God's decision to appoint males as leaders of the church, and current traditionalists generally do not. The great theologians of the past did not appeal to God's raw decree and then fall silent.

By contrast, the Scotist tendency in recent complementarian thought suffers from its refusal to give reasons. Why do Moo, Hurley and others expect disasters like that in Genesis 3 to occur again when women lead (above) if Eve in no way typifies women? Does disaster occur purely because the wrong person leads? Surely that leader has to

199. Ibid., 45–46. Many popular books on codependency decry the tendency toward enmeshment. See, for example, Robin Norwood, *Women Who Love Too Much* (Los Angeles: Jeremy Tarcher, 1985), and Susan Forward and Joan Torres, *Men Who Hate Women and the Women Who Love Them* (New York: Bantam, 1986).

200. See, among others, Walter Ong, *Fighting for Life: Contest, Sexuality and Consciousness* (Ithaca, N.Y.: Cornell University Press, 1982), and Deborah Tannen, *You Just Don't Understand*, 149–87. As a Christian psychologist and feminist, Van Leeuwen stresses that men and women are far more similar than different, yet documents a number of transcultural biological and social differences between men and women.

201. This is not to say that 1 Tim. 2:8–15 is a direct response to heresy; see prior chapters.

make an erroneous decision! Do Scotists believe women possess sound judgment until they usurp leadership, when it suddenly flees? If women lack one scintilla more of a propensity toward the acceptance or tolerance of error, why should the church expect disaster if roles reverse? Do twentieth-century traditionalists want to affirm that God has ordered men to lead the church, and then give no reason for it? Has he fashioned no difference whatsoever, to fit men to lead and women to receive their guidance?

Throughout the ages the church has preferred to affirm that God has engraved reflections of his sovereign decree into human nature. This has had an ugly side, in denigrations of woman's mind and character. But we can also recognize variety in human nature, without labeling anything inferior or superior. In this view, because women generally focus on relationships more than abstract rational analysis, enmeshment in relationships could compromise a woman's willingness to uproot heresy in the church. Again, the Congruent Creation approach does not assert that all men are more rational and all women are more relational. Many women outdo their husbands, fathers, and neighbors in logical analysis and facility at disputation. Still, over the centuries, theologians have asserted that God etched traces of his sovereign decree concerning male leadership into the nature of men and women. These reflections of his decree allow men to seek leadership more readily and allow women to follow them.

No major theologian or church leader has ever believed 1 Timothy 2:12 absolutely forbids women to teach. But they have said it forbids women to teach doctrine with authority.[202] It seems to me that the Congruent Creation view best explains Paul's thinking. Paul says the teachers and guardians of doctrine should be male. He explains his dictum in two ways, saying (1) Adam was formed first (2:13), and (2) Eve was deceived, not Adam (2:14).[203] Paul never says women suffer deception

---

202. In the Pauline corpus (but not as a rule in the rest of the New Testament) the word group for teaching (διδάσκω, διδάσκολος, διδασκαλία) ordinarily means authoritative transmission of the apostolic "tradition," or doctrinal instruction. Of 15 Pauline uses of διδάσκω, seven surely refer to formal teaching of the heart of the gospel or other basic apostolic instruction (Rom. 12:7, 1 Cor. 4:17, Gal. 1:12, 2 Thess. 2:15, 1 Tim. 4:11, 1 Tim. 6:2, 2 Tim. 2:2). Five probably refer to apostolic instruction (Eph. 4:21, Col. 1:28, 2:7, Titus 1:11, and our text, 1 Tim. 2:12), and three probably refer to other teaching (Rom. 2:21, 1 Cor. 11:14, Col. 3:16). Of six uses of διδαχή, four refer to apostolic instruction (Rom. 6:17, 16:17, 2 Tim. 4:2, Titus 1:9) and two probably refer to general teaching activity (1 Cor. 14:6, 26). Notice that the pastorals use both terms for apostolic instruction in all cases, if we exclude our text from the tally. So we make something of Paul's choice of διδάσκω rather than λαλέω or λέγω, which refer to more ordinary speech. See also George Knight, *Commentary on the Pastoral Epistles* (Grand Rapids: Eerdmans, 1992), 88–89, 141.

203. See the conjunction γάρ, which Paul tends to use to give reasons for immediately preceding remarks.

more than men.[204] Yet he twice says that Eve, the first woman and mother of all women, was deceived (1 Tim. 2:14 and 2 Cor. 11:3). Further, Paul usually puts his references to historical Old Testament figures to typological use. Thus Abraham, David, Jacob, and Esau are all individuals, yet they represent, respectively, the person justified by faith, the person whose sins are forgiven, the elect and the nonelect.[205] So it seems that Paul at least alludes to woman's nature when he cites the sin of Eve. Can a skilled reader avoid entertaining the possibility of a connection between Eve and womankind? Certainly, such an allusion is consistent with Paul's practice, and the church has taken the text that way for over nineteen centuries. Since women can do some teaching, they must have the necessary rational ability. But the γάρ clause of 1 Timothy 2:13 ("for Adam . . .") proves Paul has some reason for entrusting the care of doctrine to male elders. But since women have enough ability to teach privately, we interpret the statement "for Adam was not deceived but the woman was deceived" to mean not that women have less capacity than men, but that they have different inclinations.

This view provides an alternative to the Scotism of recent traditionalists, who say men simply rule by God's decree. Yet it also rejects notions of woman's intellectual inferiority. If women were intellectually deficient, Paul should not let them teach at all. Therefore, we read 1 Timothy 2:12–14 in terms of proclivity. God created women with an orientation toward relationships more than analysis. He created men to lead in the church and that includes the defense and proclamation of the gospel.

If this is true, another hopeful convergence emerges. The data of church history indicate that women will find a way to use their gifts. Tertullian, Jerome, Calvin, Wesley and other staunch complementarians admitted it, perhaps despite themselves. Perhaps they knew that it is presumptuous to claim that every woman who reports a call for ministry is autokaletic and suffers self-deception.[206] Today, egalitarians insist on woman's freedom to perform every ministry from every office, while complementarians reserve some tasks for men. Complementari-

---

204. Paul uses the terms ἀπατάω, ἀπάτη, ἐξαπατάω to describe who deceives—sin, evil, riches—and to warn his readers not to be deceived, rather than to describe who is deceived. Paul's use of the πλανάω family is similar.

205. Rom. 4:1–25 (especially 23–24); 9:10–18. See also 1 Cor. 10:1–6, regarding the Israelites in the wilderness; Gal. 3:6–9 regarding Abraham; 4:21–31 regarding Sarah and Hagar. Paul, like other Jewish and Christian exegetes "regards Adam and Eve as historical persons, but also as archetypes of the human race" (J. N. D. Kelly, *The Pastoral Epistles* [London: Adam and Charles Black, 1963], 68). See also Leonhard Goppelt, *Typos: The Typological Interpretation of the Old Testament in the New*, trans. Donald H. Madvig (Grand Rapids: Eerdmans, 1982), 136–37.

206. Autokaletic is a new coinage, meaning self-calling or self-nominating, from αὐτο + καλέω, self + to call.

ans may stumble over the details, but they too want to affirm the gifts of women. The interpretation proposed here allows women to do all sorts of things in the church, including many kinds of teaching. But they must operate within the doctrinal guidance of the teaching office of the church, and must not claim formal teaching authority for themselves.[207]

With the traditional consensus of the church, therefore, we conclude that women should be free to listen and learn, to use their gifts in the church and be paid for it.[208] Yet God has ordered his world, and that order holds men responsible for leadership in the home and the church, and especially for the authoritative teaching of doctrine in the church. God's decree rests upon his good will, not male superiority. Nonetheless, he has pressed reflections of his will into the constitutions and inclinations of men and women. May we all recognize the callings of men and the gifts of women, that the church may serve him in unity.

207. To say women must be free to teach everything or they should be permitted to teach nothing is a false dichotomy. There is certainly a difference between formal and informal, more and less authoritative teaching.

208. From the beginning, male-governed churches have been slow to pay women for their services, even when they bore no relation to ordination. Is it just to assume that women who serve long hours are independently wealthy?

Appendix 2

αὐθεντέω in Ancient Greek Literature

H. Scott Baldwin

I. Occurrences of αὐθεντέω in Ancient Greek Literature

Literary Greeks (1st cent. B.C.—2nd cent. A.D.)

[1st cent. B.C.] Philodemus, *Rhetorica*, "those in authority" (1.) {ptc}

[2nd cent. A.D.] Ptolomey, *Tetrabiblos*, "dominates Mercury and the moon" (2.) {ptc}

[2nd cent. A.D.] Moeris, *Attic Lexicon*, "to have independent jurisdiction" (3b.) {inf}

Nonliterary Papyri (1st cent. B.C.—7th cent. A.D.)

[27 B.C.] *BGU 1208*, "I exercised authority over him" (2a.) {ptc}

[6th cent. A.D.] *PLond 1708*, "acted on his own authority" (3.) {inf}

[6th cent. A.D.] *PMasp 67151*, "to have authority in any fashion" (2.) {inf}

[6th–7th cent. A.D.] *BGU 103*, "assume authority over the matter . . . assume authority" (3a./3a.) {finite/finite}

The Church Fathers (4th cent. A.D.)

[d. A.D. 235] Hippolytus, *On the End of the World*, "have legal authority over" (2b.) {finite}

[c. A.D. 325] Eusebius, *On Ecclesiastical Theology*, "the Father ruling" (1.) {ptc}

———, *The Life of Constantine*, "God is himself the administrator of judgment" (4.) {finite}

[c. A.D. 350] Athanasius, *The Synod of the Arians in Italy*, "the Father authorizing" (2d.) {ptc}

———, *Letter to Rufinius*, "instigating unrighteousness" (4.) {finite}

———, *Testimonies from Scripture*, "the Spirit sovereignly compels" (2a.) {finite}

[A.D. 370] Saint Basil, *The Letters*, "directing the bold deed" (2.) {ptc}

———, *The Letters*, "exercise full authority in this matter" (2.) {inf}

[A.D. 375] Epiphanius, *Medicine Chest Against All Heresies*, "the Son . . . ruling" (1.) {ptc}

(x.) = meaning from table 3.2.

[c. A.D. 390] John Chrysostom, *On the Holy Pentecost*, "exercising authority" (1.) {finite}

————, *Sermons in Genesis*, "exercised authority wrongly" (2a.) {finite}

————, *Homily on Genesis*, "being in charge" (2.) {finite}

————, *Homily on Psalm 92*, "do I reign" (1.) {finite}

————, *Homilies on the Gospel of Saint Matthew*, "acted by His own power" (3.) {ptc}

————, *Homilies on the Gospel of Saint Matthew*, "authority over her Son" (2.) {finite}

————, *Homilies on the Gospel of Saint John*, "act with authority" (3.) {finite}

————, *Homilies on the Acts of the Apostles*, "as having been put in charge of them" (2.) {finite}

————, *Homilies on Romans*, "have even that [be] independent" (3.) {inf}

————, *Homilies on Colossians*, "act the despot" (2c.) {finite}

————, *Homilies on Colossians*, "to have your own way" (3.) {inf}

————, *The Heavenly Reign*, "rule absolutely" (1.) {finite}

————, *About Martha, Mary, and Lazarus*, "reigns . . . reign" (1./1.) {finite/finite}

————, *About Martha, Mary, and Lazarus*, "this One compelling" (2a.) {ptc}

————, *By the Lake of Genesareth*, "take charge!" (3a.) {finite}

————, *On the Holy Passover*, "exercise my own authority" (3.) {finite}

————, *When All Things Are Subject to Him*, "rules the will" (2.) {finite}

————, *On the Resurrection of the Lord*, "rules" (1.) {finite}

[4th cent. A.D.] Didymus the Blind, *Commentary on Job*, "control my flood of tears" (2.) {ptc}

————, *Dialogue Between a Montanist and an Orthodox*, "to control . . . controlling men" (2./2.) {inf/ptc}

[A.D. 446] Proculus Constantinopolitanus, *Oration #6*, "rules" (1.) {finite}

[A.D. 449] Leo I, *Epistle 30*, "a certain dispute instigated by Eutyches" (4.) {ptc}

[c. A.D. 450] Olympiodorus, *Excerpts*, "exercising his own authority" (3b.) {ptc}

[post A.D. 450] Socrates Scholasticus, *Church History*, "granting authorization" (2d.) {ptc}

[post A.D. 450] Socrates Scholasticus, *Church History*, "taking charge" (3a.) {ptc}

[A.D. 451] Emperor Marcian, *Letter to Leo, #1*, "you granting authorization" (2d.) {ptc}

[A.D. 451] Council of Chalcedon, *Pulcheria to Leo*, "you granting authorization" (2d.) {ptc}

[A.D. 451] Council of Chalcedon, *Eleventh Session*, "exercised their own initiative" (3.) {finite}

————, *Letter to Makarios and Mt. Sinai*, "assumed his own jurisdiction" (3b.) {finite}

[5th cent. A.D.] Ammonius Alexandrius, *Fragments of Acts*, "to act independently" (3.) {inf}

————, *Fragments of Acts*, "exercised authority" (1.) {inf}

————, *Fragments of Acts*, "all did compel others" (2a.) {finite}

[5th cent. A.D.] Eusebius of Alexandria, *Sermons*, #5, "to exercise authority over the people" (2.) {inf}

[5th cent. A.D.] Victor Antiochenus, *Chains in Mark*, "assumes his own authority" (3b.) {finite}

The Byzantines (6th cent. A.D.—12th cent. A.D.)

[c. A.D. 520] Joannes Philoponus, *About the Rational Soul*, "ignorance rules the soul" (2.) {finite}

[c. A.D. 560] Joannes Lydus, *On the Magistracies of Roman Constitution*, "of its own initiative" (3b.) {ptc}

[6th cent. A.D.] Leontius Heir., *Against the Nestorians*, "act on our own authority" (3b.) {finite}

[6th cent. A.D.] Romanus Melodus Hymnographus, *Hymn 20*, "you . . . do reign" (1.) {finite}

———, *Hymn 22*, "I rule" (1.) {finite}

[A.D. 600] Evagrius Scholasticus, *Letter to a Vigilant Tutor*, "assuming his own jurisdiction" (3b.) {ptc}

[d. A.D. 638] Sophronius Palestrinus, trans. of *On Illustrious Men*, "granting the authorization" (2d.) {ptc}

[A.D. 690] Joannes Malalas, *Chronicles*, "put pressure on the governor" (2a.) {ptc}

———, *Chronicles*, "overrruling the senate" (3c.) {ptc}

———, *Chronicles*, "flouting the authority of the senate" (3c.) {ptc}

———, *Chronicles*, "exercised their own authority" (3b.) {ptc}

———, *Chronicles*, "on his own authority" (3b.) {ptc}

———, *Chronicles*, "on his own initiative" (3b.) {ptc}

[7th cent. A.D.] *Chronicon Paschale*, "be authoritative" (2b.) {inf}

———, "be valid" (2b.) {inf}

[A.D. 790] *Second Council of Nicaea*, "Take the leading part . . . originate" (2./4.) {finite/ptc}

[A.D. 817] Theophanes, *The Chronicle*, "exercising their own authority" (3b.) {ptc}

[9th cent. A.D.] Photius, *Library*, "exercising his own authority" (3b.) {ptc}

———, *Library*, "took charge" (3a.) {ptc}

———, *Library*, "exercised his own authority" (3b.) {ptc}

[10th cent. A.D.] Scholia Vetera on Aeschylus' *Eumenides*, "murder" (5.) {ptc}

[10th cent. A.D.] Scholia Vetera on Homer's *Iliad*, "the one originating the writing" (4.) {ptc}

[10th cent. A.D.] Constantine VII, *About Strategy*, "flouting the authority of the senate" (3c.) {ptc}

———, *About Virtues and Vices*, "exercised their own jurisdiction" (3b.) {ptc}

[10th cent. A.D.] The Suda Lexicon, "be responsible for" (4.) {ptc}

[12th cent. A.D.] Michael Glycas, *Annals*, "exercise authority over the men" (2.) {finite}

[13th–14th cent. A.D.] Thomas Magister, *Attic Sayings*, " = to be with independent jurisdiction" (3b.) {inf}

[Ms from 15th cent. A.D.] Ptolemy, *Codicum Parisinorum*, "exercises authority over all" (2.) {ptc}

II. The Meanings of αὐθεντέω in Ancient Greek Literature

1. To rule, to reign sovereignly

[1st cent. B.C.] Philodemus, *Rhetorica*, "those in authority" {ptc}

[c. A.D. 325] Eusebius, *On Ecclesiastical Theology*, "the Father ruling" {ptc}

[A.D. 375] Epiphanius, *Medicine Chest Against All Heresies*, "the Son . . . ruling" {ptc}

[c. A.D. 390] John Chrysostom, *On the Holy Pentecost*, "exercising authority" {finite}

———, *Homily on Psalm 92*, "do I reign" {finite}

———, *The Heavenly Reign*, "rule absolutely" {finite}

———, *About Martha, Mary, and Lazarus*, "reigns . . . reign" {finite/finite}

———, *On the Resurrection of the Lord*, "rules" {finite}

[A.D. 446] Proculus Constantinopolitanus, *Oration #6*, "rules" {finite}

[5th cent. A.D.] Ammonius Alexandrius, *Fragments of Acts*, "exercised authority" {inf}

[6th cent. A.D.] Romanus Melodus Hymnographus, *Hymn 20*, "you . . . do reign" {finite}

———, *Hymn 22*, "I rule" {finite}

2. To control, to dominate

[2nd cent. A.D.] Ptolomey, *Tetrabiblos*, "dominates Mercury and the moon" {ptc}

[A.D. 370] Saint Basil, *The Letters*, "directing the bold deed" {ptc}

———, *The Letters*, "exercise full authority in this matter" {inf}

[c. A.D. 390] John Chrysostom, *Homily on Genesis*, "being in charge" {finite}

———, *Homilies on the Gospel of Saint Matthew*, "authority over her Son" {finite}

———, *Homilies on the Acts of the Apostles*, "as having been put in charge of them" {finite}

———, *When All Things Are Subject to Him*, "rules the will" {finite}

[4th cent. A.D.] Didymus the Blind, *Commentary on Job*, "control my flood of tears" {ptc}

———, *Dialogue beween a Montanist and an Orthodox*, "to control . . . controlling men" {inf/ptc}

[5th cent. A.D.] Eusebius of Alexandria, *Sermons, #5*, "to exercise authority over the people" {inf}

[c. A.D. 520] Joannes Philoponus, *About the Rational Soul*, "ignorance rules the soul" {finite}

[6th cent. A.D.] *PMasp 67151*, "to have authority in any fashion" {inf}

[A.D. 790] *Second Council of Nicea*, "Take the leading part " {finite}

[12th cent. A.D.] Michael Glycas, *Annals*, "exercise authority over the men" {finite}

[Ms from 15th cent. A.D.] Ptolemy, *Codicum Parisinorum*, "exercises authority over all" {ptc}

a. To compel, to influence someone/something

[27 B.C.] *BGU 1208*, "I exercised authority over him" {ptc} [c. A.D. 350] Athanasius, *Testimonies from Scripture*, "the Spirit sovereignly compels" {finite}

[c. A.D. 390] John Chrysostom, *Sermons in Genesis*, "exercised authority wrongly" {finite}

————, *About Martha, Mary, and Lazarus*, "this One compelling" {ptc}

[5th cent. A.D.] Ammonius, *Fragments of Acts*, "all did compel others" {finite}

[A.D. 690] Joannes Malalas, *Chronicles*, "put pressure on the governor" {ptc}

b. Middle voice: to be in effect, to have legal standing

[d. A.D. 235] Hippolytus, *On the End of the World*, "have legal authority over" {finite}

[7th cent. A.D.] *Chronicon Paschale*, "be authoritative" {inf}

[7th cent. A.D.] *Chronicon Paschale*, "be valid" {inf}

c. Hyperbolically: to domineer/to play the tyrant

[c. A.D. 390] John Chrysostom, *Homilies on Colossians*, "act the despot" {finite}

d. To grant authorization

[c. A.D. 350] Athanasius, *The Synod of the Arians in Italy*, "the Father authorizing" {ptc}

[A.D. 451] Emperor Marcian, *Letter to Leo, #1*, "you granting authorization" {ptc}

[A.D. 451] Council of Chalcedon, *Pulcheria to Leo*, "you granting authorization" {ptc}

[post A.D. 450] Socrates Scholasticus, *Church History*, "granting authorization" {ptc}

[d. A.D. 638] Sophronius Palestrinus, trans. of *On Illustrious Men*, "granting the authorization" {ptc}

3. To act independently

[c. A.D. 390] John Chrysostom, *Homilies on Saint Matthew*, "acted by His own power" {ptc}

————, *Homilies on the Gospel of Saint John*, "act with authority" {finite}

————, *Homilies on Romans*, "have even that [be] independent" {inf}

————, *Homilies on Colossians*, "to have your own way" {inf}

————, *On the Holy Passover*, "exercise my own authority" {finite}

[A.D. 451] Council of Chalcedon, *Eleventh Session*, "exercised their own initiative" {finite}

[5th cent. A.D.] Ammonius Alexandrius, *Fragments of Acts*, "to act independently" {inf}

[6th cent. A.D.] *PLond 1708*, "acted on his own authority" {inf}

a. To assume authority over

[c. A.D. 390] John Chrysostom, *By the Lake of Genesareth*, "take charge!" {finite}

[post A.D. 450] Socrates Scholasticus, *Church History*, "taking charge" {ptc}

[6th–7th cent. A.D.] *BGU 103*, "assume authority over the matter. . . . assume authority" {finite/finite}

[9th cent. A.D.] Photius, *Chronicles*, "took charge" {ptc}

b. To exercise one's own jurisdiction

[2nd cent. A.D.] Moeris, *Attic Lexicon*, "to have independent jurisdiction" {inf}

[c. A.D. 450] Olympiodorus, *Excerpts*, "exercising his own authority" {ptc}

[A.D. 451] Council of Chalcedon, *To Makarios and Mt. Sinai*, "assumed his own jurisdiction" {finite}

[5th cent. A.D.] Victor Antiochenus, *Chains in Mark*, "assumes his own authority" {finite}

[c. A.D. 560] Joannes Lydus, *On the Magistracies of Roman Constitution*, "of its own initiative" {ptc}

[6th cent. A.D.] Leontius Heir., *Against the Nestorians*, "act on our own authority" {finite}

[A.D. 600] Evagrius Scholasticus, *Letter to a Vigilant Tutor*, "assuming his own jurisdiction" {ptc}

[A.D. 690] John Malalas, *Chronicles*, "exercised their own authority" {ptc}

———, *Chronicles*, "on his own authority" {ptc}

———, *Chronicles*, "on his own initiative" {ptc}

[A.D. 817] Theophanes, *The Chronicle*, "exercising their own authority" {ptc}

[9th cent. A.D.] Photius, *Library*, "exercising his own authority" {ptc}

———, *Library*, "exercised his own authority" {ptc}

[10th cent. A.D.] Constantine VII, *About Virtues and Vices*, "exercised their own jurisdiction" {ptc}

[13th–14th cent. A.D.] Thomas Magister, *Attic Sayings*, " = to be with independent jurisdiction" {inf}

c. To flout the authority of

[A.D. 690] John Malalas, *Chronicles*, "overruling the senate" {ptc}

———, *Chronicles*, "flouting the authority of the senate" {ptc}

[10th cent. A.D.] Constantine VII, *About Strategy*, "flouting the authority of the senate" {ptc}

4. To be primarily responsible for or to instigate something

[c. A.D. 325] Eusebius, *The Life of Constantine*, "God is himself the administrator of judgment" {finite}

[c. A.D. 350] Athanasius, *Letter to Rufinius*, "instigating unrighteousness" {finite}

[A.D. 449] Leo I, *Epistle 30*, "a certain dispute instigated by Eutyches" {ptc}

[A.D. 790] *Second Council of Nicea*, "originate" {ptc}

[10th cent. A.D.] Scholia Vetera on Homer's *Iliad*, "the one originating the writing" {ptc}

[10th cent. A.D.] The Suda Lexicon, "be responsible for" {ptc}

5. To commit a murder

[10th cent. A.D.] Scholia Vetera on Aeschylus' *Eumenides*, "murder" {ptc}

III. Occurrences of αὐθεντέω in Ancient Greek Literature (Texts)

Literary Greeks (1st cent. B.C.—2nd cent. A.D.)

[1st cent. B.C.] Philodemus, *Rhetorica*, {ref: 133.14}

Text: Philodemus, *Philodemi: Volumina Rhetorica*, vol. 3, ed. S. Sudhaus (Leipzig, 1896), 133.

Translation:[1] H. H. Hubbell, "The Rhetorica of Philodemus," *Transactions of the Connecticut Academy of Arts and Sciences* 23 (1920): 306.

Ἀλλα' εἰ δεῖ ταληθῆ καῖ γι]νόμενα [λέγειν, οἱ ρ[ήτ]ορες καὶ μ[εγάλα βλάπτ]ουσι] πολλοὺς [καὶ μαγάλους καὶ περὶ τῶν ["δεινοῖς ἔρωσι το[ξ]ευομένων" πρὸς τοὺς ἐπιθαν[εστάτους ἑκάστοτε διαμάχονται καὶ "σὺν αὐθεντ[οῦσιν ἄν[αξιν]" ὑπὲρ τῶν ὁμοίων ὡσαύτως.

To tell the truth the rhetors do a great deal of harm to many people, and incur the enmity of powerful rulers, whereas philosophers gain the friendship of public men by helping them out of their trouble. Ought we not to consider that men who incur the enmity of *those in authority* are villains, and hated by both gods and men.[2]

[2nd cent. A.D.] Ptolemy, *Tetrabiblos*, {ref: III.13}

Text: W. G. Waddell, ed., *Manetho*, and F. E. Robbins, ed., *Ptolemy Tetrabiblos*, combined volume, Loeb Classical Library (London, 1964), 338.

Translation: same

Ὁ μὲν οὖν τοῦ κρόνου ἀστὴρ μόνος τὴν οἰκοδεσποτίαν τῆς ψυχῆς καὶ αὐθεντήσας τοῦ τε Ἑρμοῦ καὶ τῆς σελήνης, ἐὰν μὲν ἐνδόξως ἔχῃ πρόσκὸν καὶ κέντρα, ποιεῖ φιλοσωμάτους . . . ἐναντίως δὲ καὶ ἀδόξως κείμενος ῥυπαρούς. . . .

If Saturn alone is ruler of the soul and *dominates*[3] Mercury and the moon, if he has a dignified position with reference to the universe and the angels, he

---

1. Throughout the appendix I have provided English translations by someone other than myself wherever they are available.

2. Several issues bear on this perplexing text. First, while it is true that Philodemus produced "elegant but often indecent love epigrams" (Hammond and Scullard, *The Oxford Classical Dictionary*, 2nd ed. [Oxford: Clarendon, 1970], 818), even a cursory review of this prose work shows that it is a serious treatise in seven books concerning the nature and effect of rhetoric. This particular section, book 5, deals with the negative effects of rhetors and rhetoric. The assertion of C. C. Kroeger ("Ancient Heresies and a Strange Greek Verb," *Reformed Journal* [Mar. 1979]: 12–14) that the word here must have an erotic sense because it was "penned by the rhetorician and obscene epigrammatist" is inapposite.

Second, the text as given is a reconstruction by Sudhaus. It is entirely possible that αὐθεντοῦσιν could be read as αὐθενταίσιν, the Old Attic dative plural of a αὐθέντης, in which case it is a noun and not a verbal form at all.

Third, it should be remembered that Hubbell is not giving a precise translation but a paraphrase. However, C. J. Vooys, *Lexicon Philodemeum. Pars Prior* (Purmerend [The Netherlands]: Muusses, 1934), 53, accepts Sudhaus's reconstruction and gives the Latin equivalent, *dominor*, for the Greek verb, indicating the meaning, "to be lord and master." Similarly DGE lists this passage with the meaning "ejercer la autoridad" [= "exercise authority over"].

3. E. A. Sophocles, *Greek Lexicon of the Roman and Byzantine Periods* (New York: Scribner's, 1887), 276, lists this use under "be in power over, to have authority over."

makes his subjects lovers of the body . . . but if his position is the opposite and without dignity, he makes them sordid.

[2nd cent. A.D.] Moeris, Attic Lexicon

Text: Moeris, Lexicon Atticista, ed. Johannes Pierson and Georg Koch (Lipsiae: Sumptibus, 1830; reprint, Hildesheim: Olm, 1969), 54.

Translation: my own

Αὐτοδίχην, Ἀττικῶς. αὐθέντην, Ἑλληνικῶς⁴

Αὐτοδικεῖν, Attic. αὐθεντεῖν, Hellenistic

Nonliterary Papyri (1st cent. B.C.—7th cent. A.D.)

[27 B.C.] BGU 1208, {ref: line 38}

Text: F. Schubart et al., eds., Äegyptische Urkunden aus den königlichen Museen zu Berlin, vol. 4 (Berlin: Weidmannsche, 1912), 351.

Translation: John R. Werner, Wycliffe Bible Translators, International Linguistic Center, Dallas, Tex., letter as quoted by George W. Knight III, "ΑΨΘΕΝΤΕΩ in Reference to Women in 1 Timothy 2:12," NTS 30 (1984): 143–57.

Κἀμοῦ αὐθεντηκότος πρὸς αὐτὸν περιποιῆσαι Καλατύτει τῷ ναυτικῷ ἐπὶ τῷ αὐτῷ φόρῳ ἐν τῇ ὥραι ἐπεχώρησεν.

I exercised authority over him, and he consented to provide for Calatytis the Boatman on terms of full fare, within the hour.⁵

[6th cent. A.D.] PLond 1708 {ref: line 38}

Text: H. I. Bell, ed., Greek Papyri in the British Museum. Catalogue, with Texts, vol. 5 (London: British Museum, 1917), 119.

Translation: my own

. . . τον δε προειρημενον Ψατην τον ημετερον αδελφον ως μειζονα οντα ημων αφαιρεισθαι πασαν την πατρωαν και μητρωαν κληρονομιαν και αποστερησαι ημας τους δεεστερους αυτο· αδελφους ου μην αλλα και αυθεντησαι εκμισθωσαντα

---

4. The editors note that the verbs should be taken as infinitives: αὐτοδικεῖν, αὐθεντεῖν.

5. The translation of this text is disputed. G. W. Knight, 145, gives Werner's translation here. F. Preisigke, Wörterbuch der griechischen Papyrusurkunden, vol. 1 (Berlin: Erben, 1925) 235, lists this under "herr sein, fest auftreten" ("be master, to act confidently"). Liddell, Scott, Jones, A Greek-English Lexicon, with Supplement (Oxford: Clarendon, 1968) list this under "to have full power or authority over." P. B. Payne, "οὐδέ in 1 Timothy 2:12" (unpublished paper presented at the ETS annual meeting November 21, 1986), implies that the translation of Paul D. Peterson is superior: "when I had prevailed upon him to provide." Of Payne's arguments the last is the most important—the use of πρός. Payne writes that this use is "'denoting a hostile or friendly relationship—a. hostile against, with after verbs of disputing, etc.' (BAG, 717; cf. LSJ, 1497). This passage is about a hostile relationship; his action is called 'insolence' in the text. None of the other uses of πρός in the over three columns devoted to it in BAG seem to fit the text." It is difficult to evaluate the strength of Payne's argument. For all extant uses of verbal αὐθεντέω that are transitive in the Greek—nearly all are followed by a genitive noun, only twice by an accusative noun, once by the preposition περί, once by the preposition εἰς, and here alone by the preposition πρός. However, the meaning of "compel" does seem appropriate.

τας γονικας ημων οικιας και ενοικολογησαι ταυτας και οικειωσασθαι εαυτω τα προστεγα. . . .

But the aforementioned Psates, who is our elder brother, not only took to himself all the paternal and maternal inheritance and defrauded us, his own brothers, but even *acted on his own authority* and leased[6] our ancestral home and collected rents and appropriated them to himself.

[6th cent. A.D.] *PMasp 67151* {ref: line 174}

Text: Jeanne Maspero, ed., *Papyrus Grecs d'Époque Byzantine, Catalogue Général des Antiquités Égyptiennes du musée Caire*, vol. 2 (Cairo: Imp. de l'institute francois d'archéologie orientale, 1913; reprint: Osnabruck: Otto Zeller, 1973).

Translation: my own

Βουλομαι δε και κελευω την ευγενεστατην συμζιον μου γαμετην εξουσιαζειν των εαυτης και μονων των υπ εμου αυτη προδοθεντων εν ωρα των αυτης αισιων γαμων προ μιξεως, και τουτοις αρκεσθηναι και μη δυνασθαι περαιτερω τουτων επιζητειν προς οιονδηποτε κληρονομον εμον η συγκληρονομον, μητε μην αυθεντησαι και οιον δηποτε τροπον αποσπασασθαι παντελως οιονδηποτε πραγμα εκ παντοιων εμων πραγματων.

I will and command my wife, my noble-born life partner, to have authority over her own things and solely over the dowry given by me to her in the hour of our suitable wedding before our union; and that she be content with these things and not to be able to seek anything further with regard to my heirs of any kind or joint heirs neither *to have authority* in any fashion to detach outright goods of any kind from any manner of my estate.[7]

[6th cent.–7th cent. A.D.] *BGU 103*, {ref: lines 3 & 8}

Text: F. Schubart et al., eds., *Äegyptische Urkunden aus den königlichen Museen zu Berlin*, vol. 1 (Berlin: Weidmannsche, 1895), 122.

Translation: John R. Werner, Wycliffe Bible Translators, International Linguistic Center, Dallas, Tex., letter as quoted by George W. Knight III, "ΑΨΘΕΝΤΕΩ in Reference to Women in 1 Timothy 2:12," *NTS* 30 (1984): 143–57.

Ἐπιδὴ οἱ ἀδελφοὶ τοῦ μακαρίου Ἑνὼχ ἦλθαν πρὸς ἡμᾶς λέγοντες ικασθῖνε θέλωμεν μετὰ τῆς γυνεκὸς ἑαυτοῦ, καταξήωσον οὖν ἡ ὑμετέρα θεωφελία, ἐὰν αὐθεντίσεις τὼ πρᾶγμα καὶ λαβις αὐτοὺς ἐν τῇ πόλει, καὶ ἀπαλλάχουσιν πρὸς ἀλλήλους, εἰ δὲ μή γε καταχρήωσον τούτους παρασκεύασε ἀμφοτέους ἐλθῆν

6. This phrase given by Bell himself in a footnote. Preisigke lists this reference, along with *PMasp 67151.174* below, under "verfügungsberechtigt sein" ("having legitimate authority to dispose" [of something]).

7. This translation is at variance with that of C. C. and R. C. Kroeger, *I Suffer Not a Woman: Rethinking 1 Timothy 2:11–15 in Light of Ancient Evidence* (Grand Rapids: Baker, 1992), 89, who translate it "not to claim as her own [authentein] in any manner anything of my various possessions to detach it altogether from my estate." Two factors mitigate the Kroegers' translation: (1) Preisigke, renders the key passage "noch soll er berechtigt sein, irgend ein Bermögenstuck an sich zu reißen" ("neither should she be entitled to appropriate to herself any piece of property"), which is plainly "have authority to detach for herself;" and (2) the meaning "claim as one's own" is otherwise completely unattested.

ἐνταῦθα καὶ τούτους παρασκευάσωμεν αὐτοὺς ἀπαλλαγῖνε κατὰ τῶν τοῦ δικκέο καὶ κατὰ τὼ ἔθος τοῦ κτίματος. Ἀλλὰ μὴ ὑπερθῖ ἡ ὑμετέρα εὐλαβί πατρὶ διὰ θέσιν τούτους ἐκπέμψε, εἰ δὲ πάλιν αὐθεντῖς[sic] καὶ λαμβάνις αὐτοὺς ἐν τῇ πόλει, καλός, ὅτι γὰρ μετριήσειν καιόσια συντελοῦσιν ἁγιωτατῷ πατρί.

Since the brothers of the blessed Enoch have come to us saying, "We want to go to law with his wife," please be so good, Your (*pl.*) Godhelp, if you will *assume authority*[8] over the matter and receive them in the city, and they will come to terms with each other; but if not, please be so good as to have both sides come here and we shall have them come to terms in accordance with justice and in accordance with the custom of Creation. But do not defer, Your (*pl.*) Piety-to-the-Father, because of a deposit, to send them forth; but if, again, you *assume authority* and receive them into the city, fine.

The Church Fathers (4th cent. A.D.)

[d. A.D. 235] Hippolytus, *On the End of the World*, {ref: 7.5}

Text: Hippolytus, *De consummatione mundi*, in *Hippolyt's kleinere exegetische und homiletische Schriften*, ed. H. Achelis in *Die griechischen christlichen Schriftsteller*, 1.2 (Leipzig: Himrichs, 1897), 289–309.

Translation: my own

διὸ πάντες τῷ ἰδίῳ θελήματι ἐμπεριπατήσουσιν, καὶ τὰ τέκνα τοῖς γνεῦσιν ἐμβαλοῦνται χεῖρας, γυνὴ τὸν ἴδιον ἄνδρα παραδώσει εἰς θάνατον καὶ ἀνὴρ τὴν ἑαυτοῦ γυναῖκα ἐπὶ κριτήριον ἄξει ὡς ὑπεύθυνον, δεσπόται εἰς τοὺς ἰδίους δούλους ἀπάνθρωποι αὐθεντησονται[9] καὶ δοῦλοι πρὸς τοὺς δεσπότας ἀνυπότακτον διάθεσιν περιβαλοῦνται.

Therefore, everyone will walk according to his own desire, and the children will lay hands upon their parents, a wife will hand over her own husband to death and a man his own wife to judgment as deserving to render account. Inhuman masters will *have legal authority over* their servants and servants shall put on an unruly disposition toward their masters.[10]

---

8. Preisigke lists this under "beherrschen" ("rule, control, or dominate") and notes concerning the situation of the citation, "falls die Sache zu deinem Geschäftsreise gehört" ("in case the matter belongs to your business trip").

9. The text may be corrupt here. Codex **B** has πρὸς τοὺς δούλους ἀπανθρωπίαν κτήσονται ("masters shall procure inhumanity toward their servants"; κτήσονται is from the deponent κτάομαι). If the reading given above is authentic, it is the earliest of the three sole known instances of the middle voice of αὐθεντέω.

10. A. Roberts, in Hippolytus, *Discourse on the End of the World*, The Ante-Nicene Fathers of the Christian Church Series, vol. 5, ed. Philip Schaff and Henry Wace (reprint; Grand Rapids: Eerdmans, 1952), 243, translates this passage: "Wherefore, everyone all shall walk after their own will. Children will lay hands on their parents. The wife will give up her own husband to death, and the husband will bring his own wife to judgment like a criminal. Masters *will lord it over* their servants savagely, and servants will assume an unruly demeanor toward their masters."
Arguably, Roberts has missed the translation here for two reasons: (1) ἀπάνθρωποι is an adjective that modifies δεσπόται, not an adverb; (2) he has missed the importance of the middle voice. In the other two instances of the middle voice it means "to be in force, to have legal authority over" (see the *Chronicon Paschale*, below). Sophocles held the

[c. A.D. 325] Eusebius, *On Ecclesiastical Theology,* {ref: 3.5.22.1}

Text: *Eusebius, De Ecclesiastica Theologica,* ed. Kosterman and Hawsen, vol. 4 of *Eusebius Werke.*

Translation: my own

διὸ τῇ ἁγίᾳ καὶ τρισμακαρίᾳ τριάδι μόνον τοῦτο συμπαρείληπται, οὐκ ἄλλως τοῦ σωτῆρος τοῖς ἀποστόλοις αὐτοῦ διαταξαμένου τὸ μυστήριον τῆς αὐτοῦ παλιγγενεσίας πᾶσιν τοῖς ἐξ ἐθνῶν εἰς αὐτὸν πιστεύουσιν παραδιδόναι ἢ βαπτίζοντας αὐτοὺς εἰς τὸ ὄνομα τοῦ πατρὸς καὶ τοῦ υἱοῦ καὶ τοῦ ἁγίου πνεύματος· τοῦ μὲν πατρὸς αὐθεντοῦντος καὶ δωρουμένου τὴν χάριν, τοῦ δὲ υἱοῦ ταύτῃ διακονουμένου ("ἡ" γὰρ "χάρις καὶ ἡ ἀλήθεια διὰ Ἰησοῦ Χριστοῦ ἐγένετο"), τοῦ ἁγίου πνεύματος, δηλαδὴ τοῦ πρακλήτου, αὐτοῦ ὄντος τοῦ χορηγουμένου κατὰ τὰς ἐν αὐτῷ διαιρέσεις τῶν χαρισμάτων, "ᾧ μὲν γὰρ διὰ τοῦ πνεύματος δίδοται λόγος σοφίας, ἄλλῳ δὲ λόγος γνώσεως κατὰ τὸ αὐτὸ πνεῦμα, ἑτέρῳ πίστις ἐν τῷ αὐτῷ πνεύματι" καὶ τὰ τούτοις κατηριθμημένα ὁμοίως.

Therefore, to the holy and thrice-blessed Trinity alone this One [the Holy Spirit] belongs. Through no other means, seeing he has carefully arranged it, should the mystery of regeneration for all those who believe in him from among the Gentiles be handed over from the Savior to his apostles. Neither should there be without him baptizing "them in the name of the Father and Son and Holy Spirit,"—of the Father *ruling* and giving grace, of the Son who is being served by this (for "grace and truth came through Jesus Christ"), of the Holy Spirit, clearly the Comforter, himself being the provision according to distinctions of his gifts, for, "to some through the Spirit he gives a word of wisdom, to another a word of knowledge according to the same Spirit, to another faith in the same Spirit" and other verses can be reckoned with these likewise.

———, *The Life of Constantine,* {ref: 2.48.1.8}

Text: Eusebius, *Vita Constantini,* ed. F. Winkelman, vol. 1.1 of *Eusebius Werke.*

Translation: Eusebius, *Church History, Life of Constantine the Great, and Oration in Praise of Constantine,* trans. E. C. Richardson, A Select Library of Nicene and Post-Nicene Fathers of the Christian Church Series, ed. Philip Schaff and Henry Wace (reprint; Grand Rapids: Eerdmans, 1952), 512.

Διτόπερ πᾶς συνετὸς ἀνὴρ οὐκ ἄν ποτε ταραχθείη τοὺς πολλοὺς ὁρῶν ἐαντίαις προαιρέσεσι φερομένους. ἀνόητος γὰρ ἄν ἡ τῆς ἀρετῆς ἐλάνθανε χάρις, εἰ μὴ

---

middle to indicate "to be in force." If so, ours is a better translation. The case cannot be decided with certainty. The structure of the sentence does not provide the parallelism expected. If Roberts' translation of the middle voice were correct, we should expect to see (morally negative adjective—"inhuman") + (morally neutral noun—"masters") + (morally negative verb—"lord it over") paralleled by (morally negative adjective—"factious" or "rebellious" or "lazy", etc.) + (morally neutral noun—"servants") + (morally negative verb). But as it is "servant" is not modified. Therefore, the choice to translate αὐθεντοῦμαι in a morally neutral sense in this passage cannot be validated or invalidated from the structure of the passage. On balance then, the rare use of the middle, if the evidence from the *Chronicon* is taken as normative, suggests itself as the most significant factor, and αὐθεντέω should be taken here as "have legal authority over."

καταντικρὺ τὸν τῆς διεστραμμένης ἀπονοίας βίον ἡ κακία πρὀυβέβλητο. διὸ τῇ μὲν ἀρετῇ στέφανος πρόκειται, τῆς δὲ κρίθεως αὐθεντεῖ ὁ ὕψιστος θεός.

Accordingly no wise man will ever be surprised when he sees the mass of mankind influenced by opposite sentiments. For the beauty of virtue would be useless and unperceived, did not vice display in contrast with it the course of perversity and folly. Hence it is that the one is crowned with reward, while the most high God is himself *the administrator*[11] *of judgment* to the other.

[c. A.D. 350] **Athanasius**, *The Synod of the Arians in Italy and Seleucia of Isauria* {ref: 27.3.26}

Text: Athanasius, *De Synodis Arimini in Italia et Seleuciae in Isauria*, ed. H. G. Opitz, in *Athanasius Werke*, vol. 2.1 (Berlin: de Gruyter, 1940). This text reappears in Athanasius, *Symboule Sirmium, Anathema XVIII*, MPG 26:737(XVIII).

Translation: Athanasius, *Selected Treatises of S. Athanasius, Archbishop of Alexandria, in Controversy with the Arians*, trans. J. H. Parker (Oxford: J. H. Parker, 1842), 121.

Εἴ τις ἀκούων κύριον τὸν πατέρα καὶ τὸν υἱὸν κύριον καὶ κύριον τὸ πατέρα καὶ τὸν υἱόν, ἐπεὶ κύριος ἐκ κυρίου, δύο λέγοι θεούς, ἀνάθεμα ἔστω. οὐ γὰρ συντάσσομεν υἱὸν τῷ πατρί, ἀλλ᾽ ὑποτεταγμένον τῷ πατρί. οὔτε γὰρ κατῆλθεν ἐπὶ Σόδομα ἄνευ βουλῆς τοῦ πατρὸς οὔτε ἔβρεξεν ἀφ᾽ ἑαυτοῦ, ἀλλὰ παρὰ κυρίου αὐθεντοῦντος δηλαδὴ τοῦ πατρός, οὔτε κάθηται ἐκ δεξιῶν ἀφ ἑαυτοῦ ἀλλ᾽ ἀκούει λέγοντος τοῦ πατρός· "κάθου ἐκ δεξιῶν μου".

Whosoever hearing that the Father is Lord and the Son Lord and the Father and Son Lord, for there is Lord from Lord, says there are two Gods, be he anathema. For we do not place the son in the Father's order, but as subordinate to the Father; for he did not descend upon Sodom without the Father's will, not did he rain [fire] from Himself, but from the Lord, that is the Father *authorizing it*. Nor is He of Himself set down on the right hand, but he hears the Father saying, "Sit thou on My right hand."

————, *Letter to Rufinius* {ref: 78.8}

Text: Athanasius, *Epistulae ad Rufinium*, in *Fascido IX. Discipline général antique (iie–ixe s.)*, vol. 2, *Les canons des pères grecs*, ed. P. Joannou (Rome: Italo-Orientale, 1963), 76–80.

Translation: my own

Καὶ ἤρεσεν ὅπερ ὧδε καὶ πανταχοῦ, ὥστε τοῖς μὲν καταπεπτωκόσι καὶ προϊσταμένοις τῆς ἀσεβεῖς συγγινώσκειν μὲν μετανοοῦσι, μὴ διδόναι δὲ αὐτοῖς τόπον κλήρου· τοῖς δὲ μὴ αὐθεντοῦσι μὲν τῆς ἀσεβείας, παρασυρεῖσι δὲ δι᾽ ἀναγκην καὶ βίαν, ἔδοξε δίδοσθαι μὲν συγγνώμην, ἔχειν δὲ καὶ τὸν τόπον τοῦ κλήρου, μάλιστα ὅτι ἀπολογίαν πιθανήν ἐκομίσαντο, καὶ ἔδοξε τοῦτο πως οἰκονομικῶς γεγενῆσθαι·

And indeed he strove in this manner to please much in this and every way, so as on the one hand to make allowance upon their repentance for the ones who had fallen and the ones being directors of impiety, but not to give to them a place among the clergy. But to the ones not *instigating unrighteousness*,[12] but

---

11. Here the sense of "be primarily responsible for" is apposite.

being sweeping away because of force and violence, he deemed to give to them lenient judgment, and even to have a place among the clergy, especially because they made a credible apology, and these he somehow deemed as having become part of the household again.

————, *Testimonies from Scripture (The Essential Community of Father and Son and Holy Spirit)* [ref: 28.41.31][13]

Text: Athanasius, *Testimonia e Scripturia (de communi essentia patris et filii et spiritus sancti)*, in H. G. Opitz, *op cit.*

Translation: my own

Περὶ τοῦ Πνεύματος ἐν ταῖς Πράξεσι λέγει· "Οἱ μὲν οὖν ἀποσταλέντες ὑπὸ τοῦ ἁγίου Πνεύματος ἦλθον εἰς Σελεύκειαν." Εἰ τοίνυν Θεοῦ τὸ προσκαλεῖσθαι, διὰ τί τὸ Πνεῦμα διὰ τῶν προφητῶν λέγει· "Τάδε λέγει Κύριος;" Καὶ πάλιν τὸ Πνεῦμα τοῖς ἐν Ἀντιοχείᾳ ἁγίοις· "Ἀφορίσατε δή μοι τὸν Παῦλον καὶ Βαρνάβαν εἰς τὸ ἔργον ὃ προσκέκλημαι αὐτούς;" Μάθε οὖν τὴν δύναμιν τῆς Τριάδος. Ὁ Πατὴρ νομοθετεῖ· ὁ Υἱὸς κελεύει· τὸ Πνεῦμα αὐθεντεῖ. Ἄκουε λέγοντος τοῦ Θεοῦ· "Εὐαγγελιζόμενοι ἥξουσιν, οὓς ὁ Κύριος προσκέκληται."

Concerning the Spirit in the Acts [of the Apostles] it says, "The ones sent out by the Holy Spirit came to Seleucia." If therefore the act of being called is of God, why does the Spirit through the prophet say, "Thus says the Lord?" And again the Spirit [says] to the saints in Antioch, "Set aside for me Paul and Barnabas to the work which I have called them." Learn therefore the power of the Trinity. The Father gives the law, the Son commands, the Spirit sovereignly *compels.* Hear the one speaking of God, "The ones preaching good news will come, whom the Lord has called."

[A.D. 370] **Saint Basil**, *The Letters*, [ref: #51, line 24]

Text: Saint Basil, *The Letters*, vol. 3, ed. Roy J. Deferrari, Loeb Classical Library Series (Cambridge, Mass.: Harvard University Press, 1952), 322.

Translation: Ibid., 323.

Ἐγὼ δέ, εἰπέ μοι, τὸν μακαριώτον Διάνιον ἀνεμάτισμα; τοῦτο γὰρ ἡμῶν κατήγγειλαν. ποῦ ἢ πότε; τίνων παρόντων; ἐπὶ ποίᾳ προφάσει; ψιλοῖς ῥήμασιν ἢ ἐγγράφοις; ἑτέροις ἀκολουθῶν, ἢ αὐτὸς κατάρχων καὶ αὐθεντῶν τοῦ τολμήματος; ὦ τῆς ἀναιδείας τῶν πάντα φθεγγομένων ῥαδίως.

Tell me, did I anathematize the most blessed Dianius? For this is the charge they made against us. Where or when? In whose presence? On what pretext? Was it bare words or in writing? Was I merely quoting others, or myself originating and *directing the bold deed?*[14] Oh, the shamelessness of those who are ever ready to say anything!

12. Sophocles uses this citation as one of two (the other is the Second Council of Nicea) to substantiate a meaning of "to be the originator of anything" for αὐθεντέω. Lampe lists this under "be primarily responsible for, instigate, authorize."

13. This is believed not to be one of the genuine works of Athanasius, and therefore may be of a much later date.

14. Kroegers, *I Suffer Not a Woman*, 103, render this "profess himself to be its author." On the astonishing creativity of the rendering "profess him to be," see A. Wolters, review of *I Suffer Not a Woman*, by C. C. and R. C. Kroeger, in *Calvin Theological Journal* 28 (1993): 210. Lampe lists this under "be primarily responsible for, etc."

————, *The Letters*, {ref: #69, line 45}

Text: Saint Basil, *The Letters*, vol. 4, ed. Roy J. Deferrari, Loeb Classical Library Series (Cambridge, Mass.: Harvard University Press, 1952), 40, 42.

Translation: Ibid., 41, 43

ἐφάνη δὲ ἡμῖν ἀκόλουθον ἐπιστεῖλαι τῷ ἐπισκόπῳ Ῥώμης, ἐπισκέψασθαι τὰ ἐνταῦθα, καὶ δοῦναι γνώμην, ἵν᾽ ἐπειδὴ ἀπὸ κοινοῦ καὶ συνοδικοῦ δόγματος ἀποσταλῆναί τινας δύσκολον τῶν ἐκεῖθεν, αὐτὸν αὐθεντῆσαι περὶ τὸ πρᾶγμα, ἐκλεξάμενον ἄνδρας ἱκανὸς μὲν ὁδοιπορίας πόνους ὑπενεγκεῖν. . . .

It has seemed to us advisable in the circumstances, moreover, to write to the bishop of Rome, that he may examine into the state of affairs here, and give us his opinion, so that, as it is difficult to send men from Rome by a general synodical decree, he may himself *exercise full authority* in this matter, selecting men capable of enduring the hardships of a journey.

[A.D. 375] **Epiphanius**, Bishop of Salamis (Constantia), *Medicine Chest Against All Heresies*, {ref: 224.2}

Text: Epiphanius Constantiensis, *Panarion*, in *Epiphanius*, vol. 2, ed. K. Holl (Leipzig, 1922), 224.

Translation: my own

ὁρῶμεν γὰρ καὶ ἐνταῦθα ὡς περὶ αὐτοῦ τοῦ υἱοῦ εἴρηται ὅτι "ὅταν παραδιδῷ τὴν βασιλείαν τῷ θεῷ καὶ πατρί, ὅταν καταργήσῃ πᾶσαν ἀρχὴν καὶ ἐξουσίαν καὶ δύναμιν", ὡς αὐτοῦ τοῦ υἱοῦ παραδιδόντος τὴν βασιλείαν καὶ καταργοῦντος πᾶσαν ἀρχὴν καὶ τὰ ἐξῆς, καὶ τὸ δεῖ αὐτόν βασιλεύειν ἄχρις οὗ θῇ πάντας τούς ἐχθρούς ὑπὸ τοὺς πόδας αὐτοῦ", ὡς τοῦ υἱοῦ τὰ πάντα ποιοῦντος καὶ αὐθεντοῦντος καὶ ἐχουσιάζοντας καὶ τῷ πατρὶ παραδιδόντος σὺν τῇ βασιλείᾳ τοὺς ποτασσομένους.

For we see even here [i.e., in this passage] concerning with the Son himself, it says, "when he shall hand over the kingdom to the God and Father, then shall he make powerless all rule and authority and power." This means the Son himself is handing over the kingdom and rendering powerless all rule. The next, "He must reign until he should put all his enemies under his feet," means the Son is doing all things and *ruling* and exercising authority and handing over to the Father the ones who are in submission along with the kingdom."

[c. A.D. 390] **John Chrysostom**, *On the Holy Pentecost*, {ref: 50:464.35}

Text: John Chrysostom, *De Sancta Pentecosta*, MPG 50: 453–70.

Translation: my own

Καὶ βοᾷ Παῦλος λέγων· Ταῦτα πάντα ἐνεργεῖ τὸ ἕν καὶ τὸ αὐτὸ πνεῦμα, διαιροῦν ἰδίᾳ ἑκάστῳ καθὼς βούλεται. καθὼς βούλεται, θησὶν, οὐ καθὼς προστάττεται· διαιροῦν, οὐ διαιρούμενον· αὐθεντοῦν, οὐκ αὐθεντίᾳ ὑποκείμενον. Τὴν γὰρ αὐτὴν ἐξουσίαν, ἥνπερ ἐμαρτύρησε τῷ Πατρὶ, ταύτην καὶ τῷ ἁγίῳ Πνεύματι ἀνατίθησιν ὁ Παῦλος.

And Paul cries out saying, "All these the one and the same spirit works, distributing to each one just as he wills." "Just as he wills," he says, not "just as it has been determined"; "distributing," not "being distributed"; *"exercising authority,"* not "being subject to authority." For where Paul bears witness to the Father of his own authority, he attributes it even to the Holy Spirit.

————, *Sermons on Genesis*, {ref: 54.594.52}

Text: John Chrysostom, *In Genesium* (Sermons), MPG 54:581–630.

Translation: my own

Ἄκουσον πῶς καὶ Παῦλος περὶ ταύτης λέγει τῆς ὑποταγῆς, ἵνα μάθῃς πάλιν Παλαιᾶς καὶ Καινῆς τὴν συμφωνίαν. Γυνή, φησὶν, ἐν ἡσυχίᾳ μανθανέτω ἐν πάσῃ ὑποταγῇ. Εἶδες καὶ αὐτὸν ὑποτάξαντα τῷ ἀνδρὶ τὴν γυναῖκα· Ἀλλ' ἀνάμεινον, καὶ τὴν αἰτίαν ἀκούσῃ. Διὰ τί, Ἐν πάσῃ ὑποταγῇ; Γυναῖκα γὰρ, φησὶ, διδάσκειν οὐκ ἐπιτρέπω. Διὰ τί; Ἐδίδαξε γὰρ ἅπαξ κακῶς τὸν Ἀδαμ. Οὐδὲ αὐθεντεῖν του ἀνδρός. Τί δήποτε; Καὶ γὰρ ηὐθέντησεν ἅπαξ κακῶς. Ἀλλ' εἶναι ἐν ἡσυχίᾳ. Ἀλλ' εἰπὲ καὶ τὴν αἰτίαν. Ἀδαμ γὰρ, φησὶν, οὐκ ἠπατήθη, ἡ δὲ γυνὴ ἀπατηθεῖσα ἐν παραβάσει γέγονε.

Concerning this hear how Paul speaks of subordination, in order to teach again old and new [women believers] harmony. "Let a woman," he says, "learn in silence in all submission." See even he puts the woman in submission to the man. But he anticipates the reader should hear the reason. Why "in all submission"? For "A woman," he says, "I do not allow to teach." Why? Because she once taught Adam wrongly. "Neither to have authority over men." Why not at any time? Because she once *exercised authority wrongly*. "But to be in silence." Again he speaks the reason. "For Adam," he says, "was not deceived, but the woman after being deceived became the transgressor."

————, *Homily on Genesis*, {ref: 56.533.20}

Text: John Chrysostom, *In Genesium*, MPG 56:525–38.

Translation: my own

Τίς ἀνήγγειλέ σοι, ὅτι γυμνὸς εἶ, εἰ μὴ ἀπὸ τοῦ ξύλου, οὗ ἐνετειλάμην σοι, τούτου μόνου μὴ φαγεῖν, ἀπ' αὐτοῦ ἔφαγες; ἀφῆκας ἐμὲ τὸν πλάσαντα, καὶ τῷ ἐχθρῷ προσῆλθες; εἴασας ἐμὲ τὸν δημιουργήσαντα, καὶ τῷ πλάνῳ συγκατέθου; Ἐγώ σοι ἐνετειλάμην τούτου μόνου μὴ φαγεῖν, καὶ σὺ τῷ διαβόλῳ σύμβουλος γέγονας; Εἶπεν ὁ Ἀδάμ· Ἡ γυνὴ, ἣν ἔδωκας μετ' ἐμοῦ, αὕτη μοι ἔδωκεν ἀπὸ τοῦ ξύλου, καὶ ἔφαγον. Ὦ πρόφασις εὔλογον μὴ ἔχουσα! ὦ ἀπολογία μὴ ὠφελοῦσα τὸν λαλοῦντα! ὦ λέξις πικρά, μὴ διασώζουσα τὸν λέγοντα! Τὴν γυναῖκά σοι δέδωκα βοηθὸν, οὐκ αὐθεντοῦσαν· συνήγορον, οὐ δέσποιναν· ὁμογνώμονα, οὐ διδάκτριαν· σύζυγον, οὐκ ἄρχουσαν· ὑποχείριον, οὐκ ὑψηλοτέραν· συχκύπτουσάν σοι, οὐ κατακρατοῦσάν σου.

"Who told you that you are naked, except that you ate from the tree of which I commanded you, 'This alone you shall not eat?'; You forsook, me the one who molded you, and went over to the enemy; You let go of me, the one who was the craftsman, and joined the one who strayed. I commanded you of this one only not to eat and you have become co-conspirator with the devil." Adam said, "The woman which you gave to me, she gave to me of the tree and I ate." What unreasonable pretext! What excuse not worthy of being spoken! What bitter locution not justifying the speaking! The woman was given to you as a helper, not as *being in charge*; as one who agrees, not as the mistress of the manor; as of one mind, not as tutor; as yoked together, not ruling; as subject to, not highest over; as being in concert with you, not as prevailing over you.

————, *Homily on Psalm 92*, {ref: 55.615.4}

Text: John Chrysostom, *In Psalum 92*, MPG 55:611–16.

Translation: my own

Τί με φύλλα συκῆς ῥάπτειν ἐδίδαξας; τί μοι καρπὸν παγιδευτικὸν προσήγαγες, γύναι γοητόστομε, λέγουσα· Δέξαι, φάγε τοῦ φθονηθέντος σοι καρποῦ; Ἦ δ᾽ ἂν γὰρ ἡμέρα φάγῃ, διανοιχθήσονταί σου οἱ ὀφθαλμοὶ, καὶ ἔσῃ ὡς Θεὸς γινώσκων καλὸν καὶ πονηρόν. Τί ἔπραξας, γύναι; Ἐτυφλώθην, οὐ βλέπω. Τὸ κακὸν ἐποίησα, τὸ καλὸν ἀπεπήδησεν. Ὥσπερ ἡ ἀκτὶς μοχθῶ, οὐχ ὡς Θεὸς αὐθεντῶ. Ἄπιθι, γύναι, οὐκ οἶδα τίς εἶ.

Why did you teach me to sew together a bunch of fig leaves? Why did you lead me to the ensnaring fruit, Bewitching Woman, saying, "Take, eat of the fruit begrudged to you, but if you eat of it, in that day your eyes will be opened, and you will be as God, knowing good and evil?" What have you done, Woman? I am blinded, I can not see. I did evil and turned away from the good. Just like the sunbeam, I toil—but not like God *do I reign.* Disobedient One, Woman, do you not know who you are?

———, *Homilies on the Gospel of Saint Matthew,* {ref: 57.239.50}

Text: John Chrysostom, *In Mattaeum,* MPG 57:13–772

Translation: John H. Parker, *The Homilies of S. John Chrysostom on the Gospel of St. Matthew* (Oxford: J. H. Parker, 1843), 225.

Διὰ τοῦτο ὁ μυρίος νεκροὺς ἐγείρας λόγῳ μόνῳ, ἡνίκα τὸν Λάζαρον ἐκάλει, καὶ εὐχὴν προσέθηκεν· εἶτα, ἵνα μὴ τοῦτο ἐλάττονα αὐτὸν δείξῃ τοῦ γεγεννηκότος, διορθούμενος τὴν ὄχλον τὸν περιεστῶτα, ἵνα πιστεύσωσιν ὅτι σύ με ἀπέστειλας. Καὶ οὔτε πάντα ὡς αὐθεντῶν ἐργάζεται, ἵνα τὴν ἐκείνων ἀσθένειαν διορθώσηται· οὔτε τάντα εὐχόμενος ποιεῖ, ἵνα μὴ τοῖς μετὰ ταῦτα καταλίπῃ πονηρᾶς ὑποψίας ὑπόθεσιν, ὡς ἀσθενῶν καὶ ἀδυνάτως ἔχων· ἀλλὰ μίγνυσι ταῦτα ἐκείνοις, κἀκεινα τούτοις.

For this cause He who had raised thousands of the dead with a word only, when He was calling Lazarus, added also a prayer; and then, lest this should make Him appear less than Him that begat Him, He, to correct this suspicion, added, "I said these things, because of the people which standeth by, that they may believe that Thou hast sent Me." And neither doth He work all things as one who *acted by His own power,* that He might thoroughly correct their weakness; nor doth He all things with prayer, lest He should leave matter of evil suspicion to them that should follow, as though He were without strength or power: but He mingles the latter with the former, and those again with these.

———, *Homilies on the Gospel of Saint Matthew,* {ref: 57.465.1}

Text: John Chrysostom, *In Mattaeum,* MPG 57:13–772.

Translation: John H. Parker, *The Homilies of S. John Chrysostom on the Gospel of St. Matthew* (Oxford: J. H. Parker, 1843), 608.

[In reference to Matt. 12:46–49 and Mary:] Καὶ γὰρ ὅπερ ἐπεχείρησε, φιλοτιμίας ἦν περιττῆς· ἐβούλετο γὰρ ἐνδείξασθαι τῷ δήμῳ, ὅτι κρατεῖ καὶ αὐθεντεῖ τοῦ παιδὸς, οὐδὲν οὐδέπω περὶ αὐτοῦ μέγα φανταζομένη· διὸ καὶ ἀκαίρως προσῆλθεν.

For in fact that which she assayed to do, was of superfluous vanity; in that she wanted to shew the people, that she *hath power and authority over her Son,* imagining not as yet any thing great concerning him; whence also her unseasonable approach.

————, *Homilies on the Gospel of Saint John,* {ref: 59.367.45}

Text: John Chrysostom, *In Joannen,* MPG 59:23–482.

Translation: John H. Parker, *The Homilies of S. John Chrysostom on the Gospel of St. John* (Oxford: J. H. Parker, 1842), 587.

[In reference to John 12:21:] Τῆς φήμης οὖν διαδοθείσης, λέγουσι· Θέλομεν τὸν Ἰησοῦν ἰδεῖν. Ὁ δὲ Φίλιππος παραχωρεῖ τῷ Ἀνδρέᾳ, ἅτε πρὸ αὐτοῦ ὄντι, καὶ πρᾶγμα αὐτῷ κοινοῦται. Ἀλλ᾽ οὐδὲ οὗτος ἁπλῶς αὐθεντεῖ· ἤκουσε γὰρ, ὅτι Εἰς ὁδὸν ἐθνῶν μὴ ἀπέλθητε. Διὰ τοῦτο μετὰ τοῦ μαθητοῦ κοινωσάμενος, τῷ διδασκάλῳ ἀναφέρει· ἀμφότεροι γὰρ εἶπον αὐτῷ.

When the report concerning him was imparted to them, they say, "We would see Jesus." Philip gives place to Andrew as being before him, and communicates the matter to him. But neither doth he at once *act with authority;* for he heard that saying, "Go not into the way of the Gentiles": therefore having communicated with the disciple, he refers the matter to his Master. For they both spoke to Him.

————, *Homilies on the Acts of the Apostles,* {ref: 60.37.13}

Text: John Chrysostom, *In Acta Apostelorum,* MPG 60:13–384.

Translation: John H. Parker, *The Homilies of S. John Chrysostom on the Gospel of St. John* (Oxford: J. H. Parker, 1841), 43.

[In reference to Acts 1:15–26 and Peter:] Ὅρα γὰρ, ἑκατὸν εἴκοσιν ἦσαν, καὶ ἕνα αἰτεῖ ἀπὸ παντὸς τοῦ πλήθους· εἰκότως. Πρῶτος τοῦ πράγματος αὐθεντεῖ, ἅτε αὐτὸς πάντας ἐγχειρισθείς. Πρὸς γὰρ τοῦτον εἶπεν ὁ Χριστός· καὶ σύ ποτε ἐπιστρέψας, στήριξον τοὺς ἀδελφούς σου.

For observe, they were an hundred and twenty, and he asks for one out of the whole body: with good right, *as having been put in charge of them*: for to him had Christ said, "And when thou art converted, strengthen thy brethren."

————, *Homilies on Romans,* {ref: 60.525.41}

Text: John Chrysostom, *In Epistulam ad Romanos,* MPG 60:391–682.

Translation: John H. Parker, *The Homilies of S. John Chrysostom on the Epistle of St. Paul to the Romans* (Oxford: J. H. Parker, 1841), 587.

[With reference to Rom. 8:14:] Οὗτος γὰρ πάλιν πολλῷ τοῦ προτέρου μείζων ὁ στέφανος. Διὸ οὐδὲ ἁπλῶς εἶπεν, Ὅσοι γὰρ Πνεύματι Θεοῦ ζῶσιν, ἀλλ᾽, Ὅσοι Πνεύματι Θεοῦ ἄγονται, δεικνὺς ὅτι οὕτω βούλεται αὐτὸ κύριον εἶναι τῆς ἡμετέρας ζωῆς, ὡς τὸν κυβερνήτην τοῦ πλοίου, καὶ τὸν ἡνίοχον τοῦ ζεύγους τῶν ἵππων. Καὶ οὐχὶ τὸ σῶμα μόνον, ἀλλὰ καὶ αὐτὴν τὴν ψυχὴν ὑποβάλλει ταῖς τοιαύταις ἡνίαις. Οὐδὲ γὰρ ἐκείνην βούλεται αὐθεντεῖν, ἀλλὰ καὶ ἐκείνης τὴν ἐξουσίαν ὑπὸ τῇ τοῦ Πνεύματος ἔθηκε δυνάμει.

Now this is again a much greater honor than the first. And this is why he does not say merely, "as many as live by the Spirit of God," but, "as many as are led by the Spirit of God," to shew that he would have Him use such power over our life as a pilot doth over a ship, or a charioteer over a pair of horses. And it is not the body only, but the soul, itself too, that he is for setting under reins of this sort. For he would not *have even that independent*, but place its authority also under the power of the Spirit.

————, *Homilies on Colossians*, [ref: 62.366.29]

Text: John Chrysostom, *In Epistulam ad Colossenses*, MPG 62:299–392.

Translation: John H. Parker, *The Homilies of S. John Chrysostom on the Epistle of St. Paul to the Philippians, Colossians and Thessalonians* (Oxford: J. H. Parker, 1879), 294–295.

Τὸ μὲν οὖν ἀγαπᾶν τῶν ἀνδρῶν ἐστι, τὸ δὲ εἴκειν ἐκείνων. Ἐὰν οὖν ἕκαστος τὸ ἑαυτοῦ εἰσενέγκῃ, ἕστηκε πάντα βέβαια. Ἀπὸ μὲν γὰρ τοῦ ἀγαπᾶσθαι γίνεται καὶ ἡ γυνὴ φιλική· ἀπὸ δὲ τοῦ ὑποτάσσεσθαι ὁ ἀνὴρ ἐπιεικής. Ὅρα δὲ ὅτι καὶ ἐν τῇ φύσει οὕτω κατεσκεύασται, ὥστε τὸν μὲν φιλεῖν, τὴν δὲ ὑπακούειν. Ὅταν γὰρ ὁ ἄρχων τὸ ἀρχόμενον φιλῇ, τότε τὰ πάντα συνέστηκεν. Οὐχ οὕτως ἡ παρὰ τοῦ ἀρχομένου ἀγάπη, ὡς ἡ παρὰ τοῦ ἄρχοντος ζητεῖται πρὸς τὸν ἀρχόμενον· Παρ' ἐκείνου γὰρ ἡ ὑπακοή. Τὸ γὰρ ἐν ὥρᾳ εἶναι τὴν γυναῖκα, τοῦτον δὲ ἐν ἐπιθυμίᾳ, οὐδὲν ἄλλο δείκνυσιν, ἀλλ' ἢ ὅτι διὰ τὴν ἀγάπην οὕτω γεγένηται. Μὴ τοίνυν, ἐπειδὴ ὑποτέτακται ἡ γυνή, αὐθέντει· μεδὴ σύ, ἐπειδὴ ὁ ἀνὴρ ἀγαπᾷ, φυσιοῦ. Μήτε ἡ τοῦ ἀνδρος φιλία τὴν γυναῖκα ἐπαιρέτω, μήτε ἡ τῆς γυναικὸς ὑποταγὴ φυσάτω τὸν ἄνδρα. Διὰ τοῦτό σοι ὑπέταξεν αὐτήν, ἵνα μᾶλλον φιλῆται· διὰ τοῦτό σε φιλεῖσθαι ἐποίησεν, ὦ γύναι, ἵνα εὐκόλως φέρῃς τὸ ὑποτετάχθαι.

To love therefore is the husbands' part, to yield is theirs. If then each one contributes his own part, all stands firm. For from being loved, the wife too becomes affectionate; and from her being submissive, the husband becomes gentle. And see how in nature also it hath been so ordered, that the one should love, the other obey. For when the governing party loves the governed, then every thing stands fast. Love from the governed is not so requisite, as from the governing to the governed; for from the other obedience is due. For that the woman hath beauty, and the man desire, shews nothing else than that for the sake of love it hath been made so. Do not therefore, because thy wife is subject to thee, *act the despot*; nor because thy husband loveth thee, be thou puffed up. For this cause hath He subjected her to thee, that she may be loved the more. For this cause He hath made thee to be loved, O wife, that thou mayest easily bear thy subjection.

————, *Homilies on Colossians*, [ref: 62.376.1]

Text: John Chrysostom, *In Epistulam ad Colossenses*, MPG 62:299–392.

Translation: John H. Parker, *The Homilies of S. John Chrysostom on the Epistle of St. Paul to the Philippians, Colossians and Thessalonians* (Oxford: J. H. Parker, 1879), 309.

Ἀλλ' ἴδωμεν τὴν σύνεσιν Παύλου. Ἐν σοφίᾳ, φησί, περιπατεῖτε πρὸς τοὺς ἔξω, τὸν καιρὸν ἐξαγοραζόμενοι. Τουτέστιν, Οὐκ ἔστιν ὑμέτερος ὁ καιρός, ἀλλ' ἐκείνων ἐστί· μὴ τοίνυν βούλεσθε αὐθεντεῖν, ἀλλ' ἐξαγοράζετε τὸν καιρόν. Καὶ οὐκ εἶπεν ἁπλῶς, Ἀγοράζετε, ἀλλ', Ἐξαγοράζετε, δηλῶν, ὅτι Οὕτω διατιθέμενοι, ὑμέτερον αὐτὸν ποιεῖτε ἑτέρως.

But let us see the wisdom of Paul. "Walk in wisdom," he saith, "towards them that are without, redeeming the time." That is, the time is not yours, but theirs. Do not then wish *to have your own way* (i.e. in the world, as men of the world), but redeem the time. And he said not simply, "Buy," but "redeem," making it your own after another manner.

————, *The Heavenly Reign*, {ref: 59.583.46}

Text: John Chrysostom, *In Illud: Regnum Caelorum Patri Filius*, MPG 59:577–86.

Translation: my own

[The householder of Matt. 20 addresses the others about the eleventh-hour worker]. Οὐ δύναμαι οὖν τὸν οὕτω με ποθήσαντα, τὸν οὕτω μοι πιστεύσαντα, μὴ τιμῆσαι πάσῃ σπουδῇ καὶ τιμῇ. Ὡς ἐπίστευσας, ἐπίστευσεν· ὡς εὐπόρησας, εὐπόρησεν· ὡς προσεκύνησας, προσεκύνησεν· ὡς ἐβασίλευσεν· ἐβασίν· ὡς ἔκαμες, οὐκ ἔκαμεν, ἀλλ᾽ ἐγὼ τῇ χάριτι τὸ λεῖπον ἀνεπλήρωσα. Ἢ οὐκ ἔξεστί μοι ποιῆσαι, ὃ θέλω, ἐν τοῖς ἐμοῖς; μὴ γὰρ τὰ σὰ δαπανῶ; Τὰ ἐμὰ χορηγῶ. Μὴ γὰρ ἐν τοῖς σοῖς φιλοτιμοῦμαι; Ἐν τοῖς ἐμοῖς αὐθεντῶ. Μὴ γὰρ ἐπίτροπόν σε τῆς ἐμῆς κατέστησα γνώμης; Μισθωτόν σε ἔλαβον ὡς ἐξ ἀρχῆς. Μὴ γὰρ κύριόν σε τῆς ἐμῆς ἐξουσίας ἐχειροτόνησα; Ὡς φιλάνθρωπος κοινωνόν ἐποιησάμην τῶν ἐμαυτοῦ.

Therefore, am I not unable not to honor, by every honor and with all diligence, the one desiring me thus, the one believing in me thus? As you believed, he believed; as you abounded, he abounded; as you worshipped, he worshipped; as you reigned, he reigned; as you were afflicted, were we not afflicted? But I, by grace, will fill up what is lacking. Is it not lawful for me to do, what I will among my own? Do I take what is yours? I provide out my own resources. For not by means of your property do I seek glory. I *rule absolutely* by means of my own. For I did not appoint you as a guardian of my opinion. I received you as a hireling from the beginning. For I did not appoint you as lord of my authority. As a lover of mankind I share with my own.

————, *About Martha, Mary, and Lazarus*, {ref: 61.706.19,20}

Text: John Chrysostom, *In Martham, Miriam et Lazarus*, MPG 61:705–10.

Translation: my own

[Elijah cries out:] Λύτρωσαί με, Κύριε, τῆς ὀχλήσεως ταύτης· θέατρόν μοι περιέστησαν, αἰσχύνην μοι περιέθηκε, θλίψιν μοι πολλὴν ἐπήγαγε. Δὸς τὴν ψυχήν, καὶ παρέχω τὴν βροχήν· πληροφόρησον τὴν χήραν, καὶ ἀρδεύω τὴν χώραν· δὸς τοῦ παιδὸς τὴν παλαιβίωσιν, καὶ κινῶ τὴν γλῶτταν πρὸς ὀμβροδοσίαν. Ταῦα μέντοι διὰ τὴν προρρηθεῖσαν τοῦ Λαζάρου νεκρεγεσίαν, καὶ τὴν τῶν Ἰουδαίων ἀντιλογίαν, ὅτι ἄλλως Δεσπότης αὐθεντεῖ, καὶ ἄλλως δοῦλος ἐγείρει. Ἡλίας ἤγειρε νεκρὸν, ἀλλ᾽ ὅμως οὐκ ηὐθέντησεν.

"Set me free me, Lord, from this mob! He put around me gawkers. He placed around me disgraceful ones. He brought upon me much tribulation. Give life and I will supply the rain. Give full measure of bereavement and I will irrigate the land with tears. Give the old manner of discipline and I will stir up the tongue for a shower of tears." These things occurred rather, for the sake of prophecy of the resurrection of Lazarus and the controversy with the Jews—because another Lord *reigns* and another servant raises the dead. Elijah raised the dead, but nevertheless he did not *reign*.

————, *About Martha, Mary, and Lazarus*, {ref: 61.706.57}

Text: John Chrysostom, *In Martham, Miriam et Lazarus*, MPG 61:705–10.

Translation: my own

Τίς οὗτος ὁ καλῶν; τίς οὗτος ὁ αὐθεντῶν; τίς ὁ ἀναπλάττων διαλελυμένον χοῦν; τίς ὁ ἐξυπνίζων νεκρὸν ὡς ἐξ ὕπνου; τίς ὁ ἀδαμαντίνας πύλας διαῤῥήσσων; τίς ὁ βοῶν, Λάζαρε, δεῦρο ἔξω; ἡ φωνὴ μὲν ἀνθρωπόφθογγος, καὶ ἡ δύναμις θεοδύναμος. Τίς ὁ καλῶν; οὐκ ἔστιν ἄνθρωπος· τὸ μὲν σχῆμα ἀνθρώπου, ἡ δὲ φωνὴ Θεοῦ.

Who is this one who is calling? Who is *this one compelling*? Who is this one forming again the one shamefully cast into a sepulchre? Who is this one waking the dead as from sleep? Who is the one sundering the adamantine gates? Who is this one crying, "Lazarus, come out!" The voice sounds like a man, but the power is the power of God. Who is the one calling? It is not man; it is the form of man, but the voice of God.

——, *By the Lake of Genesareth,* {ref: 64.52.15}

Text: John Chrysostom, *In lacum Genesarth et in Sanctum Petrum Apostolum*, MPG 64:47–52.

Translation: my own

Ὁ Μωϋσῆς αὐτὸν ὕβριζεν, ἀλλ᾽ ὁ Χριστὸς ἐθεράπευσεν. Ὧδε θεραπεύεται, κἀκεῖ τὰ δῶρα τῆς θεραπείας προσφέρειν κελεύεται. Διὰ τί; Ἵνα καὶ τοῦ Δεσπότου Χριστοῦ τὸ φιλάνθρωπον γνωσθῇ, καὶ τῶν φιλαργύρων Ἰουδαίων τὸ φιλέμπορον φανῇς. Τί οὖν κακοδόξων ἔλεγχος λεπρός. Κύριε, ἐὰν θέλῃς, δύνασαί με καθαρίσαι. Οὐ λέγω, παρακάλεσον, ἀλλ᾽ αὐθέντισον· οὐ λέγω, πρόσθευξαι, ἀλλ᾽ ἴασαι. Ἴδιον γὰρ Θεοῦ ἰδίῳ θελήματι θεραπεύειν, οὐχὶ δὲ ἀλλοτρίῳ πνεύματι. Κύριε, ἐὰν θέλῃς, δύνασαί με καθαρίσαι. Ἤκουσα γὰρ τοῦ προφήτου λέγοντος· Ὁ Θεὸς ἡμῶν ἐν τῷ οὐρανῷ καὶ ἐν τῇ γῇ πάντα ὅσα ἠθέλησεν ἐποίησεν.

Moses insulted him, but Christ healed. Thus he is healed, and there the gift of treating the sick is command to come forth. Why? In order that love of mankind by the Lord Jesus should be made known and the incessant love of money of the Jews should appear. Why the infamous reproach of the leper, "Lord, if you wish you are able to heal me"? I do not say, "comfort!," but *take charge!*"; I do not say "to pray!" but "to heal!" To heal his own by God's own will, but not by another spirit. "Lord, if you will, you are able to make me clean." For he heard the word of the prophet, "Our God does what ever he has willed in heaven and all earth."

——, *On the Holy Passover,* {ref: line 25}

Text: John Chrysostom, C. Baur, "Drei unedierte Chrysostums-Text, bzw," *Traditio* 9 (1953): 108–10.

Translation: my own

"Λύσατε τὸν ναὸν τοῦτον καὶ ἐν τρισὶν ἡμέραις ἐγερῶ αὐτόν." Οὐκ εἶπεν· ἐγερεῖ αὐτὸν ὁ Πατήρ, ἵνα μὴ Ἄρειος ἐπιπηδήσῃ τῷ λόγῳ ἀλλ᾽· Ἐγὼ ἐγερῶ αὐτόν· ἐγὼ δι᾽ ἐμαυτοῦ αὐθεντῶ οὐ κελευόμενος. Διὰ τί δὲ μὴ παραχρῆμα, ἀλλὰ μετὰ τρεῖς ἡμέρας; ἐρωτᾷς διὰ τί μὴ πραχρῆμα ἀνίσταται, ἀλλὰ μετὰ τρεῖς ἡμέρας· τοῦ προφήτου Ἰωνᾶ τὸν τύπον παραλύσῃ.

"Destroy this temple and in three days I will raise it." He did not say, "The Father will raise it," in order that you, Ares, do not pounce upon the word; But, "I will raise it. I, not being commanded, *exercise my own authority.*" But why not immediately instead of after three days? You ask, "Why does he not rise immediately, but after three days?" In order that he should not vitiate the type of Jonah the prophet.

————, *When All Things Are Subject to Him,* {ref: 160.25}

Text: John Chrysostom, *In Illud: Quando ipsi subicietomnia,* ed. S. Haidacher, "Drei unedierte Chrysostomus-Texte einer Baseler handscrift," *Zeitschrift für Katholische Theologie* 31 (1907): 150–67.

Translation: my own

Ἀλλ' οὐδὲν τούτων ὁ σωτὴρ εἶπε πρὸς τὸν γνησίως αὐτῷ προσελθόντα ἀλλ' ἀποδεξάμενος αὐτοῦ τὸ εἰλικρινὲς τῆς πίστεως εἰλικρινῆ καὶ σίαν αὐτῷ δίδωσι τὴν σωτηρίαν· προσῆλθες ἐμοὶ πιστῶς, δέχου πιστῶς τὸ φάρμακον· θελήματι τῷ ἐμῷ ἐπιγράφεις τὴν εὐεργεσίαν, ἐκ τοῦ θελήματός μου κομίζου τὴν σωτηρίαν. Κύριε, ἐὰν θέλῃς, δύνασαί με καθαρίσαι· Θέλω, καθαίσθητι. Μὴ ἔστηκε τοῖς αἱρετικοῖς τῆς ἀσεβείας ὅρος. Ὁρᾷς, ὅτι λόγῳ ὑπόκειται, ἐξ οἰκείου δὲ θελήματος αὐθεντεῖ; Ταῦτα δὲ ὅταν εἴπω, οὐκ ἀπεσχοινισμένον εἰσάγω τοῦ υἱοῦ τὸ θέλημα τοῦ πατρικοῦ θελήματος.

But nothing of this did the Savior say to the one who came to him sincerely, but after praising him for the sincerity of his faith, pure and genuine, he gave him salvation. "You have come to me faithfully. Receive faithfully the remedy. By my will you inscribe the good deed, from my will receive salvation." "Lord, if you will, you are able to make me clean." "I will be clean." Do not stand with the factious at the borders of impiousness; You see that he is subject to the word, but for the members of the Household, he *rules the will*; but when I say these things, I bring in and do not exclude from the Son the will of the Paternal Will.

————, *On the Resurrection of the Lord,* {ref: line 42}

Text: John Chrysostom, *In Resurrectionen Domini,* ed. C. Datema and P. Allen, "Text and Tradition of Two, etc," *Jahrbuch der österreichischen Byzantinistik* 30 (1981): 94–97.

Translation: my own

Καθολικὴν ἑορτὴν πανηγυρίζομεν σήμερον, ὁμοῦ τὸν νόμον πληροῦντες καὶ τὴν χάριν κυροῦντες, ὅτι ὁ νόμος διὰ Μωσέως ἐδόθη, ἡ χάρις καὶ ἀλήθεια διὰ Ἰησοῦ Χριστοῦ ἐγένετο. Ὅπου δοῦλος ἐκεῖ τὸ ἐδόθη, ὅπου ἐλεύθερος ἐκεῖ τὸ ἐγένετο, ὅτι ὁ δοῦλος μὲν διακονεῖ, ὁ δεσπότης δὲ αὐθεντεῖ.

Today we celebrate the universal feast together, fulfilling likewise the law and confirming grace, "because the law was given through Moses, but grace and truth came through Jesus Christ." Where there is a servant, there is a "was given"; but where there is freedom, there is a "came," because the servant serves, but the Lord *rules*.

[4th cent. A.D.] Didymus the Blind, *Commentary on Job,* {ref: 285.4}

Text: Didymus Caecus, *Didymos der Blinde. Kommentar zu Hiob,* pt. 3, ed. U. Hegendorn, D. Hagendorn, and L. Koenen (Bonn: Habelt, 1968), 2–220.

Translation: my own

Τοῦτο δὲ οὐκ ὑπεροψίᾳ, ἀλλὰ φανερώσει τῆς ἐπιβουλῆς· εἴρηται. πάλιν γὰρ μεταβαλὼν δεινῶς με ὀλέκεις. παρίστησιν, ὅτι εἰ καὶ ἀγρεύομαι ὥσπερ λέων, τοσούτων μοι περιεστηκότων, ἀλλ' οὐκ αὐθεντοῦσιν αὐτοὶ τῆς ἐπιφορᾶς·

But this thing he does not ignore, but he makes plain the plot. It says, "Thus changing again marvelously you destroy me." It proves that even if I should be hunted like a lion, having been surrounded by such ones, they themselves do not *control* my deliverance.

————, *Dialogue Between a Montanist and an Orthodox,* {ref: 457.2; 457.8}

Text: Didymus Caecus, *Dialexis Montanistae et orthodoxi,* in "Widerlegung eines Montanisten," *Zeitschrift für Kirchengeschichte* 26 (1905): 449–58

Translation: my own

Ἡμεῖς τὰς προφητείας τῶν γυναικῶν οὐκ ἀποστρεφόμεθα, καὶ ἡ ἁγία Μαεία προεφήτευσε λέγουσα· "Ἀπὸ τοῦ νῦν μακαριοῦσί με πᾶσαι αἱ γενεαί." Καὶ ὡς καὶ αὐτὸς εἶπας ἦσαν τῷ ἁγίῳ Φιλίππῳ θυγατέρες προφητεύουσαι, καὶ Μαία ἡ ἀδελφὴ Ἀαρὼν προεφήτευεν. Ἀλλ᾽ οὐκ ἐπιτρέπομεν αὐταῖς λαλεῖν ἐν ἐκκλησίαις οὐδὲ αὐθεντεῖν ἀνδρῶν, ὥστε καὶ βίβλους ἐξ ὀνόματος αὐτῶν γράφεσθαι. Τοῦτο γὰρ ἐστιν ἀκατακαλύπτως αὐτὰς προσεύχεσθαι καὶ προφητεύειν, καὶ οὐ κατήσχυνε τὴν κεφαλὴν τουτέστιν τὸν ἄνδρα. Μὴ γὰρ οὐκ ἠδύνατο ἡ ἁγία Θεοτόκος Μαρία ἐξ ὀνόματος ἑαυτῆς βιβλία γράψαι; Ἀλλ᾽ οὐκ ἐποίησεν, ἵνα μὴ καταισχύνη τὴν καφαλὴν αὐθεντοῦσα τῶν ἀνδρῶν.

We do not shun the prophecies of women. Even the holy Mary prophesied saying, "From now on all generations will bless me." And even as you say the holy Philip had prophesying daughters, and Miriam, the sister of Aaron, prophesied. But we do not allow them to speak in church nor *to control* men so that books be written in their name. For this is "uncovered": for women to pray and to prophesy, but not to dishonor the head, that is, the man. For the holy Mother of God, Mary, was not unable to write a book under her own name; but she did not do it in order not to dishonor the head by *controlling* men.

[A.D. 446] Proculus Constantinopolitanus, *Oration #6,* {ref: 65.816 A}

Text: Proculus Constantinopolitanus, *Oratio VI,* MPG 65:692ff.

Translation: my own

πόση τοῦ νόμου καὶ τῆς χάριστος ἡ διαφορά· πῶς ὁ μὲν κατακρίδὲ συγχωρεῖ· ὁ μὲν κολάζει, ἡ δὲ διασώζει· ὁ μὲν ὑπερετεῖ, ἡ δὲ αὐθεντεῖ· ὁ μὲν τὴν ἁματίαν ἐπιτρίβει, ἡ δὲ τὴν ἁμαρτίαν ἐξαφανίζει·

How much is the difference between law and grace! How the one condemns, but the other unites; the one punishes, but the other saves completely; the one serves, but the other *rules*; the one afflicts with sin, but the other utterly destroys sin.

[A.D. 449] Leo I, Pope, *Epistle #30 (To Pulcheria),* {ref: 54.788 A}

Text: Leo Magni, *Epistulae XXX,* MPL 54.788ff

Translation: my own (Cpr. *Epistle XXXI,* trans. C. L. Feltoe, in *The Nicene and Post-Nicene Fathers,* Second Series, ed. P. Schaff and H. Wace, [Grand Rapids: Eerdmans, 1979]).

Τούτου τοῦ ἁγίου Πνεύματος οἰδάσκοντος μεμαθήκατε. Τούτῳ τὴν ὑμετέραν ἐξουσίαν ὑπετάξατε. Διὰ ταύτης τῆς δωρεᾶς, καὶ τῆς ἐκδικίας βασιλεύετε, Ὅθεν ἐπείπερ κατὰ τῆς ἀκεραίου πίστεως τῶν χριστιανῶν διχόνοιαν τινα ἐν τῇ Ἐκκλησίαι τῇ κατὰ Κωνσταντινούπολιν Εὐτιχοῦς αὐθεντοῦντος γεγενῆσθαι, τοῦ ἀδελφοῦ μου, καὶ συνεπισκόπου Φλαυιανοῦ διὰ τῆς ἀναφορᾶς ἔγνων. . . .

You have been taught by this vaunting Holy Spirit. To him you have submitted your authority. Through his gifts and his favors you rule. Hence, seeing that, I knew through the report of my brother and fellow bishop Flavian, a certain dispute, *instigated* by Eutyches, in the Church of Constantinople, has arisen against the pure faith of Christianity.

[c. A.D. 450] Olympiodorus, *Excerpt from the History of Olypiodorus*, [ref: 456.3]

Text: Olympiodorus, *Ex Historia Olympiodori Excerpta*, in *Dexippi, Eunapii, Petri Patricii, Prisci, Malchi*, et al., ed. B. G. Niebuhre, I. Bekker, et al. (Bonnae: Weberi, 1829), 456.

Translation: my own

Ἄρχεται δὲ ἡ δευτέρα ὧδε· ὅτι Ἰοβῖνος παρὰ γνώμην Ἀδαούλφου τὸν ἴδιον ἀδελφὸν Σεβαστιανὸν βασιλέα χειροτονήσας, εἰς ἔχθραν Ἀδαούλφῳ κατέστη. καὶ πέμπει Ἀδάουλφος πρὸς Ὀνώριον πρέσβεις, ὑποσχόμενος τάς τε τῶν τυράννων κεφαλὰς καὶ εἰρήνην ἄγειν. ὧν ὑποστρεψάντων, καὶ ὅρκων μεσιτευσάντων, Σεβαστιανοῦ μὲν πέμπεται τῷ βασιλεῖ ἡ κεφαλή· Ἰοβῖνος δὲ ὑπο Ἀδαούλφου πολιορκούμενος, ἑαυτὸν ἐκδίδωσι, καὶ πέμπεται κἀκεῖνος τῷ βασιλεῖ, ὃν αὐθεντήσας Δάρδανος ὁ ἔπαρχος ἀναιρεῖ.

The second part begins here: For Jobinos, making his own brother Sebastian king, contrary to the wishes of Adaulfo, made Adaulfo his enemy. And Adaulfo sent ambassadors to Honorios, and he promised to bring peace—and the heads of the tyrants. They returned and promised with oaths, and the head of Sebastian was sent to the king. But being besieged by Adaulfo, Jobinos surrendered himself, and he was sent to the king. Dardanos, the governor, *exercising his own authority*, killed him.

[post A.D. 450] Socrates Scholasticus, *Church History*, [ref: 2.30.63]

Text: *Socrates' Ecclesiastical History*, 2nd ed., ed. W. Bright (Oxford: Clarendon, 1893), 1–330.

Translation: my own [compare J. H. Parker's translation of Athanasius, *Controversy with the Arians* (above)]

Οὐ γὰρ συντάσσομεν τὸν Υἱον τῷ Πατρὶ, ἀλλ᾽ ὑποτεταγμένον τῷ Πατρί· οὔτε γὰρ κατῆλωεν εἰς σῶμα ἄνευ βουλῆς τοῦ Πατρός· οὐδὲ ἔβρεχεν ἀθ᾽ ἑαυτοῦ, ἀλλὰ "παρὰ Κυρίου" αὐθεντοῦντος, δηλαδὴ τοῦ Πατρός.

For the Son does not dictate to the Father, but is in submission to the Father. Neither does he descend to a body without the Father's will; nor did he rain [sic] from himself, but from the Lord, that is, the Father *granting authorization*.

———, *Socrates*, [ref: 2.34.6]

Text: *Socrates' Ecclesiastical History*, 2nd ed., ed. W. Bright (Oxford: Clarendon, 1893), 1–330.

Translation: my own

ὥστε οὐκ εἰς μακρὰν ὁ σκοπὸς αὐτοῦ ὑπὸ Κωνσταντίου κατάφωρος ἐγένετο. Δομετιανὸν γὰρ τὸν τότε ἔπαρχον τῆς ἑῴας, καὶ Μάγνον κυαίστωρα αὐθεντήσας ἀνεῖλε, μηνύσας τῷ Βασελεῖ τὸν σκοπὸν αὐτοῦ.

So that, not long after, his spy was detected by Constantine. For Domitian, *taking charge*, confined the then commander of the East and Magnos, the quaestor, informing the king about his spy.

[A.D. 451] **Emperor Marcian**, *Letter to Leo, #1*, {ref: 54.900 B}

Text: Marcianus Imperator, *Epistulae ad Leonem, I*, MPL 54.900ff.

Translation: my own

διὰ τὸ καὶ τὴν ἡμετέραν πρόσθεσιν, καὶ τὸν πόθον τοιοῦτον ὑπάρχειν, ὥστε πάσης ἀσεβοῦς πλάνης ἀποκινηθείσης, διὰ τῆς συγκροτηθείσης ἧς συνόδου, σοῦ αὐθεντοῦντος, μεγίστη εἰρήνη περὶ πάντας τοὺς ἐπισκόπους τῆς καθολικῆς [?], παντὸς μύσους καθαρὰ καὶ ἄσπιλος γενομένη.

On account of our application, and the existence of all the foregoing matters, so that, every unrighteous wanderer having been put away through the well-disciplined ones of this synod, *you granting authorization*, great peace with respect to the bishops of the catholic faith will come about, and the pollutions of all will be clean and spotless.

[A.D. 451] **Council of Chalcedon**, *Letter of Empress Pulcheria to Leo I*, {ref: 2,1,1.9.34}

Text: *Concilium universale Chalcedonese anno 451*, vol. 2.1.1–2.1.2, ed. E. Schwartz (Berlin: de Gruyter, 1933; reprint, 1962)

Translation: my own

...ἵνα πάντες καὶ πάσης τῆς Ἀνατολῆς οἱ ἐπίσκοποι Θράικης τε καὶ Ἰλλυρικοῦ, καθὼς καὶ τῷ ἡμετέρῳ δεσπότῃ τῷ εὐσεβεστάτῳ βασιλεῖ τῷ ἐμῷ συζύγῳ ἀρέσκει, εἰς μίαν πόλιν τὴν ταχίστην ἀπὸ τῶν Ἀνατολικῶν μερεῶν παραγένωνται κἀκεῖσε γενομένης συνόδου περί τε καθολικῆς ὁμολογίας καὶ περὶ τούτων τῶν ἐπισκόπων οἵτινες πρὸ τούτου ἐχωρίσθησαν, καθὼς ἡ πίστις καὶ ἡ Χριστιανικὴ εὐσέβεια ἀπαιτεῖ, σου αὐθεντοῦντος ὁρίσωσιν.

In order that all, even every bishop of Anatolia, Thrace, and even Illyricum, just as indeed it pleases our most holy king, should appear to my yoke fellow in one city of the region of Anatolia, and there convene a synod concerning the Catholic Confession and concerning these bishops who have separated themselves from it, just as faith and Christian piety demand and they should determine, *you granting authorization*.

———, *Eleventh Session of Chalcedon*,[15] 29 October 451, {ref: 2,1,3.48.12}

Βασσιανὸς τῆς εὐλαβέστατος εἶπεν· Εὐάζων ποτὲ ἐγὼ οὔτε ἐγενόμην οὔτε ἀπῆλθον, ἀλλὰ βιασθεὶς ὠνομάσθην ἐπίσκοπος. οἱ κανόνες φανερὰ ἔχουσιν. εἴπωσιν οἱ πατέρες ἐὰν πρόκριμά ἐστι τὸ χειροτονηθῆναι καὶ μὴ ἀπελθεῖν. αὐτοὶ εἴπωσιν· οἴδαν τοὺς κανόνας. παρακαλῶ, ἀκούσατέ μου· τεως φανεωθῇ ἡ τόλμα ὅτι ἠυθέντησαν καὶ λαβόντες ἐνέκλεισάν με, καὶ τότε περὶ τῆς ἱερωσύνης ζητοῦμεν. βία ζητηθῇ. Στέφανος ὁ εὐλαβέστατος εἶπεν· Ἀξιῶ τοὺς κανόνας ἀναγνωσθῆναι τοὺς λέγοντας ὥστε ἐν ἑτέραι πόλει τὸν χειροτονηθέντα μὴ δύνασθαι ἐν ἑτέραι καθίστασθαι.

The Most Pious Bassianos said, "When was I ever in Evazae or went out of it? But I was declared bishop by violence! The canons are the manifest authority. The Fathers would say, 'If there is a preference, it is for the election to office,

---

15. The text titles this section "πραξις ιβ" = "Twelfth Session." C. J. Hefele, *History of the Councils of the Church*, vol. 3 (Edinburgh: T. & T. Clark, 1895), 321, records this defense as occurring in the eleventh session.

not for the vacating of it.' These would say, 'We know the canons.' I exhort you, listen to me. While this reckless deed was being done, they *exercised their own initiative* and broke into my room and seized me. Even then we only sought the priesthood. But they acted as if violence were sought!"

The Most Pious Stephen said, "Worthy are the canons to be read which say that the election to office in one city is without force in another."

————, *Letter to Bishop Makarios and the Monastery on Mt. Sinai,* [ref: 2,1,3.131.26]

ἐντεῦωέν τε ἑαυτῷ πλῆθος τῶν ἀπατηθέντων ἀθροίσας καὶ τὴν τῶν ἀελῶν ὡς εἰπεῖν ἄγνοιαν κτησάμενος σύμμαχον τὴν Αἰλιέων κατατρέχει πόλιν, ἐμπρησμοὺς οἰκιῶν, φόνους εὐλαβῶν ἀνδρῶν, ἀφέσεις τῶν ἐπὶ τοῖς ἐσχάτοις ἐγκλήμασιν ἑαλωκότων τολμῶν, δι' ὧν εὐλαβοῦς τινος δόξαν θηρώμενος ἐπικινδύνως ηὐθέντησεν, καὶ τὰς εἱρκτὰς ἀναρρηγνύς, ἵνα τῶν ὑπευθύνων τό γε ἐπ' αὐτῷ τῆς δίκης ἐλευθερωθέντων πᾶσιν ὡς εἰπεῖν τοῦ πλημμελεῖν ἀνεύθυνον παράσχῃ τὴν εὐχέρειαν.

Then gathering to himself multitudes of the deceivers and acquiring as allies the ignorant-of-the-simple-truth-as-it-is-spoken, he overran the Ailiean city, burning homes, murdering righteous men, committing the rash deeds which were condemned in the last indictment. During these acts, hunting down the notably pious as dangerous criminals, he *assumed his own jurisdiction* and broke into the prisons in order to put in his power the facility to release those subject to trial, that is to say, to offend the guiltless.

[5th cent. A.D.] Ammonius Alexandrius, *Fragments of Acts,* [ref: 85: 1537 B]

Text: Ammonius Alexandrius, *Fragmenta Acti,* MPG 85:1524ff.

Translation: my own

καὶ φωνήσαντες ἐπυνθάνοντο, εἰ Σίμων ὁ ἐπικαλούμενος Πέτρος ἐνθάδε ξενίζεται. Τοῦ δὲ Πέτρου διανουμένου περὶ τοῦ ὁράματος, εἶπε τὸ Πνεῦμα αὐτῷ. Σημειωτέον ὅτι οὐ δεῖ τινα ἑαυτῷ αὐθεντεῖν καὶ καινοτομίας εἰσάγειν ἐν τῇ πίστει· ὅπου μετὰ ὀπτασίαν ὁ Πέτροςτοσοῦτον διηπόρει, ὥστε καὶ Πενεῦμα αὐτὸν προστρέψασθαι.

And when they called, they were inquiring if Simon, the one called Peter, were a guest there. But while Peter was thinking over the vision, the Spirit spoke to him. One must note that it is not necessary for one *to act independently* by himself[16] and to lead into innovations in the faith; whereas Peter was at a loss after such a vision, the Spirit turned his ear to him.

————, *Fragments of Acts,* [ref: 85: 1549 A]

Text: Ammonius Alexandrius, *Fragmenta Acti,* MPG 85:1524ff.

Translation: my own

Καὶ ὅτι τοσοῦτον ἦν αὐτοῖς ὠφεληθῆναι διὰ λόγων, ὅτι οὐκ ἀπώκνησαν οἱ ἀπὸ Ἀντιοχείας πέμψαι εἰς Ἰερουσαλὴν καὶ ἐρωτῆσαι τὸ ἀμφιβαλλόμεν· καίτοι μὴ πρωτοτύπως περὶ Θεότητος ἢ τῆς τοῦ γιοῦ οἰκονομικῆρκώσεως ἢ περὶ τοῦ Πνεύματος, ἢ ἀγγέλων, ἢ ἀρχῶν, ἢ οὐρανοῦ, ἢ ἄλλου τοιούτου ζητηθέντος, ἀλλὰ

---

16. Lampe lists this under "assume authority, act on one's own authority."

περιτομῆς, μέρους ἐλαχίστου τῶν ἀσχημόνων τοῦ σώματος τοῦ ἀνθρώπου· ἢ δεισαν γὰρ ὅτι ἰῶτα ἕν ἢ μία κεραία τοῦ νόμου πνευματικῆς ἔγεμεν (sic) ἐμφάσεως· οἱ ἐν Ἀντιοχείᾳ μαθηταὶ αὐθεντῆσαι· ἀλλὰ τοσοῦτον ἐφρόντιζον καὶ τῶν δοκούντων ψιλῶν εἶναι ζητημάτων, ὅτι δὴ οἱ μὲν ἀπὸ Ἀντιοχείας ἀπέστειλαν Βαρνάβαν καὶ Παῦλον ἐρωτήσοντας τοὺς ἐν Ἱεροσολύμοις.

Because such things were of profit to them through the word, the Antiochenes did not shrink from sending to Jerusalem to ask concerning these matters. And these were not issues of the original Deity, or of the fleshly nature of the Son, or concerning the Spirit, or angels, or rulers, or heaven, or another such living creature, but concerning circumcision, an infinitesimal, unseemly part of the body of man. For it was necessary that one jot and one tittle of the spiritual law be fulfilled. The disciples of Antioch *exercised authority*. But they considered such things—even the evaluation of nakedness—to be the subject of inquiry. For just so they sent Barnabas and Paul from Antioch to ask those who were in Jerusalem.

————, *Fragments of Acts*, [ref: 85: 1552 A]

Text: Ammonius Alexandrius, *Fragmenta Acti*, MPG 85:1524ff.

Translation: my own

Ἔδοξεν ἡμῖν γενομένοις ὁμοθυμαδόν Σημειωτέον ὅτι οὔτε Ἰάκωβος οὔτε Πέτρος ἐτόλμησαν, καίτοι κρίναντες αὐτὸ καλὸν εἶναι, δίχα πάσης τῆςκκλησίας δογματίσαι τὰ περὶ τῆς περιτομῆς· ὅπουγε οὔτε πάντες ηὐθέντησαν, εἰ μὴ ἐπείσθησαν ὅτι τοῦτο δοκεῖ καὶ τῷ ἁγίῳ Πνεύματί· οὗ καὶ προέταξαν τὴν αὐθεντείαν ἐν τῇ ἐπιστολῇ εἰπόντες· "'δοξε τῷ ἁγίῳ Πνεύματι καὶ ἡμῖν," Βαρνάβᾳ καὶ Παύλῳ, ἀνθρώποις παραδεδωκόσι τὰς ψυχὰς αὐτῶν ὑπὲρ τὸ ὀνόματος τοῦ κυρίου·

For it seems to us who are of one accord, Semeioteos, that neither James nor Peter was audacious to judge it to be good, apart from all of the church, to decree the things concerning circumcision. Wherefore, neither did all *compel others*, unless they were persuaded that it seemed so also to the Holy Spirit. They determined this authority in the epistle saying, "It seemed good to the Holy Spirit and to us," to Barnabas and to Paul, to men who handed over their lives for the sake of the Lord.

[5th cent. A.D.] Eusebius of Alexandria, *Sermons*, #5, [ref: 86.348 D]

Text: Eusebius Alexandrini, *Sermones*, V, MPG 86:309ff.

Translation: my own

Λοιπὸν καὶ περὶ διακόνων τὸν λόγον παραθήσομαι. Ὁ διάκονος τοίνυν ὀφείλει τάντα κατὰ γνώμην πρεσβυτέρου πράττειν, καὶ εἰς τὸν κανόνα καὶ εἰς τὰς ἐκκλησιαστικὰς χρείας· εἰς τὸν λαὸν δὲ μὴ αὐθεντεῖν, ἀλλὰ πάντα τῇ κελεύσει τοῦ πρεσβυτέρου ποιεῖν. παρόντος δὲ τοῦ πρεσβυτέρου, οὐδὲ ἀφορίσας τινὰ ἐξουσίαν ἔχει ἤ τι ἕτερον ποιῆσαι·

And finally I will set forth the word concerning deacons. The deacon ought to accomplish everything in accordance with the intention of the elder, and for the rules and for the needs of the church; not *to exercise authority over* the people, but to do everything by the command of the elder. But the elder being at hand, neither does he have authority to banish or to do the like.

[5th cent. A.D.] Victor Antiochenus, *Chains in Mark,* {ref: 292.29}

Text: Victor Antiochenus, *Catenae in Evangelia S. Matthaei et S. Marci ad fidem Codd. MSS.*, vol. 1 of *Catenae Graecorum Patrum in Novum Testamentum,* ed. J. A. Cramer (Oxford, 1840; reprint Hildesheim: Olms, 1967).

Translation: my own

Μέμνηται δι οἰκείως τοῦ Δαβίδ, δόξαντος ἄν καὶ αὐτοῦ μὴ κατὰ τό τεθράφθαι, ὅτε τῶν ἱερατικῶν ἥψατο τροθῶν καὶ τοῖς μεθ᾽ ἑαυτοῦ ἔδωκεν, ἵνα ἡ πρὸς ἐκεῖνον αἰδὼς ἐπισχῇ τὴν κατὰ τῶν Ἀποστόλων συκοφατίαν. εἰ γὰρ προφήτης αὐθεντεῖ κατὰ τοῦ νόμου συμπεριαγόμενος τῇ ἐνδείᾳ καὶ τῇ χρείᾳ ἐπακολυθῶ καίτοι ὑπὸ ὑπάρχων, ἐάν μου τοὺς μαθητὰς ἴδητε διὰ τὸ μὴ ἔχειν ἄρτους τὴν παράθεσιν τῶν σπερμάτων ἑαυτοῖς ἀντὶ τραπέζης παρατιθέντας, ἀγανακεῖτε καὶ ἐκδικεῖτε τὸν νόμον; ἢ οὐκ οἴδατε ὅτι Δαβίδ μὲν δοῦλος ἦν τοῦ νόμου; ἐγὼ δὲ υἱὸς ἀνθρώπου Κύριος εἰμὶ τοῦ σαββάτου.

He [Jesus] naturally recalled David, who reckoned he should not live according to the law when he took the priestly food and gave it to the ones with him, in order that he [Jesus] should multiply the shame of the one snitching on the Apostles. "For if a prophet *assumes his own authority* against the law, being led to it by the wants and needs of the followers who indeed are under the law, if you see my disciples on account of not having bread, setting a table with a meal of seeds for themselves, should you be vexed and judge the law? Or do you not know that David was a servant of the law?—but I, the Son of Man, am Lord of the Sabbath."

The Byzantines (6th cent. A.D.–12th cent. A.D.)

[c. A.D. 520] Joannes Philoponus, *About the Rational Soul,* {ref: 487.12}

Text: [c. A.D. 520] Joannes Philoponus, *De Anima,* ed. M. Hayduck, vol. 15, *Commentaria in Aristoelem Graeca* (Berlin: Reiner, 1897).

Translation: my own

Τούτου δὲ αἴτιον ἡ γένεσις καὶ ἡ ἐν τῇ ὕλῃ ἀμβλυωπία τῆς ψυχῆς. ὥσπερ γὰρ τῶν ἐν λοιμώδει χωρίῳ ὄντων πλείους νοσοῦσι τῶν ὑγιαινόντων, οὕτω καὶ τῶν ἐν γενέσει ψυχῶν μᾶλλον αὐθεντεῖ ἄγνοια ἤπερ γνῶσις. ἐπειδὴ οὖν μᾶλλον ἀπατώμεθα, ἐχρῆν αὐτὸν πλέον περὶ ἀπάτης διαλεχθῆναι· οὐδὲ γὰρ ὁ Ἐμπεδοκλῆς δοξάζει μὴ εἶναι ἀπάτην. αὐτὴ γὰρ ἡ δόξα ἡ λέγουσα μὴ εἶναι ἀπάτην ἠλέγχθη ὑπὸ Πλάτωνος.

But the cause of this is the inexperience and the dimness of soul in the matter. For just as, when the healthy ones are in a pestilential country, they suffer many things, so ignorance rather than knowledge *rules the soul* in birth. Since therefore we are deceived, it was necessary for him to discourse more concerning guile. For neither did Empedocles form the opinion "not to be beguiled." For this opinion, the saying "not to be beguiled," was refuted by Plato.

[c. A.D. 560] Joannes Lydus, On the Magistracies of the Roman Constitution, {ref: 3.42}

Text: Joannes Lydus, *Ioannis Lydi, De Magistratibus Populi Romani,* vol. 3, ed. R. Wünsch (Leipzig, 1903), 131.

Translation: T. F. Carney, *Bureaucracy in Traditional Society: Romano-Byzantine Bureaucracies Viewed from Within*, 3 vols. in 1, no. 3, "John the Lydian, On the Magistracies of the Roman Constitution" (Lawrenceville, Kans., 1971).

Νόμον γὰρ ἀντιγράφειν ὁ βασιλεὺς ἀνεπείσθη πάσης ἀφαιρούμενον ἐχουσίας τὴν ἐπαρχότητα· ἡ γὰρ ἄρτι καὶ κουφίσαι φόρους καὶ σιτήθεις καὶ φῶτα καὶ θέας καὶ ἀνανεώσεις ἔργων αὐθεντοῦσα ταῖς πόλεσιν ἐπιδοῦναι οὐκ ἤρκεσε τὸ λοιπὸν οὐδὲ ἐτόλμησε μικρᾶς γ' οὖν τινος παραψυχῆς ἐκ τῶν δημοσίων μεταδοῦναί τινι.

For the emperor was prevailed upon to write with his own hand a law that stripped the prefecture of all authority. For the magistracy which but recently *of its own initiative*[17] both lightened the tribute and made additional grants to the cities for foodstuffs, lighting, shows and renovations of public works, was not capable hereafter (and did not dare to do so) of making anyone a grant of at least some tiny recompense.

[6th cent. A.D.] Leontius Hierosolymitanus, *Against the Nestorians, Book 5*, {ref: 86:1720 D}

Text: Leontius Hierosolymitanus, *Adversus Nestorianos, Lib. V*, MPG 86:1400ff.

Translation: my own
Θεοτόκον τὴν Μητέρα τοῦ Ἰησου λέγειν ἡμεῖς οὐκ αὐθεντήσομεν, τῆς ἁγίας Γραφῆς οὐδαμοῦ αὐτὴν ὅτω προσαγορευούσης, ἀλλ' οὐδὲ τὶς τῶν πατέρων.

We will not *act on our own authority* to call the Mother of Jesus, "Theotokos,"[18] the Holy Scriptures nowhere addressing her thus, nor any one of the Fathers.

[6th cent. A.D.] Romanus Melodus Hymnographus, *Hymn 20*, {ref: 13.6}

Text: Romanus, *Romanos le Mélode. Hymnes*, vol. 2, ed. J. Grosdidier de Matons (Paris: Cerf, 1965).

Translation: my own
πάσης τῆς γῆς ἐδεσπόζομεν, πάντα αἰχμάλωτα εἴχομεν·
σὺ δὲ ὡς μέγας αὐτοκράτωρ
ἐπελθὼν αὐθεντεῖς, ἀπελαύνων ἡμᾶς ὧν κεκτήμεθα
ὡς πάντων δεσπότης.

All the earth we ruled, all booty we have;
But you as a great sovereign
coming upon them, *do reign*, leading us away
who are completely the property of the master

———, *Hymn 22*, {ref: 17.8}

Text: Romanus, *Romanos le Mélode. Hymnes*, vol. 3, ed. J. Grosdidier de Matons (Paris: Cerf, 1965).

Translation: my own
Καὶ δυνάστης ὑπάρχω καὶ βούλομαι σῶσαι·
διὰ τοῦτο προστάττω, αὐ[θεν]τῶ καὶ λέγω· "Θέλω, καθαρίθητι."
I am powerful and I will to save,
Therefore I command, I *rule* and I say, "I will, be clean"

17. Plainly the sense here is that of "relying on its own authority."
18. Lampe lists this under "presume on one's own authority."

[A.D. 600] Evagrius Scholasticus, *Letter to a Vigilant Tutor*, {ref: 86.2564 E}

Text: Evagrius Scholasticus, *Epistula ad Vigilium Papam*, MPG 86:2416ff.

Translation: my own

οὗτος γὰρ, ἵνα τὰ πολλὰ παραλίπωμεν, Εὐτυχῆ τὸν ὁμόδοξον αὐτῷ καθαιρεθέντα κανονικῶς παρὰ ἰδίου ἐπισκόπου, τοῦ ἐν ἁγίοις φαμὲν πατρὸς ἡμῶν καὶ ἀχιεπισκόπου Φλαβιανοῦ, αὐθεντήσας ἀκανονίστως εἰς κοινωνίαν ἀνεδέξατο, πρὶν ἢ συνεδρεῦσαι ἐν τῇ Ἐφεσίων μετὰ τῶν θεοφιλῶν ἐπισκόπων.

For this fellow took upon himself the communion, in order to neglect the many, being of the same mind as the Eutychians, having been legally deposed by his own bishop—the one we among the saints think of as our father, even the archbishop Flavian—*assuming his own jurisdiction* without regulation in order to receive communion before sitting in council in Ephesus with the God-loving bishops.

[d. A.D. 638] Sophronius Palestrinus, Greek translation of the Latin work, Hieronymus Stridonensis, *On Illustrious Men*.

Text: Hieronymus Stridonensis, *De viris illustribus*, in O. von Gebhart, *Texte und Untersuchungen zur Geschichte der Altchrislichen Literatur (Leipzig)*, 14[1b] (1896), as quoted by G. W. H. Lampe, *Patristic Greek Lexicon* (Oxford: Clarendon, 1961), 262.

Translation: my own

Μάρκος . . . βραχὺ συνέταξεν εὐαγγέλιον, ὧπερ ἐντυχὼν Πέτρος ἐδοκίμασε καὶ τῇ ἐκκλησίᾳ ἀναγνωσθησόμενον αὐθεντήσας ἐξέδωκε.

Mark . . . briefly composed a gospel, which thing Peter, approved, and *granting authorization*, he published what will be read by the church.

[A.D. 690] Joannes Malalas, *Chronicles*, {ref: 257.15}

Text: Joannes Malalae, *Chronographia* (Bonnae: Weberi, 1831).

Translation: Elizabeth Jeffreys, Michael Jeffreys, and Roger Scott, *The Chronicle of John Malalas: A Translation* (Melbourne: Australian Association for Byzantine Studies, 1986), 136.

Ἔπεμψε δὲ κατὰ τῆς Ἰουδαίας καὶ τῆς Ἱερουσαλὴμ ὁ αὐτὸς βασιλεὺς νέρων, καὶ πᾶσι κακῶς ἐχρήσατο, πολλοὺς φονεύσας στρατιωτικῇ συμβολῇ, ὅτι τυραννίδι φερόμενοι ἐξεφώνησαν ὑβριστικὰς φωνὰς κατὰ τοῦ Νέρωνος, διότι ἀπεκεφάλισε τὸν Πιλᾶτον ὡς εἰς ἐκδίκησιν Χριστοῦ· καὶ ἦλθεν εἰς αὐτὸν οὐ μὴν ἀλλὰ ὅτι καὶ αὐθεντήσαντες τὸν ἡγεμόνα ἐσταύρωσιν τὸν Χριστόν· καὶ διὰ τοῦτο ἠγανάκτει κατ' αὐτῶν ὡς τυράννων.

The emperor Nero sent an expedition against Judea and Jerusalem and treated all the inhabitants badly, killing many in a pitched battle, since they had behaved rebelliously and had shouted insults against Nero, because he had beheaded Pilate to avenge Christ. Pilate had come before Nero for no other reason than that they had *put pressure on*[19] their governor when they had crucified Christ. So Nero was angry with them because they were rebels.

19. Sophocles lists this under the heading "to compel." Here, as in BGU 1208, the idea of "to compel/influence" is in view.

————, *Chronicles*, {ref: 291.12}

Text: *Chronographia*.
Translation: Jeffreys, *Malalas*, 155.

Ἐπὶ δὲ τῆς αὐτοῦ βασιλείας ἐτυράννησεν Ἀλβῖνος ὁ συγκλητικός· ὅντινα ὁ στρατός, ὡς πολεμεῖ τοῖς Γήπεδι πεμφθεὶς παρὰ τοῦ πρὸ αὐτοῦ βασιλέως Διδίου, ἀνηγόρευσε βασιλέα αὐθεντήσας τὴν σύγκλητον. καὶ κατεδίωξεν αὐτὸν ὁ Σέβηρος ἐν τῇ Θρᾴκῃ, καὶ παραλαβὼν αὐτὸν ἐφόνευσεν.

During his reign the senator Albinos rebelled. The army, which had been sent by the previous emperor Didius to fight against the Gepids, proclaimed Albinus emperor, *overruling* the senate. Severus pursued him into Thrace, captured him, and put him to death.

————, *Chronicles*, {ref: 341.15}

Text: *Chronographia*.
Translation: Jeffreys, *Malalas*, 185.

Μετὰ δὲ τὴν βασιλείαν Βαλεντινιανοῦ τοῦ μεγάλου τοῦ ἀποτόμου ἐποίησεν ὁ στρατὸς βασιλέα αὐθεντήσας τὴν σύγκλητον Εὐγένιον ὀνόματι· καὶ ἐβασίλευσεν ἡμέρας εἴκοσι δύο καὶ ἐσφάγη εὐθέως.

After the reign of Valentinian the Great, the Ruthless, the army made a man named Eugenios emperor, *flouting the authority* of the senate. He reigned twenty-two days and was immediately assassinated.

————, *Chronicles*, {ref: 359.13}

Text: *Chronographia*.
Translation: Jeffreys, *Malalas*, 196.

Κατ᾽ ἐκαῖνον δὲ τὸν καιρὸν παρρησίαν λαβόντες ὑπὸ τοῦ ἐπισκόπου οἱ Ἀλεξανδρεῖς ἔκαυσαν φρυγάνοις αὐθεντήσαντες Ὑπατίαν τὴν περιβόητον φιλόσοφον. περὶ ἧς μεγάλα ἐφέρετο· ἦν δὲ παλαιὰ γυνή.

At that time the Alexandrians, given free rein by their bishop, [*exercising their own authority*[20]] seized and burnt on a pyre of brushwood Hypatia the famous philosopher, who had a great reputation and who was an old woman.

————, *Chronicles*, {ref: 416.14}

Text: *Chronographia*.
Translation: Jeffreys, *Malalas*, 235–36.

ὅστις προεβλήθη ἐπὶ τῆς πρώτης ἰνδικτιῶνος, καὶ κατεδυνάστευσε τῆς δημοκρατίας τῶν Βυζαντίων, τιμωρησάμενος πολλοὺς τῶν ἀτάκτων κατὰ κέλευσιν τοῦ βασιλέως Ἰουστίνου. ἐν οἷς συνελάβετο Θεοδόσιόν τινα τὸν ἐπικλὴν Ζτικκάν, ὅστις ἐν πολλῇ εὐπορίᾳ ὑπῆρχε, καὶ τῇ ἀξίᾳ ὢν ἰλλούστριος, καὶ τοῦτον αὐθεντήσας ανεῖλε, μὴ ἀναγαγὼν τῷ βασιλεῖ. καὶ ἀγανακτηθεὶς ὑπὸ τοῦ βασιλέως ἐπαύθη τῆς ἀρχῆς καὶ ἀπεζώσθη τῆς ἀξίας, κελευσθεὶς ἐξελθεῖν ἐπὶ τὴν ἀνατολήν.

---

20. The translators evidently did not find it necessary to translate the participle here. But it seems that αὐθεντήσαντες refers to an action by the Alexandrians distinct from λαβόντες παρρησίαν. One could wish for more context here to decide how Malalas viewed their action. Unfortunately there is none.

He [Theodotos, a city prefect] was appointed during the first indication and restored order over the rioting among the Byzantines by punishing many of the rioters at the emperor Justin's command. Among these he arrested a certain Theodosios, nicknamed Ztikkas, who was very wealthy and held the rank of illustris. Theodotos, *on his own authority*, put him to death without reporting this to the emperor. This met with the emperor's anger and he was dismissed from office, deprived of his rank and ordered into exile in the East.

————, *Chronicles*, {ref: 462.12}

Text: *Chronographia*.
Translation: Jeffreys, *Malalas*, 270.
Ὁ δὲ μάγιστρος Ῥωμαίων καταλαμβὼν τὴν Ἱεράπολιν, καὶ μαθὼν ὅτι εἰς τὰ Ῥωμαϊκὰ ἐσκήνωσαν οἱ Πέρσαι, ἐξελθὼν πρὸς Βελισάριον πλησίον ὄντα τῶν Περσῶν μετὰ Στεφάνου καὶ Ἄψκαλ ἐξάρχων καὶ Σίμμα τοῦ δουκὸς μετὰ χιλιάδων τεσσάρων, ἐπὶ Βαρβαισισσον τὴν πόλιν· καὶ ἀγανακτήσαντος Βελισαρίου κατὰ Σουνίκα, διότι αὐθεντήσας ἐπῆλθε τῷ Περσικῷ στρατῷ, καὶ φθάσαντος τοῦ μαγίστου ἐποίησεν αὐτοὺς γενέσθαι φίλους, προτρεψάμενος ὁρμῆσαι κατὰ Περσῶν.

The Roman magister[21] came to Hierapolis, and learnt that the Persians had encamped on Roman territory. He went off to Belisarios who was near the Persians at the city of Barbalissos, together with Stephanos and Apskal, the exarchs, and the dux Simmas, with 4,000 men. Belisarios was angry with Sounikas because he had attacked the Persian army *on his own initiative*. When the Roman magister arrived he reconciled them, urging them to advance on the Persians.

[7th cent. A.D.] Anonymous, *Chronicon Paschale*, {ref: 619.9}

Text: anonymous, *Chronicon Paschale*, ed. Dindorf (Bonnae: Weberi, 1832).
Translation: anonymous, *Chronicon Paschale*, ed. Michael and Mary White (Liverpool: Liverpool University Press, 1989), 110.
Ἰνδ. ζ΄. β΄. ὑπ. Δεκίου μόνου.
Τούτῳ τῷ ἔτει ὁ Ἰουστινιανὸς κῶδιξ ἀνεπληρώθη καὶ ἐκελεύσθη αὐθεντεῖσθαι ἀπὸ τῆς πρὸ ις΄ καλανδῶν ἀπριλίων τῆς ἐνεστώσης ζ΄ ἐπινεμή
Τούτῳ τῷ ἔτει κατὰ Θεοῦ φιλανθρωπίαν γέγονε τὸ μέγα θανατικόν.
Indication 7, year 2, sole consulship of Decius.
In this year the Justinianic Codex was completed and it was ordered that it *be authoritative* from the 16th day before Kalends of April [17 March] of the current tax period 7.
In this year in accordance with God's clemency there occurred the Great Death.

————, *Chronicon Paschale*, {ref: 634.1}

Text: anonymous, *Chronicon Paschale*, ed. Dindorf (Bonnae: Weberi, 1832).
Translation: anonymous, *Chronicon Paschale*, ed. Michael and Mary White (Liverpool: Liverpool University Press, 1989), 110.

---

21. Minister in charge of miscellaneous administrative duties in the imperial household and especially foreign affairs (cf. Jeffreys, *Malalas*, 316).

καὶ ἐκελεύσθη τῆς προτέρας ἐκδόσεως σχολαζούσης αὐθεντεῖσθαι ἀπὸ τῆς πρὸ δ καλανδῶν ἰανουρίων ἰνδικτιῶνος ιγ.

And it was ordered that, the previous edition being made void, it should *be valid* from the 4th day before Kalends of January [29 Dec], in indication 13.

[A.D. 789] Second Council of Nicea {ref: 721 D}

Text: Nicolao (Sebastian) Coleti, ed., *Sacrosancta Concilia ad Regium Additionem exacta*, vol. 8 (Venice, 1728–33).[22]

Translation: *The Seventh General Council, The Second Council of Nicaea*, ed. John Mendham (London: Painter, undated).

ὅμως καὶ αὖθις ἀναγνωθήτω ἡ αὐτὴ πρὸς Ρουφινιανὸν ἐπιστολὴ τοῦ αὐτοῦ πατρός. Ἀναγινωσκομένου δὲ τοῦ χωρίου τοῦ λέγοντος. ὥστε τοῖς καταπεπτωκόσι καὶ προϊσταμένοις τῆς ἀσεβείς συγγινώσκειν μὲν μετανοῦσι, μὴ διδόναι δὲ αὐτοῖς τόπον κλήρου· τοῖς δὲ μὴ αὐθεντοῦσι μὲν τῆς ἀσεβείας, ὑποσυρεῖσι δὲ δι᾽ ἀνάγκην καὶ βίαν, ἔδοξε δίδοσθαι μὲν συγγνώμην,[23] ἔχειν δὲ καὶ τὸν τόπον τοῦ κλήρου. μάλιστα ὅτι ἀπολογίαν πιθανήν ἐκομίσαντο, καὶ ἔδοξε τοῦτο πως οἰκονομικῶς γεγενῆσθαι·.... Ὁ μὲν πατὴρ τοὺς μὴ αὐθεντήσαντας τῆς αἰέσεως, ἀλλ᾽ ὑποσυρέντας καὶ βίαν παθόντας ἀποδέχεται εἰς σύνη. μόνας δὲ τοὺς προϊσταμένους ἢ γεγυνήτορας τοῦ αἱρέσεως, αὐτὸς εἰς ἱερωσύνη οὐ προσδέξατο.[24]

"However, let this same Epistle to Rufinius be read once more." And the following passage was read which declares:—"That they who had so fallen as to become very leaders of impiety should, indeed, be pardoned on repentance, but should no longer have any place among the clergy; but that, in respect of those who had not *taken any leading part*, but had been constrained by force or violence, that they should not only meet with pardon, but should retain their place among the clergy, especially if they had a fair excuse to make for themselves. . . ."

"For the Father does admit to the Priesthood those who, not having *originated heresy*, were seduced or violently drawn aside; while he excludes those only who were the actual originators or violent promoters of the same."

[A.D. 817] Theophanes, *The Chronicle*, {ref: 372.13}

Text: Theophanes, *Chronicon* (Bonnae: Weberi, 1839).

Translation: my own

Τῷ δ᾽ αὐτῷ ἔτει οἱ Θεοδοσιανοὶ καὶ Γαϊανῖται ἐν Ἀλεξανδρείᾳ κτίζειν ἤρξαντο συνακτήρια, καὶ αὐθεντήσαντες οἱ Γαϊανῖται ἐπίσκοπον ἐν αὐτοῖς ἐχειροτόνησαν Ἐλπίδον ἀρχιδιάκονον αὐτῶν, ὃν ὁ βασιλεὺς δεδεμένον ἐλθεῖν προσέταξεν. ἐρχόμενος δὲ κατὰ τὸν Σίγριν ἀπέθανεν. Θεοδοδιανοὶ δὲ Δωρόθεον κρυπτῶς ἐν νυκτὶ ἐπίσκοπον ἑαυτοῖς ἐχειροτόνησαν.

22. Note that this is a near quotation of Athanasius's *Letter to Rufinius*.

23. The Latin of Coleti's diglot edition renders this phrase: "His autem qui auctores non fuerunt impietatis, fed per necessitatem & vim abstrahunter, placuit ut venia detur—" ("For those, however, who were not the authors of the impiety, but are drawn through compulsion and force, it seemed right that pardon be given").

24. Note that αὐθεντέω is used to parallel προϊστμμ which BAGD defines as "be at the head of, rule, direct." Mendham renders προϊστμμ variously in the passage as "be a ringleader, be the very leader, originate."

In that same year the Theodosians and the Gaianitians in Alexandria began to create an assembly, and the Gaianitians *exercising their own authority* elected Elpidios, their archdeacon, as bishop for them. The king had arranged for the replacement to come about; but coming to Sigrin he died. And the Theodosians elected Dorotheon as bishop for themselves secretly by night.

[9th cent. A.D.] Photius, *Library,* {ref: 80.59a.11}

Text: *Photius, Bibliothèque,* ed. R. Henry (Paris: Les Belles Lettres), as cited by T. L. G.

Translation: my own [Note: Photius has reproduced Olympiodorus's account (above) exactly]

Ἄρχεται δὲ ἡ δευτέρα ὧδε· ὅτι Ἰοβῖνος παρὰ γνώμην Ἀδαούλφου τὸν ἴδιον ἀδελφὸν Σεβαστιανὸν βασιλέα χειροτονήσας, εἰς ἔχθραν Ἀδούλφῳ κατέστη. καὶ πέμπει Ἀδάουλφος πρὸς Ὀνώριον πρέσβεις, ὑποσχόμενος τάς τε τῶν τυράννων κεφαλὰς καὶ εἰρήνην ἄγειν. Ὧν ὑποστρεψάντων, καὶ ὅρκων μεσιτευσάντων, Σεβαστιανοῦ μὲν πέμπεται τῷ βασιλεῖ ἡ κεφαλή· Ἰοβῖνος δὲ ὑπὸ Ἀδαούλφου πολιορκούμενος, ἑαυτὸν ἐκδίδωσι, καὶ πέμπεται κἀκεῖνος τῷ βασιλεῖ, ὃν αὐθεντήσας Δάρδανος ὁ ἔπαρχος ἀναιρεῖ.

The second part begins here: For Jobinos, making his own brother Sebastian king, contrary to the wishes of Adaulfo, made Adaulfo his enemy. And Adaulfo sent ambassadors to Honorios, and he promised to bring peace—and the heads of the tyrants. They returned and promised with oaths, and the head of Sebastian was sent to the king. But being besieged by Adaulfo, Jobinos surrendered himself, and he was sent to the king. Dardanos, the governor, *exercising his own authority,* killed him.

——, *Photius,* {ref: 80.62b.31}

Text: *Photius, Bibliothèque,* ed. R. Henry (Paris: Les Belles Lettres), as cited by T. L. G.

Translation: my own

Ὅτι Ὀνώριος ὑδερικῷ νοσήματι ἁλοὺς πρὸ ἓξ καλανδρῶν Σεπτεμβρίων τελευτᾷ· καὶ πέμπονται γράμματα πρὸς τὴν ἀνατολὴν τὸν βασιλέως θάνατον μηνύοντα. Ἐν ᾧ δὲ ταῦτα ἐπέμποντο, Ἰωάννης τις αὐθεντήσας τυραννεῖ. Ἐφ᾽ οὗ καὶ τῆς ἀναρρήσεως γινομένης ἐρρήθη ὥσπερ ἀπό τινος προρρήσεως προαχθέν·

For Honorios, stricken by a dropsy-like disease, died six days before the kalends of September [= 27 August]. And letters were sent to the East announcing the death of the king. Meanwhile a certain Joannes *took charge* and ruled tyrannically. Upon him the public proclamation was spoken just as a certain prediction had indicated.

——, *Photius,* {ref: 238.317b.7}

Text: *Photius, Bibliothèque,* ed. R. Henry (Paris: Les Belles Lettres), as cited by T. L. G.

Translation: my own [cpr. Josephus *Antiquities* 20.199–201]

Ὅτι Ἄνανος ὁ Ἀνάνου παῖς τὴν ἀρχιερωσύνην παραλαβών, ἀφαιρεθέντος αὐτὴν Ἰωσήπου, θρασὺς ἦν καὶ τολμητὴς διαφερόντως· αἵρεσιν γὰρ τὴν Σαδδουκαίων μετήει· οὗτοι γὰρ ὠμοί τε περὶ τὰς κρίσεις καὶ πρὸς πᾶσαν αὐθάδειαν ἕτοιμοι. Οὗτος οὖν ὁ ῎Ανανος, Φήστου μὲν ἐν Ἰουδαίᾳ τελευτήσαντος, Ἀλβίνου δὲ οὔπω καταλαβόντος, αὐθεντήσας καθίζει συνέδριον, καὶ Ἰάκωβον τὸν ἀδελφὸν τοῦ Κυρίου σὺν ἑτέροις, παρανομίαν αἰτιασάμενος λίθοις, ἀναιρεθῆναι παρασκευάζει.

For Ananus, son of Ananus, receiving the High Priesthood—Joseph [Joseph Cabi] being deprived of it—was rash and even more reckless. He followed the party of the Sadducees. Now these were more headstrong in judgment than all others. So this Ananus, Festus having completed his term in Judea and Albinus not yet having assumed his, *exercised his own authority* and convened the Sanhedrin. And James, the Lord's brother, along with others, he charged illegally, procuring their execution by stoning.

[10th cent. A.D.][25] "Scholia Vetera on Aeschylus's *Eumenides*, {ref: line 42a}

Text: O. L. Smith, ed., *Scholia Graeca In Aeschylum Quae Exstant Omnia*, vol. 1 (Leipzig: Tübner, 1976), 45. [For text of *Eumenides* itself, see Aeschylus, *Aeschylus*, ed. Herbert W. Smyth, Loeb Classical Library (Cambridge, Mass.: Harvard University Press, 1963), 275.]

Translation: of Scholia: my own; of Aeschylus: H. W. Smyth

[*Eumenides* lines 39–45:] ἐγὼ μὲν ἕρπω πρὸς πολυστεφῆ μυχόν· ὁρῶ δ' ἐπ' ὀμφαλῷ μὲν ἄνδρα θεομυσῆ ἕδραν ἔχοντα προστρόπαιον, αἵματι στάζοντα χεῖρας καὶ νεοσπαδὲς ξίφος ἔχοντ' ἐλαίας θ' ὑψιγέννητον κλάδον, λήνει μεγίστῳ σωφρόνως ἐστεμμένον, ἀργῆτι μαλλῷ· τῇδε γὰρ τρανῶς ἐρῶ.

[The following scholia is found at this point:] στάζοντα) ἐμφαντικῶς ⟨διὰ⟩ τούτου ⟨τὸν⟩ νεωστὶ ηὐθεντηκότα παρίστησιν.

TEXT: I was on my way to the inner shrine, enriched with many a wreath, when, on the centrestone, I beheld a man defiled before Heaven occupying the seat of the supplicants. His hands were dripping gore; he held a sword just drawn and a lofty olive branch reverently crowned with a tuft of wool exceeding large—white was the fleece; for as to this I can speak clearly.

SCHOLIA: Dripping} indicating clearly a recent *murder* occurs.

[10th cent. A.D.] Scholia on Homer, *Scholia on the Iliad*, {ref: Book 10, entry 694}

Text: *Scholia Graeca in Homeri Iliadem*, vol. 2, ed. H. Erbse (Berlin: de Gruyter, 1971) [For text of *The Iliad* itself, see Homer, *The Iliad*, ed. A. T. Murray, Loeb Classical Library (Cambridge, Mass.: Harvard University Press, 1924), 432.]

Translation: of Scholia: my own; of Homer: A. T. Murray

[*The Iliad*, IX, line 694] μάλα γὰρ κρατερῶς ἀγόρευσε.

[The following scholia is found at this point:] ὅτι ἐξ ἄλλων τόπων ἐστὶν ὁ στίχος· νῦν γὰρ οὐκ ἁρμόζει· τότε γὰρ εἴωθεν ἐπιφωνεῖσθαι, ὅταν ὁ αὐθεντῶν τοῦ λόγου καταπληκτικά τινα προενέγκηται.

---

25. This scholion is repeated with slight variations in several MSS from 10th–16th cents. A.D. However, the oldest, given here, is from the 10th cent. A.D. Smith indicates that all extant scholia vetera on Aeschylus originate from a pre-10th-cent. A.D. manuscript no longer extant. Although it is known that many of the scholia vetera date back into the Hellenistic period, the 10th cent. A.D. is the earliest sure dating possible for this scholion.

TEXT: For full masterfully did he address their gathering.

SCHOLIA: This verse is from another place. For now it does not fit properly. For then it was wont to be mentioned when *the one originating* the writing had set forth something astounding.[26]

[10th cent. A.D.] Emperor Constantine VII Porphyrogenitus, *About Strategy*, {ref: 159.33}

Text: Constantinus VII Porphyrogenitus, *De Insidiis*, ed. C. de Boor (Berlin: Weidmann, 1905), 1–228

Translation: my own

῞Οτι Μάριον τὸν βασιλέα ἡ γυνὴ αὐτοῦ κοιμώμενον ἀπέσφαξεν, ὅς οὐκ ἀνηγορεύθη βασιλεὺς ὑπὸ τῆς συγκλήτου, διότι ὁ στρατὸς αὐτὸν ἐποίησε βασιλέα αὐθεντήσας τὴν σύγκλητον.

For his wife slayed the deceased King Marion, who was not proclaimed king publicly by the assembly because the army, *controlling the assembly*, made him king.

―――, *About Virtues and Vices*, {ref: 1.160.18}

Text: Constantinius VII Porphyrogenitus, *De virtutibus et vitiis*, vol. 2, pt. 1, ed. T. Büttner-Wobst and A. G. Roos (Berlin: Weidmann, 1906), 1–361.

Translation: my own

῞Οτι Δέκιος ὁ βαιλεὺς ῾Ρωμαίων μισόχριστος ἦν· ἐν τοῖς χρόνοις γὰρ αὐτοῦ διωγμὸς ἐγένετο Χριστιανῶν μέγας καὶ ἐξεφώνησεν αὐτοῦ ἄθεον τύπον, ὥστε τοὺς εὑρίσκοντας ὅπου δήποτε τοὺς λεγομένους Χριστιανοὺς καὶ αὐθεντοῦντας καὶ φονεύοντας αὐτοὺς καὶ τὰ αὐτῶν πάντα ἁρπάζοντας ἀκιδύνους εἶναι. Καὶ πολλοὶ Χριστιανοὶ ἐφονεύθησαν ὑπὸ τῶν κατὰ πόλιν ὄχλων ὧν ἔτυχε καὶ ἐπραιδεύθησαν.

For the Emperor Decius was a Christ-hating Roman. In his time there was a great persecution of the Christians. He set up his godless image so that the ones finding those called Christians *exercised their own jurisdiction*[27] and murdered them and seized all their goods with impunity. Also many Christians were murdered by the crowds of each city who happened upon them and hauled them before the praetors.

[10th cent. A.D.] The Suda Lexicon, {ref: A 4426}

Text: *Svidae Lexicon*, pt. 1, ed. A. Adler (Reprint: Stuttgart: Tübner, 1971), 412.

Translation: my own

Αὐθέντης· ὁ αὐτόχειρ, ἢ ὁ αὐτὸν ἀναιρῶν. διὸ παρ᾽ Ἰσοκράτει αὐθέντης. Λυσίας ἰδίως αὐτὸ ἔταξεν ἐπὶ τῶν λ· καίτοι δι᾽ ἑτέρων εἰργάζοντο τοὺς φόνους. ὁ γὰρ αὐθέντης ἀεὶ τὸν αὐτόχειρα σημαίνει. καὶ Αὐθεντήσαντα, κύριον γενόμενον. μὴ ὀφείλειν αὐτὸν αὐθεντήσαντα τοὺς ὑπὸ ζώνην συνέχειν. ὅτι Μιθριδάτης διετάξατο τοὺς ῾Ρωμαίους ἀναιρεῖν καὶ ἔπεμψε γράμματα εἰς τὰς πόλεις, τὸ βασιλικὸν σφράγισμα ἔχοντα, μιᾷ τε ἡμέρᾳ τάξας ἀναγνῶναι καὶ παραχρῆμα τὰ

---

26. Murray says in a note, "Line 694 was rejected by Zenodotus, Aristophanes, and Aristarchus."

27. Or perhaps, "took justice into their own hands and. . . ."

γεγραμμμένα πρᾶξαι, ὅπως μὴ προμαθόντες τινὲς φυλάξωνται. ἀποκτεῖναι γὰρ αὐτοῖς ἐκέλυσε πάνθ' ὅντινα 'Ρωμαίους ἀναιρεῖν εὕρωσι· καὶ ἆθλα οὐ μόνον τοῖς αὐτοέντοις σφῶν ἐσομένοις, ἀλλὰ καὶ τοῖς δήμοις, παρ' οἷς ἂν ἀποθάνωσι, πρὸς τὸ πλῆθος τῶν τελευτησάντων ἔθηκε· τιμωρίαν τε τοῖς φεισομένοις τινὸς αὐτῶν μεγάλην ὥρισε.

Αὐθέντης: The one who does a thing with his own hand or the one executing a thing. Therefore with Isocrates, "αὐθέντης." Lysias himself listed it for "The 30." And indeed in others it serves for "τοὺς φόνους" [the murderers]. For "ὁ αὐθέντης" indicates "ὁ αὐτόχειρ" and "αὐθεντήσαντα" equals "κύριος γενό-μενος" [*be lord over*]. Αὐθεντήσαντα itself does not require that one wear the sword himself. For Mithridates [c. 87 B.C] set out in battle order to conquer the Romans. He sent a letter having the royal seal to the cities. In one day he arranged it and immediately what was written was carried out, so that some would not find out before hand and be on guard. For he ordered them to kill whatever Roman they should find. And he carried out his strike not only by means of the murderous slaying of the soldiers dressed for battle, but even the people they killed along with them, so that multitudes were put to death. And he assigned great punishments for some of those who spared others.

[12th cent. A.D.] Michael Glycas, *Annals*, {ref: 270.10}

Text: Michael Glycas, *Michaelis Glycae Annales*, ed. I. Bekker (Bonn, 1836), 270.

Translation: my own

παρ' 'Αγιλαίοις αἱ γυναῖκες αὐθεντοῦσιν τῶν ἀδρῶν καὶ πορνεύουσιν ὡς βούλονται, μὴ ζηλοτυπούμεναι παρὰ τῶν ἀνδρῶν αὐτῶν, γεωργίαν δὲ καὶ οἰκοδομίαν καὶ πάντα τὰ ἀνδρῶα πράττουσιν.

The women from the Agilians *exercise authority over*[28] the men and they do evil as they desire, not being jealous of men, but achieving in agriculture, and in construction, and in all manly things.

[12th–14th cent. A.D.] Thomas Magister, *Attic Sayings* {ref: 18.9}

Text: Thomas Magister, *Ecloga vocum Atticarum*, ed. F. Ritschel (Halle, 1832; reprint: Hildesheim/New York: Georg Olm, 1970).

Translation: my own

'Αυτοδικεῖν [λέγε], οὐκ αὐθεντεῖν· κοινότερον γάρ.

Say autodikein [= "to be with independent jurisdiction"[29]] not authentein, for it is more vulgar.

[Ms from 15th cent. A.D.] Ptolemy, *Codicum Parisinorum: Catalogus Codicum Astrologorum Graecorum*, {ref: 1.777.7}

Text: Ptolemy, *Codicum Parisinorum: Catalogus Codicum Astrologorum Graecorum*, vol. 7-1, ed. F. Cumont (Brussels, 1929), 177.

---

28. The Latin of this diglot edition of the text renders this phrase "apud Agilaeos feminae sua viros in potestate habent." G. W. Knight, 149, translates with the assistance of S. Kistemaker, "have in their own power (authority)."

29. LSJ, 280, also give "to have one's own courts."

Translation: John R. Werner, Wycliffe Bible Translators, International Linguistic Center, Dallas, Tex., letter (Apr. 8, 1980) as quoted by George W. Knight III, "ΑΥΘΕΝΤΕΩ in Reference to Women in 1 Timothy 2.12," *NTS* 30 (1984): 143–57.

ἐὰν δὲ ἐν ὁρίοις Κρόνου, ἀπὸ κλοπῆς ἢ παρύγρων φροντιστήν, ἀγαθοποιῶν δὲ τετραγωνιζόντων, τὸν πάντων αὐθεντοῦντα ἐν τῇ τέχνῃ καὶ μηδὲν κτώμενον.

But if [Mercury is] in the regions of Saturn, [that signifies that the newborn baby will be] one who lives by his wits with theft or waterside activities. But if the Beneficent Ones are in the quartile aspect, [that signifies that the newborn will be] the one who *exercises authority over* all [others who are in the trade and pays no consequences (or, acquires nothing)].

Bibliography

Books

Albertz, Martin. *Die Botschaft des Neuen Testaments*. Zollikon-Zürich: Evangelischer Verlag, 1954.

Alföldy, Géza. *The Social History of Rome*. London: Croom Helm, 1985.

Aman, Kenneth, ed. *Border Regions of Faith*. Maryknoll, N.Y.: Orbis, 1987.

Ameling, Walter, ed. *Die Inschriften von Prusias ad Hypium*. Bonn: Rudolf Habelt, 1985.

Arendell, Terry. *Mothers and Divorce*. Berkeley: University of California Press, 1986.

Arnold, Clinton E. *Ephesians: Power and Magic. The Concept of Power in Ephesians in Light of Its Historical Setting*. SNTSMS 63. Cambridge: Cambridge University Press, 1989.

Arnold, Franz X. *Woman and Man: Their Nature and Mission*. Trans. R. Brennan. New York: Herder & Herder, 1963.

Augustine. *On Christian Doctrine*. Trans. D. W. Robertson Jr. Indianapolis: Bobbs-Merrill, 1983.

Baird, William. *History of New Testament Research*. Vol. 1. Minneapolis: Fortress, 1992.

Balch, David L. *Let Wives Be Submissive: The Domestic Code in 1 Peter*. Society of Biblical Literature Monograph Series 26. Atlanta, Ga.: Scholars Press, 1981.

Bammer, Anton. *Führer durch das archäologische Museum in Selçuk-Ephesos*. Vienna: ÖAI, 1974.

———. *Das Heiligtum der Artemis von Ephesos*. Graz, Austria: Akademische Druck, 1984.

Barrett, C. K. *The Pastoral Epistles*. Oxford: Clarendon, 1963.

Barth, Karl. *Die kirchliche Dogmatik*. 4th ed. Zürich: Evy-Verlag, 1970.

Barthes, Roland. *Elements of Semiology*. Trans. A. Lavers and C. Smith. New York: Hill & Wang, 1968.

Bellah, Robert N., et al. *Habits of the Heart*. San Francisco: Harper & Row, 1986.

Berdyaev, Nicolai. *Slavery and Freedom*. Trans. R. M. French. New York: Charles Scribner's Sons, 1944.

Bernstein, Richard. *Beyond Objectivism and Relativism*. Philadelphia: University of Pennsylvania Press, 1983.

Betz, Hans Dieter. *Galatians: A Commentary on Paul's Letter to the Churches in Galatia*. Hermeneia/Philadelphia: Fortress, 1979.

Bilezikian, Gilbert. *Beyond Sex Roles. A Guide for the Study of Female Roles in the Bible*. Grand Rapids: Baker, 1985. 2d ed.: 1989.

Black, David Alan, and David S. Dockery, eds. *New Testament Criticism and Interpretation*. Grand Rapids: Zondervan, 1991.

Boardman, J., ed. *The Oxford History of Classical Art*. Oxford: Oxford University Press, 1993.

Bockmühl, Klaus. *The Challenge of Marxism*. Colorado Springs: Helmers & Howard, 1986.

Boomsma, Clarence. *Male and Female, One in Christ: New Testament Teaching on Women in Office*. Grand Rapids: Baker, 1993.

Booth, Catherine. *Female Ministry or Woman's Right to Preach the Gospel*. New York: The Salvation Army, 1959; reprinted 1975.

Bowersock, G. W. *Augustus and the Greek World*. Oxford: Clarendon, 1965.

―――. *Greek Sophists in the Roman Empire*. Oxford: Clarendon, 1969.

Brewer, David I. *Techniques and Assumptions in Jewish Exegesis before 70 CE*. Tübingen: J. C. B. Mohr (Paul Siebeck), 1992.

Bristow, John Temple. *What Paul Really Said about Women. An Apostle's Liberating Views on Equality in Marriage, Leadership, and Love*. San Francisco: HarperCollins, 1991.

Brox, Norbert. *Die Pastoralbriefe*. 4th ed. RNT. Regensburg: F. Pustet, 1969.

Bruce, F. F. *Paul: Apostle of the Heart Set Free*. Grand Rapids: Eerdmans, 1977.

Bruce, M., and Duffield, G. E. *Why Not? Priesthood and Ministry of Women: A Theological Study*. Ed. M. Bruce and G. E. Duffield; rev. and augmented ed. prepared by R. T. Beckwith. Nashville: Abingdon, 1976.

Brueggemann, Walter. *Texts under Negotiation*. Minneapolis: Fortress, 1993.

Burkert, Walter. *Greek Religion*. Cambridge, Mass.: Harvard University Press, 1985.

Burnham, Frederic B., ed. *Postmodern Theology*. San Francisco: Harper & Row, 1989.

Bushnell, Katherine C. *God's Word to Women: One Hundred Bible Studies on the Place of Women in the Divine Economy*. North Collins, N.Y.: Ray B. Munson, 1919; reprinted 1976.

Bynum, Caroline. *Jesus as Mother: Studies in the Spirituality of the High Middle Ages*. Berkeley: University of California Press, 1982.

Calvin, John. *Commentary on the Epistles of Paul the Apostle to the Corinthians*. Trans. John Pringle. Edinburgh: Calvin Translation Society, 1848.

―――. *Commentary on the First Epistle to Timothy*. Trans. John Pringle. Edinburgh: Calvin Translation Society, 1848.

Carnap, Rudolf. *The Logical Syntax of Language*. London: Kegan, 1937.

Carson, D. A., Douglas J. Moo, and Leon Morris. *An Introduction to the New Testament*. Grand Rapids: Zondervan, 1992.

Cavanaugh, John. *Following Christ in a Consumer Society*. Maryknoll, N.Y.: Orbis, 1989.

Cherlin, Andrew J. *Marriage, Divorce, Remarriage*. Rev. ed. Cambridge, Mass.: Harvard University Press, 1992.

Clapp, Rodney. *Families at the Crossroads*. Downers Grove: InterVarsity, 1993.

Clark, Elizabeth, and Herbert Richardson, eds. *Women and Religion: A Feminine Sourcebook of Christian Thought*. New York: Harper & Row, 1977.

Clark, Stephen B. *Man and Woman in Christ: An Examination of the Roles of Men and Women in Light of Scripture and the Social Sciences*. Ann Arbor, Mich.: Servant, 1980.

Clouse, Bonnidell, and Robert G., eds. *Women in Ministry: Four Views*. Downers Grove: InterVarsity, 1989.

Cobern, Camden M. *New Archeological Discoveries*. 2d ed. New York: Funk & Wagnalls, 1917.

Contarella, Eva. *Pandora's Daughters*. Baltimore: Johns Hopkins University Press, 1987.

Cooper, John W. *A Cause for Division? Women in Office and the Unity of the Church*. Grand Rapids: Calvin Theological Seminary, 1991.

Daniélou, Jean. *The Ministry of Women in the Early Church*. Trans. Glen Symon. New York: Faith Press, 1961.

Dayton, Donald. *Discovering an Evangelical Heritage*. Peabody, Mass.: Hendrickson, 1976.

Deininger, Jürgen. *Die Provinziallandtage der römischen Kaiserzeit*. Munich: C. H. Beck, 1965.

De Yong, P., and D. R. Wilson. *Husband and Wife: The Sexes in Scripture and Society*. Grand Rapids: Zondervan, 1979.

Dewey, John. *Liberalism and Social Action*. New York: Capricorn, 1935.

Dibelius, Martin, and Hans Conzelmann. *The Pastoral Epistles*. Hermeneia. Trans. Philip Buttolph and Adela Yarbro. Philadelphia: Fortress, 1972.

Dill, Samuel. *Roman Society from Nero to Marcus Aurelius*. London: Macmillan, 1905.

Donfried, Karl P., and I. Howard Marshall, eds. *The Theology of the Shorter Pauline Epistles*. Cambridge: Cambridge University Press, 1993.

Eckenstein, Lina. *Women under Monasticism*. New York: Russell & Russell, 1896.

Edwards, David L. with a response from John Stott. *Evangelical Essentials: A Liberal-Evangelical Dialogue*. Downers Grove: InterVarsity, 1988.

Elliger, W. *Ephesos: Geschichte einer antiken Weltstadt*. Stuttgart: Kohlhammer, 1985.

Elliot, Elisabeth. *Let Me Be a Woman*. London: Hodder & Stoughton, 1979.

Ellis, E. Earle. *Pauline Theology, Ministry and Society*. Grand Rapids: Eerdmans, 1989.

Erickson, Millard J. *Evangelical Interpretation: Perspectives on Hermeneutical Issues*. Grand Rapids: Baker, 1993.

Evans, Mary. *Woman in the Bible*. Downers Grove: InterVarsity, 1983.

Feder, T. *Great Treasures of Pompeii and Herculaneum*. New York: Abbeville, 1978.

Fee, Gordon D. *1 & 2 Timothy, Titus*. NIBC. Peabody, Mass.: Hendrickson, 1988.

———. *Gospel and Spirit*. Peabody, Mass.: Hendrickson, 1991.

Fee, Gordon D., and Douglas Stuart. *How to Read the Bible for All Its Worth*. Grand Rapids: Zondervan, 1982.

Ferguson, Everett. *Backgrounds of Early Christianity*. 2d ed. Grand Rapids: Eerdmans, 1993.

Fiorenza, Elisabeth Schüssler. *In Memory of Her: A Feminist Theological Reconstruction of Christian Origins*. New York: Crossroad, 1985.

Fleischer, Robert. *Artemis von Ephesos und verwandte Kultstatuen aus Anatolien und Syrien*. Leiden: E. J. Brill, 1973.

Foh, Susan T. *Women and the Word of God*. Grand Rapids: Baker, 1979.

Forward, Susan, and Juan Torres. *Men Who Hate Women and the Women Who Love Them*. New York: Bantam, 1986.

Franke, Peter Robert. *Kleinasien zur Römerzeit: Griechisches Leben im Spiegel der Münzen*. Munich: C. H. Beck, 1968.

Friesen, Steven J. *Twice Neokoros: Ephesus, Asia, and the Cult of the Flavian Imperial Family*. Leiden: E. J. Brill, 1993.

Funk, Robert, R. Hoover, and the Jesus Seminar. *The Five Gospels*. New York: Macmillan, 1993.

Gardner, Jane F. *Women in Roman Law and Society*. Bloomington: Indiana University Press, 1991.

Garfinkel, Irwin, and Sara McLanahan. *Single Mothers and Their Children*. Washington, D.C.: Urban Institute Press, 1986.

Gies, Frances and Joseph. *Women in the Middle Ages*. New York: Harper & Row, 1978.

Grant, Michael. *Greek and Latin Authors*. New York: Wilson, 1980.

———. *A Social History of Greece and Rome*. New York: Charles Scribner's Sons, 1992.

Grenz, Stanley J. *Revisioning Evangelical Theology: A Fresh Agenda for the 21st Century*. Downers Grove: InterVarsity, 1993.

Gritz, Sharon Hodgin. *Paul, Women Teachers, and the Mother Goddess at Ephesus: A Study of 1 Timothy 2:9–15 in Light of the Religious and Cultural Milieu of the First Century*. Lanham, Md.: University Press of America, 1991.

Groothuis, Rebecca. *Women Caught in the Conflict*. Grand Rapids: Baker, 1994.

Gryson, Roger. *The Ministry of Women in the Early Church*. Trans. Jean Laporte and Mary Louise Hall. Collegeville, Minn.: Liturgical Press, 1976.

Guthrie, Donald. *New Testament Introduction*. Rev. ed. Downers Grove: InterVarsity, 1990.

———. *The Pastoral Epistles*. TNTC. Grand Rapids: Eerdmans, 1957.

Guthrie, W. K. C. *The Greeks and Their Gods*. Boston: Beacon, 1950.

Hammond, N., and H. Scullard, eds. *The Oxford Classical Dictionary*. 2d ed. Oxford: Clarendon, 1970.

Hanson, A. T. *The Pastoral Epistles*. NCB. Grand Rapids: Eerdmans, 1982.

Harper, Michael. *Equal and Different: Male and Female in Church and Family*. London: Hodder & Stoughton, 1994.

Harris, James F. *Against Relativism: A Philosophical Defense of Method*. LaSalle, Ill.: Open Court, 1992.

Harris, William V. *Ancient Literacy*. Cambridge, Mass.: Harvard University Press, 1989.

Hasler, Victor. *Die Briefe an Timotheus und Titus*. Zürich: Theologischer Verlag, 1978.

Hauerwas, Stanley. *Unleashing the Scripture*. Nashville: Abingdon, 1993.

Hauke, Manfred. *Women in the Priesthood? A Systematic Analysis in Light of the Order of Creation and Redemption*. Trans. D. Kipp. San Francisco: Ignatius, 1988.

Hayter, Mary. *The New Eve in Christ: The Use and Abuse of the Bible in the Debate about Women in the Church*. Grand Rapids: Eerdmans, 1987.

Head, Barclay V. *Catalogue of the Greek Coins in the British Museum: Ionia*. Reprint edition: Bologna, 1964.

―――. *Historia Numorum: A Manual of Greek Numismatics*. Chicago: Argonaut, 1967 [1911].

Hicks, E. L., ed. *The Collection of Ancient Greek Inscriptions in the British Museum*. Part 3. Oxford: Clarendon, 1890.

Hill, David. *New Testament Prophecy*. Atlanta: John Knox, 1979.

Hölbl, Günther. *Zeugnisse ägyptischer Religionsvorstellungen für Ephesos*. Leiden: E. J. Brill, 1978.

Holtz, Gottfried. *Die Pastoralbriefe*. THKNT. Berlin: Evangelische Verlagsanstalt, 1972.

Horton, Robert F., ed. *The Pastoral Epistles: Timothy and Titus*. Edinburgh: T. C. & E. C. Jack, 1901.

Houlden, J. L. *The Pastoral Epistles: I and II Timothy, Titus*. TPINTC. Philadelphia: Trinity Press International, 1976.

Howe, E. Margaret. *Women and Church Leadership*. Grand Rapids: Zondervan, 1982.

Hull, Gretchen. *Equal to Serve: Women and Men in the Church and Home*. Old Tappan, N.J.: Fleming H. Revell, 1987.

Hunt, A. S., and C. C. Edgar. *Select Papyri*. LCL. 2 vols. Cambridge, Mass.: Harvard University Press and London: William Heinemann, 1932–34.

Huntemann, Georg. *The Other Bonhoeffer*. Trans. T. Huizinga. Grand Rapids: Baker, 1993.

Hurley, James B. *Man and Woman in Biblical Perspective*. Grand Rapids: Zondervan, 1981.

Inan, Jale, and Elisabeth Rosenbaum. *Roman and Early Byzantine Portrait Sculpture in Asia Minor*. London: British Academy, 1966.

Jeremias, Joachim. *Die Briefe an Timotheus und Titus*. NTD. Göttingen: Vandenhoeck & Ruprecht, 1968.

Jewett, Paul K. *Man as Male and Female*. Grand Rapids: Eerdmans, 1975.

Johnson, Luke T. *The Writings of the New Testament: An Interpretation*. Philadelphia: Fortress, 1986.

Johnson, Philip E. *Darwin on Trial*. Downers Grove: InterVarsity, 1991.

Jones, A. H. *Essenes: The Elect of Israel and the Priests of Artemis*. New York: University Press of America, 1985.

Jones, A. H. M. *The Greek City*. Oxford: Clarendon, 1940.

Kassian, Mary A. *Women, Creation and the Fall*. Westchester, Ill.: Crossway, 1990.

―――. *The Feminist Gospel: The Movement to Unite Feminism with the Church*. Wheaton, Ill.: Crossway, 1992.

Keener, Craig S. *Paul, Women and Wives: Marriage and Women's Ministry in the Letters of Paul*. Peabody, Mass.: Hendrickson, 1992.

Kelly, J. N. D. *A Commentary on the Pastoral Epistles*. Grand Rapids: Baker, 1963.

Kern, O. *Die Inschriften von Magnesia am Maeander*. Berlin: W. Spemann, 1900.

Klein, William W., Craig L. Blomberg, and Robert L. Hubbard Jr. *Introduction to Biblical Interpretation*. Dallas: Word, 1993.

Knibbe, Dieter. *Forschungen in Ephesos. 9.1.1. Der Staatsmarkt. Die Inschriften des Prytaneions. Die Kureteninschriften and sonstige religiöse Texte*. Vienna: Österreichische Akademie der Wissenschaften, 1981.

Knibbe, Dieter, and B. Iplikçioglu. *Ephesos im Spiegel seiner Inschriften*. Vienna: Schindler, 1984.

Knight, George W., III. *The Pastoral Epistles*. NIGTC. Grand Rapids: Eerdmans, 1992.

———. *The Role Relationship of Men and Women: New Testament Teaching*. Phillipsburg, N.J.: Presbyterian & Reformed, 1985.

Kraemer, Ross. *Her Share of the Blessings: Women's Religions among Pagans, Jews, and Christians in the Greco-Roman World*. New York: Oxford University Press, 1992.

Kreeft, Peter. *Christianity for Modern Pagans*. San Francisco: Ignatius, 1993.

Kroeger, Catherine Clark and Richard Clark. *I Suffer Not a Woman: Rethinking 1 Timothy 2:11–15 in Light of Ancient Evidence*. Grand Rapids: Baker, 1992.

Kroner, Richard. *The Primacy of Faith*. New York: Macmillan, 1943.

Langley, Myrtle S. *Equal Woman: A Christian Feminist Perspective*. London: Marshall, Morgan & Scott, 1983.

Lefkowitz, Mary, and Maureen Fant, eds. *Women's Life in Greece and Rome: A Source Book in Translation*. Baltimore: Johns Hopkins University Press, 1982.

Lewis, C. S. "Priestesses in the Church?" In *God in the Dock*, 234–39. Grand Rapids: Eerdmans, 1970.

Lock, Walter. *A Critical and Exegetical Commentary on the Pastoral Epistles*. ICC. Edinburgh: T. & T. Clark, 1936.

Longenecker, Richard N. *New Testament Social Ethics for Today*. Grand Rapids: Eerdmans, 1984.

Luther, Martin. *A Commentary on St. Paul's Epistle to the Galatians*. London: James Clarke, 1953.

———. *Works*. In *Lectures on Genesis, Chapter 1–5*, vol. 1, ed. Jaroslav Pelikan. St. Louis: Concordia, 1958.

Magie, David. *Roman Rule in Asia Minor*. 2 vols. Princeton: Princeton University Press, 1950.

Mahowald, Mary B., ed. *Philosophy of Woman: An Anthology of Classic and Current Concepts*. 2d ed. Indianapolis: Hackett, 1983.

Maier, Gerhard. *Biblical Hermeneutics*. Trans. Robert Yarbrough. Wheaton, Ill.: Crossway, 1994.

Malherbe, A., ed. *The Cynic Epistles*. SBLSBS 12. Atlanta: Scholars Press, 1977.

Marrou, H. I. *A History of Education in Antiquity*. New York: Sheed & Ward, 1956. Reprinted: Mentor, 1964.

Martin, Faith. *Call Me Blessed*. Grand Rapids: Eerdmans, 1988.

McGrath, Alister. *The Mystery of the Cross*. Grand Rapids: Zondervan, 1988.

Meade, David G. *Pseudonymity and Canon: An Investigation into the Relationship of Authorship and Authority in Jewish and Earliest Christian Tradition*. Grand Rapids: Eerdmans, 1987.

Meiselman, Moshe. *Jewish Woman in Jewish Law*. New York: Ktav, 1978.

Merk, Otto. *Biblische Theologie des Neuen Testaments in ihrer Anfangszeit*. Marburg: N. G. Elwert, 1972.

Mickelsen, Alvera, ed. *Women, Authority and the Bible*. Downers Grove: InterVarsity, 1986.

Mitchell, Stephen. *Anatolia*. Oxford: Clarendon, 1993.

Mollenkott, Virginia R. *Women, Men and the Bible*. Nashville: Abingdon, 1977.

Mommsen, Theodor. *The Provinces of the Roman Empire*. London, 1909. Reprinted 1974.

Morford, Mark P. O., and Robert J. Lenardon. *Classical Mythology*. 4th ed. New York: Longman, 1991.

Morgan, Robert, with John Barton. *Biblical Interpretation*. Oxford: Oxford University Press, 1988.

Morris, Joan. *The Lady Was a Bishop: The Hidden History of Women with Clerical Ordination and the Jurisdiction of Bishops*. New York: Macmillan, 1973.

Mueller-Vollmer, Kurt, ed. *The Hermeneutics Reader*. New York: Continuum, 1985.

Neuer, Werner. *Man and Woman in Christian Perspective*. Trans. Gordon J. Wenham. Wheaton, Ill.: Crossway, 1991.

Newsom, Carol, and Sharon Ringe, eds. *The Women's Bible Commentary*. London: SPCK/Westminster/John Knox, 1992.

Noll, Mark A. *A History of Christianity in the United States and Canada*. Grand Rapids: Eerdmans, 1992.

Norwood, Robin. *Women Who Love Too Much*. Los Angeles: Jeremy Tarcher, 1985.

Nugent, M. Rosamond. *Portrait of the Consecrated Woman in Greek Christian Literature of the First Four Centuries*. Washington, D.C.: Catholic University Press, 1941.

Oden, Thomas C. *First and Second Timothy and Titus*. Louisville: John Knox, 1989.

Osborne, Grant R. *The Hermeneutical Spiral*. Downers Grove: InterVarsity, 1991.

Oster, Richard E. *A Bibliography of Ancient Ephesus*. ATLABS 19. Metuchen: Scarecrow, 1987.

Ozawa, Martha N. *Women's Life Cycle and Economic Insecurity*. New York: Praeger, 1989.

Pagels, Elaine. *The Gnostic Gospels*. New York: Random, 1979.

Pantel, Pauline Schmitt, ed. *A History of Women in the West I: From Ancient Goddesses to Christian Saints*. Cambridge, Mass.: Belknap Press of Harvard University, 1992.

Piper, John, and Wayne Grudem, eds. *Recovering Biblical Manhood and Womanhood: A Response to Evangelical Feminism*. Wheaton, Ill.: Crossway, 1991.

Poythress, Vern. *The Church as Family*. Wheaton, Ill.: Council of Biblical Manhood and Womanhood, 1990. Reprinted in *Recovering Biblical Manhood and Womanhood*, ed. John Piper and Wayne Grudem. Wheaton, Ill.: Crossway, 1991, 233–47.

Price, S. R. F. *Rituals and Power: The Roman Imperial Cult in Asia Minor*. Cambridge: Cambridge University Press, 1984.

Pritchard, J. B., ed. *The Harper Atlas of the Bible*. New York: Harper & Row, 1987.

Quasten, Johannes. *Music and Worship in Pagan and Christian Antiquity*. Trans. B. Ramsay. Washington, D.C.: National Association of Pastoral Musicians, 1983.

Ramsay, William. *Cities and Bishoprics of Phrygia*. Oxford: Clarendon, 1895.

———. *The Teaching of Paul in Terms of the Present Day*. 2d ed. London: Hodder & Stoughton, 1914.

———. *A Historical Commentary on St. Paul's Epistle to the Galatians*. Grand Rapids: Baker, 1965 [1900].

———. *Asian Elements in Greek Civilisation*. Chicago: Ares, 1976. Reprint of 1927 edition.

Reardon, B. P., ed. *Collected Ancient Greek Novels*. Trans. Graham Anderson, et al. Berkeley: University of California Press, 1989.

Renié, J., *Les origines de l'humanité d'après la Bible*. Lyon: Emmanuel Vitte, 1950.

Riesner, R. *Apostolischer Gemeindebau. Die Herausforderung der paulinischen Gemeinden*. Giessen-Basel, 1978.

Rogers, Guy M. *The Sacred Identity of Ephesos*. London: Routledge, 1991.

Roloff, Jürgen. *Der erste Brief an Timotheus*. EKK. Zürich: Benziger, 1988.

Ruether, Rosemary R., ed. *Religion and Sexism: Images of Woman in the Jewish and Christian Traditions*. New York: Simon & Schuster, 1974.

Ryrie, Charles C. *The Role of Women in the Church*. Chicago: Moody, 1970.

Saller, R. P. *Personal Patronage under the Early Empire*. Cambridge: Cambridge University Press, 1982.

Scanzoni, Letha Dawson, and Nancy A. Hardesty. *All We're Meant to Be: Biblical Feminism for Today*. 3d ed. Grand Rapids: Eerdmans, 1992 (1974).

Schlatter, Adolf. *Die Theologie des Neuen Testaments*. Vol. 2, *Die Theologie der Apostel*. 2d ed. Stuttgart: Calwer, 1922.

————. *The Church in the New Testament Period.* Trans. Paul P. Levertoff. London: SPCK, 1955.

————. *Die Kirche der Griechen im Urteil des Paulus.* 2d ed. Stuttgart: Calwer, 1958.

Scholder, Klaus. *The Birth of Modern Critical Theology.* Trans. John Bowden. London: SCM/Trinity Press International, 1990.

Schreiner, Thomas. *The Law and Its Fulfillment.* Grand Rapids: Baker, 1993.

————. *Interpreting the Pauline Epistles.* Grand Rapids: Baker, 1990.

Sherwin-White, A. N. *The Letters of Pliny: A Historical and Social Commentary.* Oxford: Clarendon, 1966.

Smith, M., et al., eds. *The Holman Book of Biblical Charts, Maps, and Reconstructions.* Nashville: Broadman & Holman, 1993.

Spicq, Ceslaus. *Saint Paul les épitres pastorales.* 2 vols. 4th ed. E. Bib. Paris: J. Gabalda, 1969.

Stagg, Evelyn and Frank, eds. *Women in the World of Jesus.* Edinburgh: St. Andrew, 1978.

Stauffer, Ethelbert. *New Testament Theology.* Trans. John Marsh. London: SCM, 1955.

Stendahl, Krister. *The Bible and the Role of Women: A Case Study in Hermeneutics.* Facet Books Biblical Series 15. Trans. E. Sander. Philadelphia: Fortress, 1966.

Stott, John R. W. *Decisive Issues Facing Christians Today.* Old Tappan, N.J.: Fleming H. Revell, 1990.

Swartley, Willard M. *Slavery, Sabbath, War and Women.* Scottsdale, Pa.: Herald, 1983.

Sweet, Waldo E. *Sport and Recreation in Ancient Greece.* New York: Oxford University Press, 1987.

Taylor, Henry Osborn. *The Medieval Mind.* Cambridge, Mass.: Harvard University Press, 1949.

Terrien, Samuel. *Till the Heart Sings: A Biblical Theology of Manhood and Womanhood.* Philadelphia: Fortress, 1985.

Thielicke, Helmut. *The Evangelical Faith.* Vol. 1, *Prolegomena: The Relationship of Theology to Modern Thought Forms.* Trans. Geoffrey Bromiley. Grand Rapids: Eerdmans, 1974.

Thiselton, Anthony C. *New Horizons in Hermeneutics.* Grand Rapids: Zondervan, 1992.

Thomas, Rosalind. *Oral Tradition and Written Record in Classical Athens.* Cambridge: Cambridge University Press, 1989.

Towner, Philip H. *The Goal of Our Instruction.* JSNTSup 34; Sheffield: JSOT Press, 1989.

————. *1–2 Timothy & Titus.* IVP New Testament Commentary. Downers Grove: Inter-Varsity, 1994.

Tucker, Ruth A. *Women in the Maze: Questions and Answers on Biblical Equality.* Downers Grove: InterVarsity, 1992.

Tucker, Ruth A., and Walter Liefeld. *Daughters of the Church: Women and Ministry from New Testament Times to the Present.* Grand Rapids: Zondervan, 1987.

Van Leeuwen, Mary Stewart. *Gender and Grace.* Downers Grove: InterVarsity, 1989.

Verner, David C. *The Household of God: The Social World of the Pastoral Epistles.* SBLDS 71. Chico, Calif.: Scholars Press, 1983.

Voegelin, Ernst. *Science, Politics, and Gnosticism.* Chicago: Regnery, 1968.

Wallerstein, Judith S., and Sandra Blakeslee. *Second Chances.* New York: Ticknor & Fields, 1989.

Wankel, Hermann, et al. *Die Inschriften von Ephesos.* 8 vols. Bonn: Rudolf Habelt, 1979–84.

Willard, Frances E. *Women in the Pulpit.* Boston: D. Lothrop, 1888.

Witherington, Ben. *Women and the Genesis of Christianity.* Cambridge: Cambridge University Press, 1990.

————. *Women in the Earliest Churches.* SNTSMS 59. Cambridge: Cambridge University Press, 1988.

———. *Women in the Ministry of Jesus*. SNTSMS 51. Cambridge: Cambridge University Press, 1984.

Wright, Conrad. *The Beginnings of Unitarianism in America*. Hamden, Conn.: Shoe String Press, 1976.

Zaidman, Louise Bruit, and Pauline Schmitt Pantel. *Religion in the Ancient Greek City*. Trans. P. Cartledge. Cambridge: Cambridge University Press, 1992.

Ziegler, K., and W. Sontheimer, eds. *Der Kleine Pauly*. 5 vols. Munich: Deutscher Taschenbuch Verlag, 1979.

Journal Articles and Essays

Aland, Kurt. "The Problem of Anonymity and Pseudonymity in the Christian Literature of the First Two Centuries." *Journal of Theological Studies* 12 (1961): 39–49.

Albertz, Martin. "Die Krisis der sogenannten neutestamentlichen Theologie." *Zeichen der Zeit* 8 (1954): 371–75.

Allen, Diogenes. "Christianity and the Creed of Postmodernism." *Christian Scholars Review* 23 (1993): 117–26.

Aurenhammer, Maria. "Römische Porträts aus Ephesos: Neue Funde aus dem Hanghaus 2." *Jahreshefte des Österreichischen Archäologischen Institutes in Wien* 54 (1983): 105–12.

Barclay, John M. G. "Mirror-Reading a Polemical Letter: Galatians as a Test Case." *Journal for the Study of the New Testament* 3 (1987): 73–93.

Barnett, Paul W. "Wives and Women's Ministry (1 Timothy 2:11–15)." *Evangelical Quarterly* 61 (1989): 225–38.

———. "*Authentein* Once More: A Response to L. E. Wilshire." *Evangelical Quarterly* 66 (1994): 159–62.

Barron, Bruce. "Putting Women in Their Place: 1 Timothy 2 and Evangelical Views of Women in Church Leadership." *Journal of the Evangelical Theological Society* 33 (1990): 451–59.

Bartchy, Scott. "Power, Submission, and Sexual Identity among the Early Christians." In *Essays in New Testament Christianity*, ed. C. Robert Wetzel, 50–80. Cincinnati: Standard Publishing, 1978.

Bauckham, Richard. "Pseudo-Apostolic Letters." *Journal of Biblical Literature* 107 (1988): 469–94.

Baugh, Steven M. "The Apostle Paul among the Amazons." *Westminster Theological Journal* 56 (1994): 153–71.

———. "Feminism at Ephesus: 1 Timothy 2:12 in Historical Context." *Outlook* 42 (May 1992): 7–10.

———. "Paul and Ephesus: The Apostle among His Contemporaries." Ph.D. diss., University of California, Irvine, 1990.

Beckwith, R. T. "The Office of Women in the Church to the Present Day." In *Why Not? Priesthood and Ministry of Women: A Theological Study*. Ed. M. Bruce and G. E. Duffield; rev. and augmented ed. prepared by R. T. Beckwith, 26–39. Nashville: Abingdon, 1976.

Blum, G. G. "Das Amt der Frau im Neuen Testament." *Novum Testamentum* 7 (1965): 142–61.

Börker, Christian. "Eine pantheistische Weihung in Ephesos." *Zeitschrift für Papyrologie und Epigraphik* 41 (1981): 181–88.

Boucher, Madeleine. "Some Unexplored Parallels to 1 Cor 11, 11–12 and Gal 3,28: The NT on the Role of Women." *Catholic Biblical Quarterly* 31 (1969): 50–57.

Bowman, Ann L. "Women in Ministry: An Exegetical Study of 1 Timothy 2:11–15." *Bibliotheca Sacra* 149 (1992): 193–213.

Bratt, John. "The Role and Status of Women in the Writings of John Calvin." In *Renaissance, Reformation, Resurgence: Colloquium on Calvin and Calvin Studies*, ed. Peter DeKlerk, 1–17. Grand Rapids: Calvin Theological Seminary, 1976.

Broughton, T. R. S. "Roman Asia Minor." In *An Economic Survey of Ancient Rome*, ed. T. Frank, 4:499–950. Baltimore: Johns Hopkins University Press, 1938.

Bruce, F. F. "Women in the Church: A Biblical Survey." In *A Mind for What Matters*, 259–66, 323–25. Grand Rapids: Eerdmans, 1990.

Bultmann, Rudolf. "Das Problem einer theologischen Exegese des Neuen Testaments." In *Das Problem der Theologie des Neuen Testaments*, ed. Georg Strecker, 249–77. Darmstadt: Wissenschaftliche Buchgesellschaft, 1975.

Butler, Christine. "Was Paul a Male Chauvinist?" *New Blackfriars* 56 (1975): 174–79.

Cameron, Averil. "Neither Male Nor Female." *Greece and Rome* 27 (1980): 60–68.

Cardman, Francis. "The Medieval Question of Women and Orders." *The Thomist* 42 (1978): 588–90.

Carson, D. A. "Reflections on Christian Assurance." *Westminster Theological Journal* 54 (1992): 1–29.

Casarico, L. "Donne ginnasiarco." *Zeitschrift für Papyrologie und Epigraphik* 48 (1982): 117–23.

Clowney, Edmund P. "The Biblical Theology of the Church." In *The Church in the Bible and the World*, ed. D. A. Carson, 13–87. Grand Rapids: Baker, 1987.

Cohen, David. "Seclusion, Separation, and the Status of Women in Classical Athens." *Greece and Rome* 36 (1989): 3–15.

Cole, Susan Guettel. "Could Greek Women Read and Write?" In *Reflections of Women in Antiquity*, ed. H. Foley, 219–45. New York: Gordon & Breach Science, 1981.

Coloumbis, Angela E. "New Report Finds Youth Deaths by Homocide [sic] Doubled since 1985." *Christian Science Monitor* (Monday, April 25, 1994): 18.

Danet, A.-L. "I Timothée 2,8–15 et le ministère pastoral féminin." *Hokhma* 44 (1990): 23–44.

DeBoer, Willis P. "Calvin on the Role of Women." In *Exploring the Heritage of John Calvin: Essays in Honor of John H. Bratt*, ed. D. E. Holwerda, 236–72. Grand Rapids: Baker, 1976.

Detienne, Marcel. "The Violence of Wellborn Ladies: Women in the Thesmophoria." In *The Cuisine of Sacrifice among the Greeks*, ed. Marcel Detienne and J.-P. Vernant, 129–47. Chicago: University of Chicago, 1989.

Dex, Shirley. "Objective Facts in Social Science." In *Objective Knowledge*, ed. Paul Helm, 167–90. Leicester: InterVarsity, 1987.

Díaz, J. A. "Restricción en algunos textos paulinos de las reivindicaciones de la mujer en la Iglesia." *Estudios Eclesiásticos* 50 (1975): 77–93.

Ellis, E. Earle. "Pseudonymity and Canonicity of New Testament Documents." In *Worship, Theology and Ministry in the Early Church: Essays in Honor of Ralph P. Martin*, ed. Michael J. Wilkins and Terence Paige, 212–24. Sheffield: JSOT Press, 1992.

Elshtain, Jean Bethke. "Family Matters: The Plight of America's Children." *Christian Century* (July 14–21, 1993): 710–12.

Engelmann, H. "Zu Inschriften aus Ephesos." *Zeitschrift für Papyrologie und Epigraphik* 26 (1977): 154–56.

———. "Zum Kaiserkult in Ephesos." *Zeitschrift für Papyrologie und Epigraphik* 97 (1993): 279–89.

Falconer, Robert. "1 Timothy 2:14–15: Interpretive Notes." *Journal of Biblical Literature* 60 (1941): 375–79.

Fee, Gordon D. "Reflections on Church Order in the Pastoral Epistles, with Further Reflection on the Hermeneutics of *Ad Hoc* Documents." *Journal of the Evangelical Theological Society* 28 (1985): 141–51.

———. "Issues in Evangelical Hermeneutics, Part III: The Great Watershed—Intentionality and Particularity/Eternality: 1 Timothy 2:8–15 as a Test Case." *Crux* 26 (1990): 31–37.

———. "Women in Ministry: The Meaning of 1 Timothy 2:8–15 in Light of the Purpose of 1 Timothy." *Journal of the Christian Brethren Research Fellowship* 122 (1990): 11–18.

Fleischer, Robert. "Artemis von Ephesos und verwandte Kultstatuen aus Anatolien und Syrien Supplement." In *Studien zur Religion und Kultur Kleinasiens*, ed. S. Sahin et al., 324–31. Leiden: E. J. Brill, 1978.

Ford, J. Massingberd. "A Note on Proto-Montanism in the Pastoral Epistles." *New Testament Studies* 17 (1970–71): 338–46.

French, David. "Acts and the Roman Roads of Asia Minor." In *The Book of Acts in Its First Century Setting: The Book of Acts in Its Graeco-Roman Setting*, 55–57. Grand Rapids: Eerdmans and Carlisle: Paternoster, 1994.

Fung, Ronald Y. K. "Ministry in the New Testament." In *The Church in the Bible and the World*, ed. D. A. Carson, 154–212. Grand Rapids: Baker, 1987.

Geivett, R. Douglas. "Is Jesus the Only Way?" In *Jesus Under Fire*, ed. Michael J. Wilkins and J. P. Moreland, 177–205. Grand Rapids: Zondervan, 1995.

Giles, Kevin. "The Biblical Case for Slavery: Can the Bible Mislead?" A Case Study in Hermeneutics." *Evangelical Quarterly* 66 (1994): 3–17.

Gill, D. W. J. "Corinth: A Roman Colony in Achaea [*sic*]." *Biblische Zeitschrift* 37 (1993): 259–64.

Gordon, T. David. "Equipping Ministry in Ephesians 4?" *Journal of the Evangelical Theological Society* 37 (1994): 69–78.

Graf, Fritz. "An Oracle against Pestilence from a Western Anatolian Town." *Zeitschrift für Papyrologie und Epigraphik* 92 (1992): 267–79.

Grayston, Kenneth, and G. Herdan. "The Authorship of the Pastorals in the Light of Statistical Linguistics." *New Testament Studies* 6 (1959): 1–15.

Greeven, H. "Propheten, Lehrer, Vorsteher bei Paulus." *Zeitschrift für die neutestamentliche Wissenschaft* 44 (1952–53): 1–43.

Grey, M. "'Yet Women Will Be Saved through Bearing Children' (1 Tim 2.15): Motherhood and the Possibility of a Contemporary Discourse for Women." *Bijdragen* 52 (1991): 58–69.

Gritz, Sharon Hodgin. "The Role of Women in the Church." In *The People of God: Essays on the Believers' Church*, 299–314. Nashville: Broadman, 1991.

Grudem, Wayne. "Prophecy—Yes, But Teaching—No: Paul's Consistent Advocacy of Women's Participation without Governing Authority." *Journal of the Evangelical Theological Society* 30 (1987): 11–23.

Hardwick, Lorna. "Ancient Amazons—Heroes, Outsiders or Women?" *Greece and Rome* 37 (1990): 14–36.

Harris, Timothy J. "Why Did Paul Mention Eve's Deception? A Critique of P. W. Barnett's Interpretation of 1 Timothy 2." *Evangelical Quarterly* 62 (1990): 335–52.

Heschel, Susannah. "Jewish and Christian Feminist Theologies." In *Critical Issues in Modern Religion*, ed. Robert A. Johnson et al., 309–45. 2d ed. Englewood Cliffs, N.J.: Prentice Hall, 1990.

Hill, A. "Ancient Art and Artemis: Toward Explaining the Polymastic Nature of the Figurine." *JANES* 21 (1992): 91–94.

Hommes, N. J. "Let Women Be Silent in Church." *Calvin Theological Journal* 4 (1969): 5–22.

Horsley, G. H. R. "The Inscriptions of Ephesus and the New Testament." *Novum Testamentum* 34 (1992): 105–68.

House, H. Wayne. "A Biblical View of Women in the Ministry." *Bibliotheca Sacra* 145 (1988): 301–18.

Hugenberger, Gordon P. "Women in Church Office: Hermeneutics or Exegesis? A Survey of Approaches to 1 Tim 2:8–15." *Journal of the Evangelical Theological Society* 35 (1992): 341–60.

Huizenga, Hilde. "Women, Salvation, and the Birth of Christ: A Reexamination of 1 Timothy 2:15." *Studia Biblica et Theologica* 12 (1982): 17–26.

Jagt, Krijn A. van der. "Women Are Saved through Bearing Children (1 Timothy 2.11–15)." *The Bible Translator* 39 (1988): 201–8.

————. "Women Are Saved through Bearing Children: A Sociological Approach to the Interpretation of 1 Timothy 2.15." In *Issues in Bible Translation*, ed. Philip C. Stine, 287–95. UBSMS 3. New York: United Bible Societies, 1988.

Jebb, S. "A Suggested Interpretation of 1 Ti 2.15." *Expository Times* 81 (1970): 221–22.

Jenkins, C. "Documents: Origen on I Corinthians." *Journal of Theological Studies* 10 (1909): 29–51.

Johnson, P. F. "The Use of Statistics in the Analysis of the Characteristics of Pauline Writing." *New Testament Studies* 20 (1973): 92–100.

Kampen, J. "A Reconsideration of the Name 'Essene.'" *HUCA* 57 (1986): 61–81.

Karris, Robert J. "The Background and Significance of the Polemic of the Pastoral Epistles." *Journal of Biblical Literature* 92 (1973): 549–64.

Karwiese, Stefan. "Ephesos: Numismatischer Teil." *PW Suppl.* 12 (1970): 297–364.

Kearsley, R. A. "Women in Public Life." In *New Documents Illustrating Early Christianity*, ed. S. R. Llewelyn, 6:24–27. North Ryde, Australia: Macquarie University, 1992.

Kimberly, David R. "1 Timothy 2:15: A Possible Understanding of a Difficult Text." *Journal of the Evangelical Theological Society* 35 (1992): 481–86.

Knibbe, Dieter. "Ephesos: Historisch-epigraphischer Teil." *PW Suppl.* 12 (1970): 248–97.

————. "Ephesos—Nicht nur die Stadt der Artemis: die 'anderen' ephesischen Götter." In *Studien zur Religion und Kultur Kleinasiens*, ed. S. Sahin et al., 2:489–503. Leiden: E. J. Brill, 1978.

————. "Eine neue Kuretenliste aus Ephesos." *Jahreshefte des Österreichischen Archäologischen Institutes in Wien* 54 (1983): 125–27.

Knibbe, Dieter, et al. "Der Grundbesitz der ephesischen Artemis im Kaystrostal." *Zeitschrift für Papyrologie und Epigraphik* 33 (1979): 139–46.

Knibbe, Dieter, and Wilhelm Alzinger. "Ephesos vom Beginn der römischen Herrschaft in Kleinasien bis zum Ende der Principatszeit." In *Aufstieg und Niedergang der römischen Welt* II.7.2, 748–830. Berlin: Walter de Gruyter, 1980.

Knibbe, Dieter, and B. Iplikçioglu. "Neue Inschriften aus Ephesos VIII." *Jahreshefte des Österreichischen Archäologischen Institutes in Wien* 53 (1981–82): 87–150.

————. "Neue Inschriften aus Ephesos IX." *Jahreshefte des Österreichischen Archäologischen Institutes in Wien* 55 (1984): 107–35.

————. "Neue Inschriften aus Ephesos X." *Jahreshefte des Österreichischen Archäologischen Institutes in Wien* 55 (1984): 137–45.

Knibbe, Dieter, H. Engelmann, and B. Iplikçioglu. "Neue Inschriften aus Ephesos XI." *Jahreshefte des Österreichischen Archäologischen Institutes in Wien* 59 (1989): 163–237.

————. "Neue Inschriften aus Ephesos XII." *Jahreshefte des Österreichischen Archäologischen Institutes in Wien* 62 (1993): 113–50.

Knight, George W., III. "ΑΥΘΕΝΤΕΩ in Reference to Women in 1 Timothy 2.12." *New Testament Studies* 30 (1984): 143–57.

Köstenberger, Andreas J. "Gender Passages in the New Testament: Hermeneutical Fallacies Critiqued." *Westminster Theological Journal* 56 (1994): 259–83.

Kraabel, A. Thomas. "*Hypsistos* and the Synagogue at Sardis." *Greek, Roman and Byzantine Studies* 10 (1969): 81–93.

Kroeger, Catherine Clark. "Ancient Heresies and a Strange Greek Verb." *Reformed Journal* 29 (1979): 12–15.

————. "Women in the Church: A Classicist's View of 1 Tim 2:11–15." *Journal of Biblical Equality* 1 (1989): 3–31.

Kuske, D. F. "An Exegetical Brief on 1 Timothy 2:12 (*oude authentein andros*)." *Wisconsin Lutheran Quarterly* 88 (1991): 64–67.

Lacey, W. K. "Patria Potestas." In *The Family in Ancient Rome*, ed. B. Rawson, 121–44. Ithaca, N.Y.: Cornell University Press, 1986.

Lane, William L. "1 Tim. iv.1–3: An Early Instance of Over-Realized Eschatology?" *New Testament Studies* 11 (1965): 164–67.

Lassman, E. "1 Timothy 3:1–7 and Titus 1:5–9 and the Ordination of Women." *Concordia Theological Quarterly* 56 (1992): 291–95.

Lefkowitz, Mary. "Influential Women." In *Images of Women in Antiquity*, ed. Averil Cameron and A. Kuhrt, 49–64. Detroit: Wayne State University Press, 1983.

Libby, J. A. "A Proposed Methodology and Preliminary Data on Statistically Elucidating the Authorship of the Pastoral Epistles." M.Div. Thesis, Denver Seminary, 1987.

LiDonnici, Lynn. "The Images of Artemis Ephesia and Greco-Roman Worship: A Reconsideration." *Harvard Theological Review* 85 (1992): 389–415.

Liefeld, Walter. "Women and the Nature of Ministry." *Journal of the Evangelical Theological Society* 30 (1987): 49–61.

Lightfoot, N. "The Role of Women in Religious Services." *Restoration Quarterly* 19 (1976): 129–36.

Lips, Hermann von. "Die Haustafel als 'Topos' im Rahmen der urchristlichen Paränese." *New Testament Studies* 40 (1994): 261–80.

Luick, J. "The Ambiguity of Kantian Faith." *Scottish Journal of Theology* 36 (1983): 339–46.

MacMullen, Ramsay. "Woman in Public in the Roman Empire." *Historia* 29 (1980): 208–18.

Mancha, Rita. "The Woman's Authority: Calvin to Edwards." *Journal of Christian Reconstruction* 6 (1979–80): 86–98.

Marshall, I. Howard. "The Use of the New Testament in Christian Ethics." *Expository Times* 105 (1994): 131–36.

Martin, Hubert. "Artemis." *ABD*, I:464–65.

McKenzie, D. "Kant and Protestant Theology." *Encounter* 43 (1982): 157–67.

Meinardus, Otto. "The Alleged Advertisement for the Ephesian Lupanar." *Wiener Studien* 7 (1973): 244–48.

Merkelbach, Reinhold. "Die ephesischen Dionysosmysten vor der Stadt." *Zeitschrift für Papyrologie und Epigraphik* 36 (1979): 151–56.

———. "Der Kult der Hestia im Prytaneion der griechischen Städte." *Zeitschrift für Papyrologie und Epigraphik* 37 (1980): 77–92.

Millar, Fergus. "The World of the *Golden Ass*." *Journal of Roman Studies* 71 (1981): 63–75.

Mitchell, Stephen. "Festivals, Games, and Civic Life in Roman Asia Minor." *Journal of Roman Studies* 80 (1990): 183–93.

Montgomery, Hugo. "Women and Status in the Greco-Roman World." *Studia theologica* 43 (1989): 115–24.

Moo, Douglas J. "1 Timothy 2:11–15: Meaning and Significance." *Trinity Journal* 1 n.s. (1980): 62–83.

———. "The Interpretation of 1 Timothy 2:11–15: A Rejoinder." *Trinity Journal* 2 n.s. (1981): 198–222.

———. "What Does It Mean Not to Teach or Have Authority over Men?" 1Timothy 2:11–15." In *Recovering Biblical Manhood and Womanhood—A Response to Evangelical Feminism*, ed. John Piper and Wayne Grudem, 179–93. Wheaton, Ill.: Crossway, 1991.

Motyer, Steve. "Expounding 1 Timothy 2:8–15." *Vox Evangelica* 24 (1994): 91–102.

Murphy-O'Connor, Jerome. "St. Paul: Promoter of the Ministry of Women." *Priests and People* 6 (1992): 307–11.

Osborne, Grant R. "Hermeneutics and Women in the Church." *Journal of the Evangelical Theological Society* 20 (1977): 337–52.

Osburn, Carroll D. "ΑΥΘΕΝΤΕΩ (1 Timothy 2:12)." *Restoration Quarterly* 25 (1982): 1–12.

Oster, Richard. "The Ephesian Artemis as an Opponent of Early Christianity." *Jahrbuch für Antike und Christentum* 19 (1976): 24–44.

———. "When Men Wore Veils to Worship: The Historical Context of 1 Corinthians 11.4." *New Testament Studies* 34 (1988): 481–505.

———. "Ephesus as a Religious Center under the Principate, I. Paganism before Constantine." In *Aufstieg und Niedergang der römischen Welt* II.18.3, 1661–1728. Berlin: Walter de Gruyter, 1990.

Padgett, Alan. "Wealthy Women at Ephesus: 1 Timothy 2:8–15 in Social Context." *Interpretation* 41 (1987): 19–31.

Panning, A. J. "AYΘENTEIN—A Word Study." *Wisconsin Lutheran Quarterly* 78 (1981): 185–91.

Payne, Philip B. "Libertarian Women in Ephesus: A Response to Douglas J. Moo's Article, '1 Timothy 2:11–15: Meaning and Significance." *Trinity Journal* 2 n.s. (1981): 169–97.

———. "Oὐδέ in 1 Timothy 2:12." Paper presented at the 1988 meeting of the Evangelical Theological Society.

Perriman, Andrew C. "What Eve Did, What Women Shouldn't Do: The Meaning of AYΘENTEΩ in 1 Timothy 2:12." *Tyndale Bulletin* 44 (1993): 129–42.

Phillips, Susan S. "Caring for Our Children: Confronting the Crisis." *Radix* 22 (1993): 4.

Pierce, R. "Evangelicals and Gender Roles in the 1990s: 1 Tim 2:8–15: A Test Case." *Journal of the Evangelical Theological Society* 36 (1993): 343–55.

Porter, Stanley E. "What Does It Mean to Be 'Saved by Childbirth' (1 Timothy 2.15)?" *Journal for the Study of the New Testament* 49 (1993): 87–102.

Redekop, Gloria. "Let the Woman Learn: 1 Timothy 2:8–15 Reconsidered." *Studies in Religion/Sciences Religieuses* 19 (1990): 235–45.

Ringwood, I. "Festivals of Ephesus." *American Journal of Archaeology* 76 (1972): 17–22.

Roberts, Mark D. "Woman Shall Be Saved: A Closer Look at 1 Timothy 2:15." *TSF Bulletin* 5 (1981): 4–7.

Rogers, Guy M. "Constructions of Women at Ephesus." *Zeitschrift für Papyrologie und Epigraphik* 90 (1992): 215–23.

———. "The Assembly of Imperial Ephesos." *Zeitschrift für Papyrologie und Epigraphik* 94 (1992): 224–28.

Rossner, M. "Asiarchen und Archiereis Asia." *Studii Clasice* 16 (1974): 112–42.

Ruether, Rosemary. "Misogynism and Virginal Feminism in the Fathers." In *Religion and Sexism: Images of Women in Jewish and Christian Tradition*, ed. Rosemary Ruether, 150–83. New York: Simon & Schuster, 1974.

Sandnes, K. "'. . . et liv som vinner respekt.' En sentralt perspektiv på 1 Tim 2:11–15." *Tidsskrift for Teologi og Kirke* 59 (1988): 225–37.

Saucy, Robert L. "Women's Prohibition to Teach Men: An Investigation into Its Meaning and Contemporary Application." *Journal of the Evangelical Theological Society* 37 (1994): 79–97.

Schlatter, Adolf. "The Theology of the New Testament and Dogmatics." In *The Nature of New Testament Theology*, ed. Robert Morgan, 117–66. Naperville, Ill.: Allenson, 1973.

Scholer, David. "Women in the Church's Ministry. Does 1 Timothy 2:9–15 Help or Hinder?" *Daughters of Sarah* 16, no. 4 (1990): 7–12.

Scholler [sic], David. "Women's Adornment: Some Historical and Hermeneutical Observations on the New Testament Passages." *Daughters of Sarah* 6, no. 1 (1980): 3–6.

Schreiner, Thomas R. "Did Paul Believe in Justification by Works? Another Look at Romans 2." *Bulletin for Biblical Research* 3 (1993): 131–58.

———. "Head Coverings, Prophecies and the Trinity: 1 Corinthians 11:2–16." In *Recovering Biblical Manhood and Womanhood*, ed. John Piper and Wayne Grudem, 124–39, 485–87. Wheaton, Ill.: Crossway, 1991.

Sherk, Robert K. "Eponymous Officials of Greek Cities I–V." *Zeitschrift für Papyrologie und Epigraphik* 83 (1990): 249–88; 84 (1990): 231–95; 88 (1991): 225–60; 93 (1992): 223–72; 96 (1993): 267–95.

Sigountos, James G., and Mygren Shank. "Public Roles for Women in the Pauline Church: A Reappraisal of the Evidence." *Journal of the Evangelical Theological Society* 26 (1983): 283–95.

Snodgrass, Klyne R. "The Ordination of Women—Thirteen Years Later. Do We Really Value the Ministry of Women?" *Covenant Quarterly* 48, no. 3 (1990): 26–43.

Sölle, Dorothee. "Response to H. D. Betz." In *Protocol of the Colloquy of the Center for Hermeneutical Studies in Hellenistic and Modern Culture* by Hans-Dieter Betz, 29. Berkeley, Calif.: Center for Hermeneutical Studies, 1977.

Solokowski, F. "A New Testimony on the Cult of Artemis of Ephesus." *Harvard Theological Review* 58 (1965): 427–31.

Specht, Edith. "Kulttradition einer weiblichen Gottheit: Beispiel Ephesos." In *Maria, Abbild oder Vorbild?*, ed. H. Röckelein et al., 37–47. Tübingen: Edition Diskord, 1990.

Spencer, Aída Besançon. "Eve at Ephesus. (Should Women Be Ordained as Pastors According to the First Letter of Timothy 2:1–15?)." *Journal of the Evangelical Theological Society* 17 (1974): 215–22.

Stackhouse, John G., Jr. "Women in Public Ministry in 20th-Century Canadian and American Evangelicalism: Five models." *Studies in Religion/Sciences Religieuses* 17 (1988): 471–85.

Stendahl, Krister. "The Apostle Paul and the Introspective Conscience of the West." *Harvard Theological Review* 56 (1963): 199–215.

Stowers, Stanley. "Social Status, Public Speaking and Private Teaching: The Circumstances of Paul's Preaching Activity." *Novum Testamentum* 26 (1984): 59–82.

Strecker, Georg. "Das Problem der Theologie des Neuen Testaments." In *Das Problem der Theologie des Neuen Testaments*, ed. Georg Strecker, 9–31. Darmstadt: Wissenschaftliche Buchgesellschaft, 1975.

Stuhlmacher, Peter. ". . . in verrosteten Angeln." *Zeitschrift für Theologie und Kirche* 77 (1980): 222–38.

Sullivan, Richard D. "Priesthoods of the Eastern Dynastic Aristocracy." In *Studien zur Religion und Kultur Kleinasiens*, cd. S. Sahin et al., 2.914–39. Leiden: E. J. Brill, 1978.

Taylor, L. R. "Artemis of Ephesus." In *The Beginnings of Christianity*, ed. F. Foakes Jackson and Kirsopp Lake, 5:251–56. London: Macmillan, 1933.

Theissen, Gerd. "Soziale Schichtung in der korinthischen Gemeinde." *Zeitschrift für die neutestamentliche Wissenschaft* 65 (1974): 232–72.

Thiselton, Anthony C. "Realized Eschatology at Corinth." *New Testament Studies* 24 (1978): 510–26.

Tiessen, Terrance. "Toward a Hermeneutic for Discerning Moral Absolutes." *Journal of the Evangelical Theological Society* 36 (1993): 189–207.

Trebilco, Paul. "Asia." In *The Book of Acts in Its First Century Setting: The Book of Acts in Its Graeco-Roman Setting*, 316–36. Grand Rapids: Eerdmans and Carlisle: Paternoster, 1994.

van der Jagt, Krijn. "Women Are Saved through Bearing Children: A Sociological Approach to the Interpretation of 1 Timothy 2.15." In *Issues in Bible Translation*, ed. Philip C. Stine, 287–95. UBSMS 3. New York: United Bible Societies, 1988.

———. "Women Are Saved Through Bearing Children (1 Timothy 2.11–15)." *The Bible Translator* 39 (1988): 201–8.

Waltke, Bruce K. "1 Timothy 2:8–15: Unique or Normative?" *Crux* 28 (1992): 22–23, 26–27.

Warden, Preston Duane, and Roger S. Bagnall. "The Forty Thousand Citizens of Ephesus." *Classical Philology* 83 (1988): 220–23.

Wenham, Gordon J. "The Ordination of Women: Why Is It So Divisive?" *The Churchman* 92 (1978): 310–19.

Wiebe, Ben. "Two Texts on Women (1 Tim 2:11–15; Gal 3:26–29). A Test of Interpretation." *Horizons in Biblical Theology* 16 (1994): 54–85.

Whitehead, Barbara Defoe. "Dan Quayle Was Right." *Atlantic Monthly* (April 1993): 47–84.

Wilshire, Leland E. "The TLG Computer and Further Reference to ΑΥΘΕΝΤΕΩ in 1 Timothy 2.12." *New Testament Studies* 34 (1988): 120–34.

———. "1 Timothy 2:12 Revisited: A Reply to Paul W. Barnett and Timothy J. Harris." *Evangelical Quarterly* 65 (1993): 43–55.

Wolters, Albert. "Review: *I Suffer Not a Woman.*" *Calvin Theological Journal* 28 (1993): 208–13.

———. Review article. *Calvin Theological Journal* 29 (1994): 278–85.

Wondra, E. K. "By Whose Authority? The [sic] Status of Scripture in Contemporary Feminist Theologies." *Anglican Theological Review* 74, no. 1 (1993): 83–101.

Wright, Robert. "Infidelity: It May Be in Our Genes." *Time* (August 15, 1994): 28–36.

Yamauchi, Edwin. "Ramsay's Views on Archeology in Asia Minor Reviewed." In *The New Testament Student and His Field*. New Testament Student 5. Ed. J. Skilton, 27–40. Phillipsburg, N.J.: Presbyterian & Reformed, 1982.

Yarbrough, Robert W. "I Suffer Not a Woman: A Review Essay." *Presbyterion* 18, no. 1 (1992): 25–33.

———. "New Light on Paul and Woman?" *Christianity Today* 37, no. 11 (October 4, 1993): 68–70.

Index of Scripture

Index of Ancient Authors

Index of Modern Authors

Index of Subjects